Perfect Color Choices for the

Home Decorator

by Michael Wilcox

SCHOOL OF COLOR PUBLICATIONS

www.schoolofcolor.com

Acknowledgements

A book such as this is very much a team effort and I would like to thank the undermentioned for their hard work, professionalism and dedication to what was a difficult and complex task.

I would like to thank Matthew Brown in particular. Without his massive input of effort, concentration and skill this book would not have seen the light of day. A true professional.

Publisher:
Anne Gardner

Planning, picture research and illustrations:
Matthew Brown

Scanning and color balance:
Wesley Thorne

Page design, graphics and layout:
Brian Gillespie

Finishing:
Maureen Bonas

Technical assistance:
Jo Holness and
Lucy Robinson

Research and text:
Michael Wilcox

ISBN 1-931780-20-X

Gibbet Lane, Whitchurch
Bristol BS14 OBX England
Tel: UK 01275 835500
Facsimile: UK 01275 892659
www.schoolofcolor.com

Print coordination:
Desmond Heng
and Poh Lin Neo

Printing:
Imago Productions
F.E. Singapore

Distributed to the trade and art markets in North America by:
North Light Books
F & W Publications Inc.
4700 East Galbraith Road
Cincinnati,
OH 45236
USA
Tel: (800) 289 0963

Distributed in the UK, EEC & associated territories by:
Search Press Ltd.
Wellwood, North Farm Road
Tunbridge Wells, Kent
TN2 3DR England
Tel: (01892) 510850
Facsimile (01892) 515903
Email sales@searchpress.com
Website www.searchpress.com

Distributed to the trade and art markets in Australia by:
Keith Ainsworth Pty. Ltd.
Unit 6/88 Batt Street
Penrith NSW 2750
PO Box 6061
Australia
Tel: 02 47 323411
Facsimile: 02 47 218259
Email: ainsbook@ozemail.com.au

Introduction

From the earliest of times we have sought to add to our lives through the decoration of our dwellings. From the early Egyptians to the present day, people have used color in order to achieve a wide variety of effects. These have varied from the peaceful to the strident.

This book offers suggestions on color schemes that have been used around the world and throughout the ages. I hope that you will find it to be of assistance when decorating your own home.

Michael Wilcox

Contents

Contents

Harmony through monochrome

Introduction

Without a doubt the easiest way to achieve color harmony is to use only one color. This approach is known as 'monochrome'.

Risks are certainly minimised. A large solid area of color presents little that can go wrong. However, a room decorated in one color could look extremely bland.

Actually we rarely come across an area of single, unadulterated color. Even painted walls, as in the example opposite, will show colors reflected from other objects, shadows and possibly light from a window or from an artificial light, gradually weakening over distance.

Saturation

To give a wider range to work with, the color can be *desaturated* in various ways. A color is desaturated when it is *lowered in intensity.*

The term saturation came originally from the textile industry. An easy way to visualise a fully saturated color is to imagine a new pair of blue jeans. When first dyed they would be soaked or *saturated* in color, a strong, rich blue.

As the jeans fade with age and washing the blue would becomes less intense, or *desaturated.*

If they are worn by a mechanic they would gradually become covered in black grease. Once again the color would become desaturated as it moved away from the rich, fresh blue of the new jeans.

There are several ways in which we can desaturate colored paint.

elizabethwhiting.com

Desaturating with white

The more white that is added the more the color becomes desaturated.

Desaturating with black

Black can be added to desaturate a color, although it will 'muddy' it very badly.

Desaturating with another color

The addition of yellow takes the blue away from being a fully saturated hue.

Adding blue moves the red away from a fully saturated state.

If another color is added it will also desaturate the original. Remember, to desaturate a color is to reduce its original intensity.

An easy way to remember it is to think of the pair of jeans mentioned on the previous page.

When first dyed they would be a fully saturated blue. If they faded, had black grease rubbed in or another color was added, the original bright, saturated blue would become less intense, or *desaturated.* It is an important term in color use.

Desaturating with the complementary

Adding the complementary (mixing partner) red to the green will desaturate it (see top row), and vice versa.
Underneath are the tints of each mix produced by adding white.

The addition of its complementary (mixing partner) will also desaturate a color. Only a tiny amount of the complementary should be added at a time as the color can be quickly changed. When chosen carefully, the mixing partner will desaturate the color whilst keeping it *close to its original character.* It is the best way to darken a color.

The tints (lighter versions), of such mixes, produced by adding white have a valuable contribution to make.

The beauty of this approach, as far as home decorating is concerned, is its versatility.

If, for example, you wanted a room to be in different greens, you could start off with the strong (saturated) green at top left of the swatch above. Add a 'touch' of red to darken it and plenty of white. This would give a pale, grayed green for the walls. A stronger green from the same range could be used for the skirting boards and another for the doors perhaps. All could harmonise beautifully.

A monochrome scheme involves the use of a single color or color group. One of two approaches can be taken:

A single color

The complete room to be decorated in a single color. This could simply be one color painted everywhere, or, for additional interest, a single color could be used together with *variations in its saturation.*

As covered on the previous page, *whatever* the base color, the saturation can be varied either by adding white or a touch of the complementary color (its mixing partner). *Or both at the same time.*

From now on I will refer to a color's complementary simply as its 'mixing partner'.

A single color

The same hue group

Alternatively, several variations of a single hue can all be worked together. Different types of blue for example:

Maybe a violet-blue and a greenish blue. With each type of blue being applied at *different saturations* perhaps. A 'blue room' such as this could appear to be very calm and 'cool'.

Such arrangements can be harmonised with ease and 'moods' can be set without difficulty.

In the example to the right, several types of orange have been used. From a yellowish orange on the far wall to redder oranges under the stairs, in the stonework and in the flooring.

This arrangement will bring a very 'warm' feel to the scene as well as adding visual interest.

elizabethwhiting.com

Harmony through monochrome

A single color

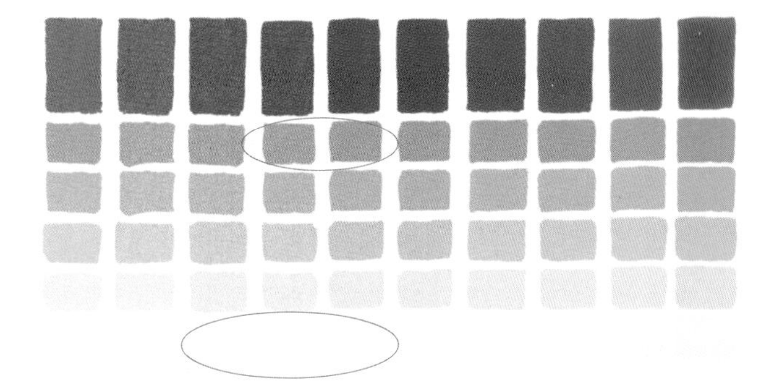

As discussed on the previous page, a single color can be used with variations in its saturation.

The walls of the room above were painted in *very pale*, dull green. Similar to the type of pale, dulled green shown (circled in blue) above.

A small amount of orange-red was added to a bluish green. Plenty of white was then introduced.

A darker green (circled in orange), was then mixed from the same red and green but less white was added. This was used to paint the wooden ceilings.

Other desaturated greens *from the same range* were used to paint the stair rail, skirtings and doors. In this approach, none of the colors which lean towards red would be used.

If a range of varied greens, purchased ready mixed had been used, the effect could have been very inharmonious. Can you see how straightforward it is to produce a series of colors, based on a single hue, which can be harmonised with ease?

Harmony through monochrome

A single color

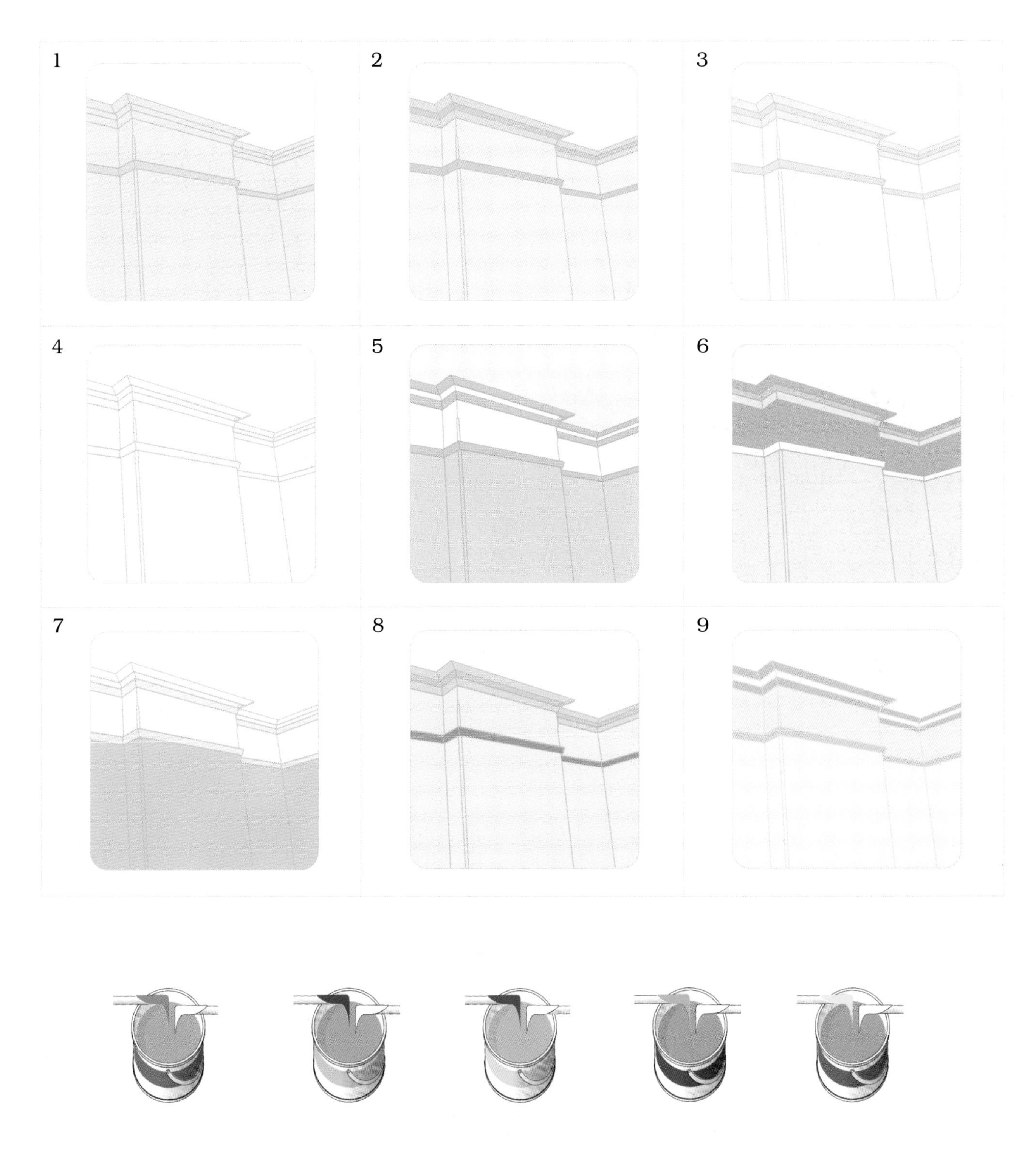

In the monochrome (one color) approach you can take any hue and simply add varying amounts of white to it. Alternatively, in order to extend the range as well as add visual interest, the base color can be desaturated with its mixing partner.

Please see page 16 for further information on mixing partners.

elizabethwhiting.com

The same hue group

Using the same hue group is very similar to using just one color at different strengths.

In the room above, rather than taking a particular orange and altering it to give a range of saturations, a *group* of oranges have been used. All are very similar.

Although the lighting plays a definite part above, the far walls, edge of the stairs and the wall to the lower floor are all in different oranges. To add to the scheme deep orange tiles have been chosen under the stairway and rich orange flooring has been used.

Harmony through monochrome

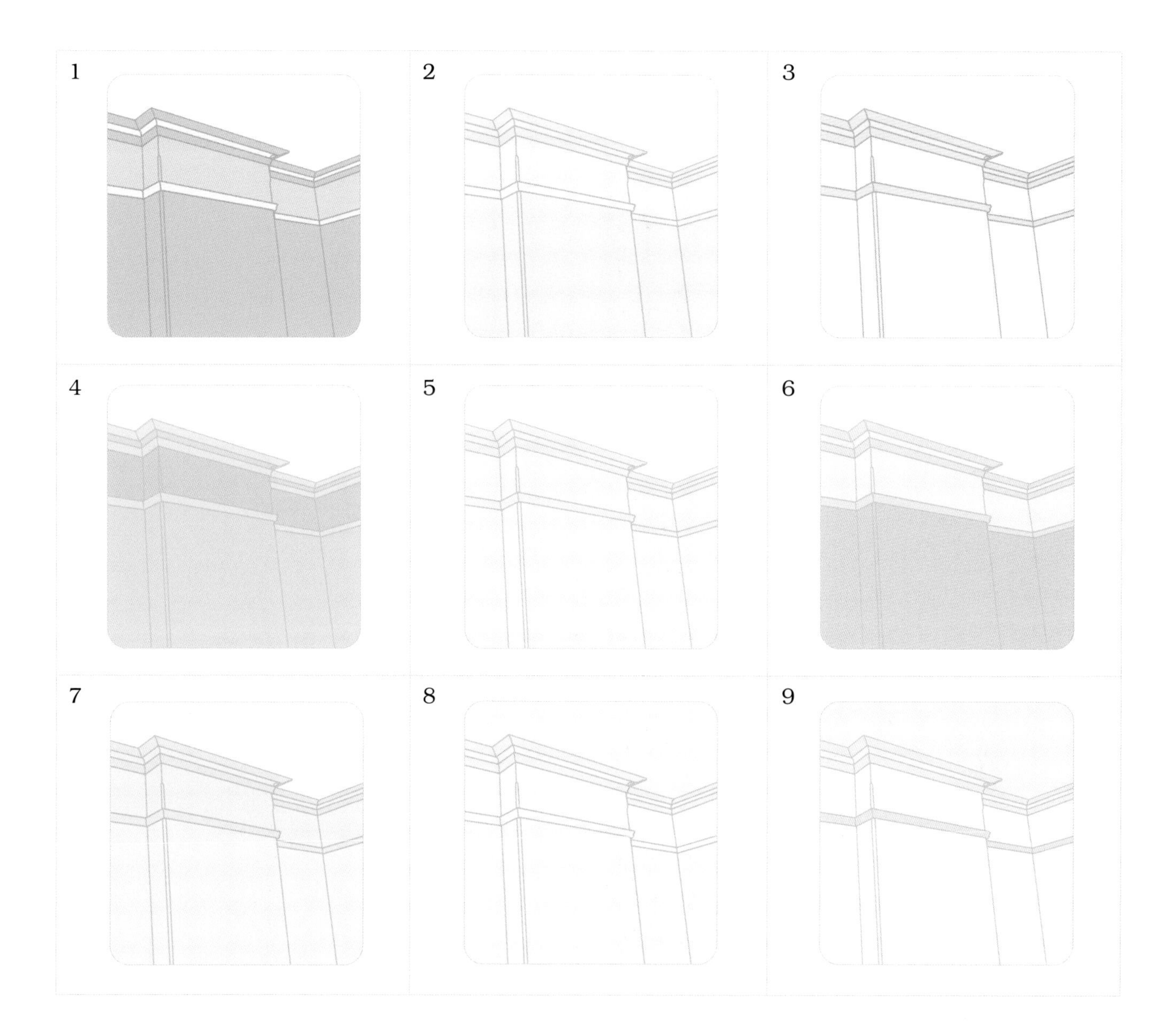

The same hue group can be extended to include fittings and furniture.

The furnishing at right could, for example, be used with the room coloring shown on the previous page, or with several of the swatches shown above.

The main drawback to this approach is that such color schemes can look a little bland if overdone. By their very nature such arrangements offer limited visual interest.

Color mixing

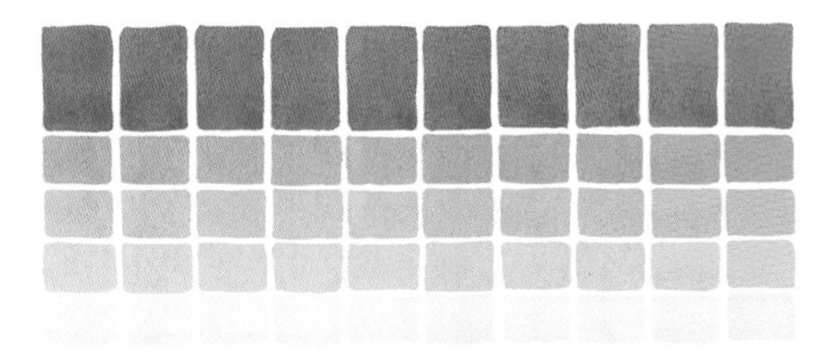

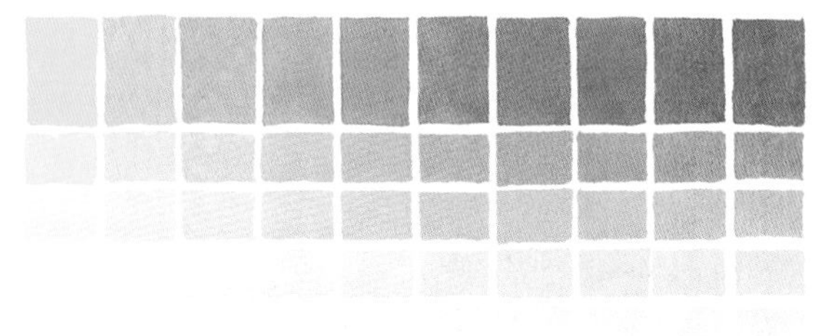

The intention of this book is to offer guidance as to possible color arrangements for the home. Although general tips on color mixing are given, this area is not covered thoroughly as many prefer to purchase ready mixed paints from the shelf.

Should you wish to prepare your own colors, our books on color mixing, such as *'Blue and Yellow Don't Make Green'* might be of interest. You will find contact details on the final page.

A considerable saving can be made by mixing your own colors and it can be very rewarding in a creative sense, but I realise that not everyone will wish to take this route.

However, the following might be of general interest: Basic greens can be mixed from various blues and yellows, the final result depending on just how much 'green' each contains.

My approach to color mixing is quite different to the normal and is based on what *actually happens* when colors are mixed. This makes accurate color mixing very easy.

Blue and yellow actually *absorb* each other when mixed, leaving behind only the green that they each contain. If they both 'carry' a lot of green the result will be a bright green. If neither 'carries' very much the mix will give a dull green, and so on.

Color mixing

Orange is not a new color created by a mix of red and yellow but is the result of the redness and yellowness absorbing each other.

They then leave behind the amount of orange that they each 'carry'. Once you know what this is it becomes very easy.

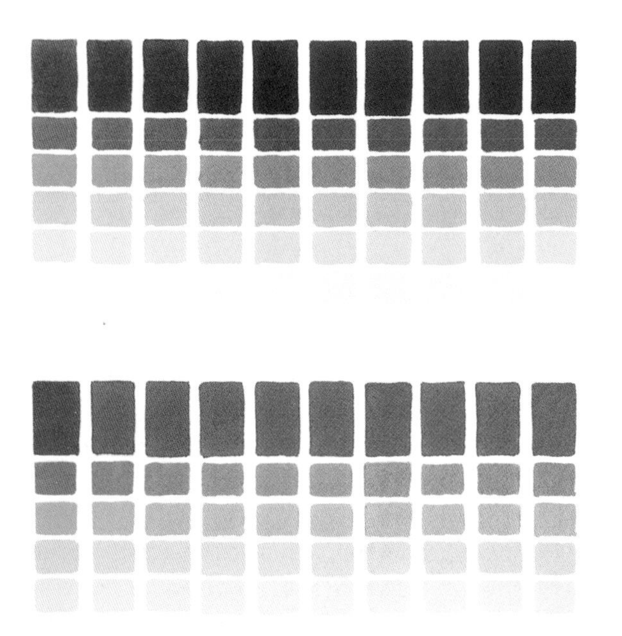

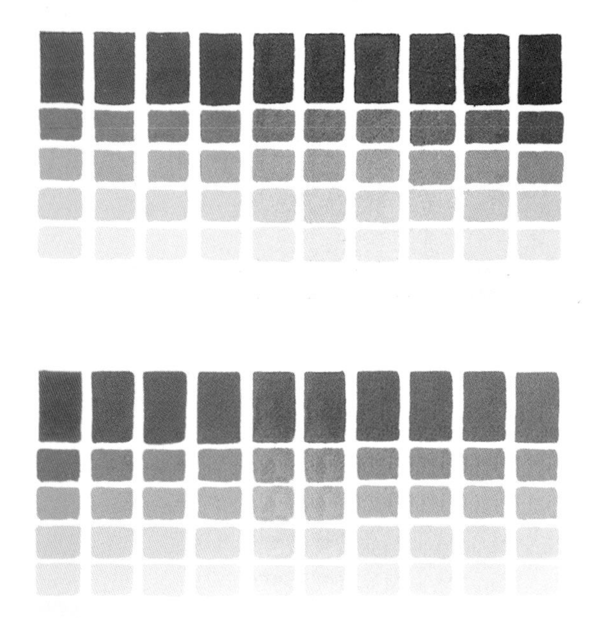

Likewise with violet. Two good 'carriers' of violet will result in a bright violet. One good and the other poor and you have a mid intensity violet.

If both are poor 'carriers' the result will be a dull violet. It is a method easily learnt within a few hours and will put a vast range of predictable mixes at your fingertips.

Color mixing

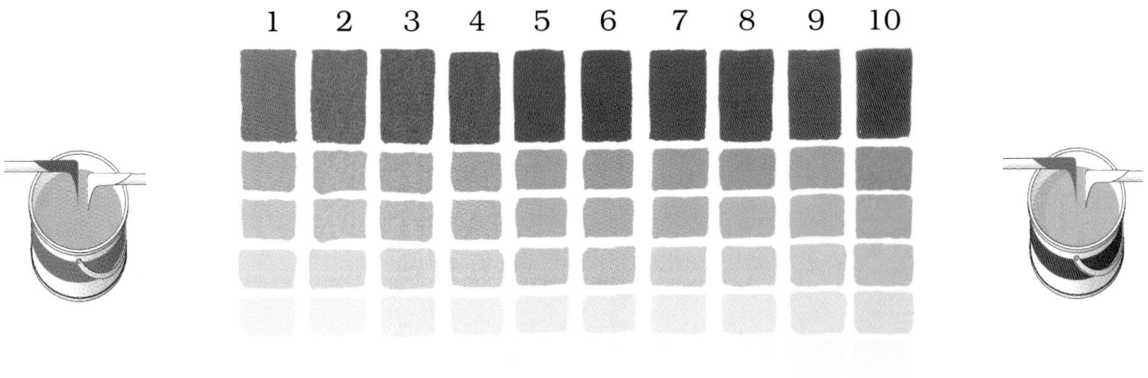

1 2 3 4 5 6 7 8 9 10

Green will absorb red and vice versa.

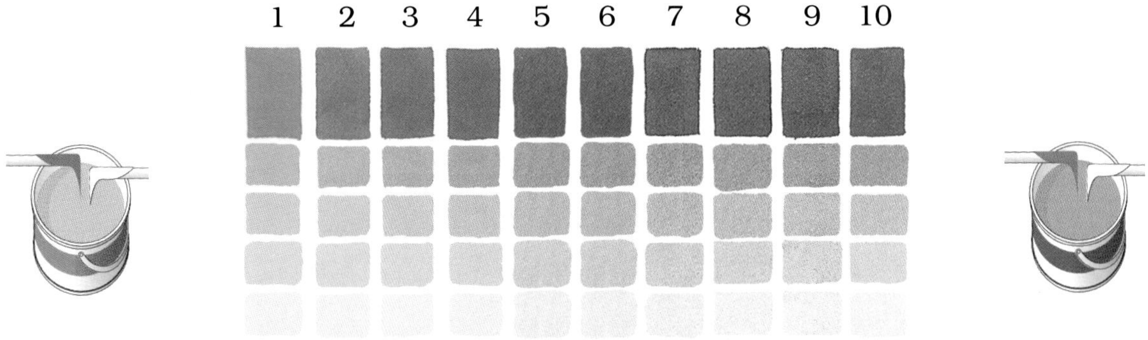

1 2 3 4 5 6 7 8 9 10

Orange and blue will also absorb each other.

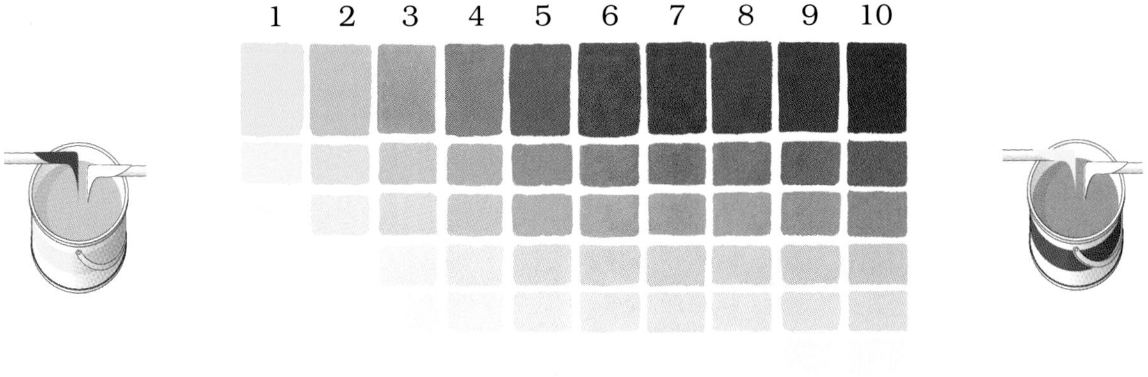

1 2 3 4 5 6 7 8 9 10

As will yellow and violet.

Red and green, blue and orange and yellow and violet are known as 'mixing partners'. When colors 1 & 10 (above) are combined they start to absorb each other. Red, for example, will 'soak up' the green and vice versa. As they absorb each other, neutralised colors are created, as in mixes 2,3,4 and 7,8 and 9. These can also be described as *dulled* or *reduced in intensity*. This is also the most accurate way to 'darken' a color. I write 'darken' this way as the color does change in character somewhat, so it is not accurate darkening. But it is the closest we can get.

Adding black simply destroys the character of a color. Black and yellow for example give a dull brownish green. Around the middle of the range, mixes 5 & 6, the two mixing partners are absorbing so much of each others color that they blend into what are known as 'colored grays'.

Color mixing

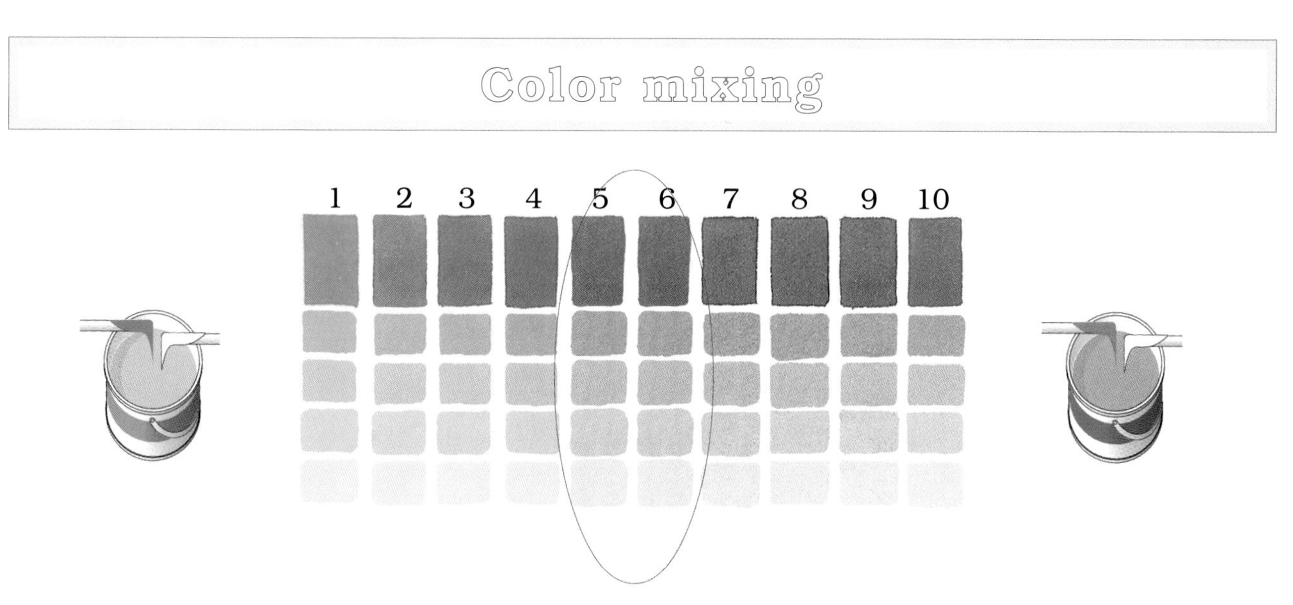

'Colored grays', circled above, are invaluable as they extend the range and can be harmonised very easily with the rest of the mixes. Under each mix a series of tints (lightened versions of a color) have been produced by adding white.

The examples on the previous page can be extended to take in a range of different greens, reds, blues, oranges, yellows and violets.

Do let us know if you would like help in this area. We can make color mixing very simple for you as we have for thousands of others.

Simply by intermixing the blue and orange and adding white where required, a vast range of harmonising color schemes will emerge.

They can be made to harmonise with ease as little can go wrong. After all, only two colors are involved.

Apart from colors 1 and 10 above, (the basic mixing hues), all the rest are mixes of these two.

Even a slight trace of one in the other will help to harmonise them when placed together, or near each other.

When mixing a color its pays to move slowly and cautiously. If you are adding blue to orange for example, add very small amounts of the blue until you have reached the desired hue. If you have put too much blue in it is easy to add small amounts of the orange to restore the color.

If you cannot quite see which way the mix is going, (perhaps it is too dark), add a little white to reveal the color.

It is only when you are satisfied with this base color that you should add it to white if you require a paler version. Even then proceed with caution, adding a little at a time.

Related colors

Introduction

© Red Cover/Graham Atkins-Hughes

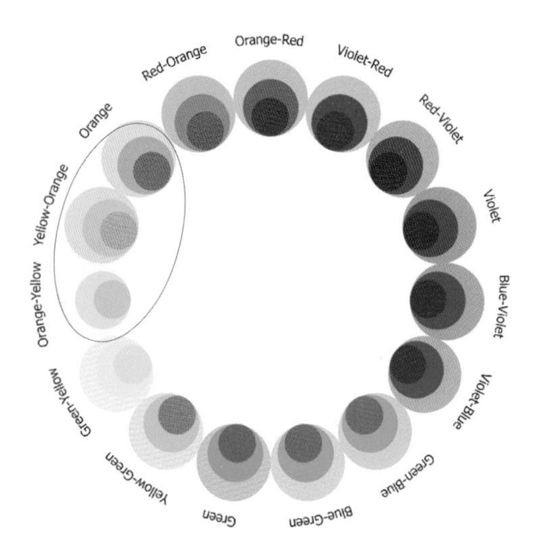

The use of a related group will provide the possibility of greater visual interest than monochrome can offer.
Up to three adjoining hues on the color wheel can be used at one time. Variation can be provided by either simply adding white or by adding white plus the mixing partner.

The three colors highlighted on the color wheel to the left have been incorporated into the color scheme shown above.
Having much in common they can be used together to provide a wide range of harmonies.

Tints, shades or a combination

With a little care, any of the possible related groupings can be worked together and remain harmonious. An added bonus is that further interest can be aroused through *varying the saturation.*

A safe approach, as far as achieving harmony is concerned, is to work within the *desaturated* ranges. When colors are used at full strength they are harder to harmonise.

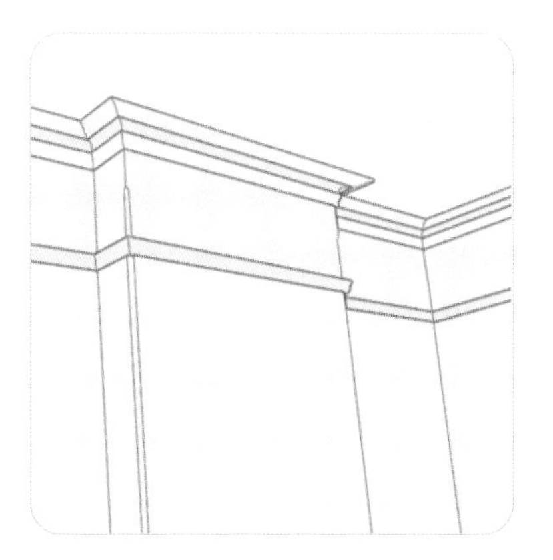

Tints of the three main colors can be used together.

Neutralised hues can be used together.

Tints, tones and neutralised hues will work well together.

If the various *tints* of the three main colors are used together they can be harmonised easily and with little danger of disruption.

In the same way, *neutralised colors* can be used together.

A wider range is available if *tones* (colors desaturated with their complementary plus white) are also introduced.

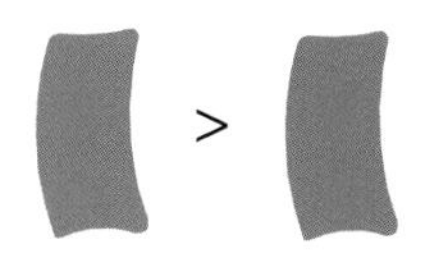

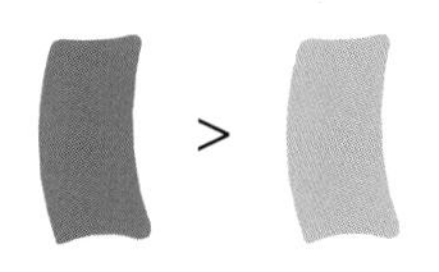

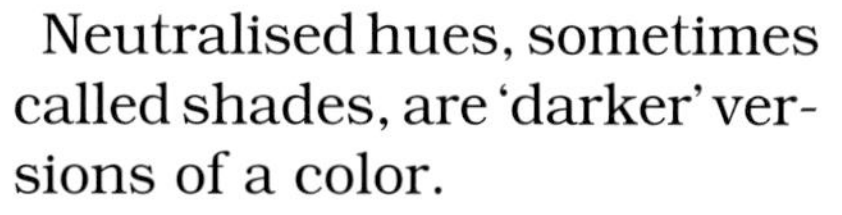

Tints are lighter versions of a color. These are normally produced by adding white.

Alternatively, but less usual in decorating, a color can be made lighter by allowing a white background to show through thinly applied paint.

Neutralised hues, sometimes called shades, are 'darker' versions of a color.

The ideal way to darken a color is to add its mixing partner. It does alter its character slightly but far less so than black would.

Tones start off as neutralised colors (a color darkened with its mixing partner), which are then normally lightened with white.

Some very subtle colors can be produced this way, pale and grayed.

With a little care, *tints, neutrals (shades) and tones* can all be used together. This will provide a wider range to work with of course, adding more potential for interest.

Related colors

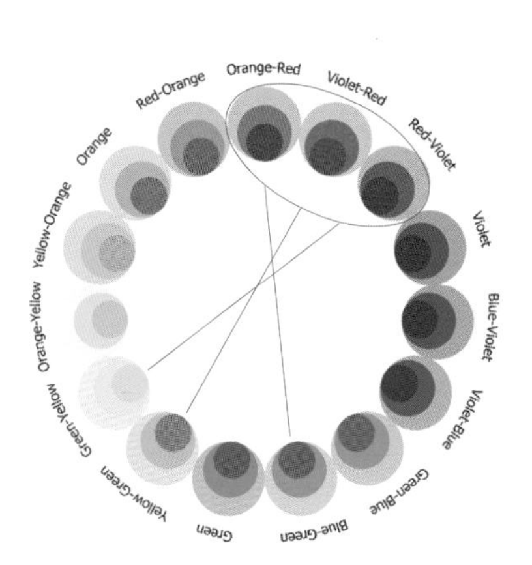

elizabethwhiting.com

Related colors can be worked together successfully because they have much in common.

In these examples the violet-red in the centre tends to hold the group together. Even so, it might be better to use the orange-red in a pale form or over smaller areas as the two types of red do not sit well together if used at strength.

Reds and violets together can evoke feelings of luxury and sumptuousness in many people. The stronger colors need to be used with some caution in most settings.

When made lighter (with white) or neutralised (with the mixing partner) these three can be made to harmonise with ease.

Related colors

Orange-red, violet-red and red-violet

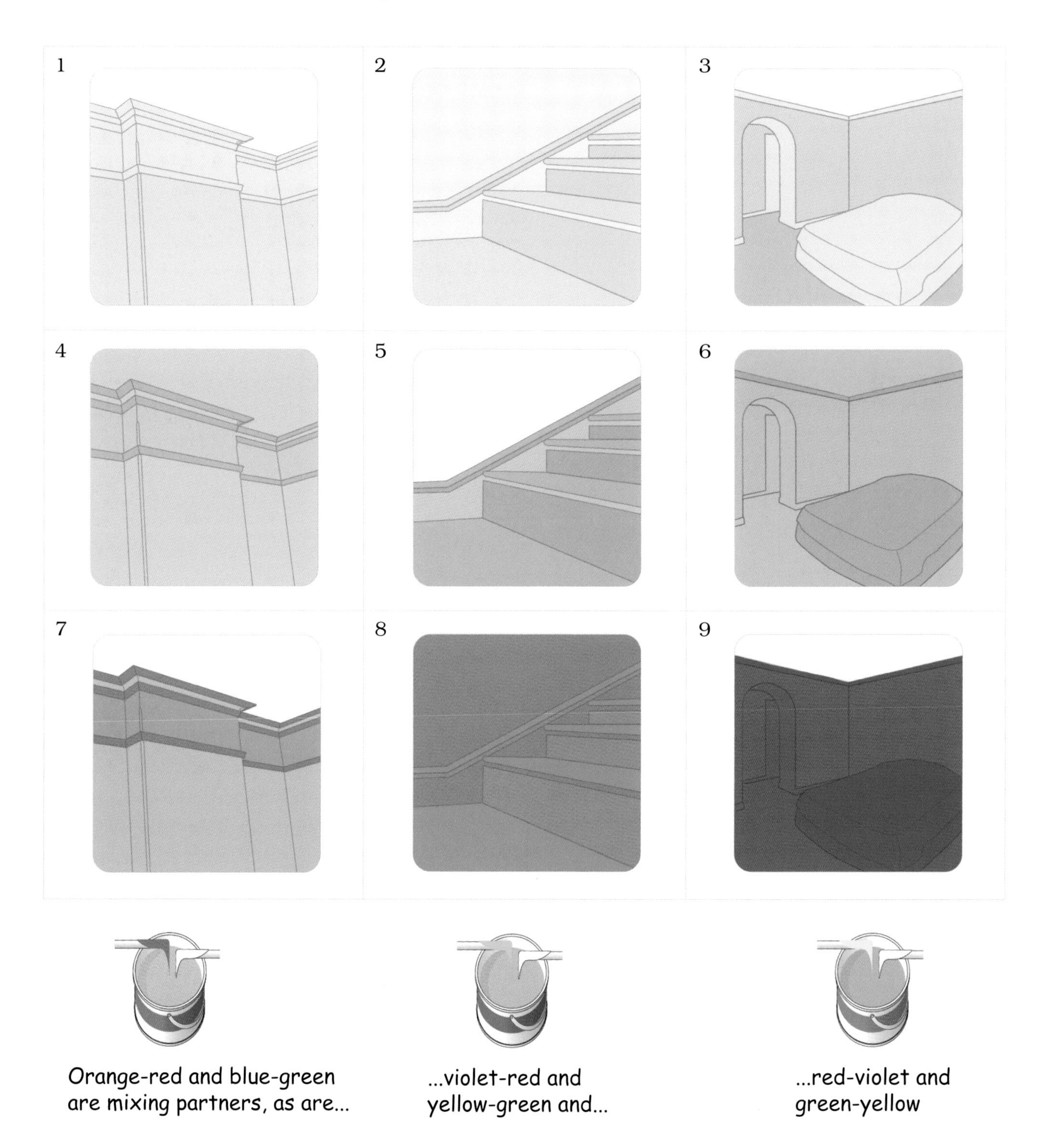

Orange-red and blue-green are mixing partners, as are...

...violet-red and yellow-green and...

...red-violet and green-yellow

The orange-red can be mixed with white to produce various pinks. Its mixing partner *blue-green* will darken it to give very deep reds.

The mixing partner of the violet-red is a *yellow-green*, that of red-violet is a *green-yellow*. Each will neutralise the other.

Related colors

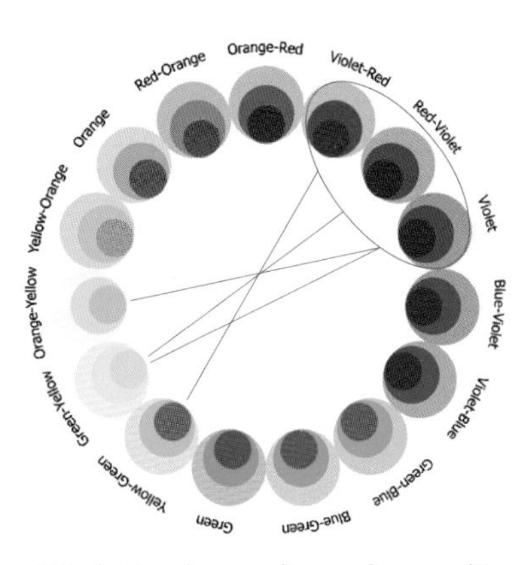

Violet, the color of royalty, can be rather overpowering if used at strength.

elizabethwhiting.com

The great cost of violet dyes in antiquity led to the color being decreed suitable only for the elite. It has been associated with royalty ever since. Having much in common, the range of colors from violet-red to violet can be harmonised quite easily. (For those who relate well to violet that is). Brighter, richer colors need to be used with some caution if you are seeking harmony. If they are a little too much try using them for small accents.

Related colors

Violet-red, red-violet and violet

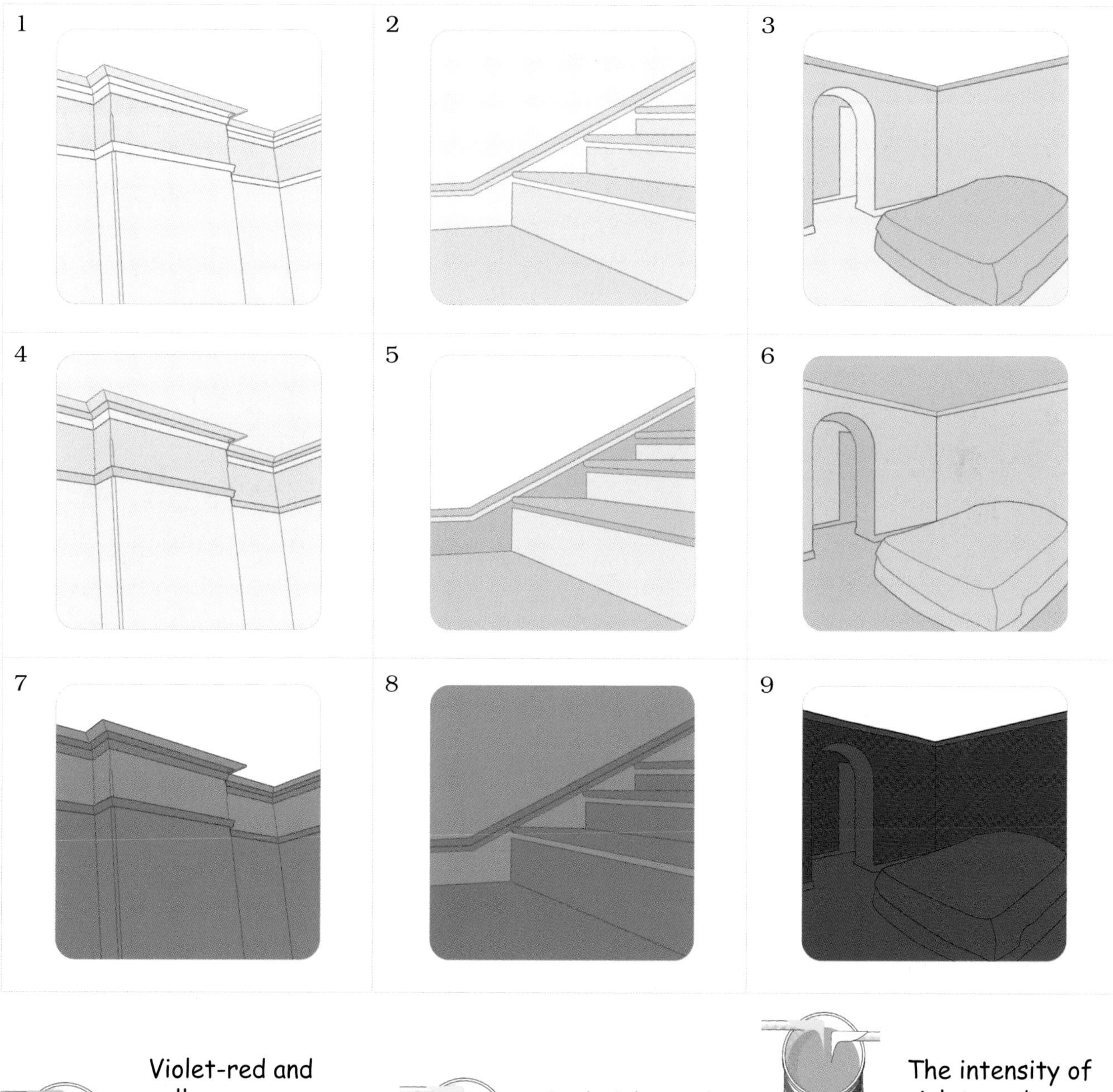

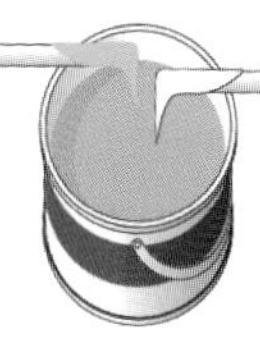

Violet-red and yellow-green are mixing partners and will reduce the strength of each other when blended.

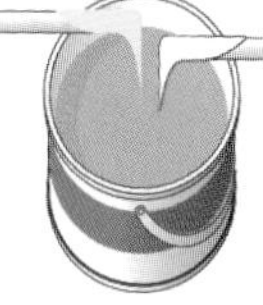

Red-violet and green-yellow are also mixing partners.

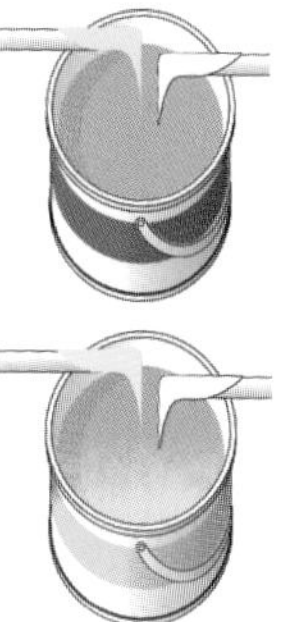

The intensity of violet can be reduced with either green-yellow or orange-yellow.

The mixing tips given above are only applicable if you wish to reduce the intensity of a color, 'darkening' it at the same time.

Although the base color will change slightly in character this is the only practical means of darkening a color. Black would quickly destroy its very nature. I write 'darkening' in this fashion because, due to a slight shift in character, the color is not darkened accurately but its the closest we can get.

Related colors

© Red Cover/Huntley Hedworth

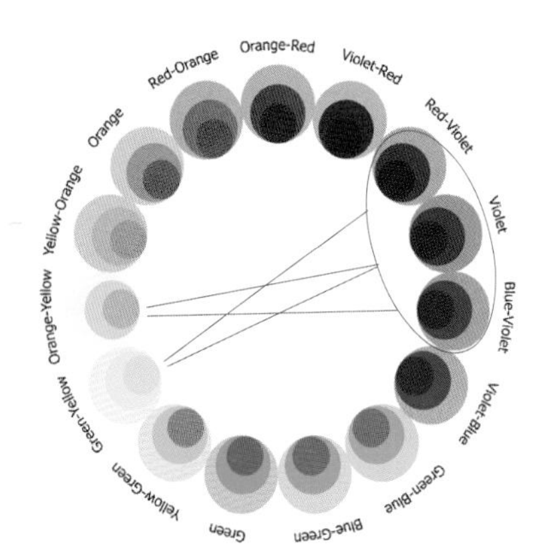

The central violet is particularly effective at holding its neighbours together. They unify readily, particularly when made lighter or darker.

This is a common color scheme in nature. If it works here perhaps it can work in your home.

As one color is made quite a lot lighter than the others, harmony can start to diminish as the contrast of light and dark sets in. This is an important contrast which can add great interest, but it can sometimes be overdone.

The overall effect starts to 'cool' slightly as the blue violet is introduced to its 'warmer' partners. This very slight contrast in temperature can add a subtle interest and might be worth cultivating.

Related colors

Red-violet, violet and blue-violet

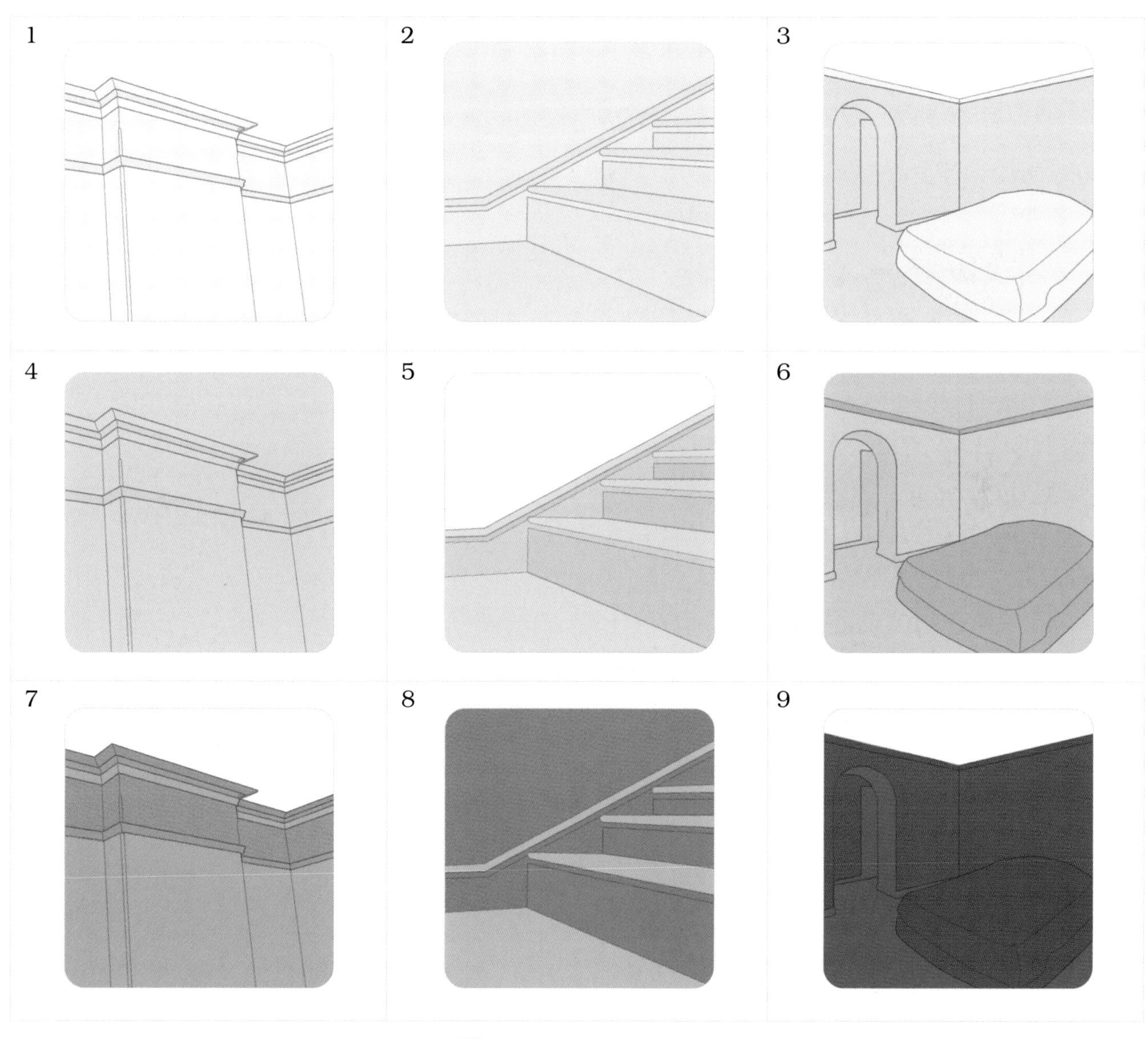

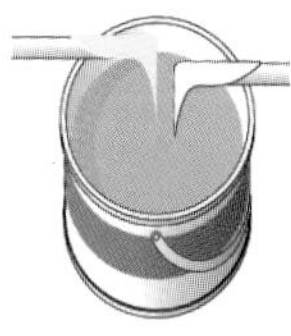

Red-violet and green-yellow are a mixing pair.

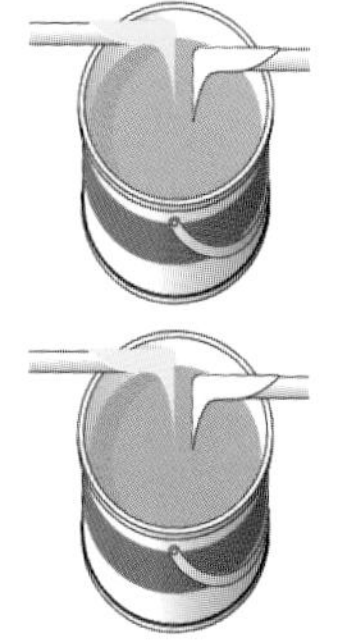

The brightness of violet can be reduced with either green-yellow or orange-yellow.

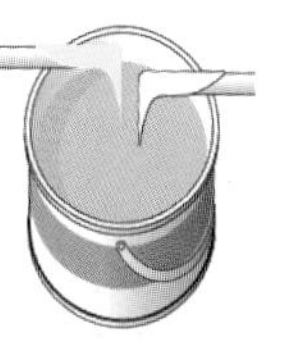

Blue-violet and orange-yellow are also mixing partners.

The colors that you have either mixed or purchased might be a little too bright for your requirements, if so:

To 'darken' and reduce a red-violet in intensity add a little green-yellow, the violet can be reduced with either green-yellow or orange-yellow and the blue-violet will darken down with orange-yellow.

White can be added to any of the mixes to create tints (lighter colors).

Related colors

© Red Cover/Huntley Hedworth

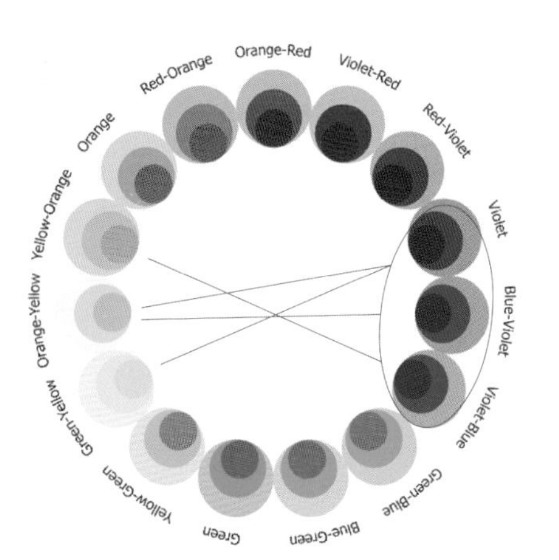

Three easily harmonised hues...

...which have many applications in the home.

These three basic hues can give well balanced arrangements which offer a very slight contrast in temperature. As the color arrangements become closer in value, (either all darker or all lighter) they tend to harmonise well but can be rather uninspiring. Interest can be added by working with a variety of values, from light to dark.

Related colors

Violet, blue-violet and violet-blue

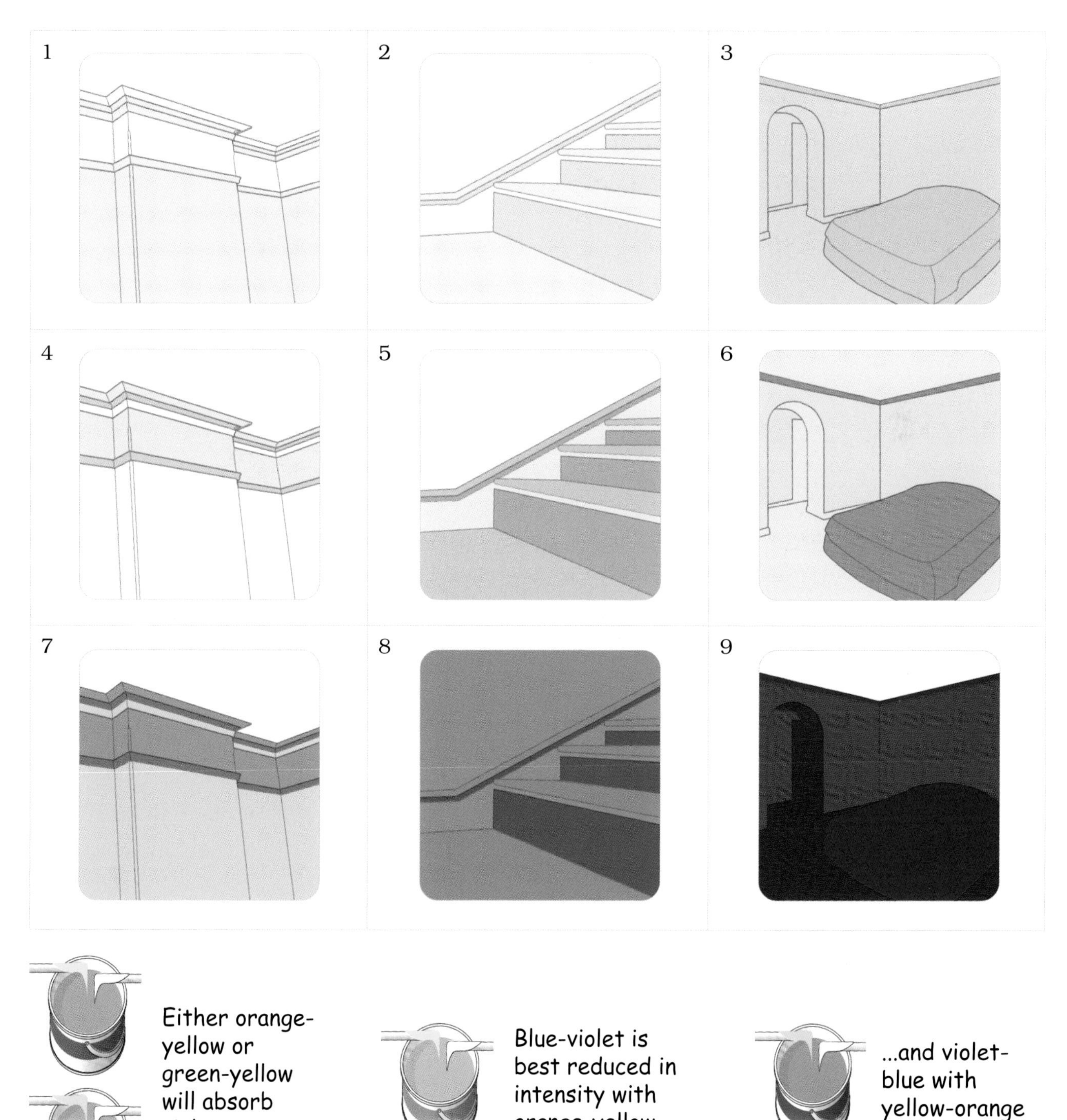

Either orange-yellow or green-yellow will absorb violet.

Blue-violet is best reduced in intensity with orange-yellow...

...and violet-blue with yellow-orange

If you are not familiar with color mixing, the terms can be a little confusing unless they are read carefully. With the above mixing tips for example; violet-blue is a type of *blue.*

Blue-violet a type of *violet.* Yellow-orange is a yellowish *orange* and orange-yellow a type of *yellow* which leans towards orange. It takes a little practice at first.

Related colors

© Red Cover/Chris Tubbs

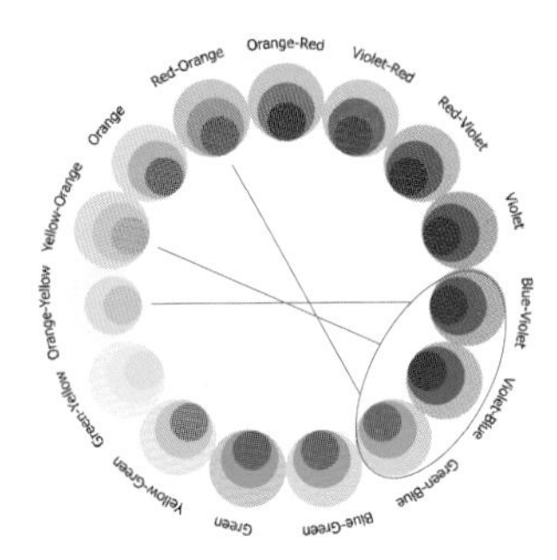

The introduction of green-blue will 'calm down' the overall effect of these arrangements when compared to page 27.

This combination of colors can be very versatile and have many applications.

The stronger, more intense colors should ideally be used sparingly with weaker neighbours. Perhaps small touches of the strong color against larger areas of its reduced neighbours.

Calm, introspective colors often found in the great outdoors.

Related colors

Blue-violet, violet-blue and green-blue

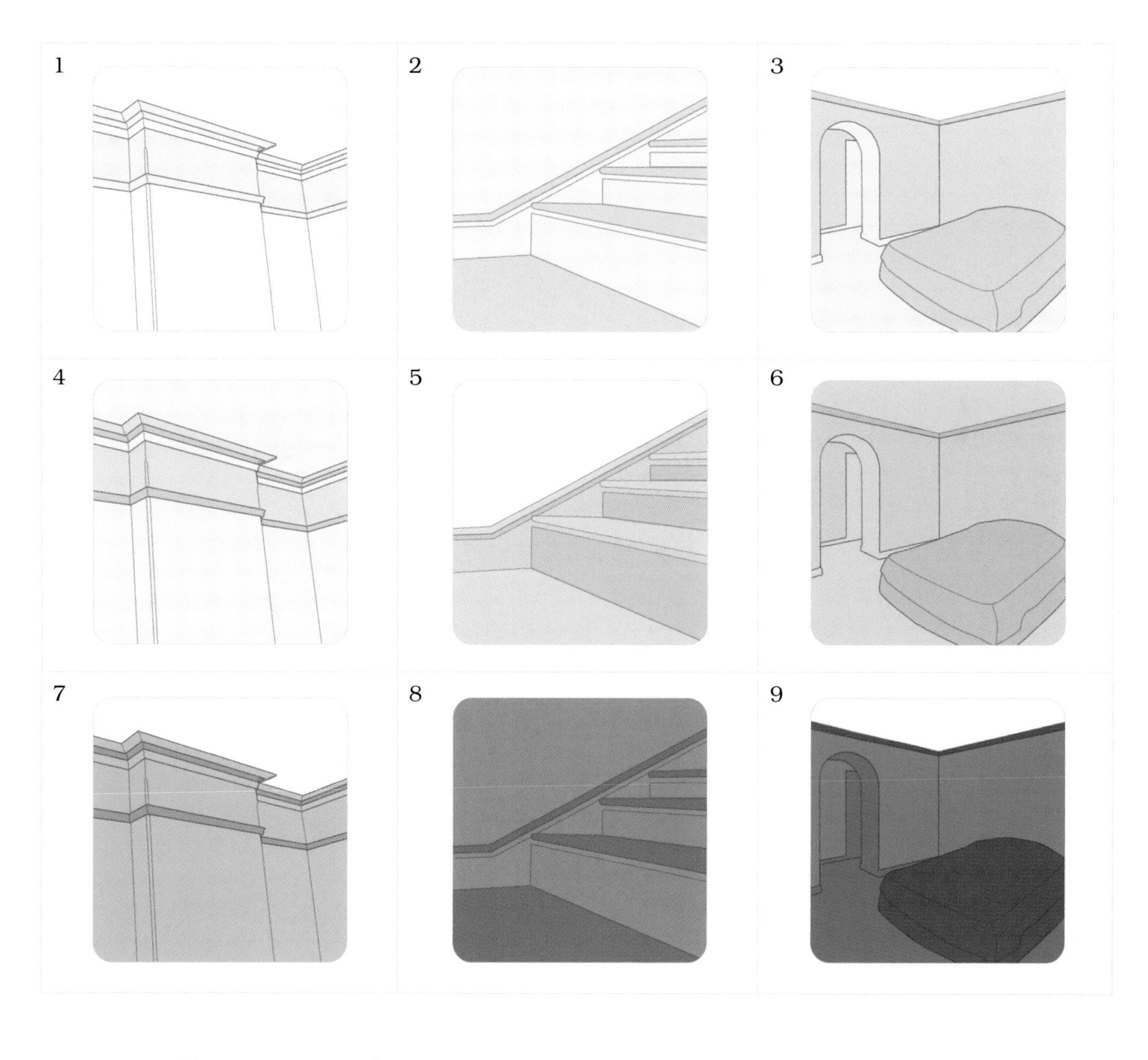

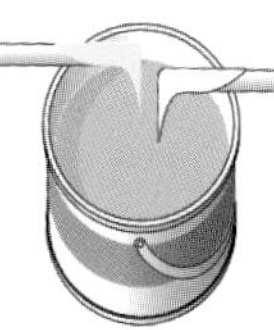

Even a very small 'touch' of orange-yellow will start to lower the intensity of blue-violet.

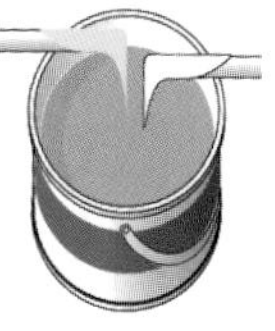

Violet-blue and yellow-orange are a mixing pair, as are...

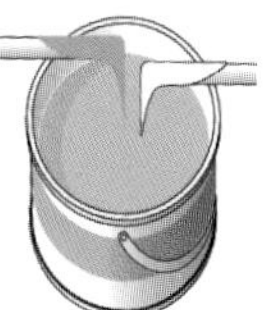

...green-blue and red-orange

To 'darken' the blue-violet add a little orange-yellow. Yellow-orange will 'darken' the violet-blue and a little reddish orange (or even a mid orange) will reduce the green-blue.

White into any of the mixes will reduce their intensity even further, allowing them to be used over larger areas. The lighter the color the larger an area it can usually be used over.

Related colors

© Red Cover/Ken Hayden

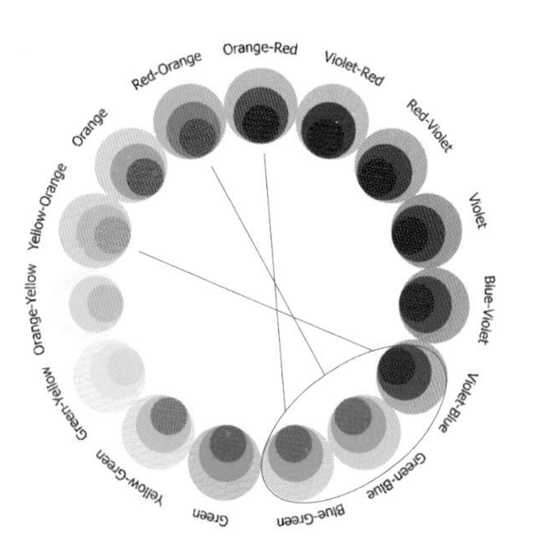

Combinations of violet-blue, green-blue and blue-green are often to be found on early pieces of oriental art. Used with skill they can provide very subtle harmonies of hue.

These particular colors tend to 'sit together' better when all three are softened with white. Stronger combinations have to be used with care as they can look rather 'hard'.

Related colors

Violet-blue, green-blue and blue-green

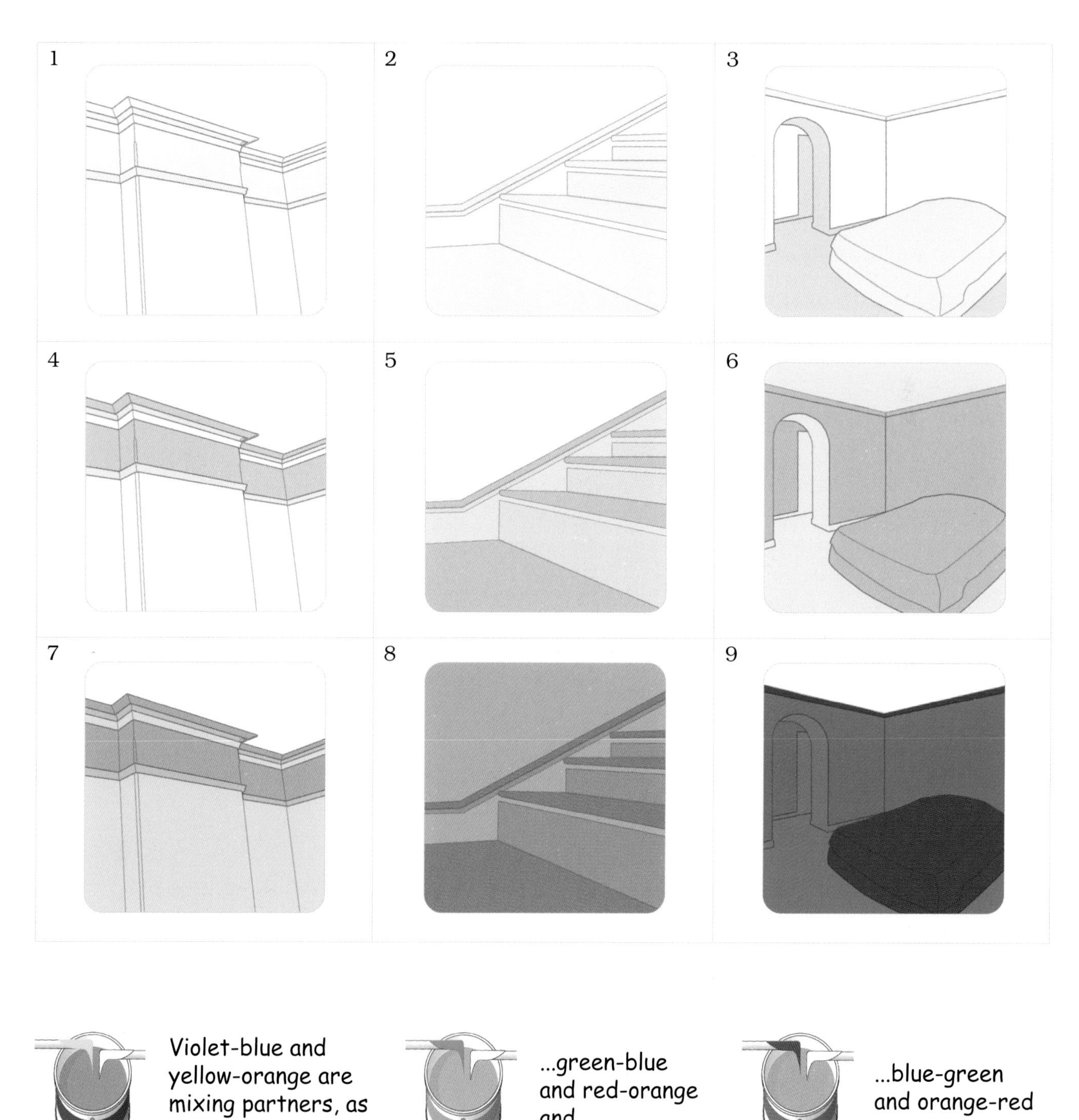

Violet-blue and yellow-orange are mixing partners, as are...

...green-blue and red-orange and...

...blue-green and orange-red

Violet-blue will darken with a little yellowish orange (or even a mid orange). Reddish orange will reduce the green-blue and orange-red will 'darken' the blue-green. White into any of the mixes will reduce the color even further. A little experimenting will soon show the way.

Related colors

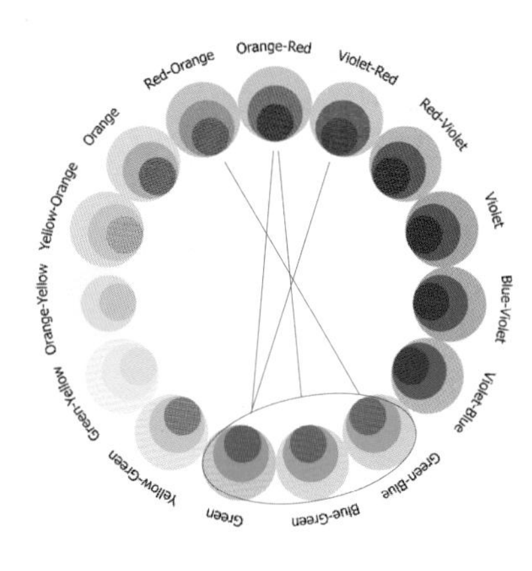

Soft, cool colors, that can be worked together very well and have many applications.

© H. Binet/arcblue.com

Many describe blue-green as a color of conformity. Cool and uncomplicated (as some of us are). These particular three can be harmonised with ease if care is taken with the stronger colors. The green, in particular, can be difficult when at or near full strength.

Related colors

Green-blue, blue-green and green

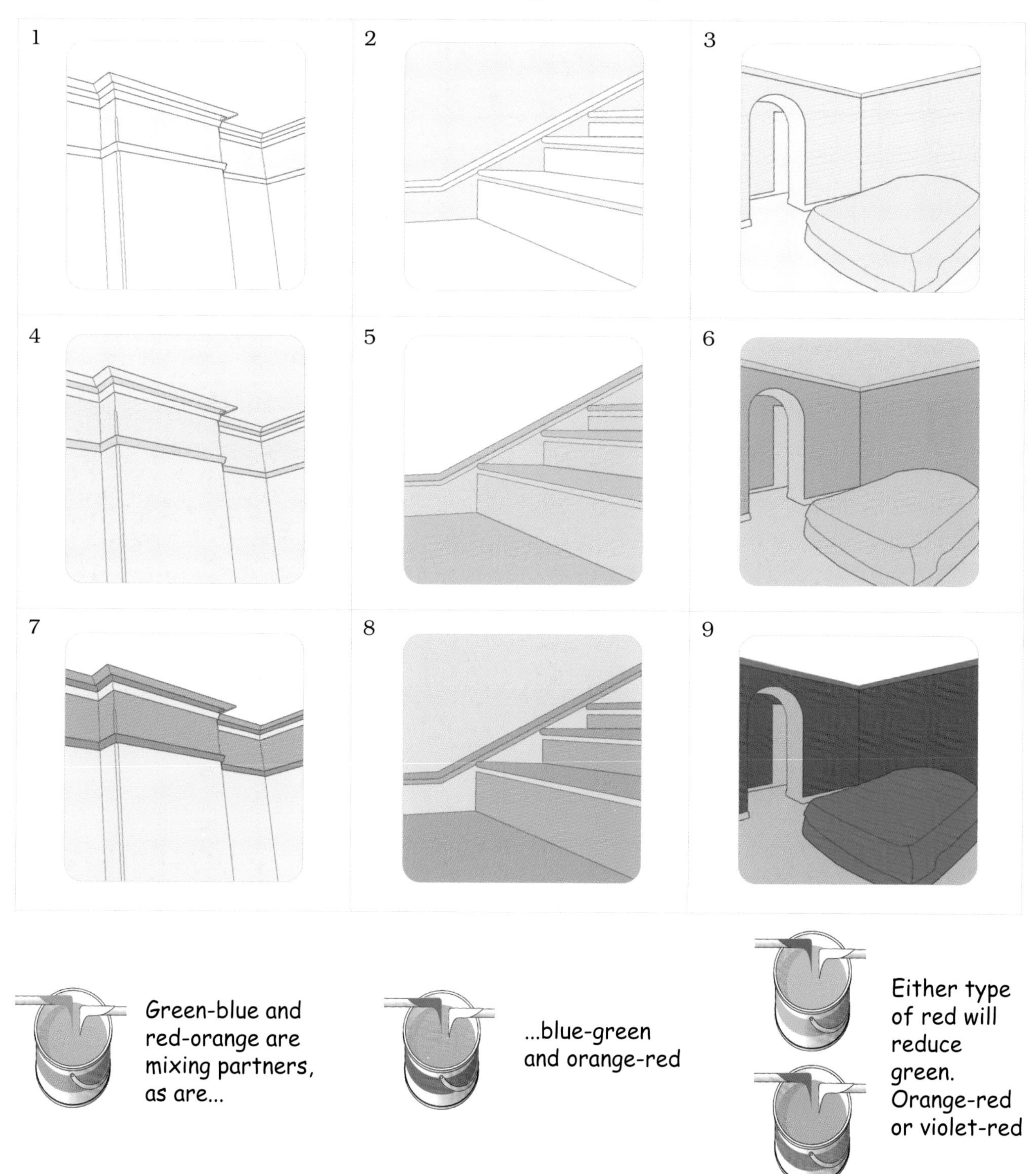

Green-blue and red-orange are mixing partners, as are...

...blue-green and orange-red

Either type of red will reduce green. Orange-red or violet-red

A reddish-orange (a type of orange), will 'darken' the green-blue and orange-red (a type of red), will darken the blue-green.

Use either type of red, (the violet or the orange-red) to reduce the mid green.

Using the mixing partner, with or without white is, of course, just one way to take a color in a different direction.

You could always add a touch of green to the green-blue for example.

Related colors

© Red Cover/David George

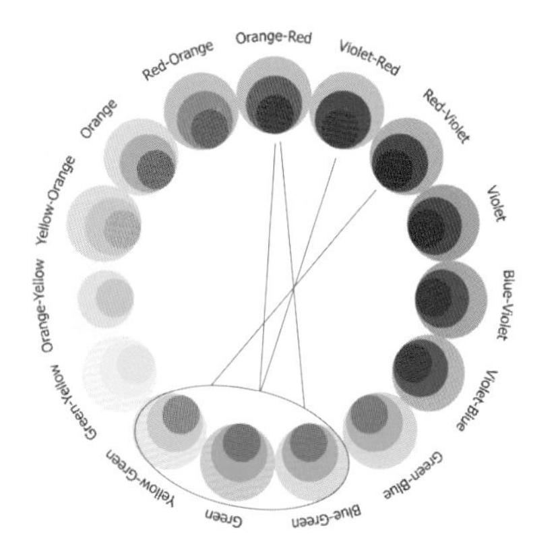

These three are seen by many as being introspective, calming colors.

Colored lighting has a definite part to play and can become one of the key hues.

Green has been described as suggesting calmness, defensiveness, envy, obstinacy and inexperience. (It's how you think really).

When lightened or darkened, these colors are easily worked together.

If any are used at or near full strength the result can be a little overpowering.

To overcome this tendency, try using strong colors in small touches against their reduced neighbours.

Related colors

Blue-green, green and yellow-green

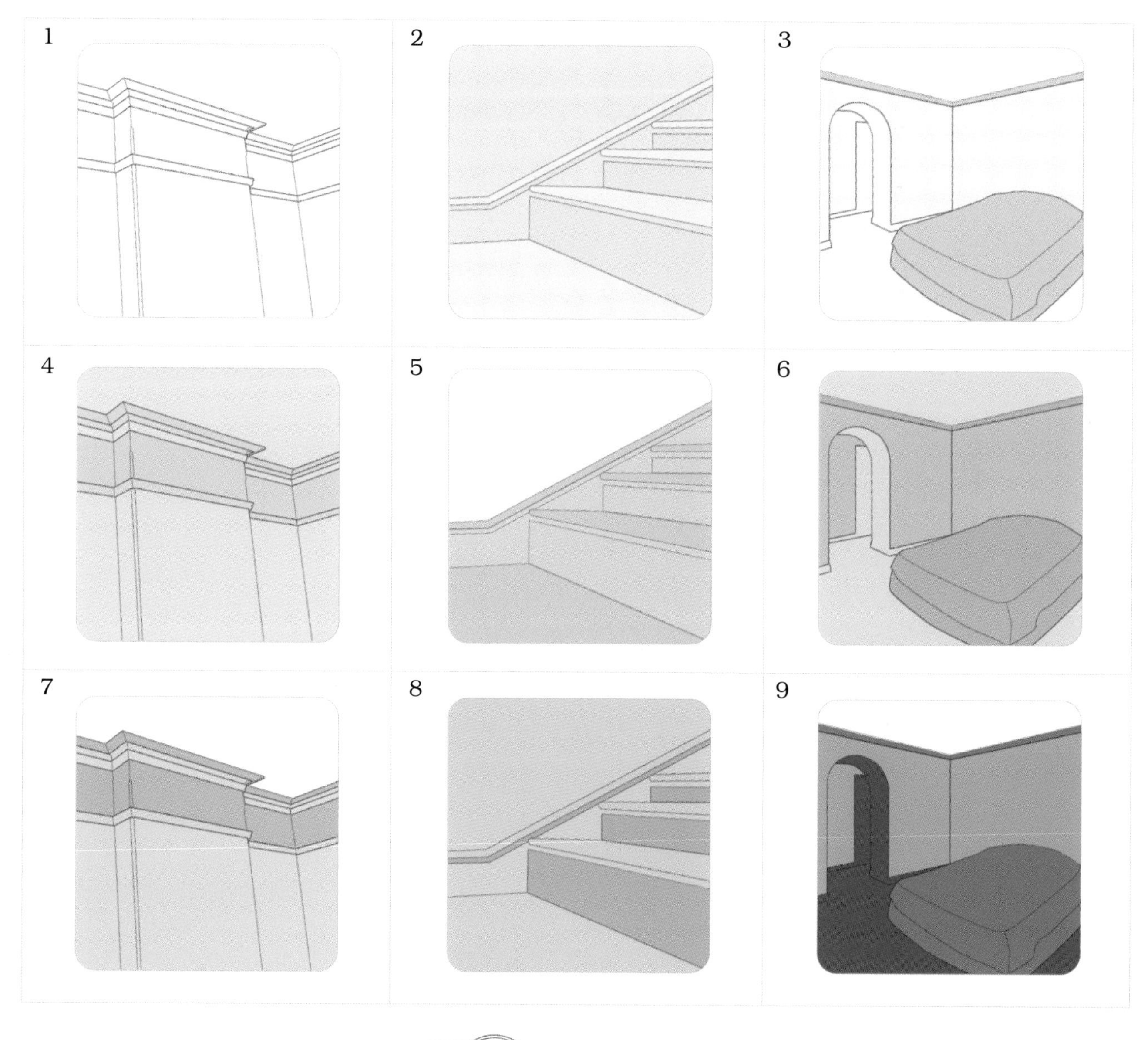

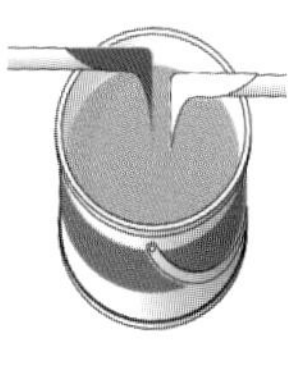

Even very small amounts of orange-red will reduce the intensity of blue-green.

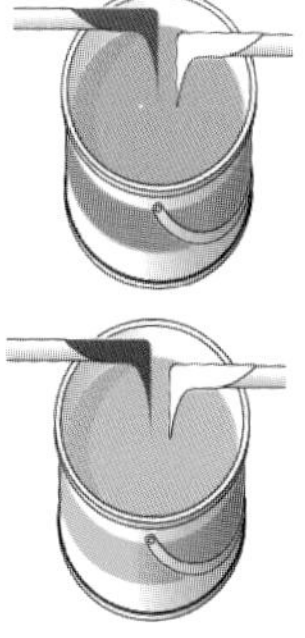

Orange-red or violet-red can be used to reduce green.

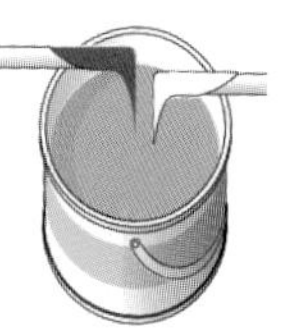

Yellow-green and violet-red are also mixing partners.

A wide range of mixed greens are available in the stores. If you decide to mix your own, you can of course proceed on a trial and error basis. If you wish to avoid the 'error' part we can help with information on color mixing at any level, from the practical to the more advanced. Please see the final page of this book for contact details.

Related colors

elizabethwhiting.com

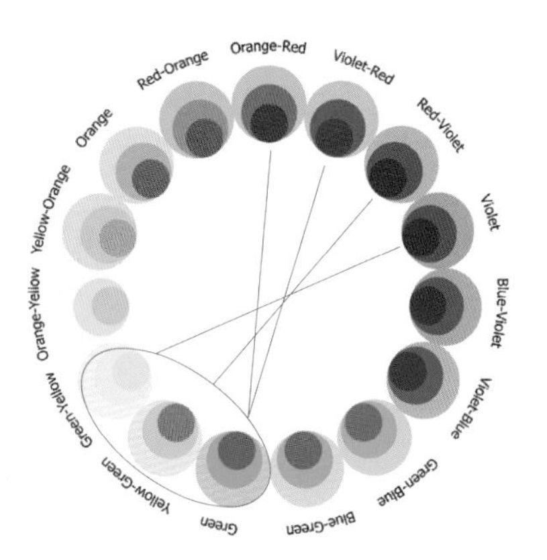

These three hues are commonly found together in nature.

The color of new plant growth, yellow-green is often described as the color of youth.

Together, these three hues can look particularly fresh. They tend to sit together better when all three are subdued with white rather than be darkened or used at full strength.

Use with caution at strength as the green-yellow is not to everyone's liking.

Related colors

Green, yellow-green and green-yellow

1

2

3

4

5

6

7

8

9

To reduce the intensity of green, add either an orange-red or a violet-red.

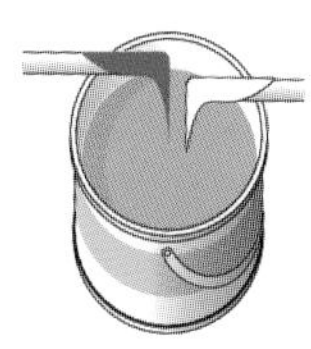

Yellow-green and violet-red will reduce each other, as will...

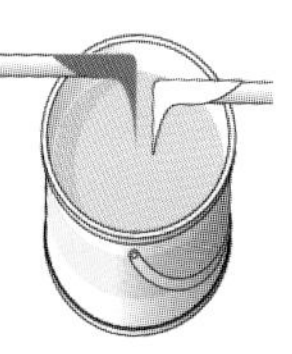

...green-yellow and violet

A wide range of harmonising colors can be built up using any of these basic hues. If a touch of either red, for example is added to green, it will start to lower its intensity and 'darken' it. A little more red and it becomes 'darker' still. A wide range of such greens can be produced with ease. If, in turn, white is added to these mixes in varying amounts an extensive range can be produced. As three basic hues are involved here you have a huge range to work with if you decide to mix or modify your own colors.

Related colors

elizabethwhiting.com

The 'cool' yellow-green gives a contrast of temperature against the 'warmer' orange-yellow.

Depending on how it is used the green-yellow can diminish or neutralise this contrast.

Not everyone finds that the two yellows sit well together. This can be an awkward combination if used without care. If using over relatively large areas it will pay to considerably reduce the yellows with white in many cases.

Related colors

Yellow-green, green-yellow and orange-yellow

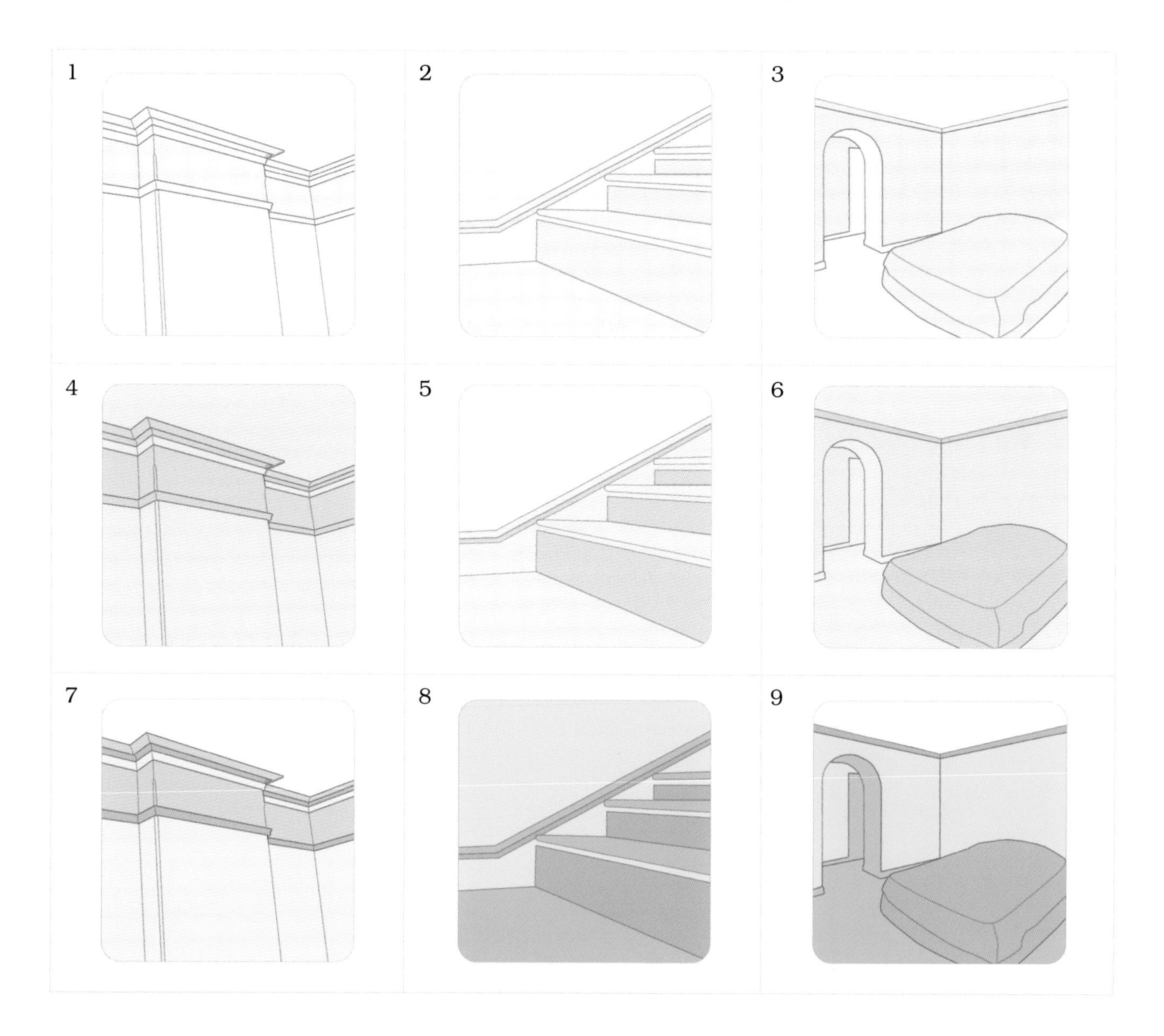

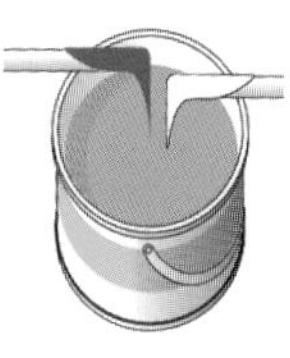

Yellow-green can be reduced in strength by violet-red.

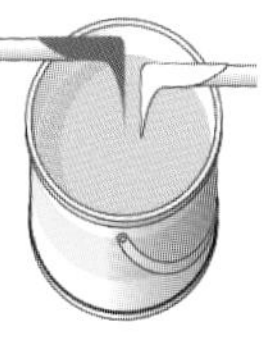

Green-yellow and red-violet are mixing partners, as are...

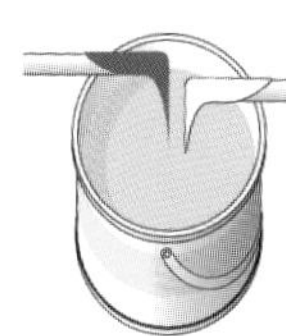

...orange-yellow and blue-violet.

Rather than mix your colors you might prefer to select from ready-mixed paints. If so, you can always match up color sample cards in the store with the color guidance swatches on these pages. The most important element is to match up the 'color-type', yellow-green, orange-yellow etc. It might take a little time but it will be worth it.

Related colors

My own interest in home decorating began with my Grandmother.

Her favourite color was yellow. In her bedroom she had yellow walls, curtains, carpets, sheets and pillows.

She then contracted yellow jaundice and we haven't been able to find her since.

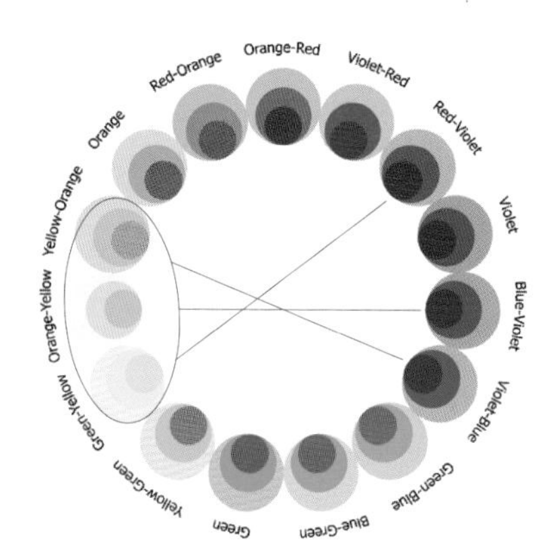

The 'cooler' green-yellow can have a slightly disruptive influence on the 'warmer' colors. It might be better to restrict its use somewhat.

When set against the orange-yellow, in particular, it can look rather awkward.

It is one of the few color pairings that many find unpleasant. In order to allow them to be worked together the strength of one or both might need to be lowered, either with plenty of white, with the mixing partner or with both.

Related colors

Green-yellow, orange-yellow, yellow-orange

1 2 3

4 5 6

7 8 9

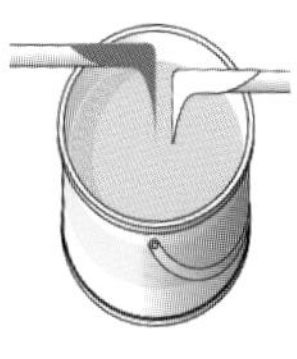

Red-violet will lower the intensity of green-yellow.

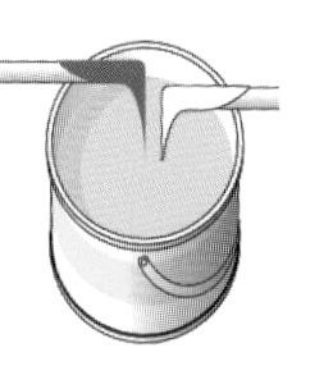

Blue-violet will reduce orange-yellow but can take it towards green quite quickly.

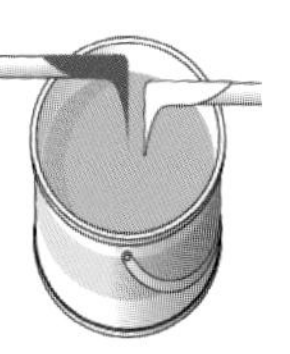

Yellow-orange and violet-blue are also mixing partners.

If you are following the mixing tips above you will need to read the color descriptions carefully as one can be confused with another. Blue-violet, for example, is a type of violet whereas violet-blue is a type of blue. With a little usage these terms will become familiar.

Related colors

© Red Cover/Adrian Wilson

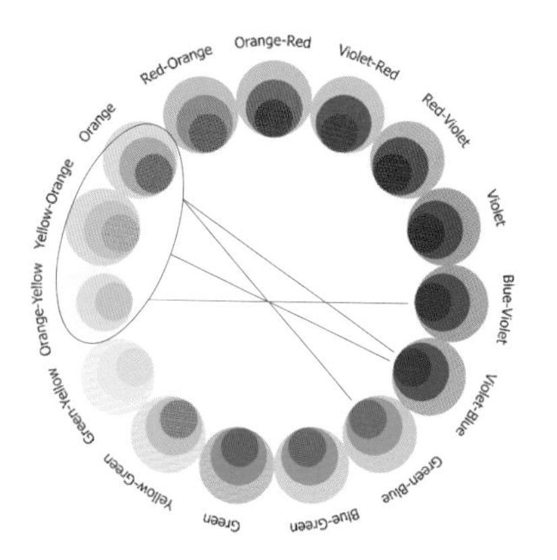

A note of caution; fully saturated orange can tend to dominate the other two hues unless used with some care.

Smaller 'touches' of bright orange can work well or alternatively, try reducing the strength by one means or another. When made lighter or darker orange tends to be more acceptable.

© Red Cover/Graham Atkins-Hughes

Warm 'sunny' colors, they can have an enlivening effect in many settings.

Related colors

Orange-yellow, yellow-orange and orange

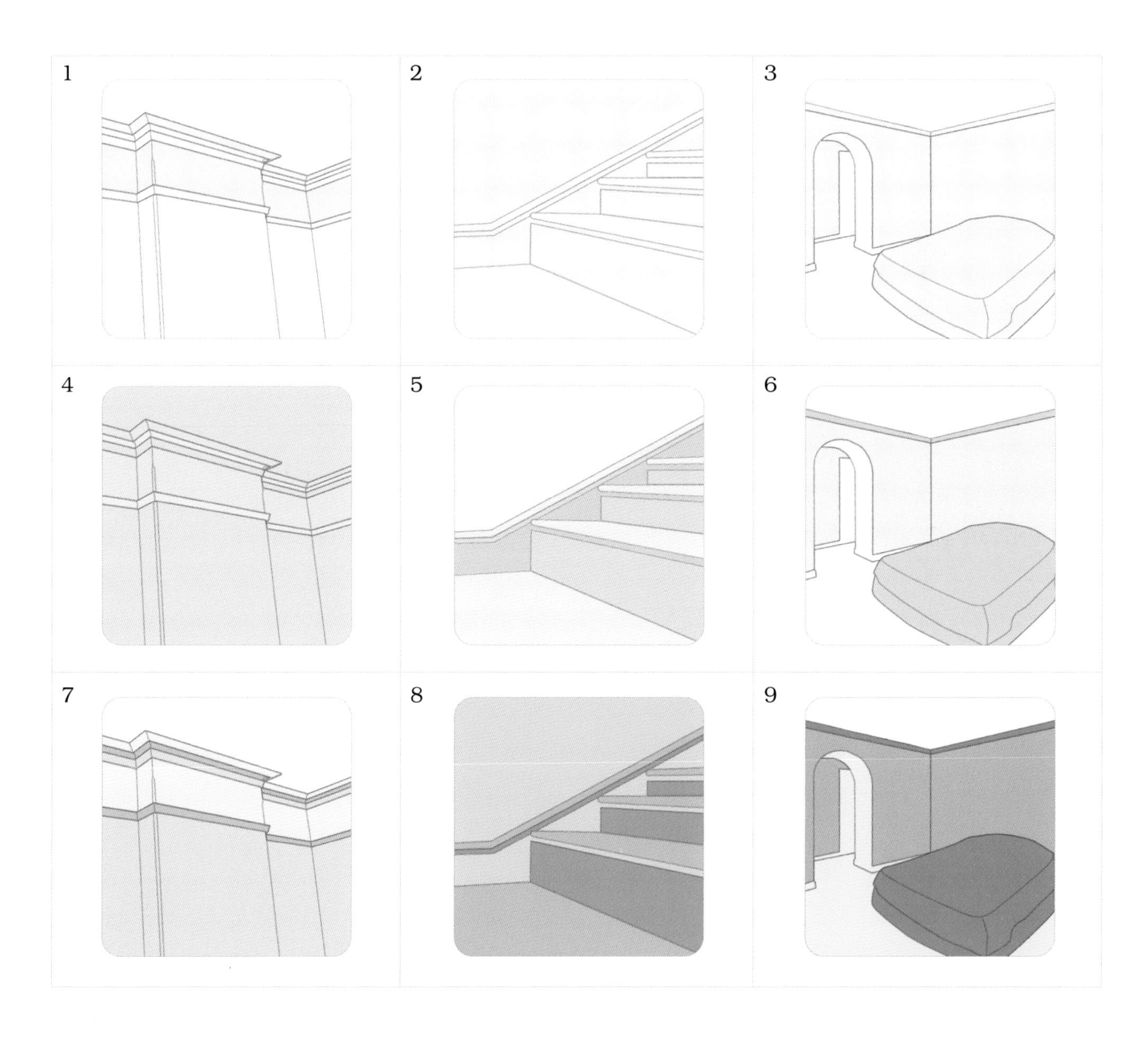

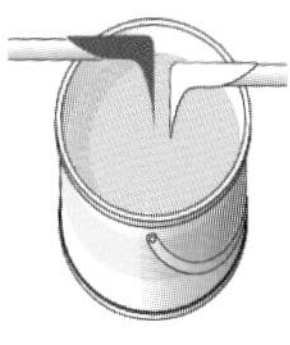

Blue-violet will reduce or neutralise orange-yellow.

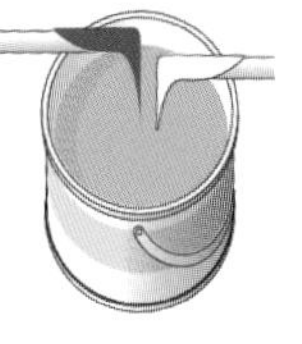

Violet-blue will absorb the strength of yellow-orange.

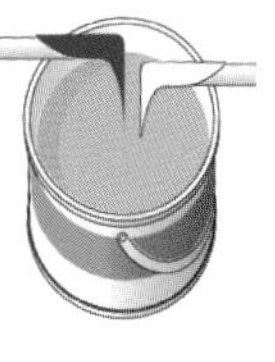

Orange and violet-blue are also mixing partners but green-blue will do a similar job.

If you wish, you can reduce the strength of these basic hues with white, with the mixing partner or with white *and* the mixing partner. For orange-yellow add blue-violet, for the yellow-orange mix in a little violet-blue and for orange add either type of blue.

Related colors

© Red Cover/Reto Guntli

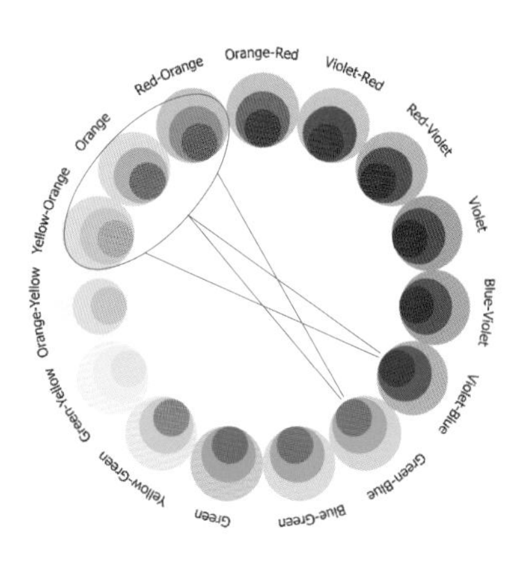

A common theme in nature,

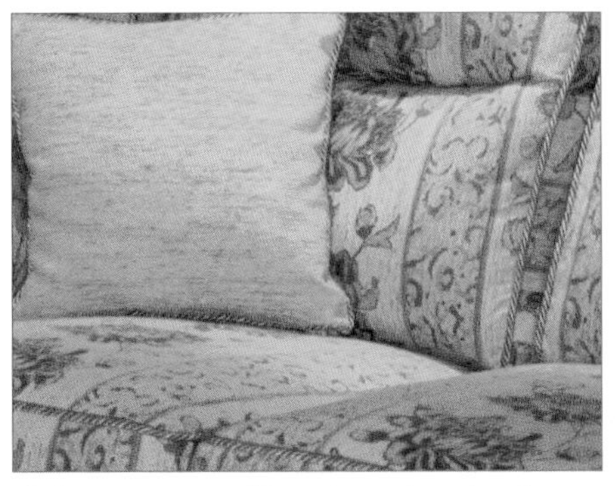

with many applications in the home.

Many people react poorly to bright orange, it is one of the least popular colors. Therefore it might be advisable to use it sparingly.

However, when reduced in intensity, by any means, it has an important role to play.

Dark orange is usually called brown and fits well in almost any color scheme. Browns are darkened yellows, oranges and reds.

Related colors

Yellow-orange, orange and red-orange

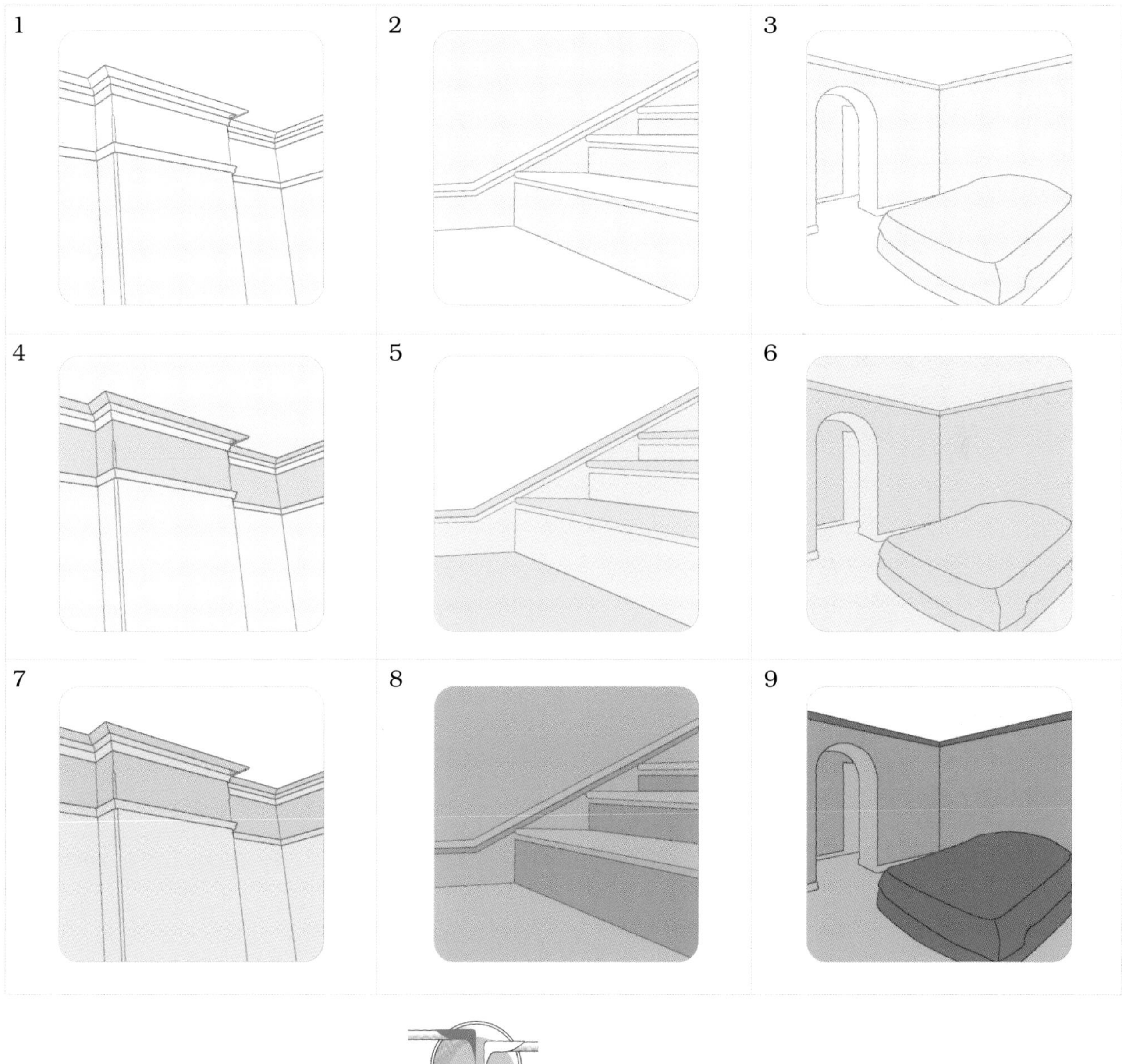

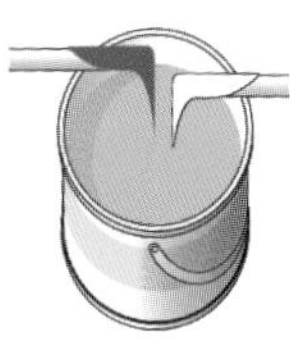

Violet-blue will reduce the strength of yellow-orange.

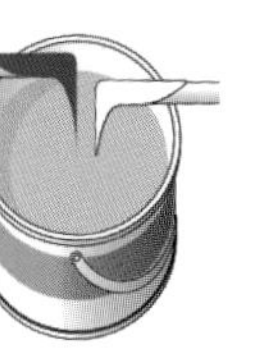

Orange can be reduced with either green-blue or violet-blue.

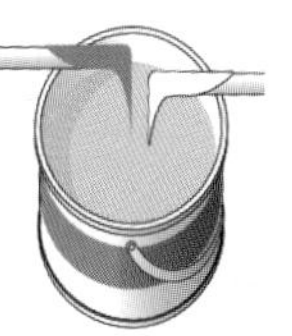

Red-orange and green-blue are also mixing partners.

If you choose to add violet-blue to the yellow-orange in order to reduce its intensity, you might find that the mix quickly moves towards green.

If this is the case, and you find it to be too green, add a tiny amount of any red. The red will reduce the greenness as it absorbs it; red and green being mixing partners.

Related colors

© A. Southall/arcblue.com

Red-Orange
Orange-Red
Violet-Red
Red-Violet
Violet
Blue-Violet
Violet-Blue
Green-Blue
Blue-Green
Green
Yellow-Green
Green-Yellow
Orange-Yellow
Yellow-Orange
Orange

The ranges available from orange to orange-red are the 'warmest' of the palette. When used at or near full strength, these colors are often employed more as accents rather than over larger areas. They can be very powerful unless moderated. Colors for the bold.

Related colors

Orange, red-orange and orange-red

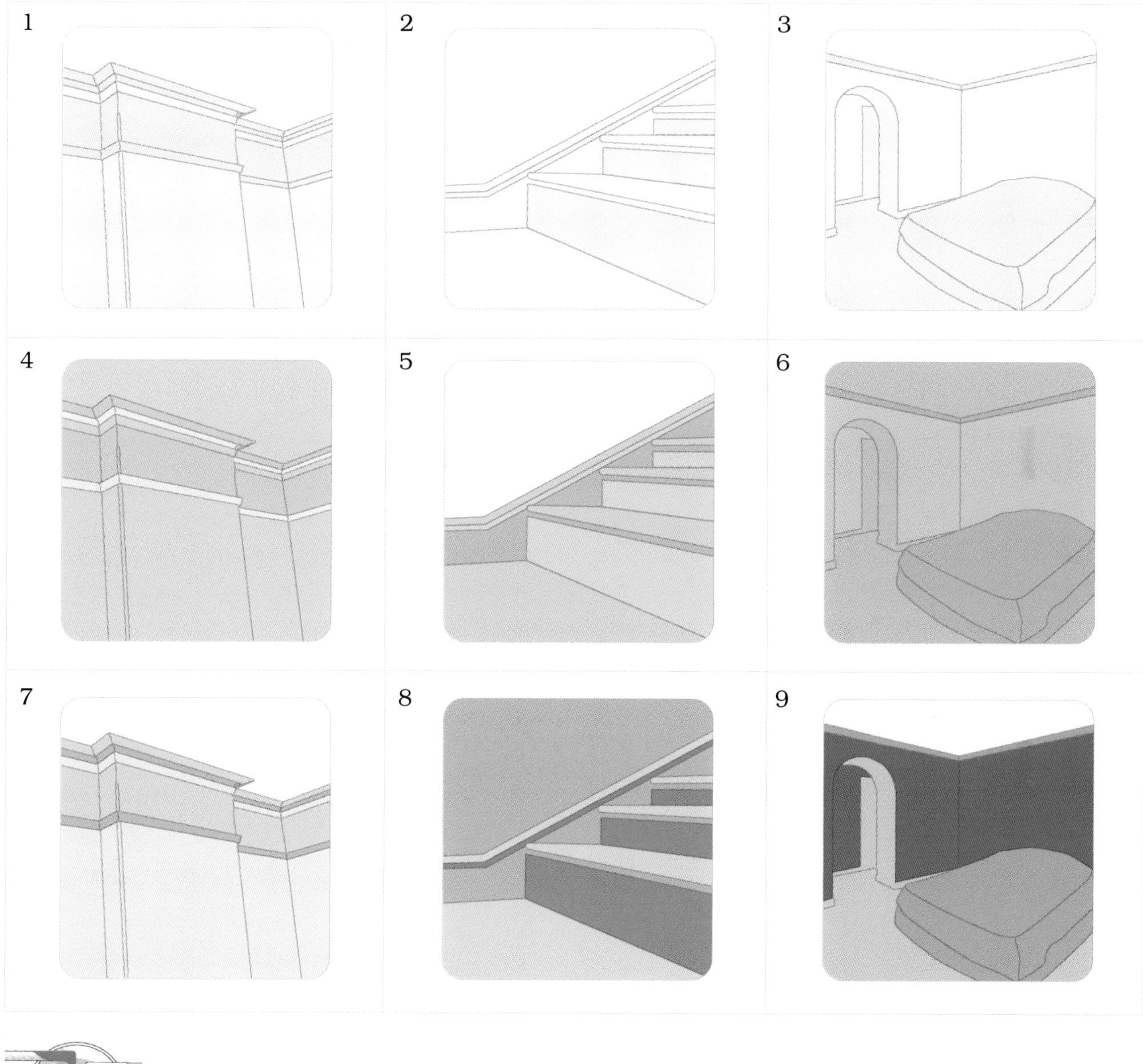

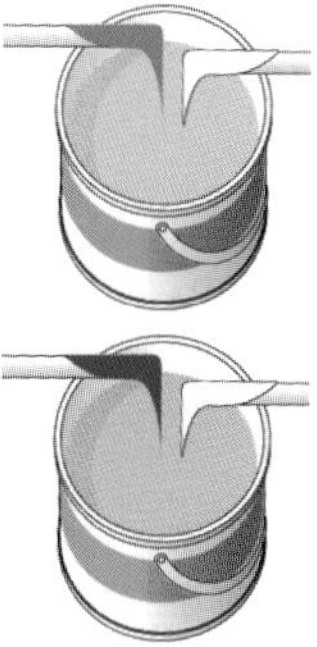

Orange can be reduced in intensity with either green-blue or violet-blue.

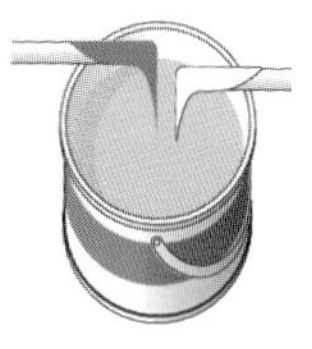

Red-orange and green-blue are a mixing pair, as are...

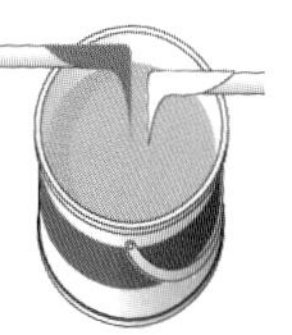

...orange-red and blue-green.

The intensity of orange can be reduced in various ways; with white, with either type of blue, or with white *and* either blue.

However, as green-blue will be used, if you reduce the intensity of the red-orange, it will be preferable to use this same type of blue with the orange. The total number of colors will be kept to a minimum this way.

Related colors

© C. Wood/arcblue.com

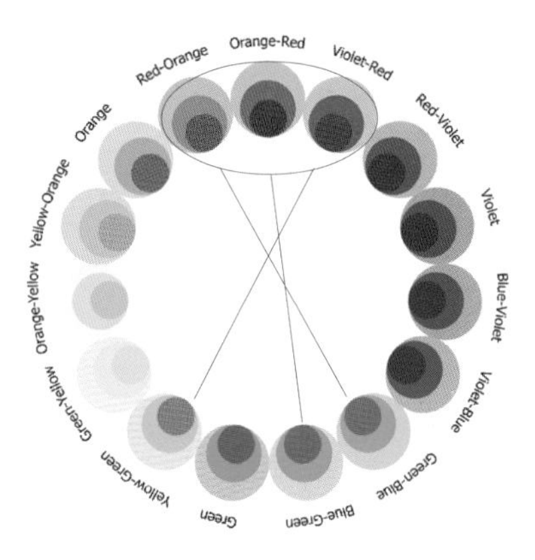

Orange-red and violet-red together can be difficult as they tend to look awkward side by side.

As the 'cooler' violet-red is introduced an element of 'temperature' contrast can add further interest, particularly if the hue is not too strong. These three colors tend to harmonise better when reduced with white or with white and the mixing partner.

When simply darkened or used at full strength they do not always work so well together.

Related colors

Red-orange, orange-red and violet-red

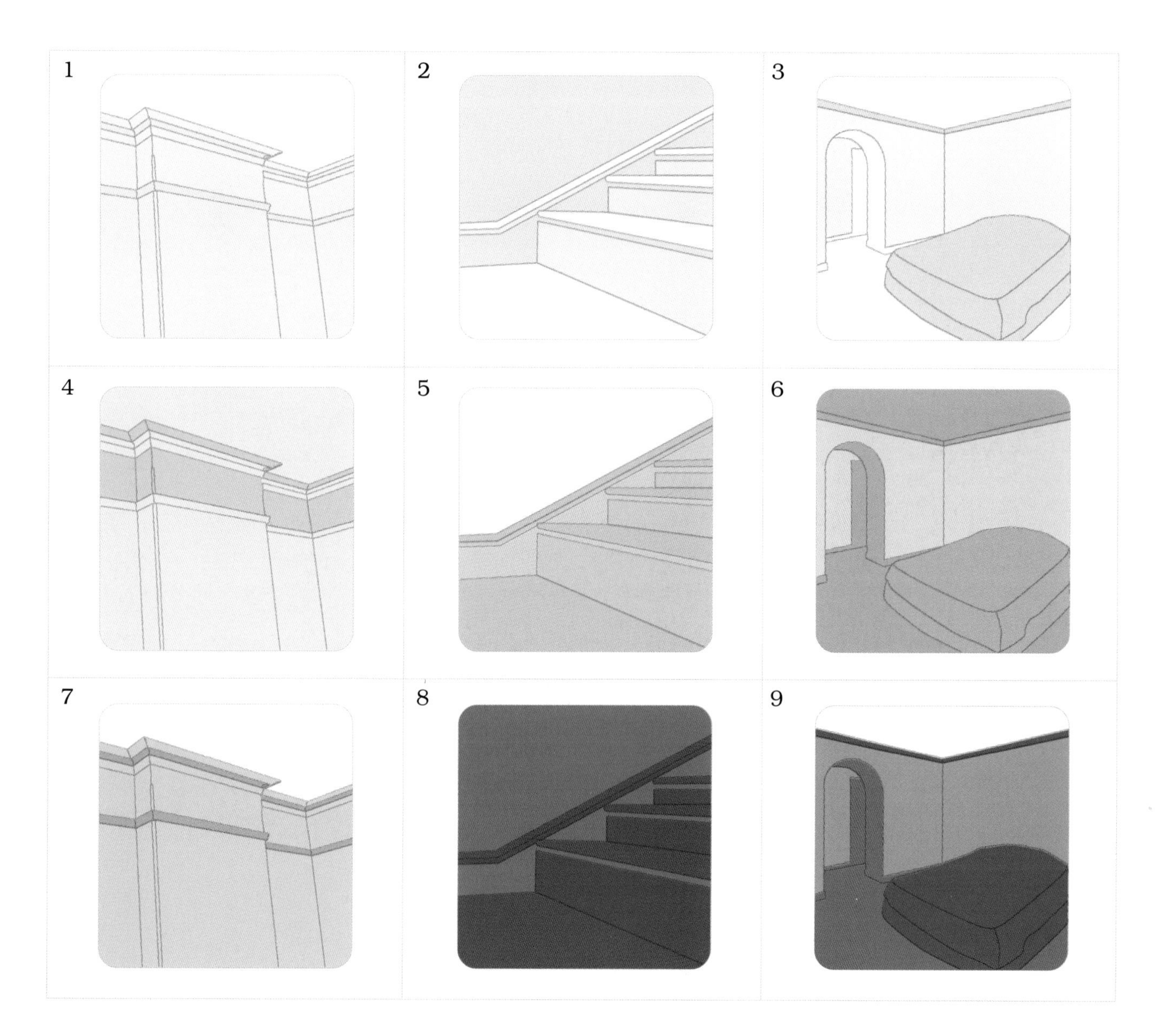

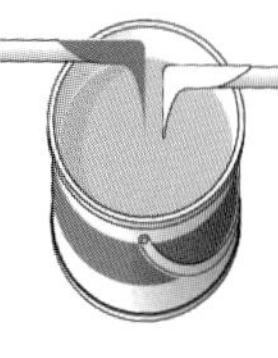

Red-orange and green-blue are mixing partners, as are...

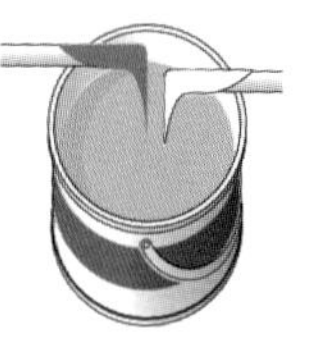

...orange-red and blue-green...

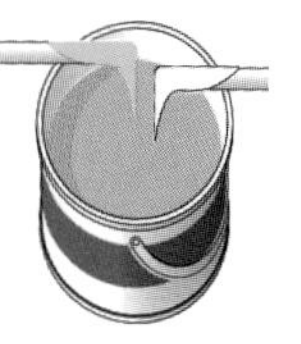

...and violet-red and yellow-green.

Desaturate the red-orange with white, with the mixing partner *green-blue*, or with white *and* the mixing partner green-blue.

The mixing partner of the orange-red is a *blue-green*, and that of violet-red a *yellow-green*.

Related colors

Summary

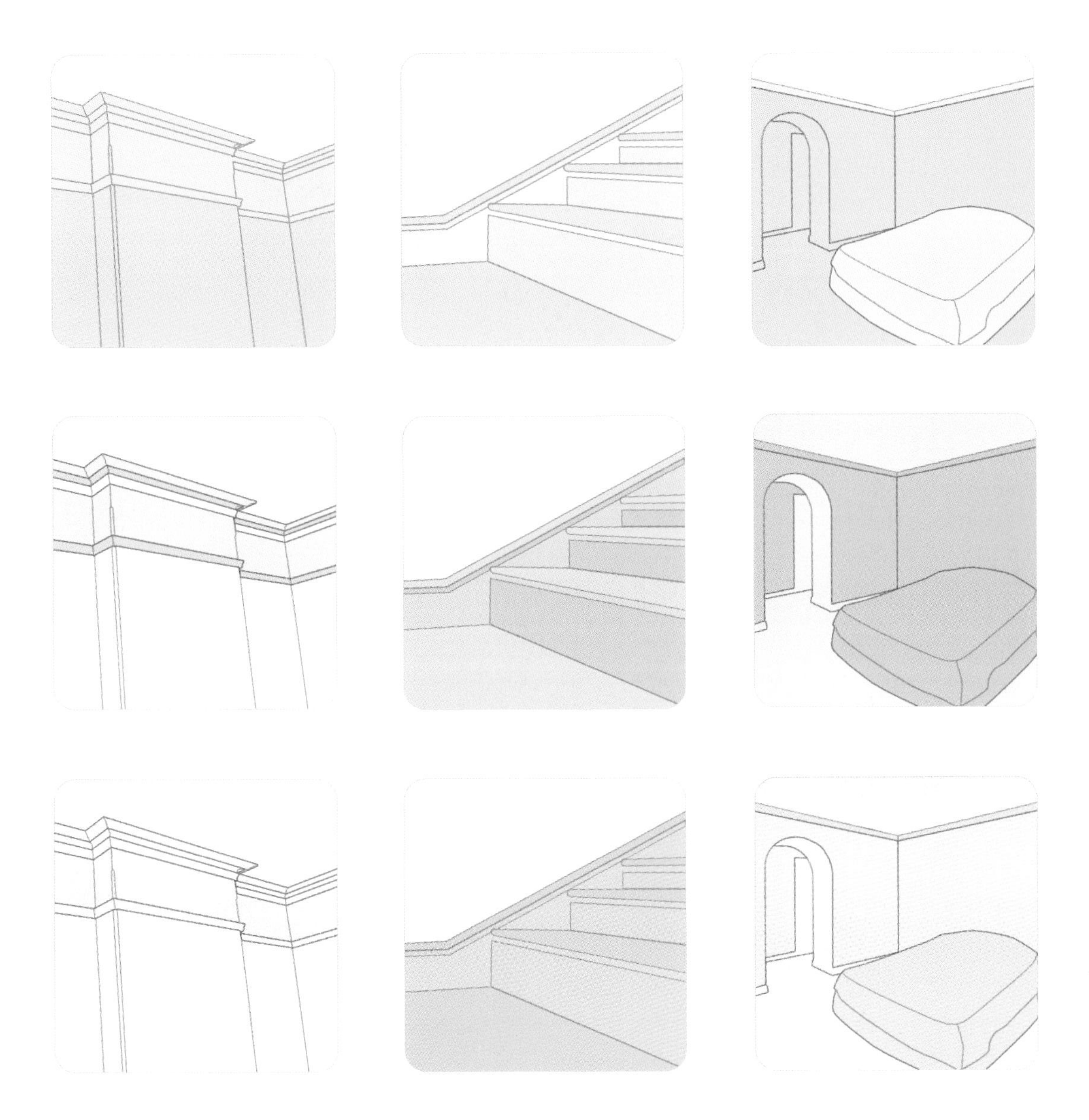

Selecting colors that are closely related will provide a wide range of combinations that are quite easy to harmonise.

Little can go wrong as the colors have so much in common. Although contrast is limited, strong visual interest can still be created.

The wider family group

Introduction

© Red Cover/Jon Bouchier

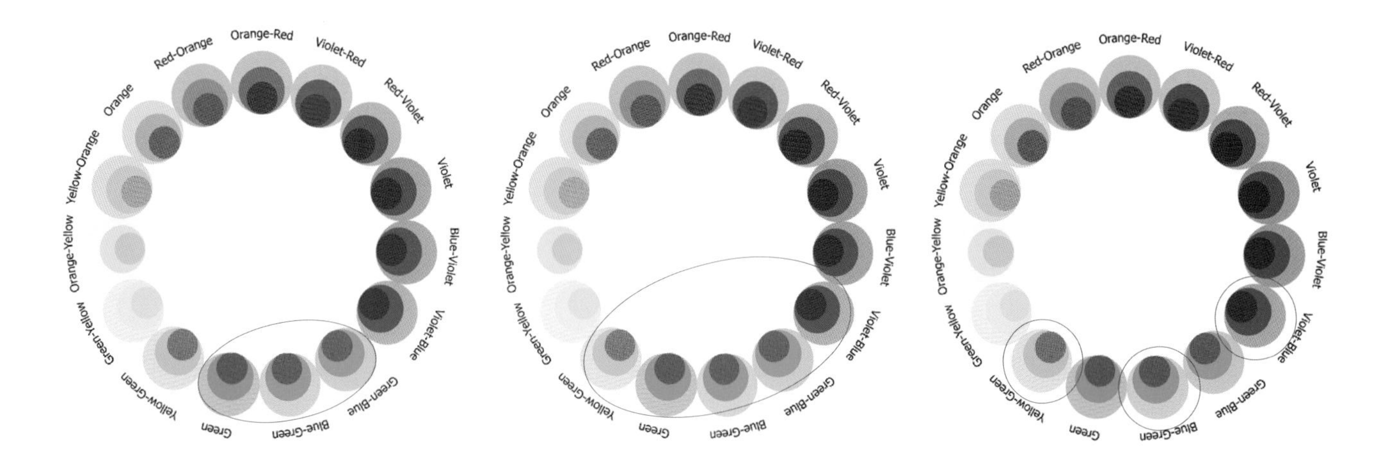

Related colors

The related color groups that we have been examining were based on three adjacent basic hues selected from the color wheel. They worked together well as they had much in common with each other.

The wider family group

This approach is taken a step further with the wider family group. In this arrangement up to *five* hues are selected.

A little more care has to be taken as the full range is not now quite so closely related.

In order to keep the color swatches which follow as simple as possible I have chosen just *three* hues from each selection instead of the full *five*.

The essential element with this approach is that the range can be selected from up to five adjacent colors.

The wider family group

elizabethwhiting.com

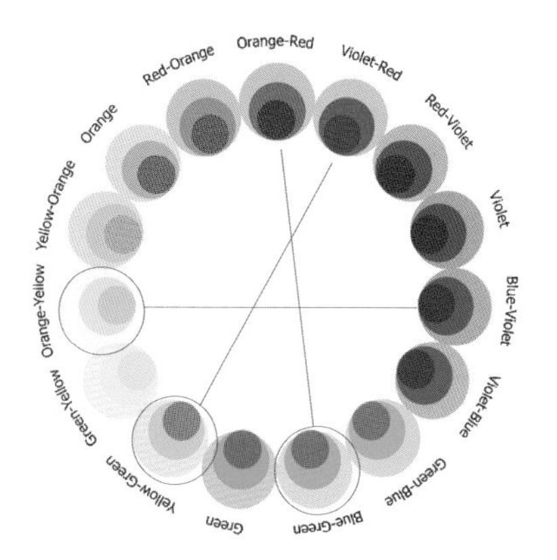

The ‘warm’ orange-yellow will contrast with its cooler partners in a more direct way than the green-yellow did in the previous exercise. This change in ‘temperature’, together with a change in character can create a strong contrast.

This need not upset harmony but could limit the use of the yellow at full saturation.

The wider family group

Blue-green, yellow-green and orange-yellow

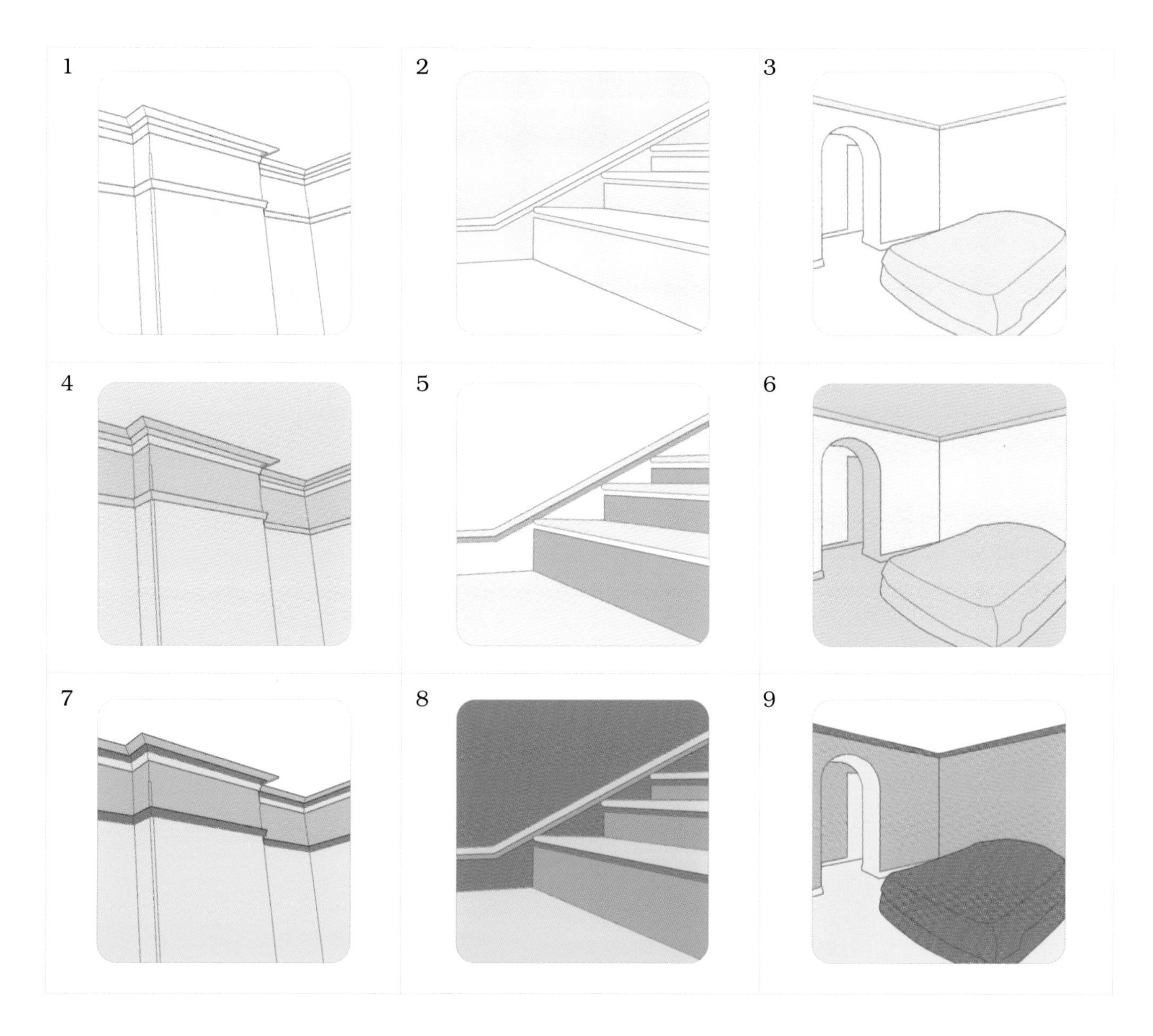

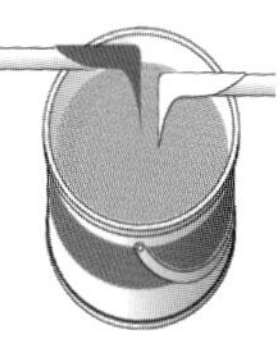

Blue-green and orange-red will 'absorb' each others color.

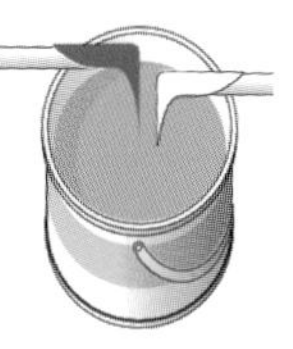

Yellow-green and violet-red are mixing partners, as are...

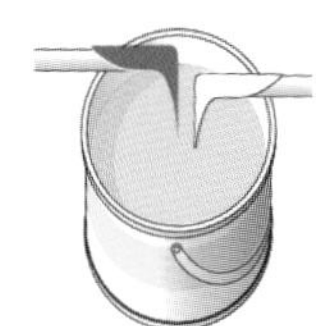

...orange-yellow and blue-violet.

In a book of this nature, intended to suggest possible color combinations, the information on color mixing is naturally limited to hints and tips.

If you wish to explore the actual mixing of color more thoroughly, you might find our books on color mixing will be of help. Please see last pages of book for further details.

The wider family group

© Red Cover/Huntley Hedworth

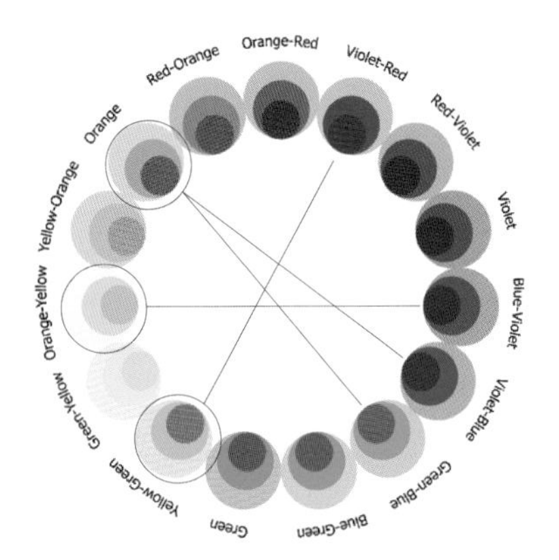

The rather powerful orange can cause discord unless it is reduced with white, desaturated with its mixing partner (either type of blue), or with white and the mixing partner.

I would suggest that you use fully saturated orange with caution as many dislike it.

© Red Cover/Graham Atkins-Hughes

Harmony can be achieved using these three basic hues, but each needs to be modified or used in very small touches at full strength.

The wider family group

Yellow-green, orange-yellow and orange

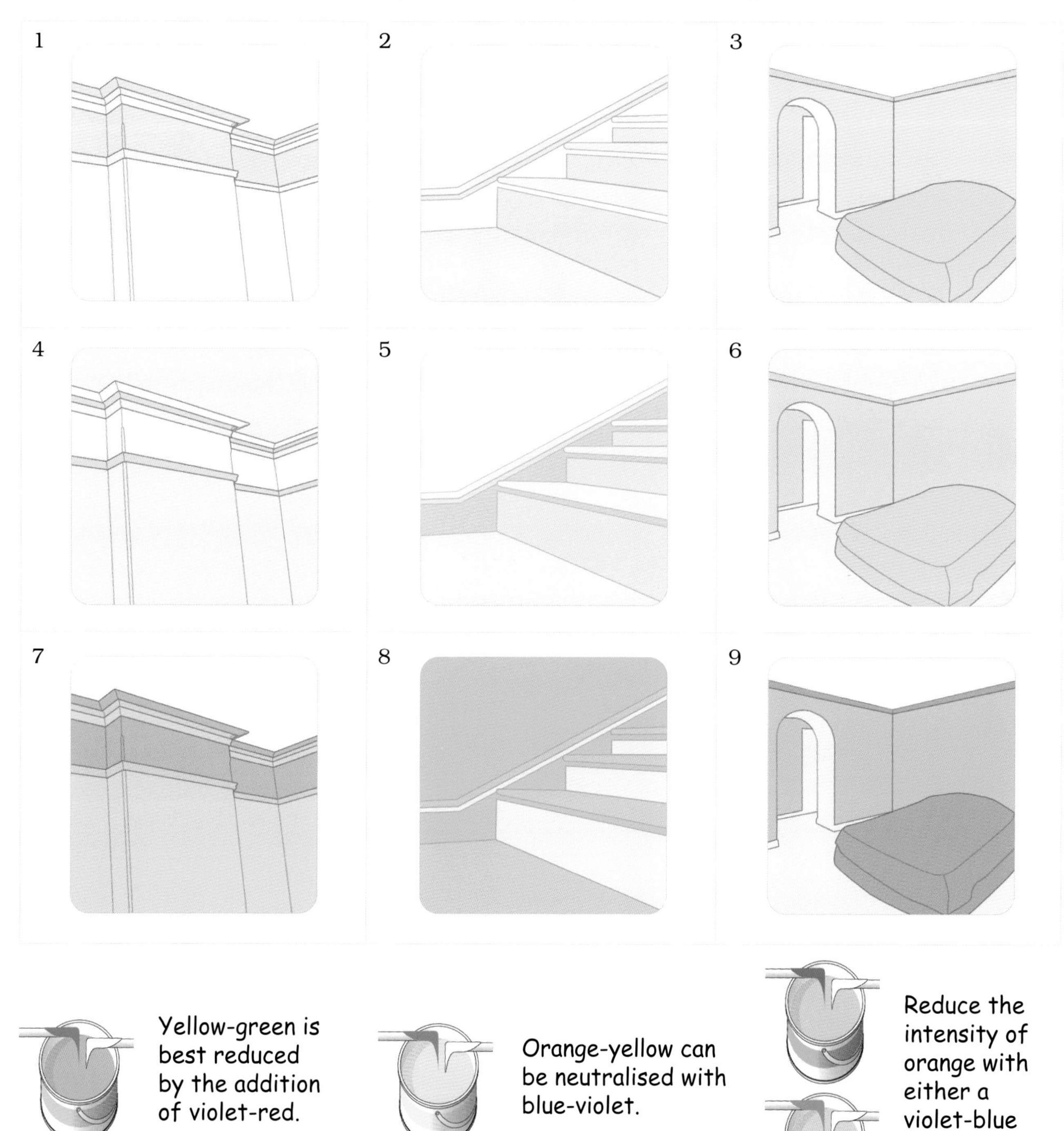

Yellow-green is best reduced by the addition of violet-red.

Orange-yellow can be neutralised with blue-violet.

Reduce the intensity of orange with either a violet-blue or a green-blue.

If neutralising the orange-yellow with blue-violet, add a touch of red if the mix moves too far towards green. The red, which need only be a drop or two, will absorb the unwanted greenness.

When mixing colors it pays to work slowly and carefully, noting the direction that the color is taken as its partner is added or if a modifier such as the red mentioned here is employed.

The wider family group

elizabethwhiting.com

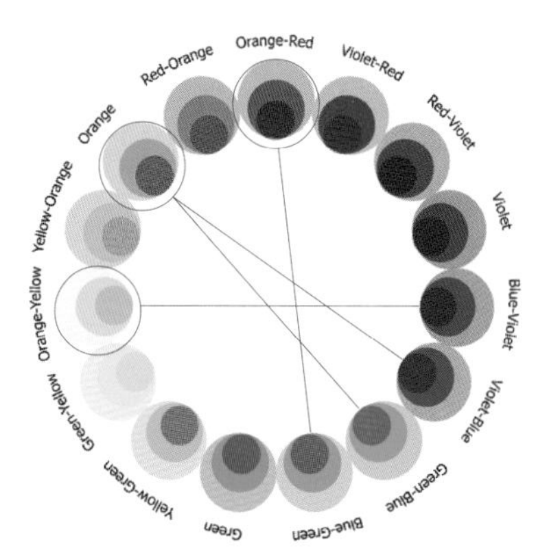

Used at near full strength these hues will give a definite feeling of warmth. If you are seeking harmony rather than contrast you will need to reduce intensities.

elizabethwhiting.com

Some bright, striking color combinations are available using these solid base colors.

The wider family group

Orange-yellow, orange and orange-red

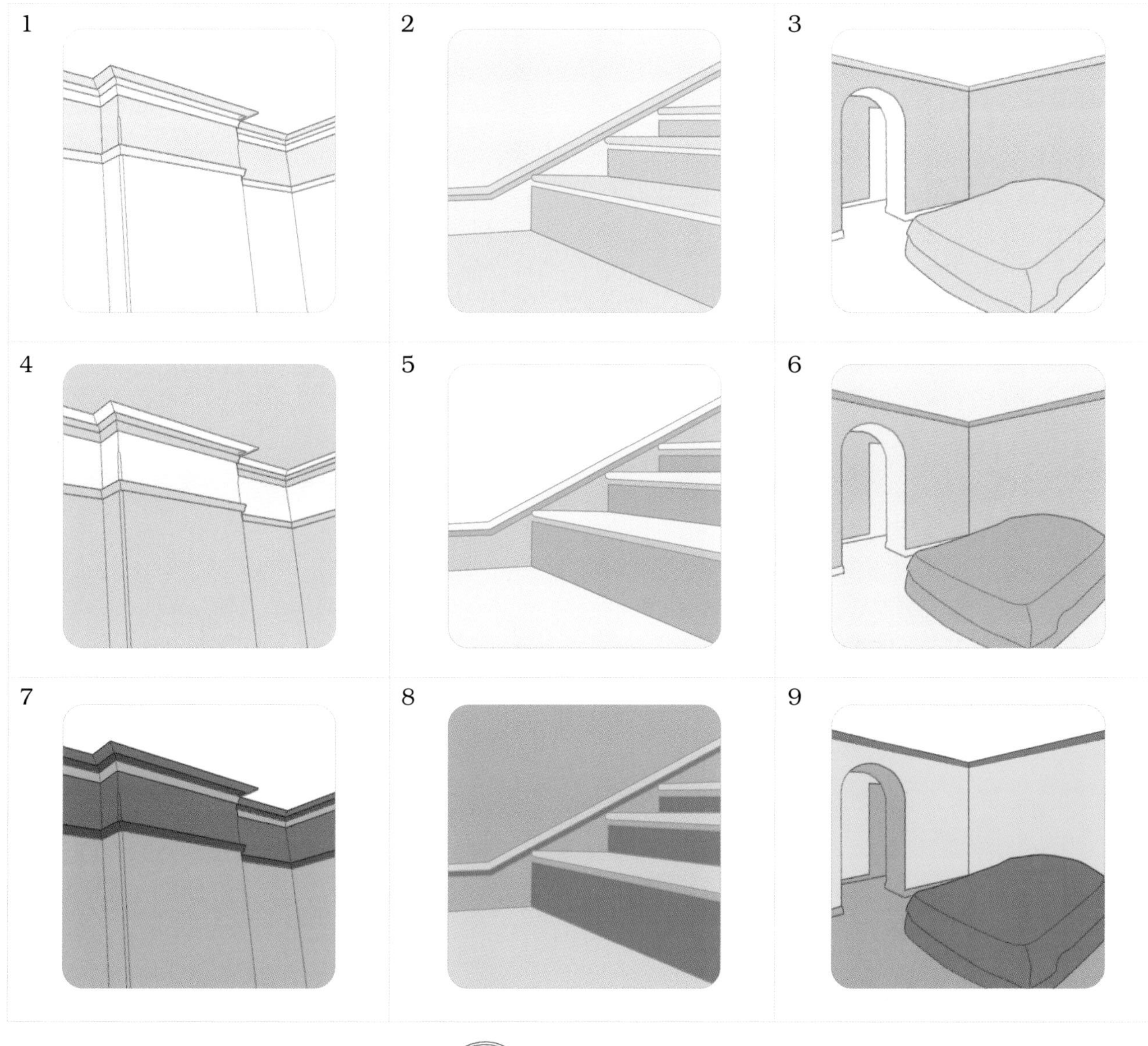

Orange-yellow and blue-violet are mixing partners and will lower the intensity of each other when blended.

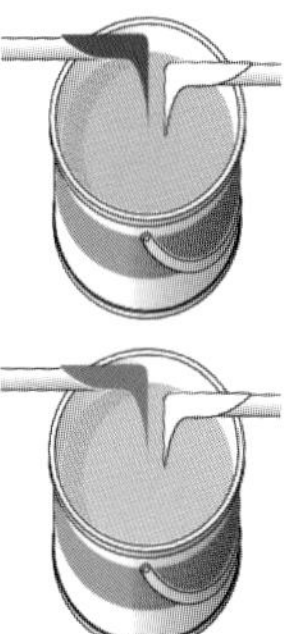

The intensity of orange can be reduced with either a violet-blue or a green-blue.

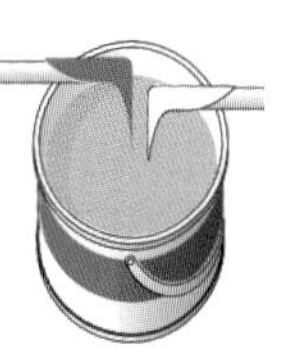

Orange-red is easily reduced with blue-green.

Yellow is the most easily altered hue of all and loses its identity very quickly. As soon as even the slightest hint of green is present we decide that the new color is green and not yellow.

You might find that only a tiny amount of the blue-violet can be added (if you are reducing its strength) before the orange-yellow becomes a yellow-green. For this reason adding white is usually the best method of reducing its strength.

The wider family group

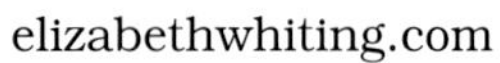
elizabethwhiting.com

Newly discovered violet dyes caused an upsurge in the use of violets and mauves during the 1800's. These once very popular hues can add an 'old fashioned' look.

Reduced in strength one way or the other and you can produce some very unusual and interesting combinations from these three basic hues.

The wider family group

Orange, orange-red and red-violet

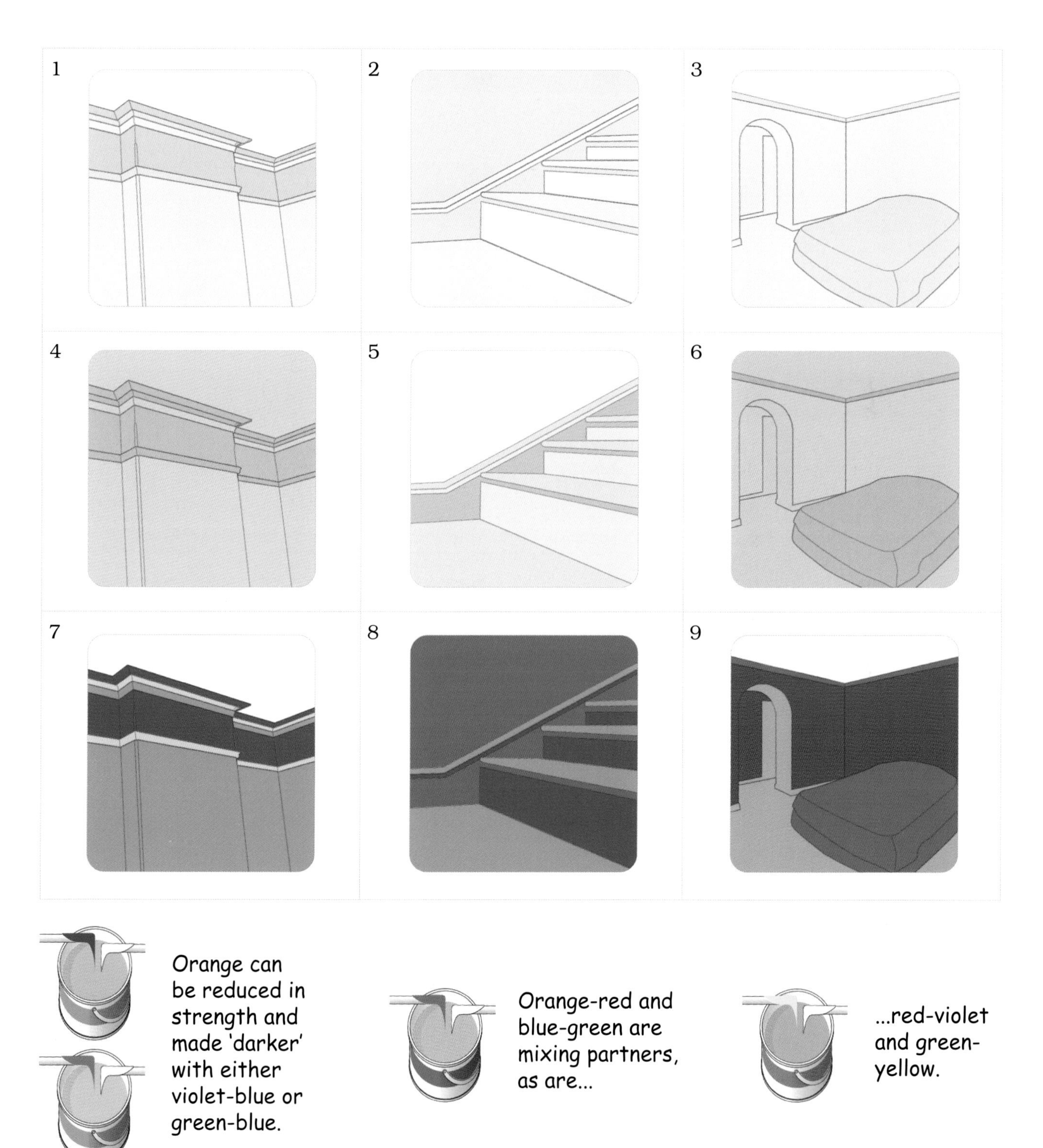

Orange can be reduced in strength and made 'darker' with either violet-blue or green-blue.

Orange-red and blue-green are mixing partners, as are...

...red-violet and green-yellow.

As the mixing partner is added it starts to remove or 'absorb' the other color.

If it is added slowly and carefully the final result can be fully controlled.

The wider family group

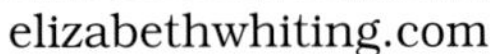
elizabethwhiting.com

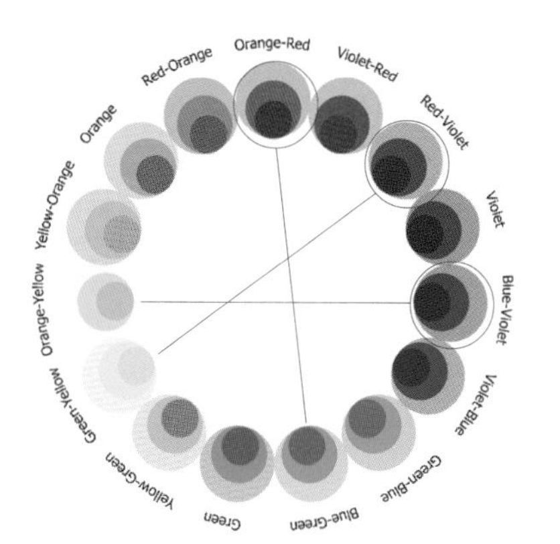

Used with care, this combination can be very effective.

Color groupings which include 'warm' hues such as orange-red and 'cool' colors like the blue-violet can be a little difficult to work together due to 'temperature' contrasts.

If required, the contrast of 'temperature' can be modified by reducing the intensities of one or all colors by the means described opposite.

The wider family group

Orange-red, red-violet and blue-violet

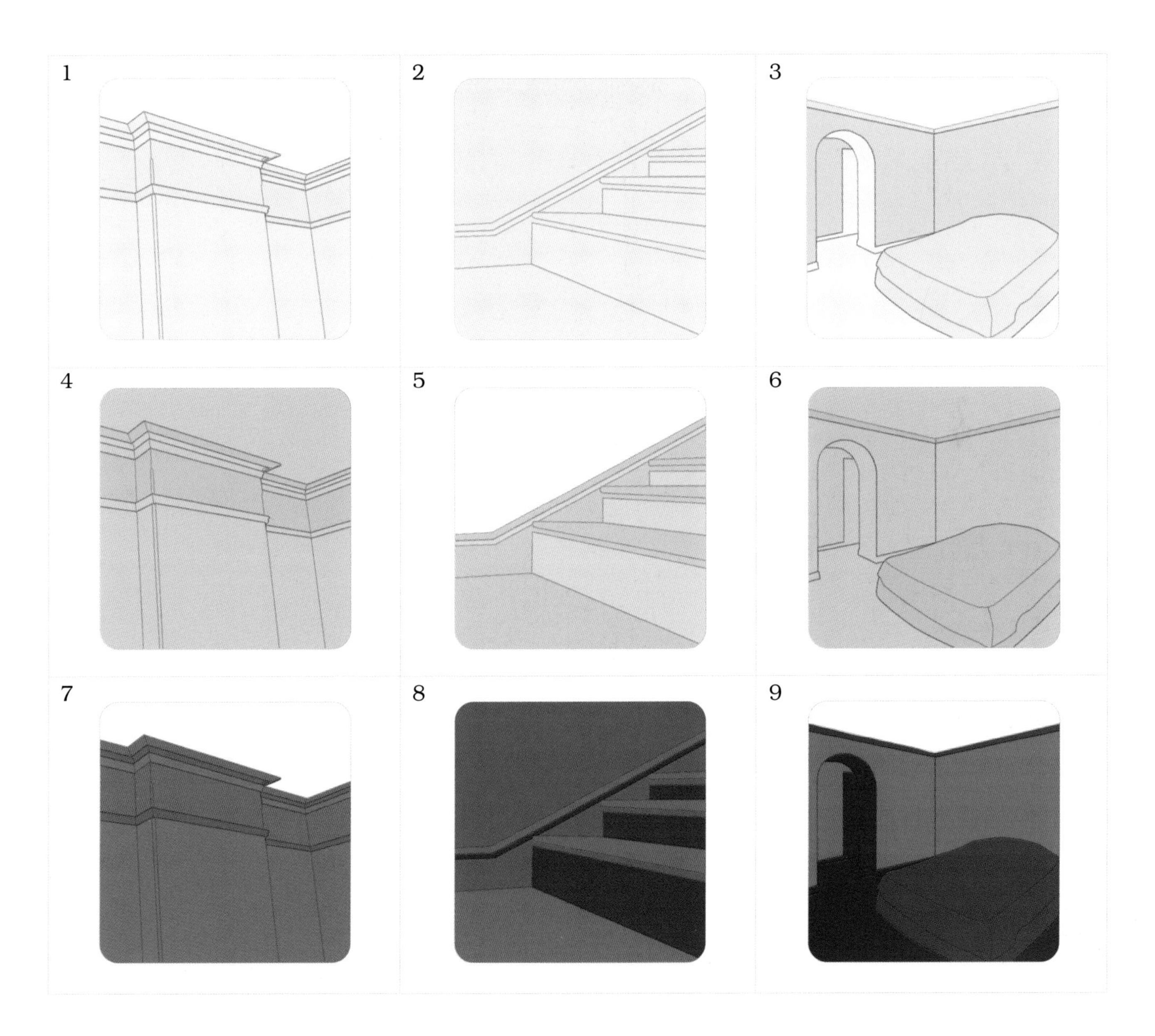

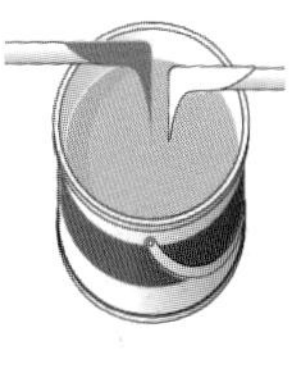

Orange-red and blue-green are mixing partners, as are....

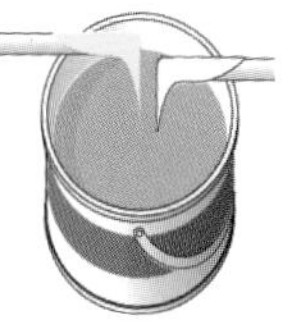

...red-violet and green-yellow.

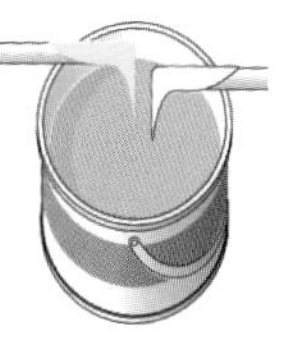

Blue-violet and orange-yellow are also a mixing pair.

The orange-red can be reduced with blue-green, red-violet with green-yellow and the blue violet with orange-yellow.

Add white as required to such reduced hues.

Alternatively use the base colors at full strength or with white alone, leaving out the mixing partner. There are many ways to alter the main color selection.

The wider family group

© Red Cover/Chris Tubbs

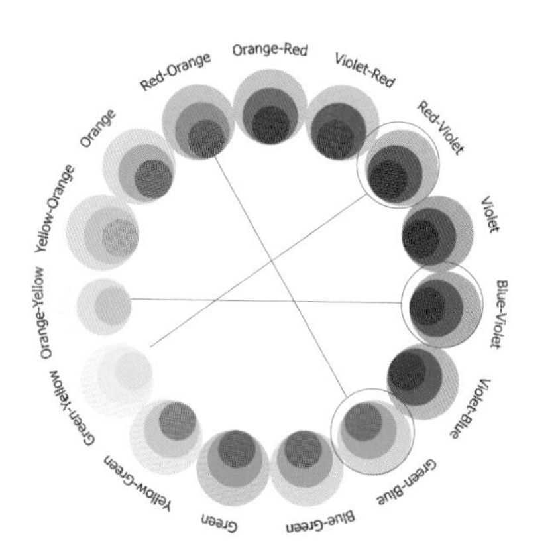

A versatile combination with many applications in the home.

The red-violet which earlier was 'cool' against the orange-red, now becomes 'warm' when compared to the green-blue. Blue-violet makes an excellent modifier.

© Red Cover/Jon Bouchier

These three hues can be worked together very satisfactorily, particularly when desaturated further with white. When lightened (made into tints), such colors can be used over large areas, the lighter the larger.

The wider family group

Red-violet, blue-violet and green-blue

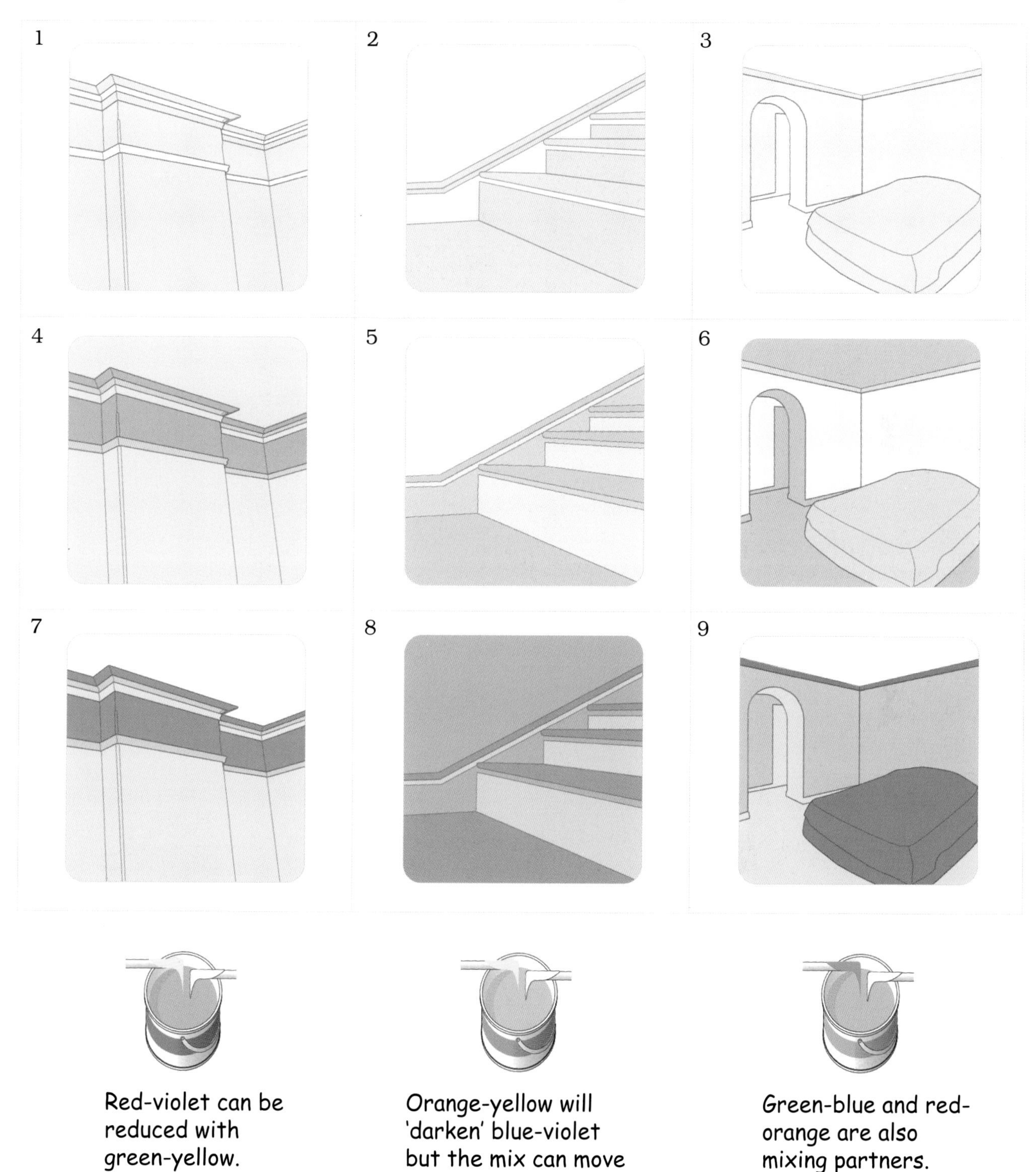

Red-violet can be reduced with green-yellow.

Orange-yellow will 'darken' blue-violet but the mix can move towards green.

Green-blue and red-orange are also mixing partners.

The mixing partner will always be found on the opposite side of the color mixing wheel.

For red-violet select a green-yellow, neutralise blue-violet with an orange-yellow and use red-orange to reduce the strength of green-blue. Add white to further reduce intensity.

The wider family group

© Red Cover/Jon Bouchier

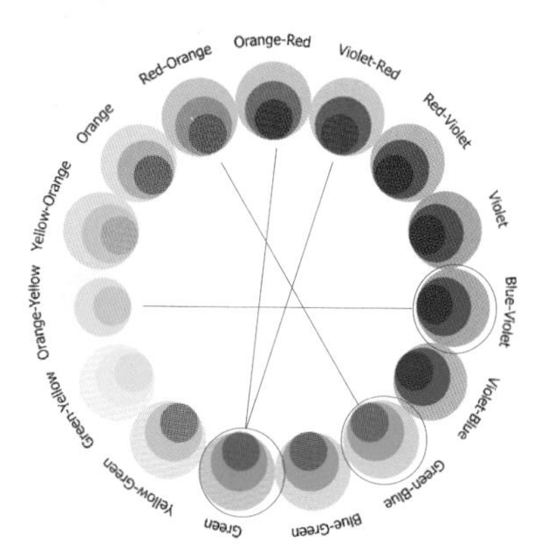

Many of the combinations of nature can be used to great effect in the home.

As all three colors come from the 'cool' area of the color wheel they can be harmonised with ease. The blue-violet could be considered to be the 'odd one out' as the other two hues are based on green. As such it should be used sparingly, especially at full strength.

The wider family group

Blue-violet, green-blue and green

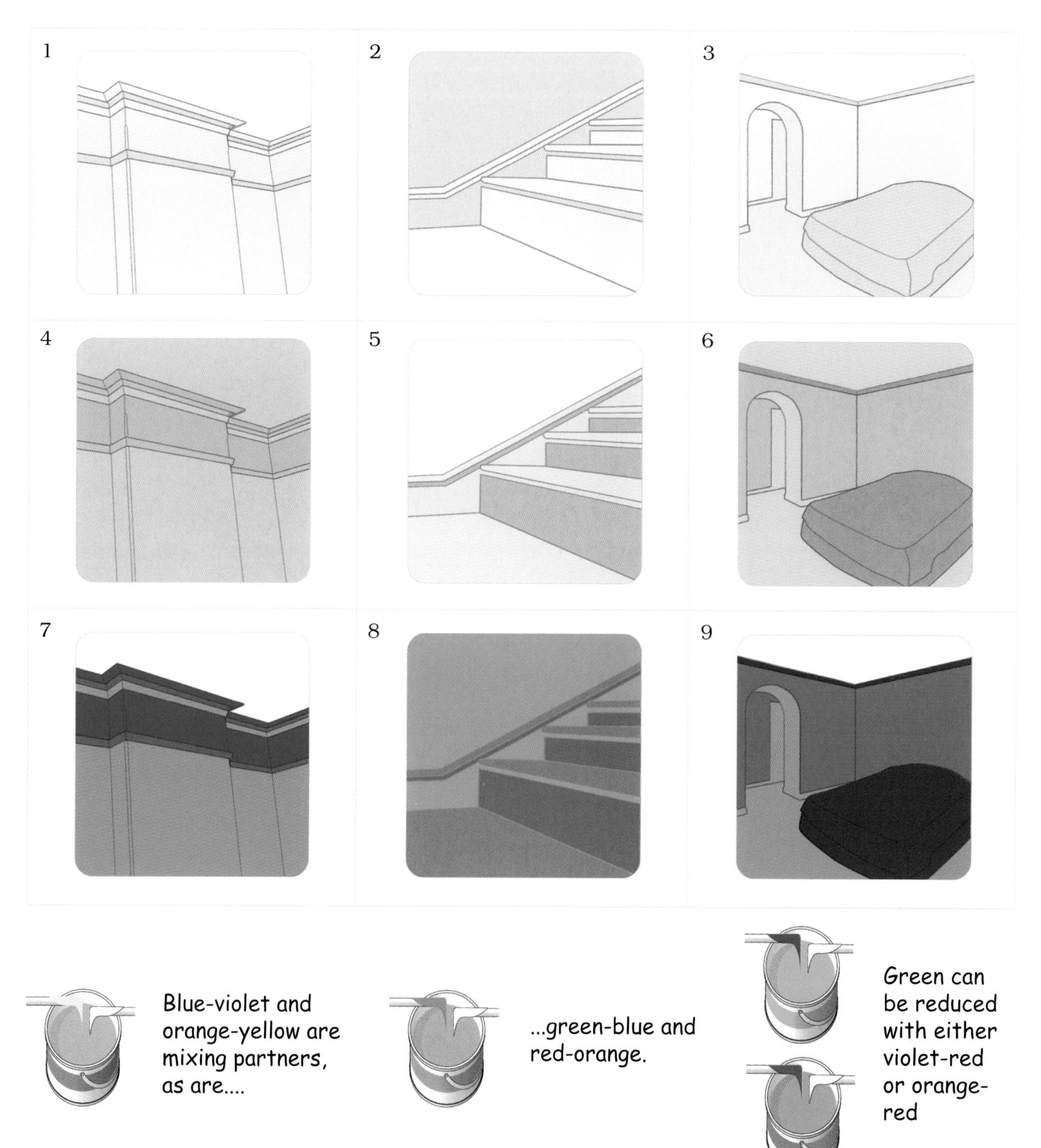

Blue-violet and orange-yellow are mixing partners, as are....

...green-blue and red-orange.

Green can be reduced with either violet-red or orange-red

If you decide to reduce the strength of a particular hue and then add white to the result, I suggest that you add the mixing partner first, carefully and slowly.

Then add this mix, very gradually, to the white. Do not hurry the process or you will possibly end up with large amounts of the wrong color. You will then blame me.

elizabethwhiting.com

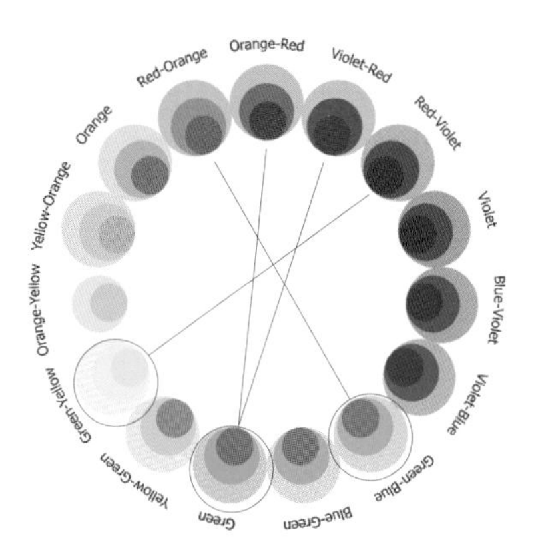

elizabethwhiting.com

Small color 'side shows' can be introduced to great effect.

Unless modified by being considerably lightened or darkened, the green-yellow can be unsettling to its partners. An 'acidic' color, it should be used with caution when set against these particular hues.

A strong light/dark contrast is easily set up with this combination. Such contrasts can move a composition away from harmony but the contrast itself can be attractive.

The wider family group

Green-blue, green and green-yellow

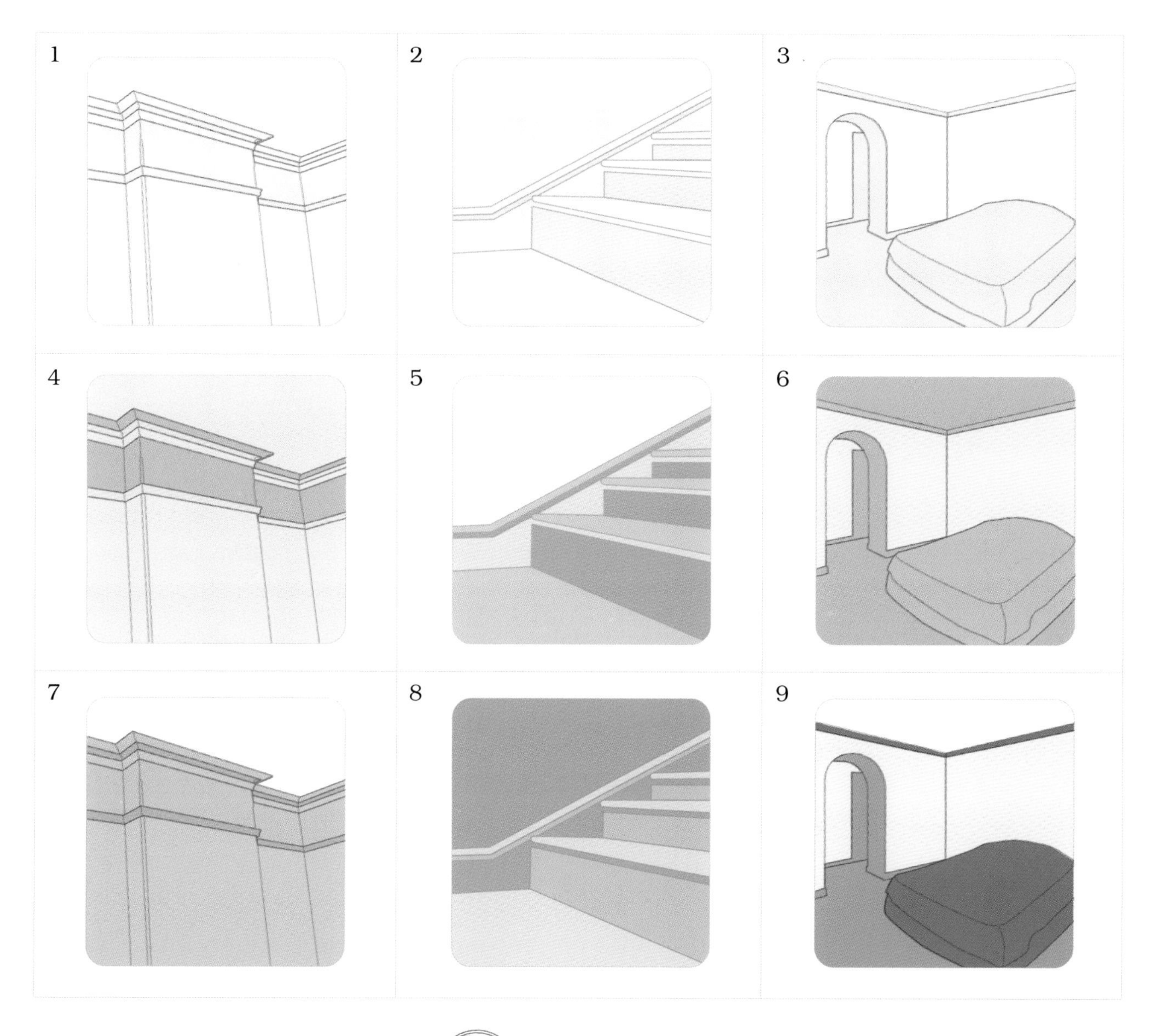

Green-blue and red-orange are mixing partners.

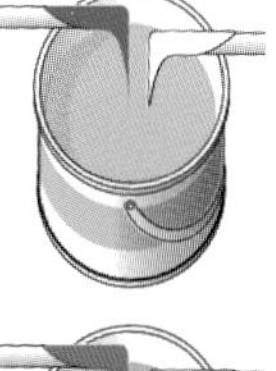

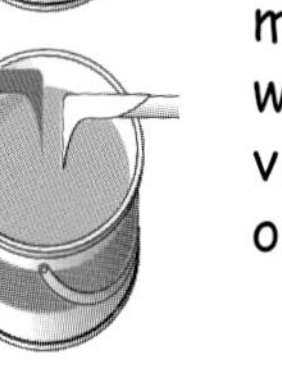

Green can be reduced in intensity and made 'darker' with either violet-red or orange-red.

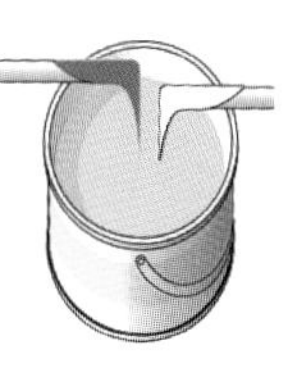

Green-yellow and red-violet will lower the intensity of each other in mixes.

The mixing partner is suggested only if you wish to dull and make 'darker' a particular color.

Once added the color can be further reduced in intensity through the addition of white.

The wider family group

© Red Cover/Chris Drake

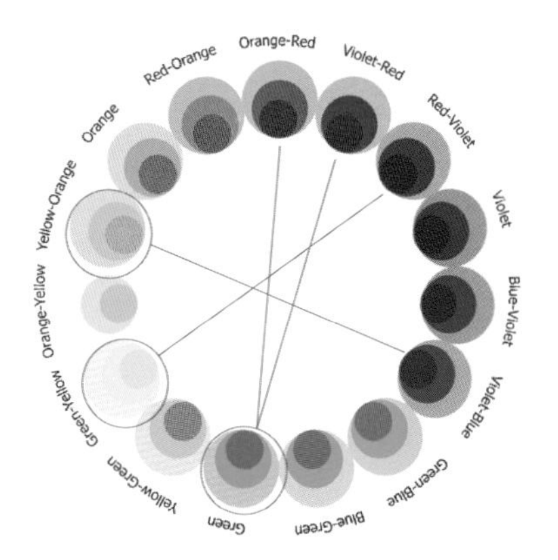

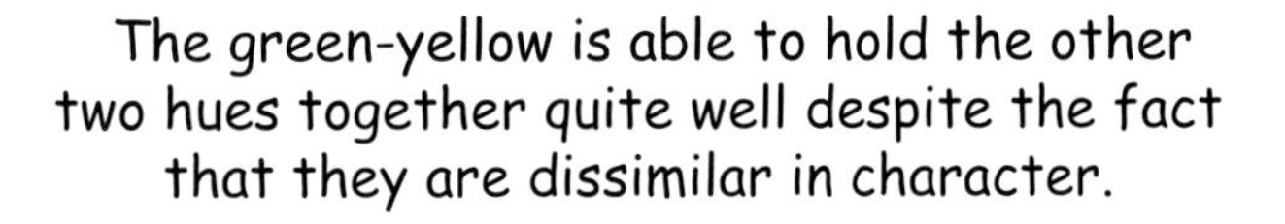

The green-yellow is able to hold the other two hues together quite well despite the fact that they are dissimilar in character.

These particular hues can give very pleasing and unusual harmonies, especially when they are reduced with white.

When used at or near full strength they can become somewhat overbearing and are seen as discordant by many.

The wider family group

Green, green-yellow and yellow-orange

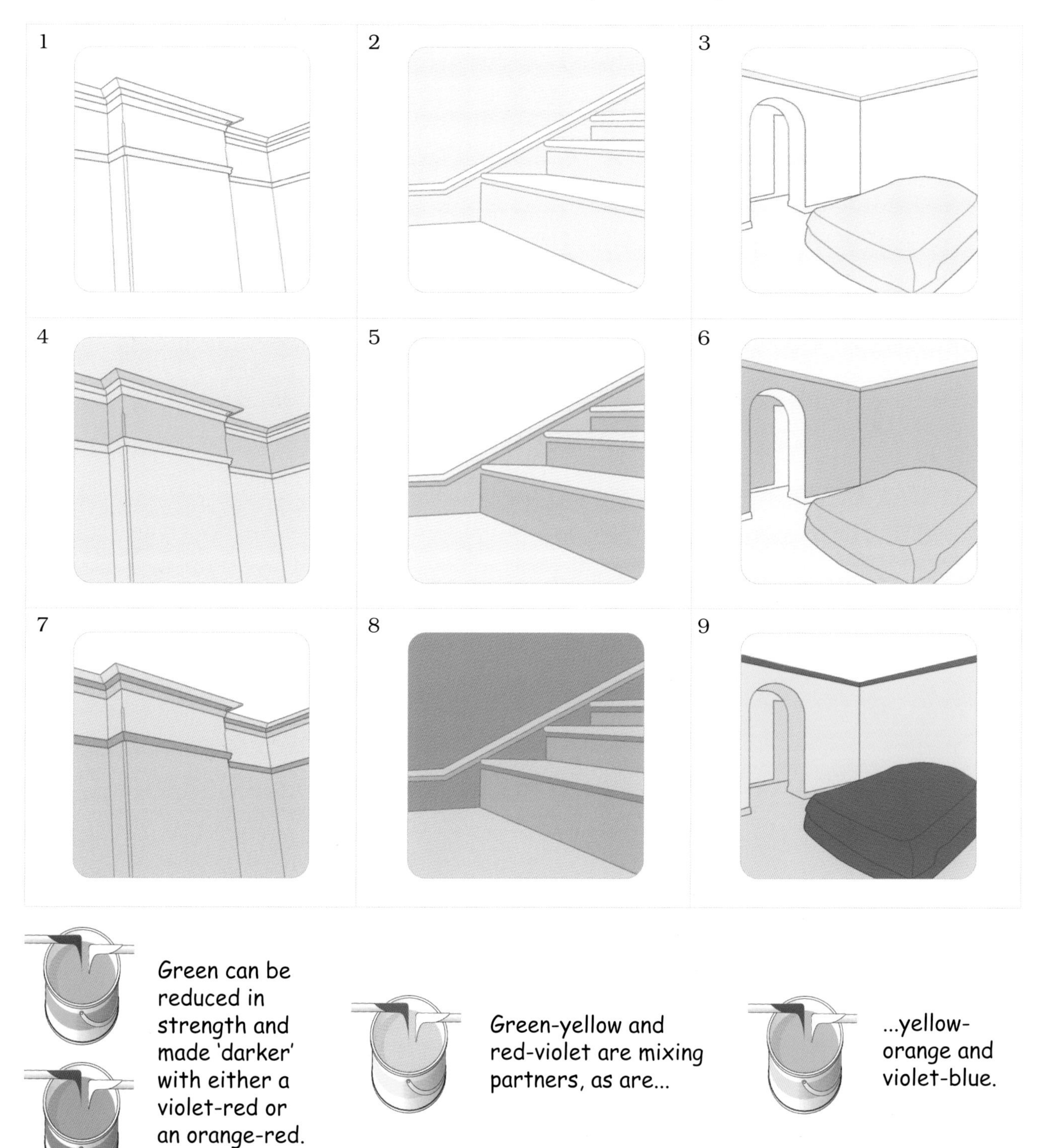

Green can be reduced in strength and made 'darker' with either a violet-red or an orange-red.

Green-yellow and red-violet are mixing partners, as are...

...yellow-orange and violet-blue.

The intention of offering the color swatches above is not to suggest color combinations which should be slavishly copied and matched exactly. They are to give ideas only.

If you decide to use one or other as guidance I suggest that you concern yourself only with selecting colors that are somewhat similar. Near enough will always be close enough.

The wider family group

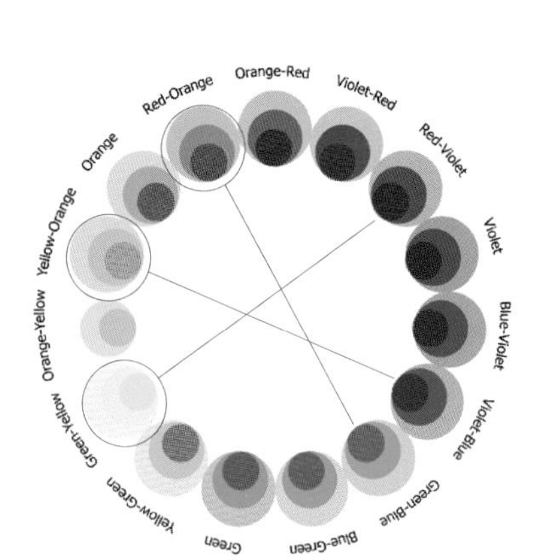

Some very subtle arrangements are possible with these hues.

© Peter Durant/arcblue.com

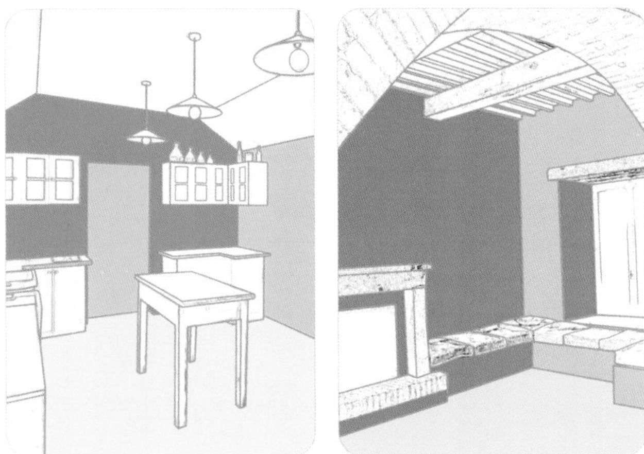

The character difference of the 'cool' green-yellow can add an interesting contrast when modified with white and/or its mixing partner.

As you will see, unless these particular hues are made either lighter of darker they tend to contrast strongly. This contrast can easily upset harmony.

The wider family group

Green-yellow, yellow-orange, red-orange

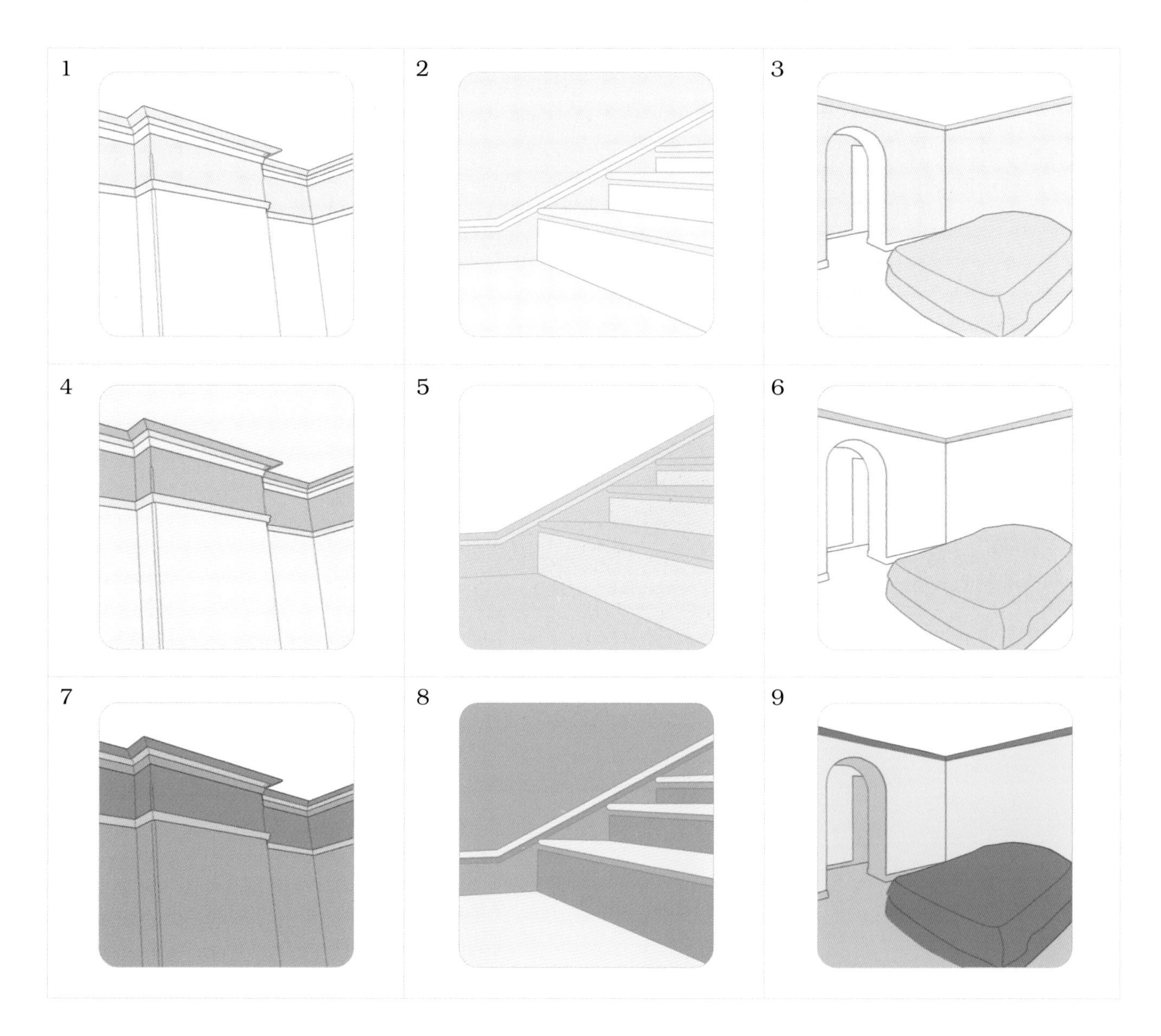

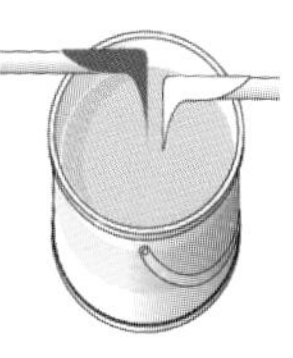

Green-yellow can be reduced with red-violet or violet.

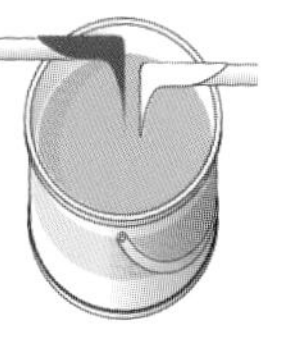

Yellow-orange and violet-blue are mixing partners, as are...

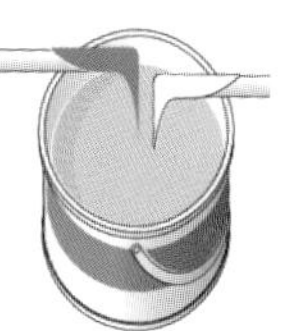

...red-orange and green-blue.

If you are lowering the intensity of the yellow-orange with its partner violet-blue and the mix moves too far towards green, try adding a small touch of red.

The red will absorb, or 'soak up' the unwanted greenness. This is because red and green are a mixing pair, one will absorb the other.

The wider family group

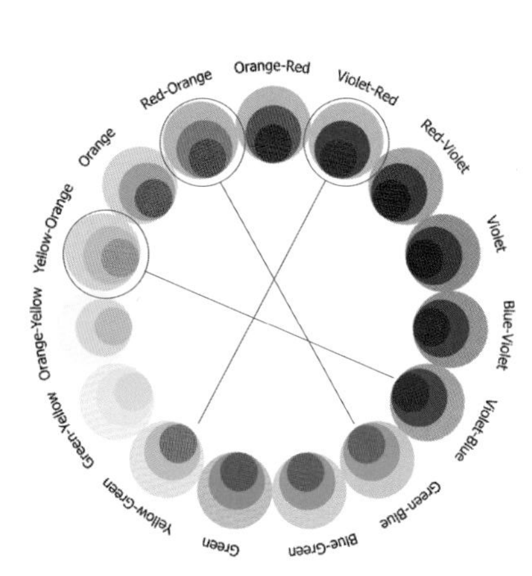

From the 'warm' oranges to the comparatively 'cool' violet-red, a range of hues are on offer which can be contrasted in temperature.

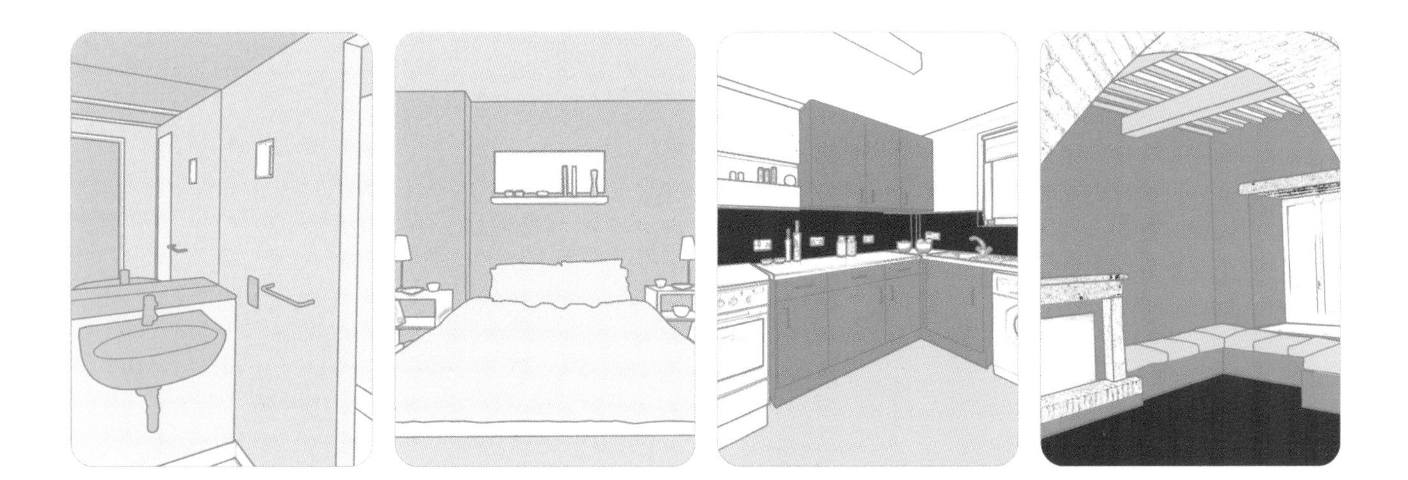

The violet-red is 'cooler' than its partners, but not dramatically so. This subtle contrast can add interest as well as harmony when used with care. The 'contrast of temperature' is covered later in the book.

If a color arrangement does not harmonise easily, try using the stronger colors as accents. Small touches here and there.

The reduced contrast can add interest and still allow color harmony.

The wider family group

Yellow-orange, red-orange and violet-red

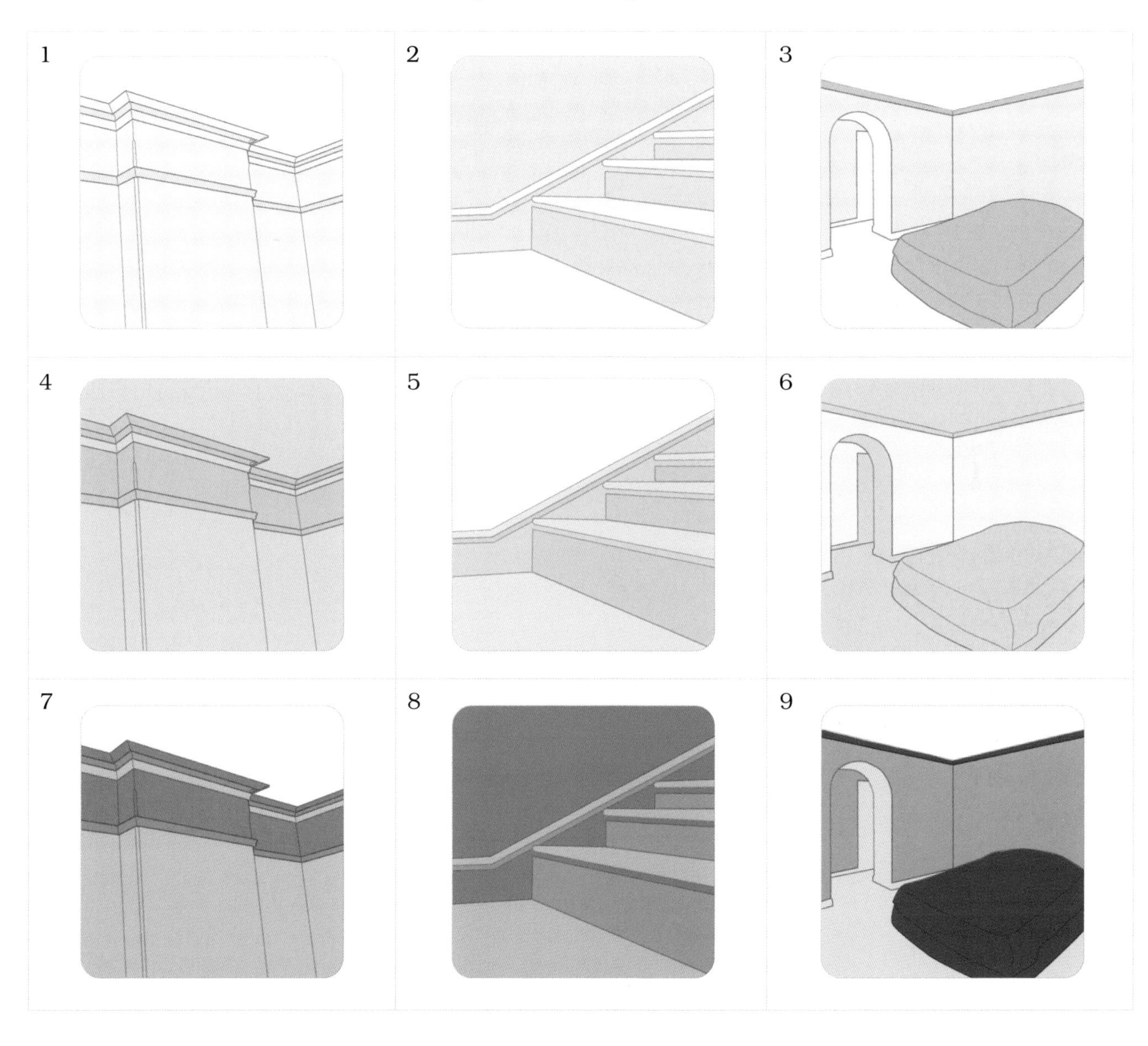

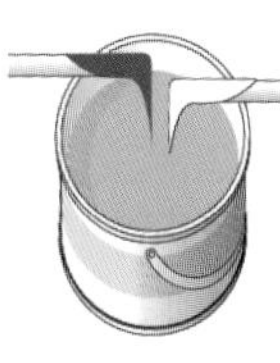

Even very small amounts of violet-blue will quickly act on the yellow-orange.

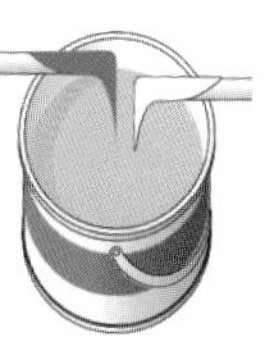

Red-orange can be neutralised by the addition of green-blue.

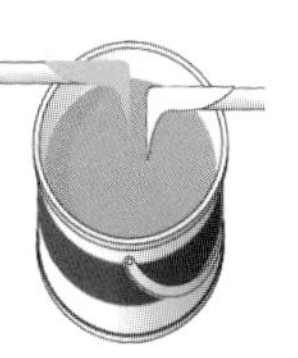

Violet-red will be reduced in intensity by the addition of yellow-green.

As one of a mixing pair is added to the other it will start to absorb its color. The original hue loses its strength and moves towards a 'darker' version of itself.

Although, strictly speaking the color does not become darker because it changes slightly in character, this is the most efficient means we have at our disposal. As more of the partner is added the mix starts to move towards a 'colored gray'

The wider family group

elizabethwhiting.com

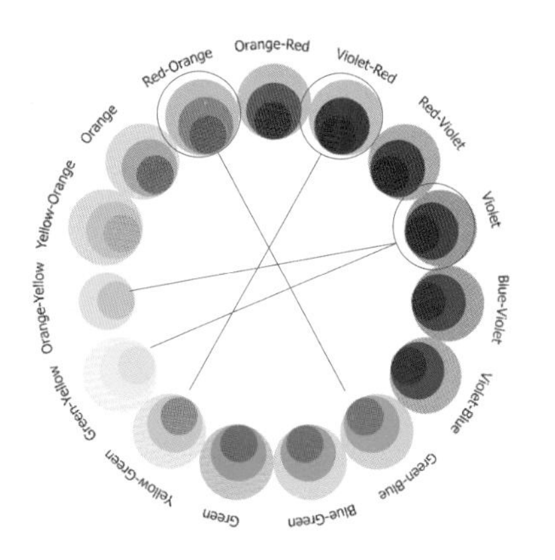

A strong contrast can be set up between the very 'warm' red-orange and its 'cooler' neighbours. This contrast can impair harmony if care is not taken. By either lightening or darkening the colors, the contrast can be modified.

© Red Cover/Brian Harrison

Alternatively very small touches of the red-orange can be employed to play down the contrast.

The wider family group

Red-orange, violet-red and violet

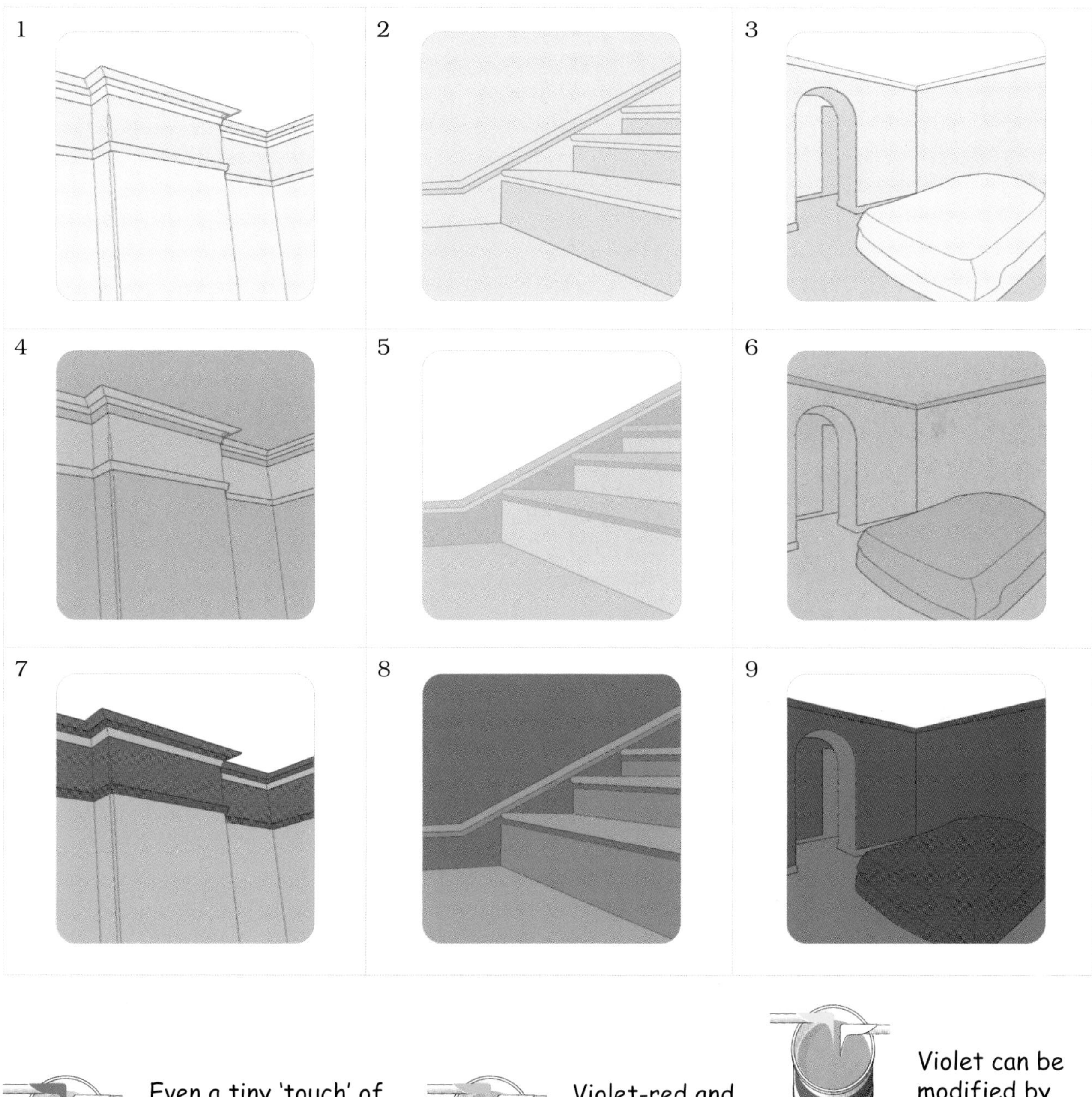

Even a tiny 'touch' of green-blue into red-orange will start to neutralise it.

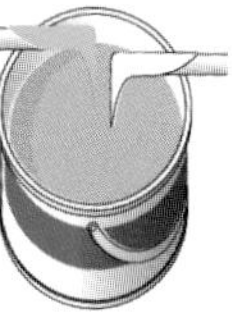

Violet-red and yellow-green are mixing partners.

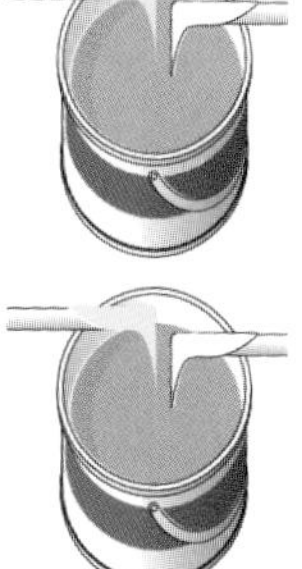

Violet can be modified by adding either green-yellow or orange-yellow.

Either type of yellow will act on the violet, causing it to become 'darker' and move towards gray. The 'colored grays' which result when any of the mixing partners are combined in similar intensities are an invaluable addition to the range of easily mixed colors.

The wider family group

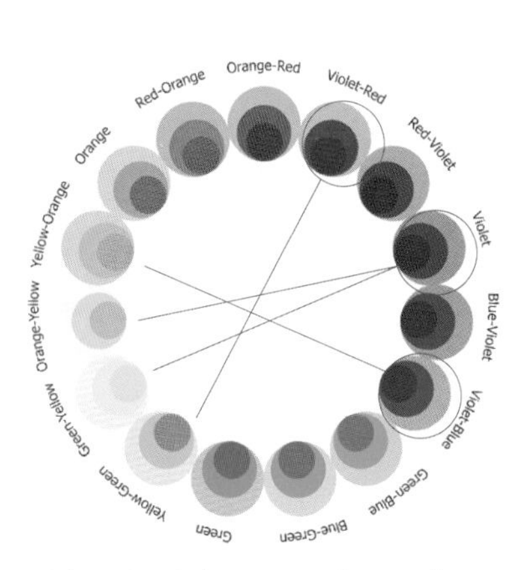

Used with care these hues will harmonise readily.

elizabethwhiting.com

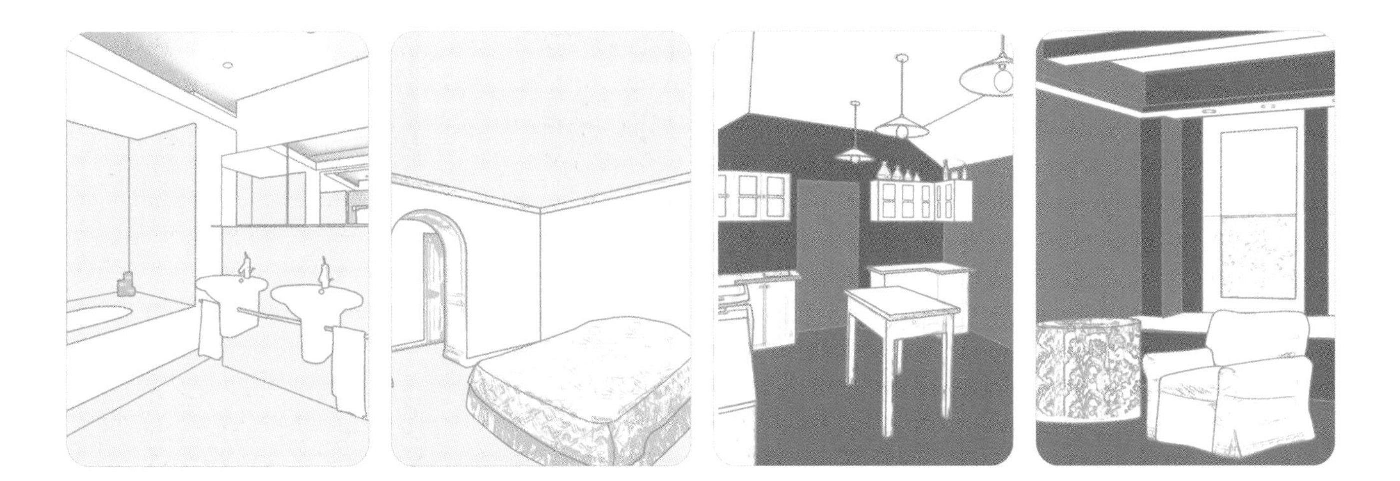

Although these basic hues all come from the 'cool' side of the color wheel, a subtle contrast is set up via the violet-red which is comparatively 'warm'. The word 'comparatively' is all important here as violet-red in isolation would not normally be considered a 'warm' color.

These particular hues can be harmonised successfully unless one or the other is applied too strongly. If anything, the violet should be modified or used in small touches rather than over larger areas, although this is not necessarily the case when it is the color of the flooring.

The wider family group

Violet-red, violet and violet-blue

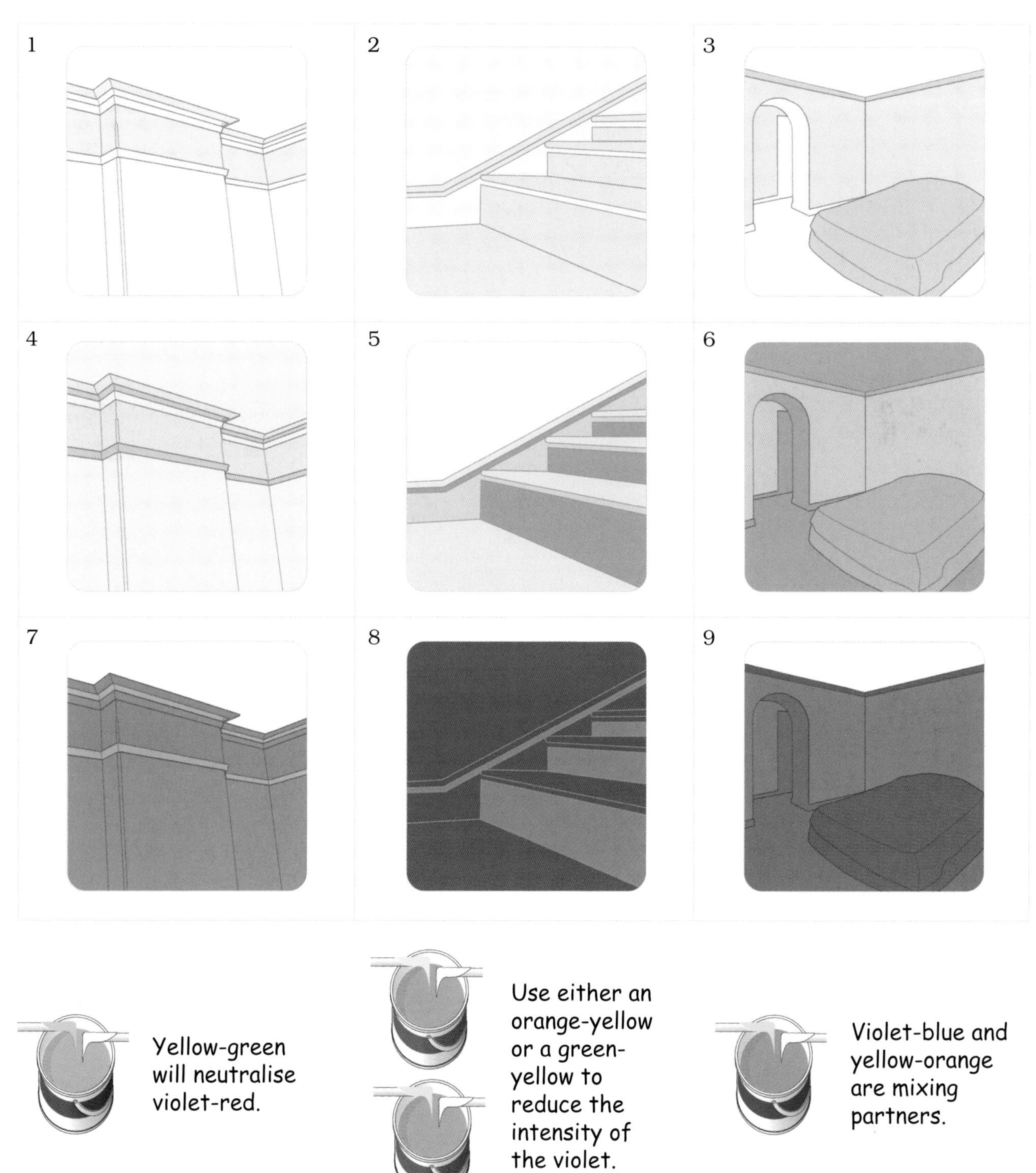

Yellow-green will neutralise violet-red.

Use either an orange-yellow or a green-yellow to reduce the intensity of the violet.

Violet-blue and yellow-orange are mixing partners.

Although white is shown in use in the mixing tips above, you might decide to lower the intensity of a color with its mixing partner alone.

The guidance above is offered only where you might wish to lower the strength of a color, 'darkening' it at the same time. You might wish to use it unmixed or blended with white.

The wider family group

© Red Cover/Chris Tubbs

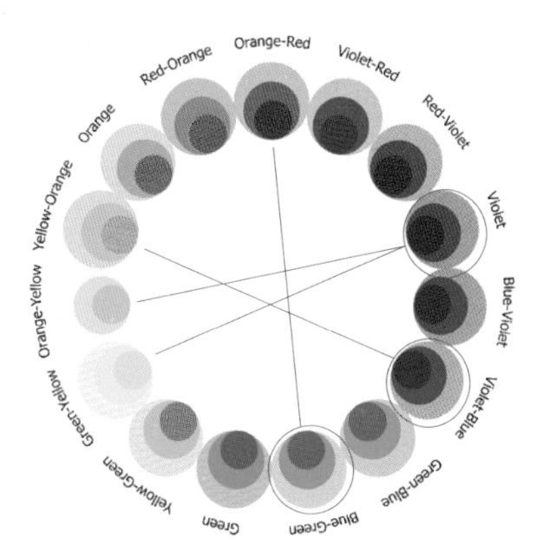

Soft, very subtle harmonies are available from these hues.

Unless the blue-green is reduced in intensity, ideally with white, it can easily dominate its partners. Darkening also makes it more workable. When used with care, these hues can be very effective, giving unusual and attractive arrangements (to many eyes). If using any of these colors at or near full strength it might be better to apply them in small touches. Larger areas can prove rather distracting.

The wider family group

Violet, violet-blue and blue-green

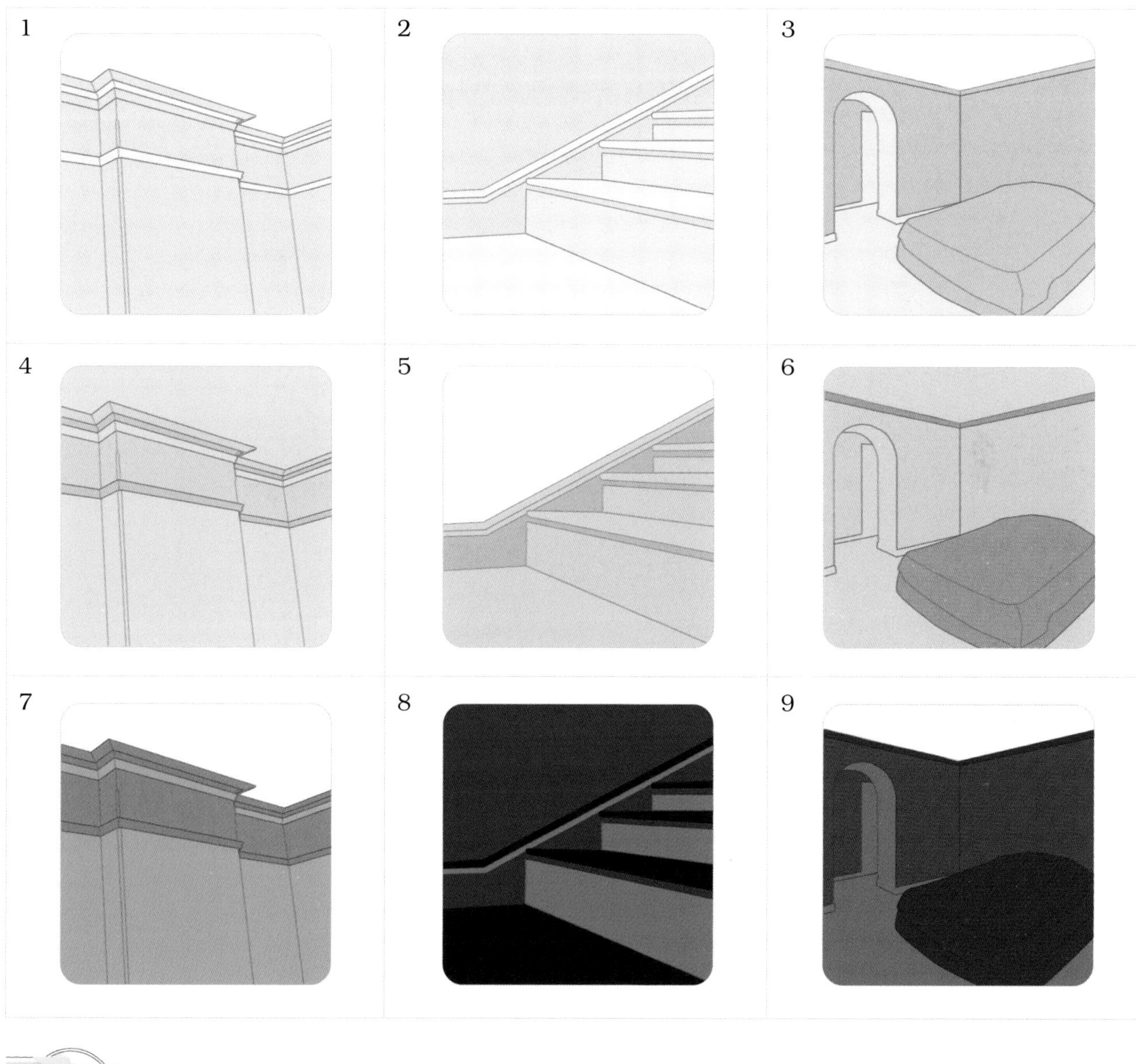

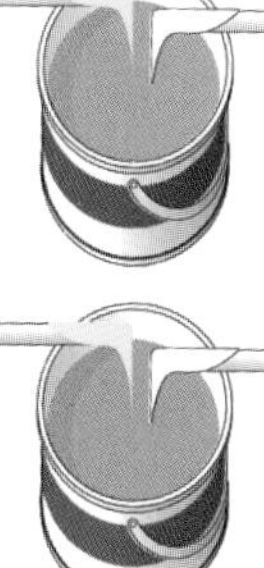

Violet can be reduced in intensity by adding either green-yellow or orange-yellow.

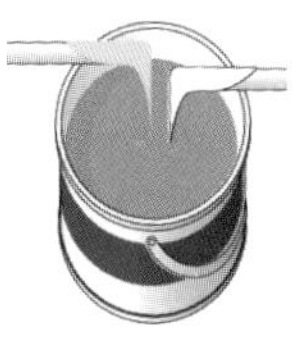

Violet-blue is best reduced by the addition of yellow-orange.

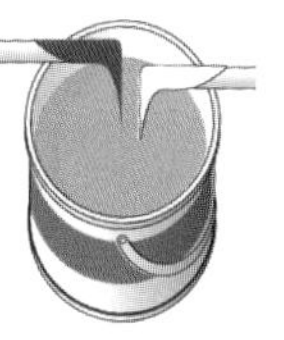

Blue-green and orange-red are a mixing pair and will neutralise each other with ease.

The violet can be desaturated with white, with the mixing partner yellow (either type), or with white and the mixing partner .

The mixing partner of the violet-blue is yellow-orange and that of blue-green, an orange-red. Instead of reducing the intensity of the colors, you might choose to use them at full strength or with the addition of white only.

The wider family group

elizabethwhiting.com

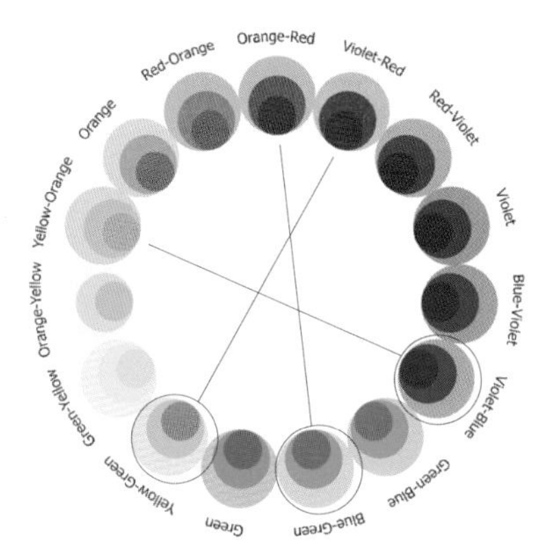

Calm, introspective color schemes are available from this range of hues.

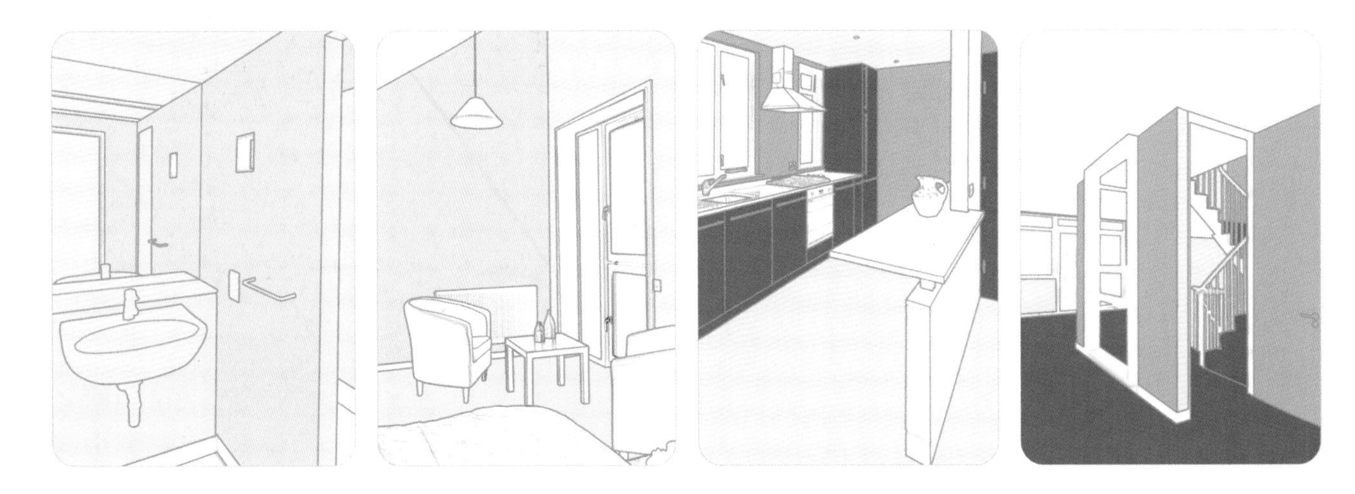

Many find that combinations from this area of the color wheel aid introspective activities such as reading and writing.

Easily harmonised, these hues find many applications. If required, a strong light/dark contrast can be set up.

The wider family group

Violet-blue, blue-green and yellow-green

1	2	3
4	5	6
7	8	9

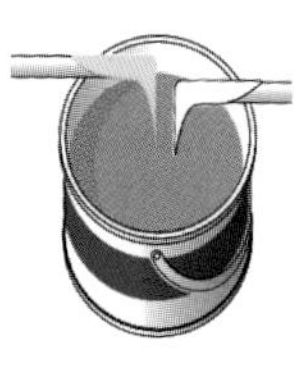

Violet-blue can be reduced with yellow-orange.

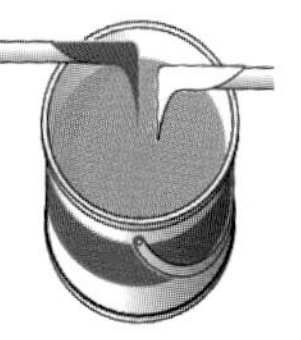

Blue-green and orange-red are mixing partners.

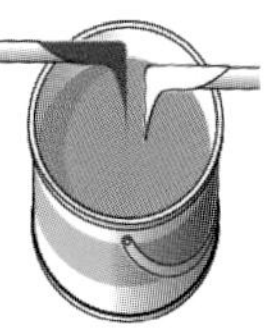

Yellow-green is best reduced in strength with violet-red.

The color mixing tips are, of course, only applicable to those who wish to mix or modify their own colors. It might well be that you decide to purchase ready mixed colors from the shelf. In which case the main color types shown should be easy to identify.

Summary

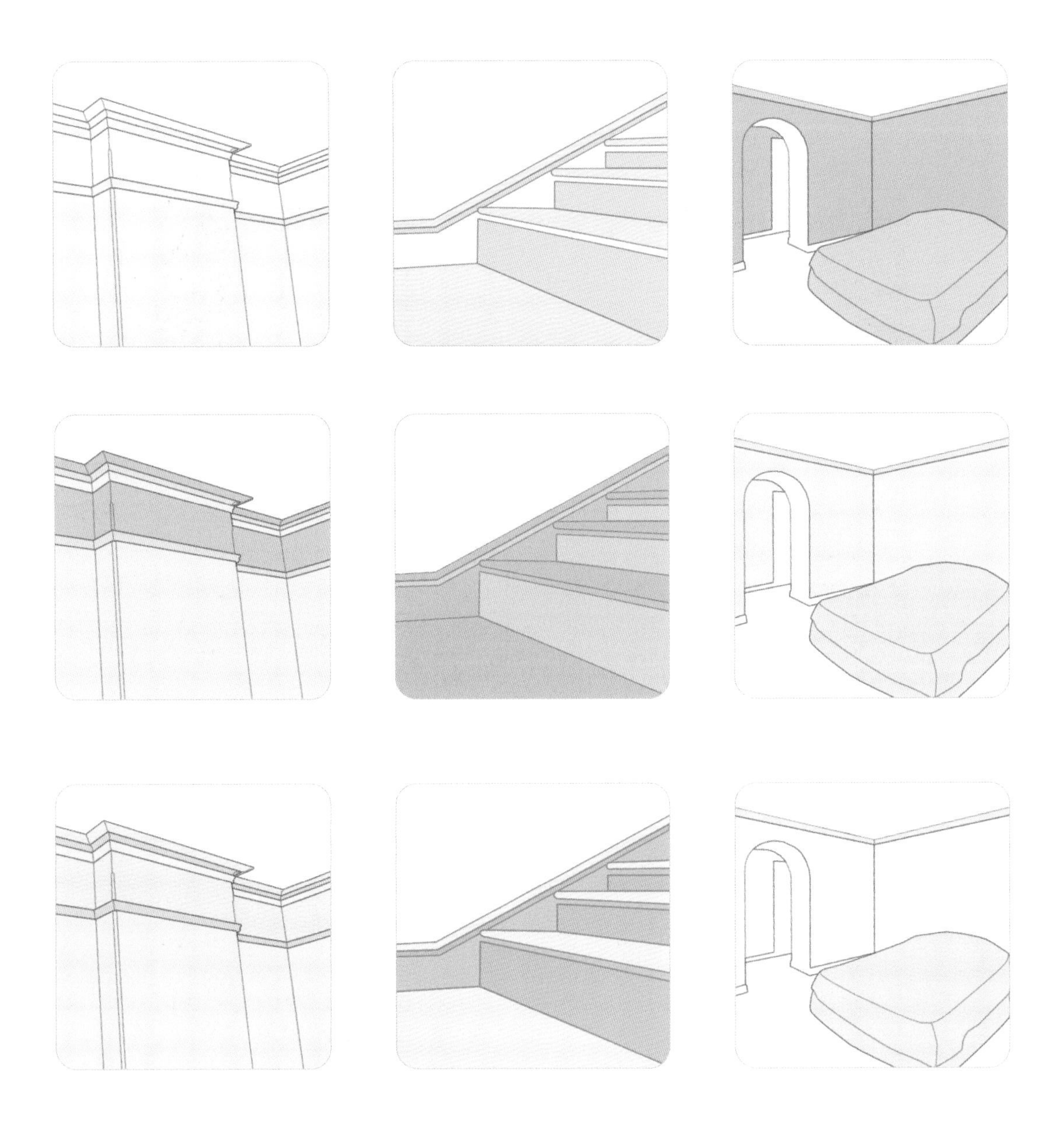

The 'wider family' approach is particularly versatile and will allow you to plan a wide range of harmonious color schemes.

As the colors are always close to each other, sitting side by side on the color wheel, they can be harmonised with ease.

The balance can be upset, however, if any of them are used in a fully saturated form (at full strength), over large areas.

A little pre-planning will avoid this possibility, unless, of course, it is what you are looking for.

Introduction

If you wish to obtain the most from color in your home, a knowledge of the optical effect known as the *after-image* will be very useful.
The *after-image* is one of the most important factors in determining the colors we perceive around us.

Descriptions such as *'optical effect' and 'after-image'* can be quickly off-putting but in fact they are easy to come to terms with. As soon as you have grasped the essentials you will find that planning your colors can not only be soundly based but also great fun.

The knowledge will also help in everyday choices; from the colors to wear, use in the garden and, for the ladies, which color make-up to select. You will also be a long way ahead of almost every professional interior designer. So, a little concentration now will pay off.

I would fully understand if you thought, 'I don't want all this, I want to get on with decorating'. If so, skip to page 109. The guidance offered in the book will take you to the same results without a full understanding. *But you could just be missing something!*

The after-image

I would like you to stare fixedly at the dot in the centre of the red shape above for about 20 seconds.

Then look at the black dot to the right of the diagram. Do you see anything? If you do, note its shape and color.

It will be the same size and shape as the red area above, but the color will, or should, have changed to a type of green.

A pale blue-green 'edge' might appear at one side or the other.

Maybe you did not see this effect, or saw it only fleetingly. If so, do not worry, many people have difficulty in seeing after-images at first. Try looking at the red strip a little longer, maybe up to a minute.

Before looking away, see if there is a bluish-green edge appearing around the red.

If so, gradually move your line of sight to the right and the entire image should follow.

If you still cannot see it, try making your eyes go slightly out of focus.

Although it may be difficult at first, you will almost certainly be able to 'pick up' the after-image with practice and patience.

The after-image

The after-image from the red shape to the left should look something like the above (given the severe limitations of conventional color printing).

Why should a pale bluish-green shape appear after the eye has been stimulated by a red area?

In general terms, what happened is that the receptors in your eyes which receive and transmit 'red' signals to the brain became fatigued; dulled from exposure to the red.

The 'green' receptors meanwhile had little to do and were fully rested.

When both the 'red' and 'green' systems focused on the black dot, the rested 'green' receptors took over, the 'reds' took a break and an image was formed.

I have greatly simplified the reasons for our perception of after-images.

For our purposes, *how* it happens is not as important as the fact that it *does*.

Go back to the red strip on the previous page, concentrate on it and then make a mental note of the properties of the resultant after-image.

Do not concern yourself with the 'type' of green, whether it is bluish or otherwise, that will come later. How else would you describe the sensation?

Do you find that the after-image is 'luminous', 'bright', 'clear', 'glowing'? Almost as if a weak colored light had been shone onto the paper?

Although not as strong as the stimulating color, being much paler, the after-image is invariably described as being more like a *light* than an area of paint or ink.

It is in fact brighter and far more luminous than any paint in use today.

The after-image

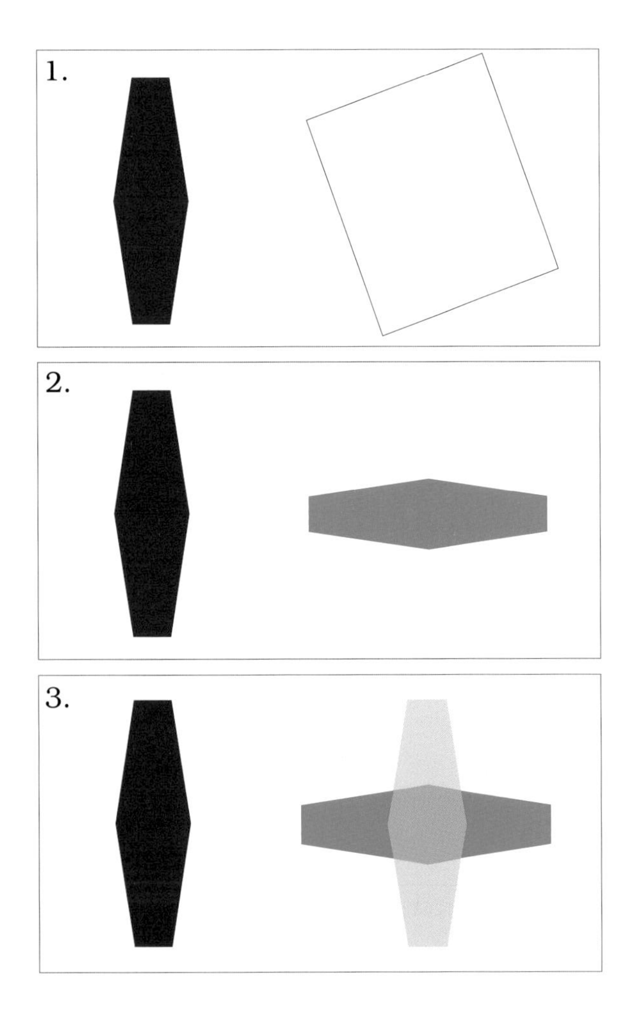

1. Now cover the green shape with a piece of paper or similar and concentrate on the red for about 20 seconds.

2. Then uncover the green and look from the red to the green.

3. Where the after-image overlaps, about the centre, the green should appear to be far brighter than the rest of the strip.

To understand the reason for this extra intensity of color, think back to the first part of this exercise. The green after-image that we transposed to the right of the page now rests on green ink instead of on a black dot.

In effect you are looking at the green ink *through* a layer of green 'light'. It is not literally light of course, but has a very similar effect.

The result can be compared with painting a wall with a second coat, only here we are over-painting with green 'light'.

The after-image will gradually wear away as the 'red receptors' in the eye overcome their 'fatigue' and start to 'work' again. The green will slowly return to its former strength.

The after-image

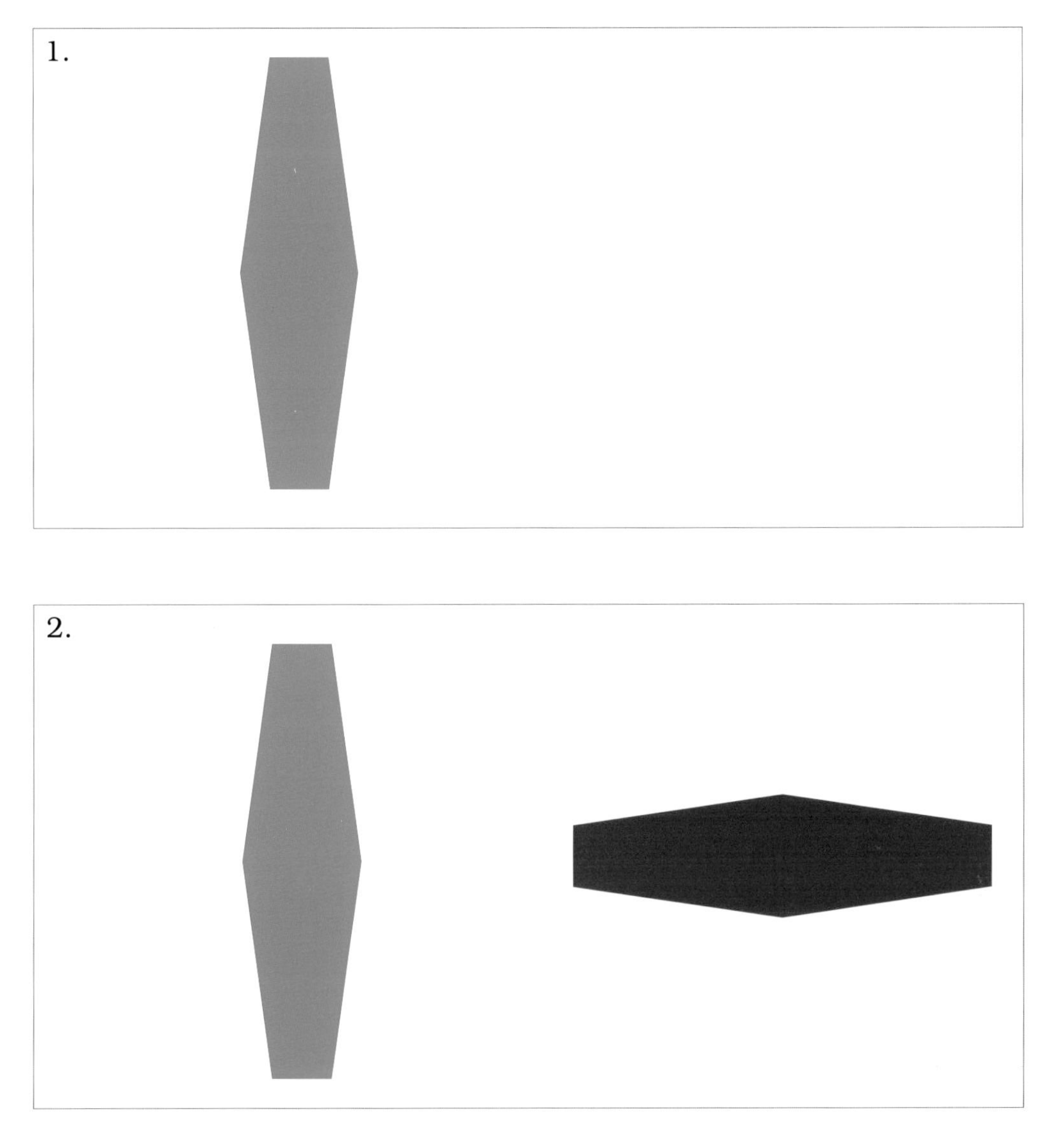

The after-image from the green should brighten the centre of the red once visually transferred.

1. Try the experiment the other way around, looking first at the green for a while and then at white paper. What do you see? There should be an after-image of red as the effect is reversed. *It will be a very pale red, more of a pink. After-images are always very pale versions of the color that they represent.*

2. This after-image will brighten the red at around its centre when you look at it. Whenever a red is concentrated upon, a green after-image will result, and vice-versa.

Red and green therefore are a pair of colors with a certain relationship to each other. That relationship is described as being *complementary.*

Whenever two colors are paired which give each others after-image they are known as *complementary colors.*

Successive color contrast

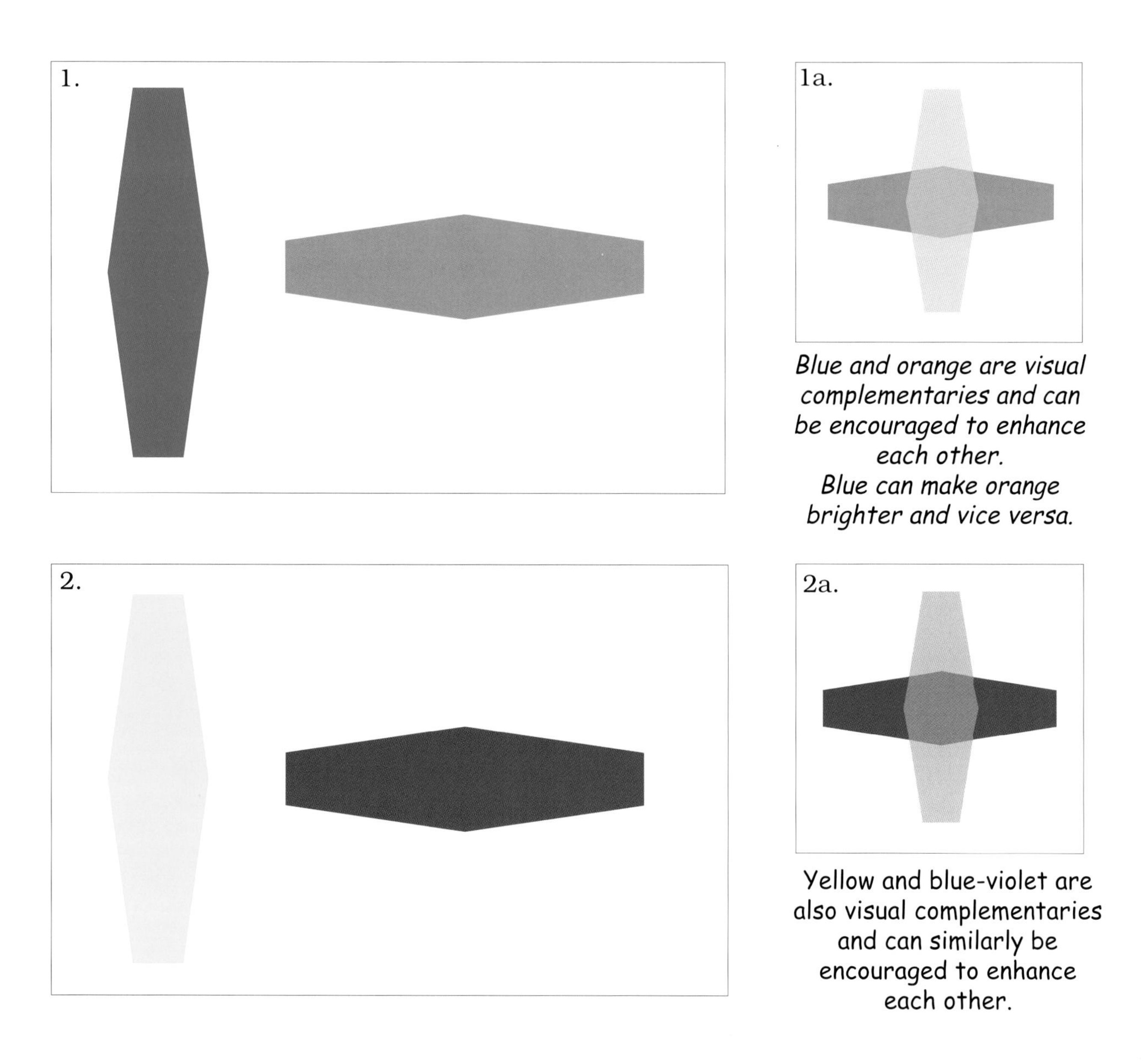

Blue and orange are visual complementaries and can be encouraged to enhance each other. Blue can make orange brighter and vice versa.

Yellow and blue-violet are also visual complementaries and can similarly be encouraged to enhance each other.

The effect of altering a color by first looking at another, as you have just been doing, is known as *successive color contrast.*

Successive contrast takes place whenever the eye moves fairly quickly from one color to another.

The effect is not confined to red and green alone. We will now look at the after-images associated with a few other colors.

After working through these exercises you will add blue and orange, yellow and blue-violet to red and green as further complementary pairs.

As already established, look first at the color on the left and take the after-image over to the color on the right. The result should be similar to 1a and 2a. Then carry out the exercise in reverse, looking first at the color to the right and taking the after-image to the color on the left.

Please bear in mind that the severe restrictions of conventional color printing will not allow for accurate illustrations. They are for guidance only. The actual after-images, of course, will appear before you as they are generated in the eye and brain.

Successive color contrast

By covering the other 'jugs' and taking the after-image from each to the black dot in the centre, you will see that *all* colors have their own after-image.

We could also say that every time you discover an after-image you are in fact looking at the complementary of the first color.

As you will discover, the after-image from this 'jug' is a pale red-orange. This suggests that the rather nondescript colored gray is in fact a dull (or neutralised) green-blue.

The after-image of a green-blue being a red-orange. This can be a useful way to discover the make up of an otherwise difficult to discern colored gray. If you actually wanted to do that, of course.

Complementaries and the color wheel

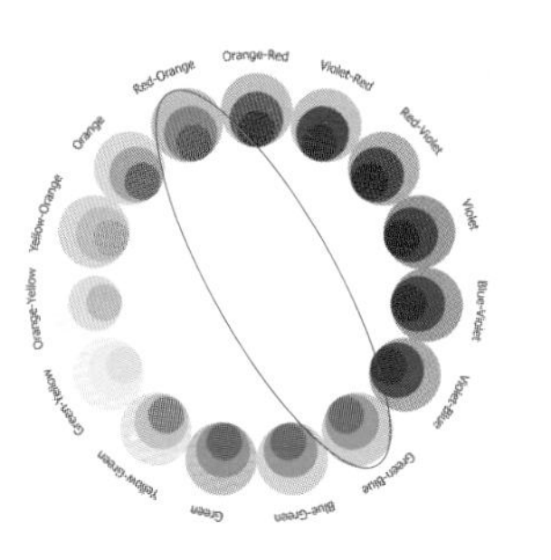

Green-blue and red-orange are a complementary pair as are...

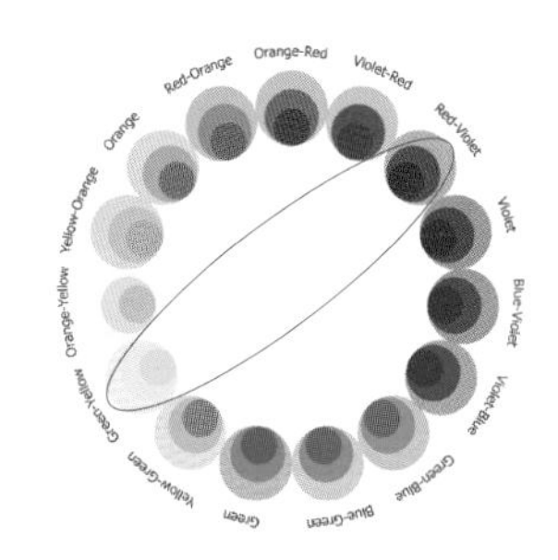

...green-yellow and red-violet.

The basic complementary pairings which we will be using throughout this book can be found opposite each other on the color wheel. They are:

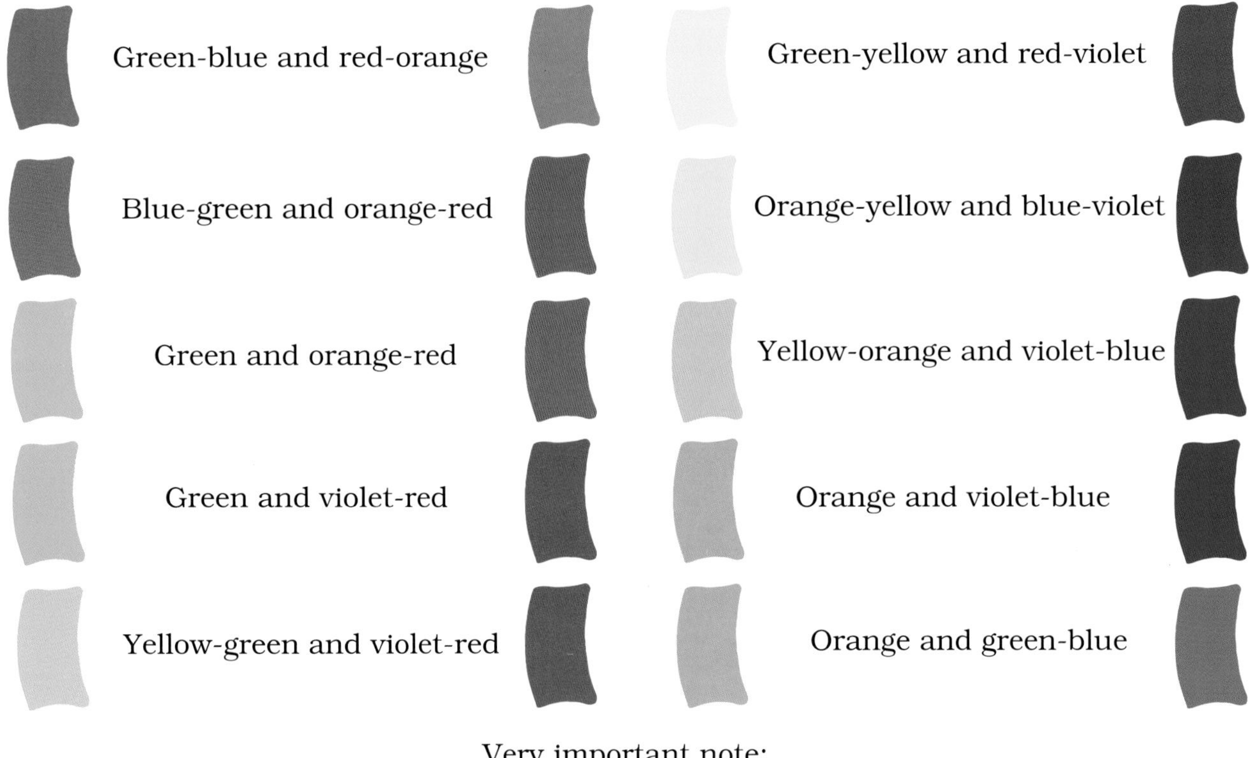

Very important note:
The complementaries shown above are also COLOR MIXING PARTNERS

Complementary pairs are found opposite each other on a comprehensive and accurate color wheel — with some reservations!

Any color wheel has to be regarded as a fairly rough and ready guide to color arrangements. For the sake of convenience and the design of the wheel, violet is placed opposite yellow, and those two colors are usually described as being complementary. The complementary of yellow, however, is more accurately described as being a *blue*-violet. When working with paints the yellow/violet approach is more practical and helps to avoid greens when mixing this complementary pair.

Multiple after-images

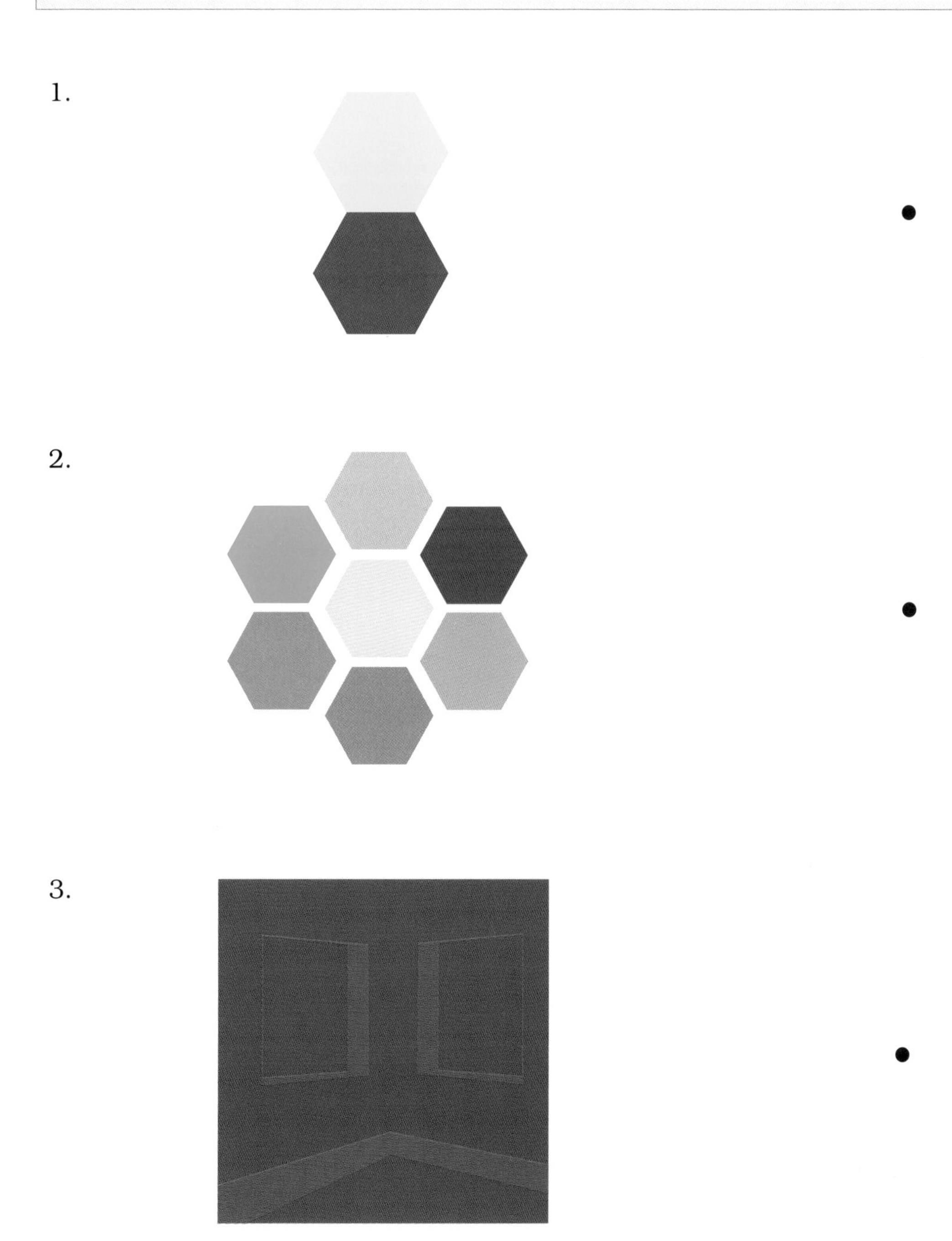

We are not confined to working with the after-image of a single color. As you will see in exercise one above, a pair of colors will provide a pair of after-images.

As you will notice, being complementaries the after-image from the yellow (top) and violet (bottom) become violet (top) and yellow (bottom). It will help if you cover the exercises not 'in use'.

In exercise two a group of colors will give a group of after-images. You will probably find that only two or three after-images will appear at first, with the rest following a few moments later.

Number 3 is a little less complicated. With a little practice you will be able to take the entire picture to one side and see it in after-image form.

Simultaneous contrast

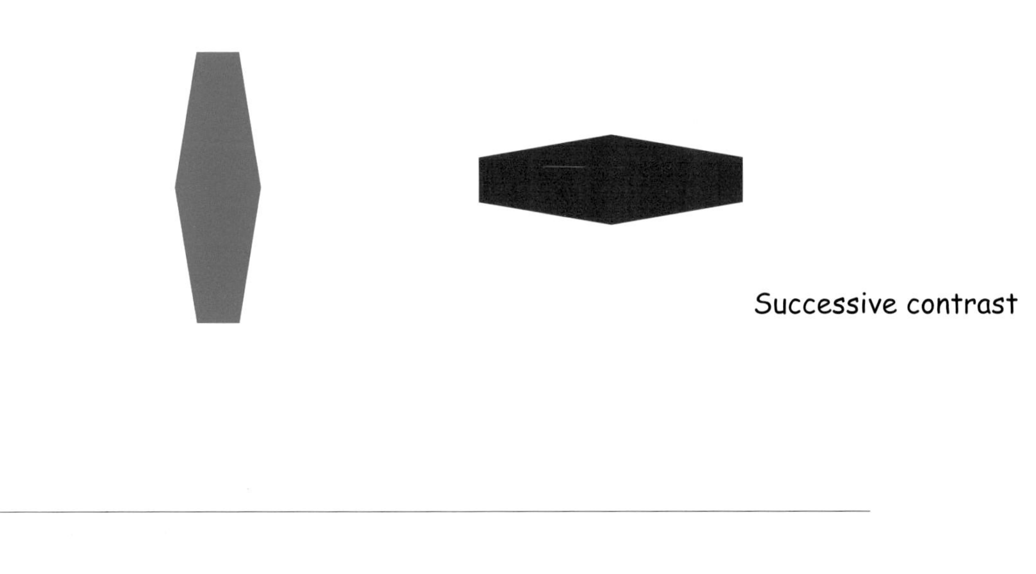

Successive contrast

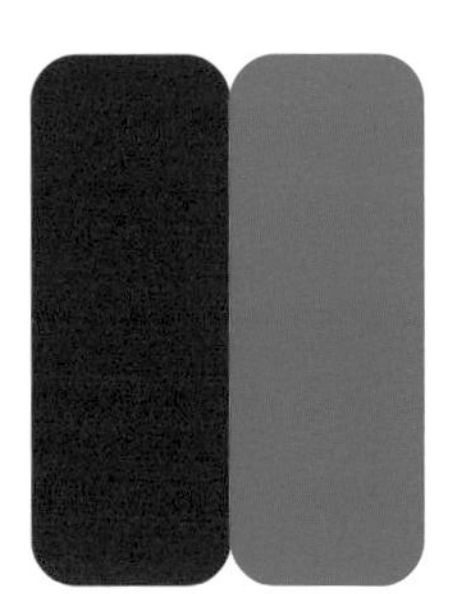

Simultaneous contrast

Simultaneous contrast

As already mentioned, altering a color visually by first looking at another (as we have been doing), is known as *successive contrast.*

Whenever colors are presented *side by side*, one area close against or surrounded by another, the optical effect that they will have on each other is known as *simultaneous contrast.*

Do not let these terms be a concern. I mention this as creative people usually want the practical information, not the technical.

For our purposes we can consider *successive* and *simultaneous contrast* to be one and the same. In fact, it is more than enough to simply be aware of the after-image and its effect.

Eye movement

The constant flickering of the eye tends to take the after-image from one color to the next. This can set up a strong contrast where one color butts up against the next.

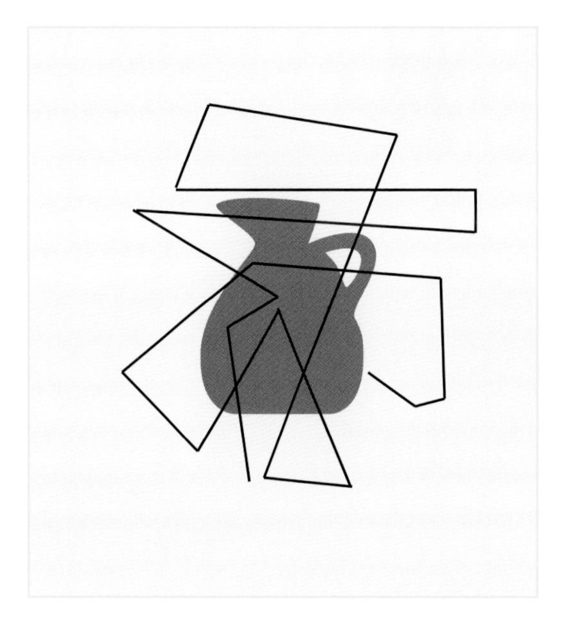

In addition to the constant flickering of the eye our focal point tends to wander around the general area, taking after-images with it to influence other colors.

If the eye dwells on the same image for more than a few seconds the receptors become fatigued and the 'picture' fades.

To overcome the tendency towards fading that occurs with a fixed stare, the eye is constantly on the move. New receptors become stimulated by a varying scene, giving a brief rest to those previously at work. This movement is quite rapid, the eye oscillating up to seventy times a second.

These constant movements of the eye are necessary for normal vision. In addition to this activity the eye will tend to wander, 'taking in the scene'.

Even when concentrating on a fixed point there is a tendency to stray away from it.

Other than complementaries

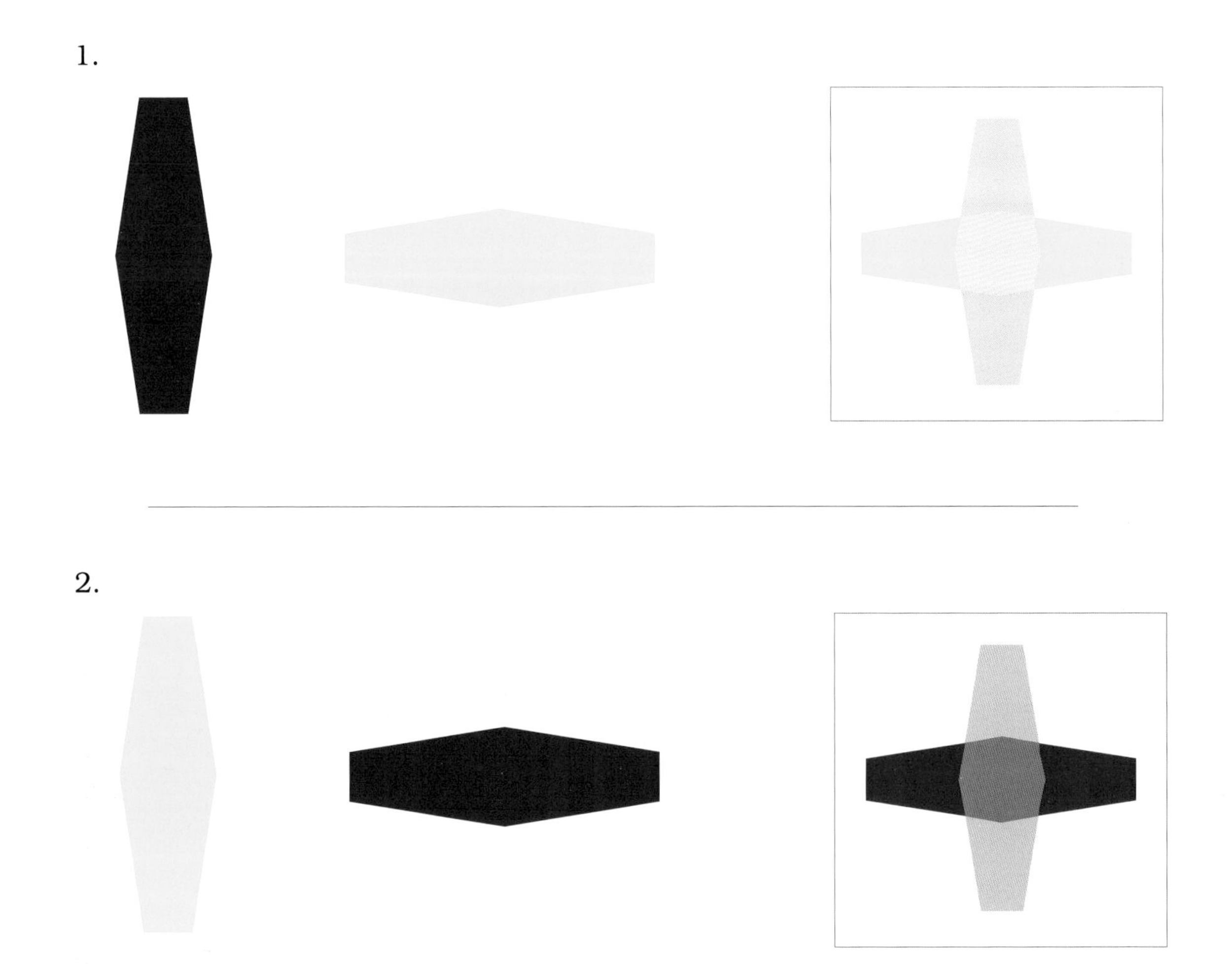

Going back to the green after-image that resulted from exposure of the eye to red, (page 84), you will recall that when the green after-image was 'taken over' to the green strip, the result was a brighter, almost luminous green.

Brighter in fact than any paint ever can be. Even the brightest paint of the future will surely be enhanced by a layer of colored 'light'. The painted area in the middle of the strip overlapped by the after-image appeared as a much brighter green. The yellow similarly enhanced the blue-violet on page 88.

Now we will see what effect the after-image resulting from the red will have on a color other than green, and the yellow on a hue other than violet.

In exercise one, impose the after-image from the red (which will be green) onto the yellow.

As you would expect, where the after-image is superimposed upon the yellow, a *yellow-green* results. Green mixed with yellow.

In the reverse sequence the blue-violet after-image from the yellow will affect the red, making it lean towards violet.

After the eye has been stimulated we can either enhance another color, (as earlier with the complementary pairs) or we can alter its character, often to its detriment.

If, as examples, you wished to place a touch of bright yellow in a vital part of a room, or add a small area of bright red, the partners shown above, (if placed close by or surrounding), would change them immediately to new and perhaps unwanted hues. The change would be permanent whilst the influence remained.

The after-image from any color can influence others similarly. It will be worth a few experiments with other combinations.

Changing by after-image

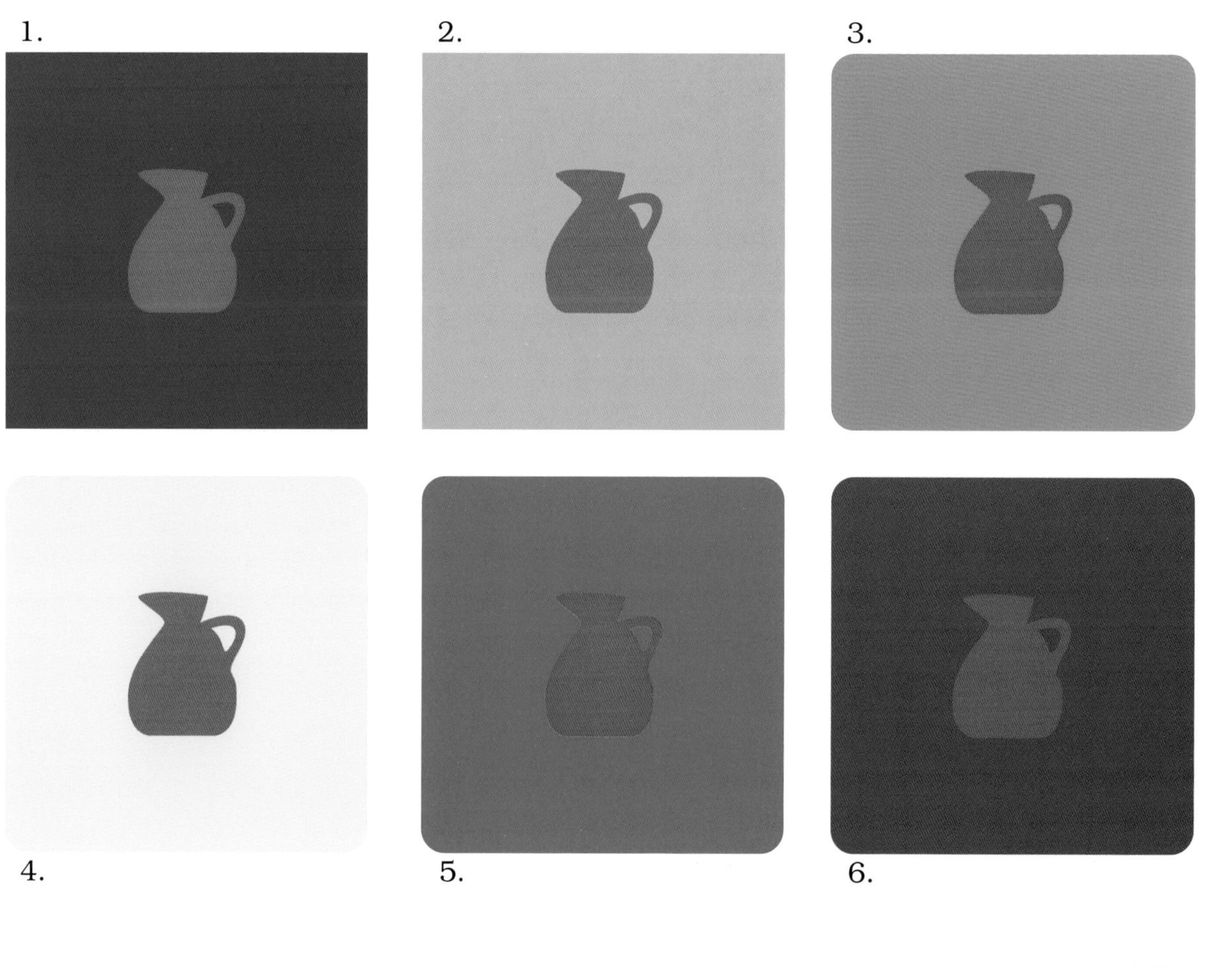

Notice how the red appears to change in the above diagrams:

1. A combination of after-image from the violet-blue (yellowish orange) and eye movement will cause the red to take on an orange bias.
2. The effect of surrounding the red with orange is probably the most dramatic, as the blue after-image makes the red appear quite dark and out of character.
3. The red will be *enhanced* due to the green.
4. The blue-violet after-image from the yellow will cause the red to move towards that color.
5. The after-image from a green-blue is a red-orange. This will have its own influence on the red in the centre.
6. As you look at this diagram the yellow after-image will flood over the area of red.

Changing by after-image

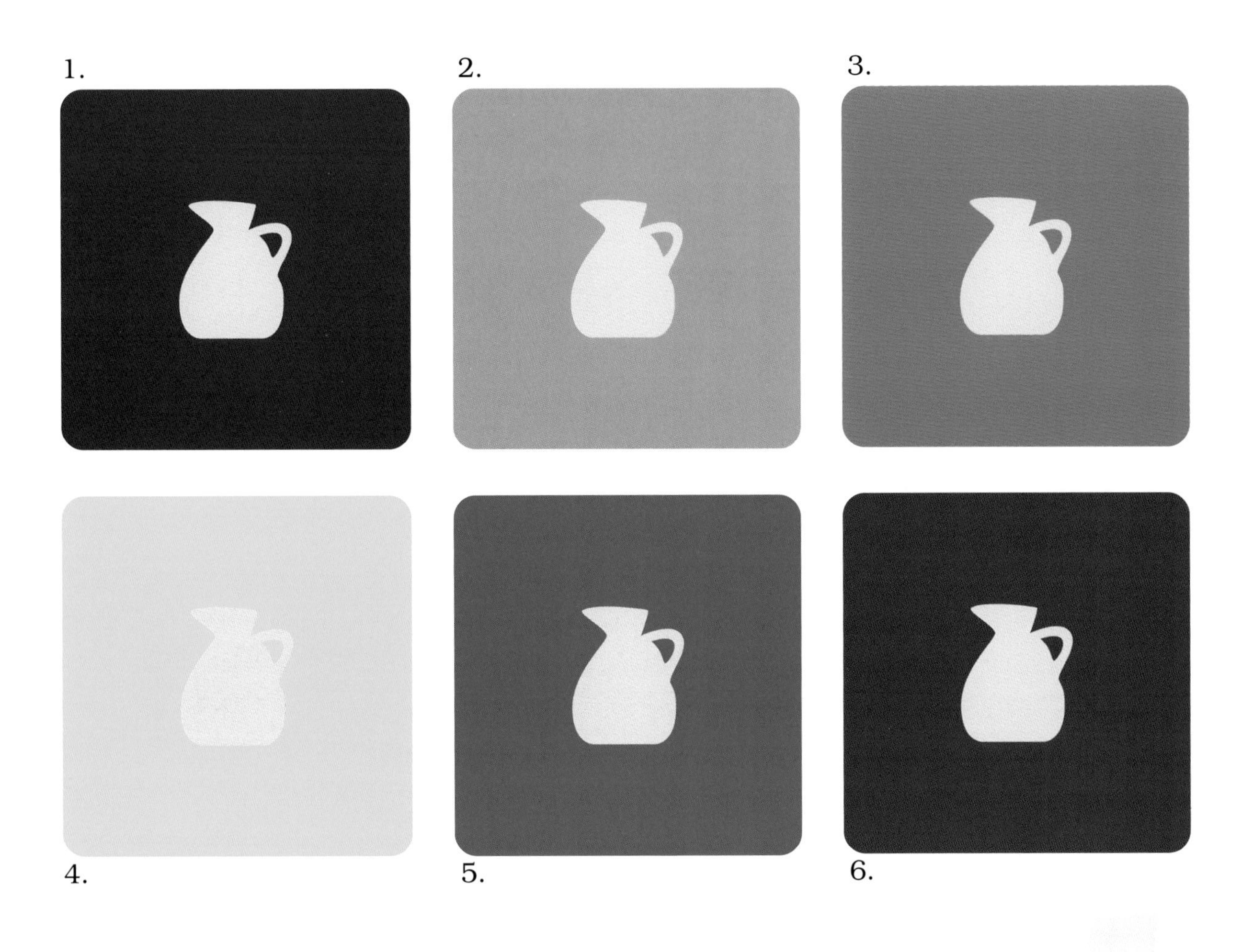

The base gray

The pale gray centre will appear slightly orange when surrounded by the violet-blue in diagram 1. I think I will leave you to decide the influence of the other surrounding colors.

Any color encompassed by another will move towards the complementary of the outer color. Such movement can be almost unnoticeable, powerful, enhancing or damaging.

It is, I believe, vital for the home decorator with an eye to contrast or harmony to have an appreciation of the effect of after-image.

Not an in-depth knowledge necessarily, but at least an awareness.

Very few who use color have this understanding. Those with it, such as yourself, are far ahead of not only most other home decorators, but virtually all professional decorators and interior designers.

Your home could look stunning with this information at your fingertips. Not only will it help in selecting a basic color scheme but you can select accessories such as cushions, curtains, ornaments and floral arrangements for sound reasons.

Changing by after-image

ABC

Any shape will give an after-image which will be exactly the same size as the influencing color.

All colors have their complementary partner, including white and black, (or light and dark).

If you take the after-image from the top diagram to the dot on the right you will, (unless you are experiencing difficulty identifying after-images), see the black and white shapes in reverse.

As they give each others after-image, we can identify them as a complementary pair.

The black will appear as a bright white and the white as a dark gray. The after-image from the white will not be a black because, as with all after-images, it is a paler version of the partner. So, light and dark (white and black) are also visual complementaries.

The contrast of visual complementaries

There are many ways in which the range of after-image complementaries can be employed. They can be made to harmonise, to clash or to add a sense of movement and excitement.

Complementary pairs, used at full strength can appear harsh and inharmonious to many, but will contrast vividly. This is particularly the case if smooth materials such as satin are used.

Although difficult to handle and suitable only for certain situations, complementaries used in this way can certainly bring interest to a room.

Subtle contrasts can be obtained by altering one color and leaving the other at full strength.

One of the hues can be 'darkened' by a small addition of the other. (This is easy to do following the color mixing tips - if using textiles etc. it will have to be done by eye).

The reduced color can be used over larger areas and will concentrate attention onto the smaller, stronger touches of color.

Alternatively, lowering the intensity with white will allow that color to be used over a greater area and will move the main interest onto the richer color. The latter is best applied in small areas.

The contrast of visual complementaries

There are many ways in which the effect of the after-image can be used in your home. All manner of accessories, from curtains, cushions, ornaments, fittings and even floral arrangements can be selected on this basis. With a little practice you will find it easy to use this approach to color selection, it is not at all difficult.

1. At full strength expect some powerful but visually interesting effects.

2. If the background is darker than its complementary partner it can be used over larger areas without a problem.

3. Likewise if the background is lighter.

The contrast of visual complementaries

Blue and orange

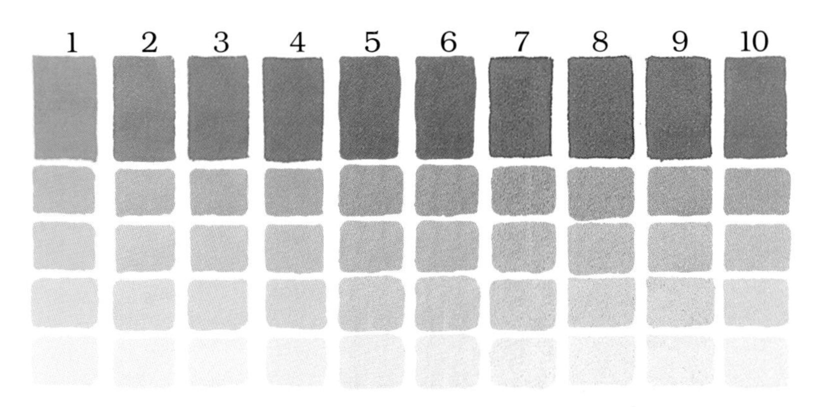

To give an idea of how this approach might work in practice: The top row of the above range can be mixed from orange and a greenish-blue paint. White has then been added progressively to each color to give the rest of the range.

If you are working with a complementary pair in paint form this guide will show the way.

But if, instead, you are working with textiles, ornaments, fittings etc. it will offer visual guidance:

Referring to the above color mixing swatch:

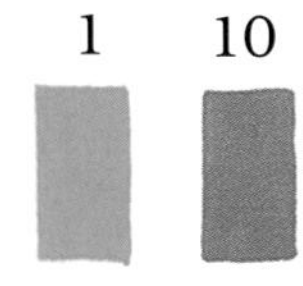

1. At full strength expect some powerful but visually interesting effects. Colors 1&10 above will provide such contrast.

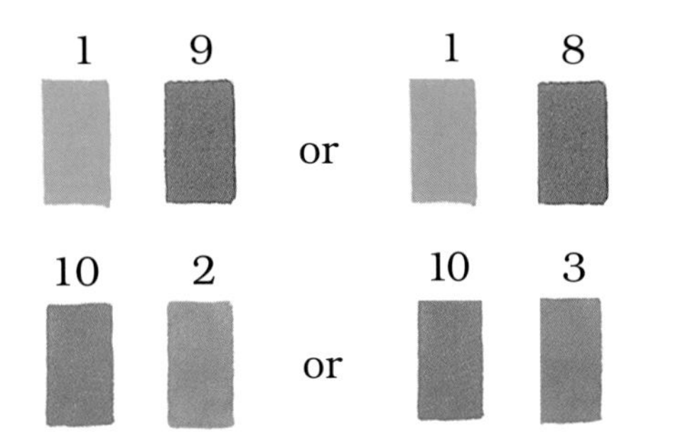

2. If the background is darker than its complementary partner it can be used over larger areas without a problem.

Colors 1 & 9 (or 1 & 8) will provide this arrangement, as will No.s 10 & 2 or 10 & 3.

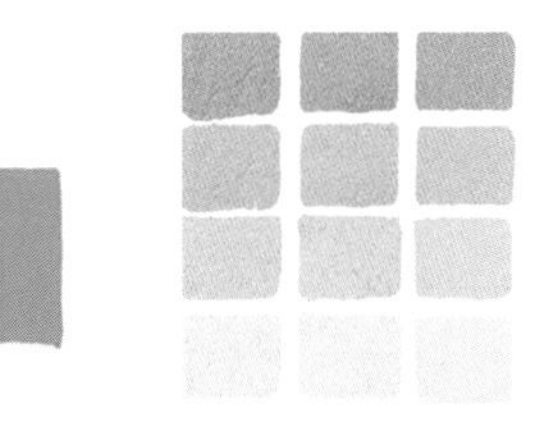

3. Likewise if the background is lighter. Color 1 with any of the tints under colors 8, 9 or 10.

Alternatively color 10 with any of the tints under colors 1, 2 or 3.

The contrast of visual complementaries

Blue and orange

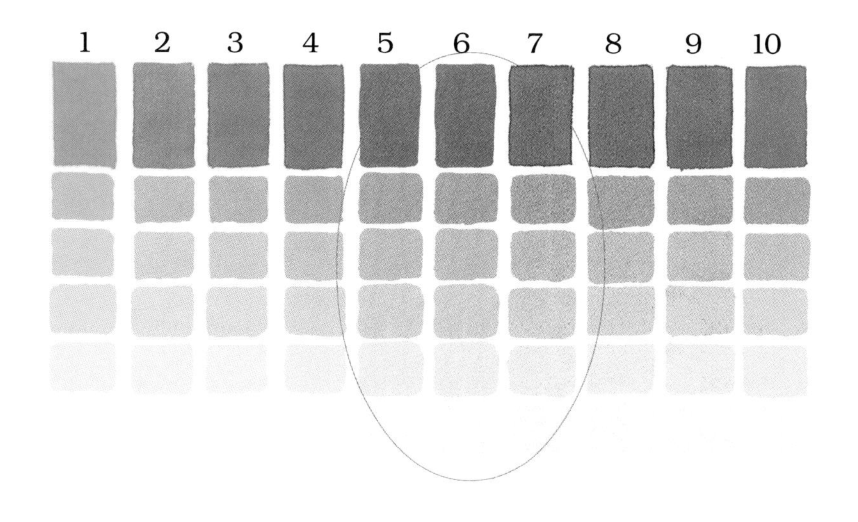

A complementary pair can be placed together in an almost endless variety of ways:

Both might be at full strength. One strong and the other reduced with white, with its mixing partner or with its partner plus white.

Both might be tints (lightened versions), or neutralised hues (a color reduced by its mixing partner).

Alternatively the 'colored grays' can be brought into play. 'Colored grays' (circled above) occur where a complementary pair (which are also mixing partners) have absorbed most of each others light.

Do not be overwhelmed by the possibilities. You only need to keep a few things in mind and the rest is experiment and practice.

Blue and orange

The contrast of visual complementaries

Red and green

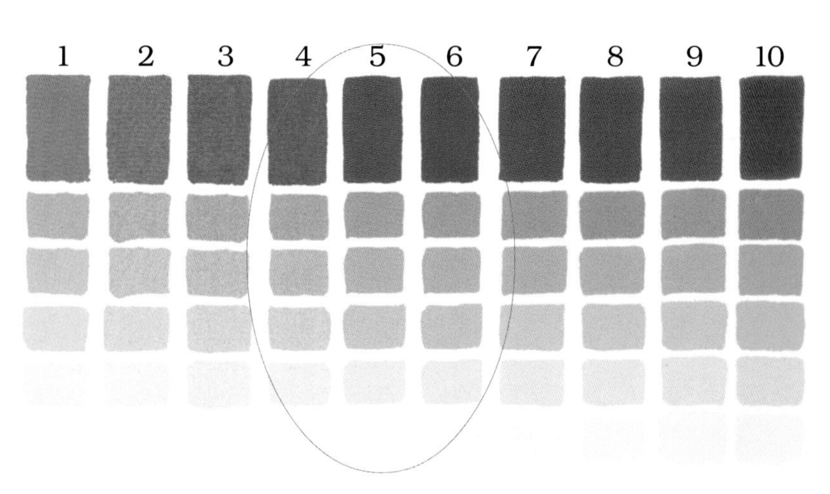

Any complementary pair can be used this way. On page 100 a greenish blue and orange were used. Blue (either a green-blue or a violet-blue) and orange are one complementary pair.

Red and green are another. In these examples I am using a bluish green and an orangish red. I could equally use a yellow-green and a violet-red. Please see suggested pairing on page 90. Remember, these are *mixing* as well as visual pairings. Once again the 'colored grays' are circled.

Red and green

Yellow and violet

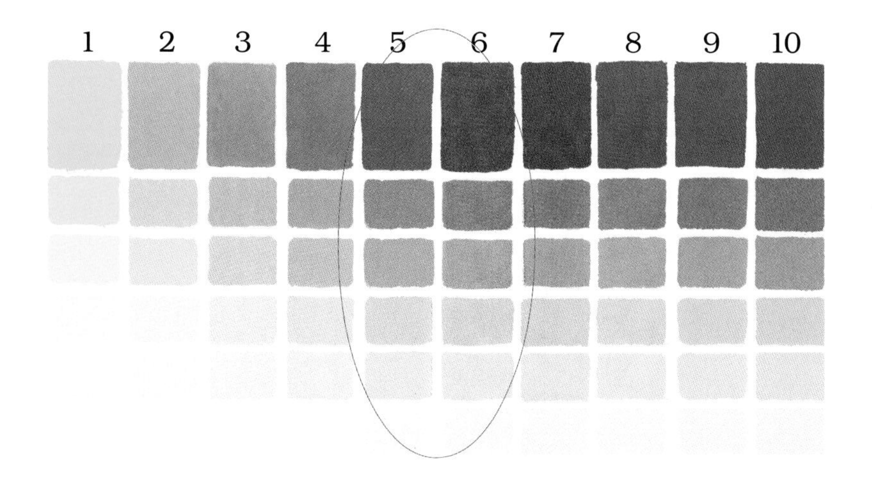

The third major complementary pair are yellow and violet. A range of yellows and violets are available. In this example I am using a mid-violet, which leans neither towards blue or yellow together with an orangish yellow.

As in the previous examples, the 'colored grays' are circled.

These grays are invaluable in all forms of color work. When they are further reduced with white they give some very subtle tints.

Yellow and violet

The complementaries in fine art

Corner of a Café-Concert 1878, Manet
© National Gallery, London

The complementaries have been used in a wide variety of ways ever since color work began because many find that they simply look good together. They have been used in interior and exterior decorating, fine art and all forms of craft work.

William Turner was possibly the first artist to understand the effect of the after-image and also exploit it in a thorough way.

Other painters followed his lead but it was left to the Impressionists to really concentrate on the subtle contrasts and harmonies that are available.

By juggling patches, strokes and dabs of various complementary pairings, by placing their color partners side by side, loosely intermingled or blended one into the other, in fact, by an almost endless variety of means, they produced work which has, it would appear, caught the imagination of more people than any other form of painting.

Their color work can still take the breath away. They produced such work not because they had an 'instinct' for color but because they studied the work of the color theorists of the day and painted with a close understanding of the effect of the after-image.

It does not take a great deal of effort to come to terms with the basics of the after-image.

With even a limited knowledge you will be able to incorporate the color schemes of your favourite artist into your home.

The complementaries in fine art

Bridge over the Dobra River, 1907, Matija Jama
National Gallery, Ljubljana, Slovenia

A favourite painting might give inspiration for a color scheme when decorating.
The actual colors of the painting can always be modified to suit the application, perhaps being made lighter or darker.

Here the artist has taken a limited number of basic hues, presented them in a myriad of saturations, played one range against the other and has repeated each color throughout the piece.

Touches of violet-blue into the orange-yellow and vice versa. Larger areas of each color have also been placed one against the other and have been scattered about.

The same approach can be taken when decorating a room. The main difference would be that instead of colors being worked one into another, it would be more usual to color walls, rails, and doors etc. in separate color areas. Unless, of course, one of the finishing techniques, such as ragging was used. Then a similar approach to that taken above might be followed.

The complementaries

Introduction

© Red Cover/Graham Atkins-Hughes

© Red Cover/David George

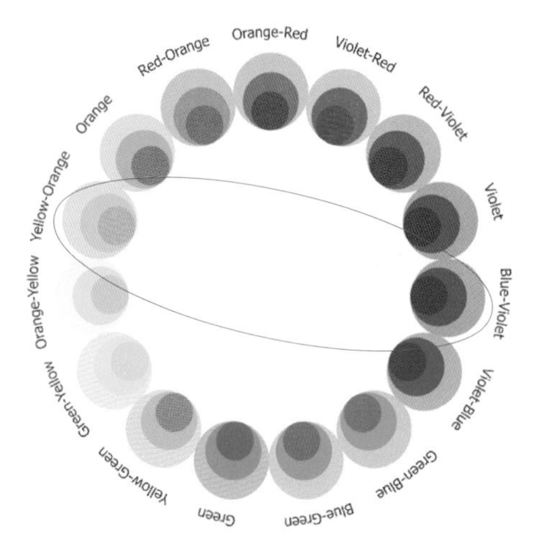

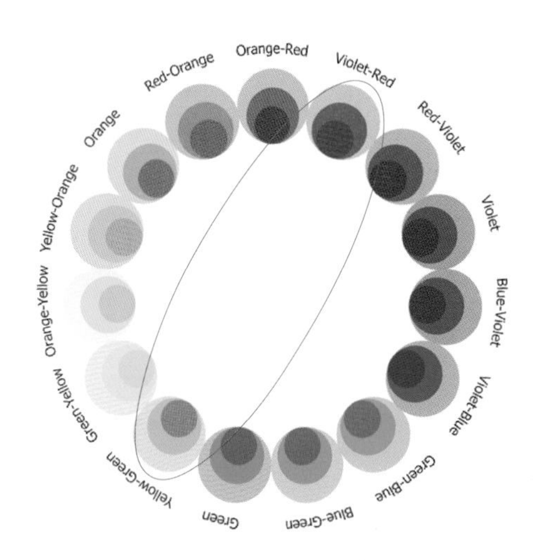

This approach to color harmony or contrast is based firmly on the after-image, the effects of which we have just been examining.

If you had decided to by-pass that particular section of the book, do not worry, the following color schemes will still be as applicable even if you are not sure why. However, it might be a good idea, at a later date, to return to that section. The more that you know about the behaviour of color the better.

elizabethwhiting.com

Although a ceiling painted in a hue, as opposed to white, can look a little 'top heavy', when it is balanced against the same hue at similar strength the effect can be very pleasing.

Blue-violet generally finds more use in interior decorating than either red-violet or violet. This, together with the fact that orange-yellow is more acceptable to many than green-yellow, makes these a very useful pair for many applications.

Orange-yellow, a bright, 'cheerful' hue, is well balanced with the much 'cooler' blue-violet. If both colors are neutralised, even slightly, a modified contrast such as this can be of great benefit when seeking color harmony.

The complementaries

Blue-violet and orange-yellow

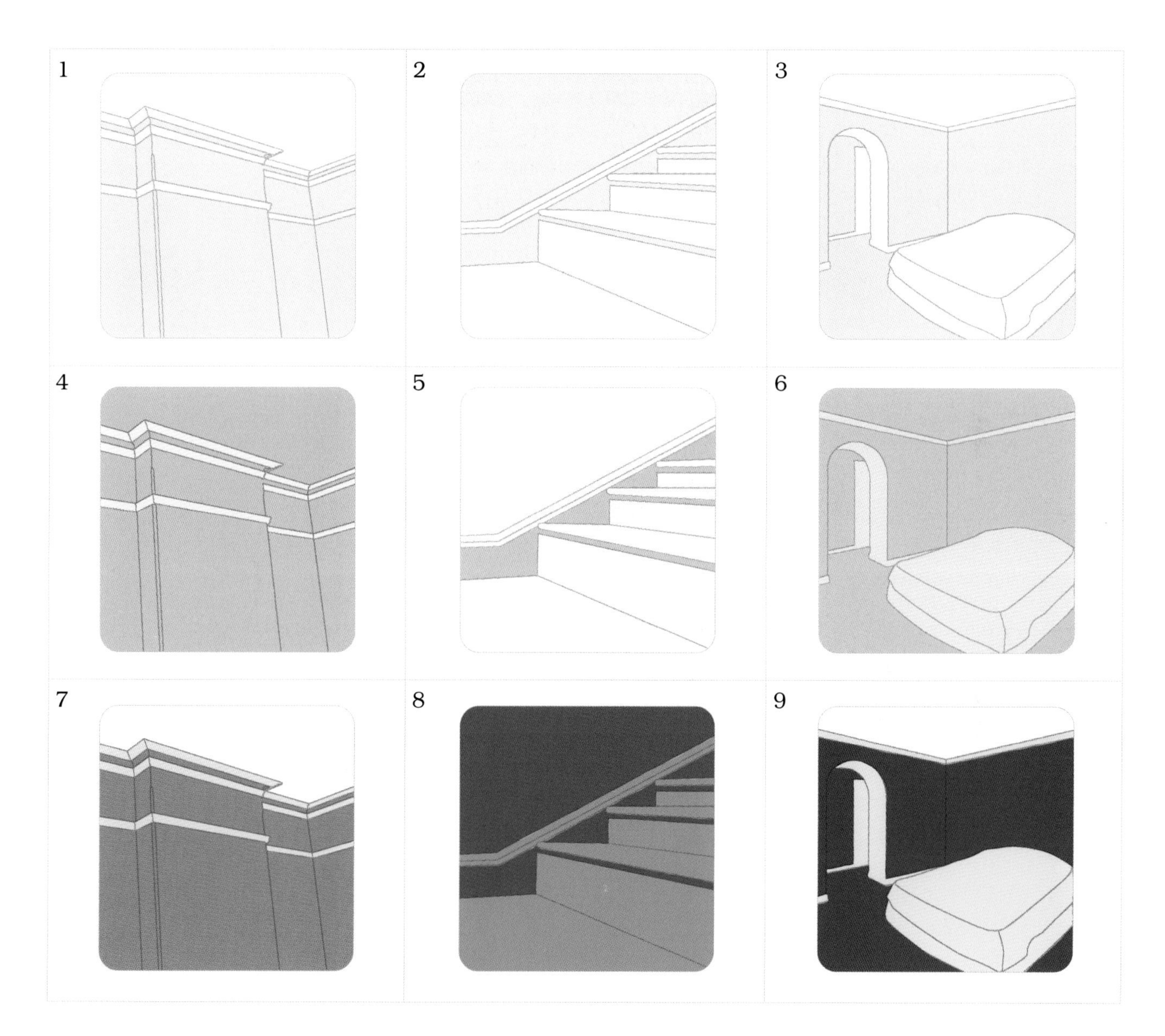

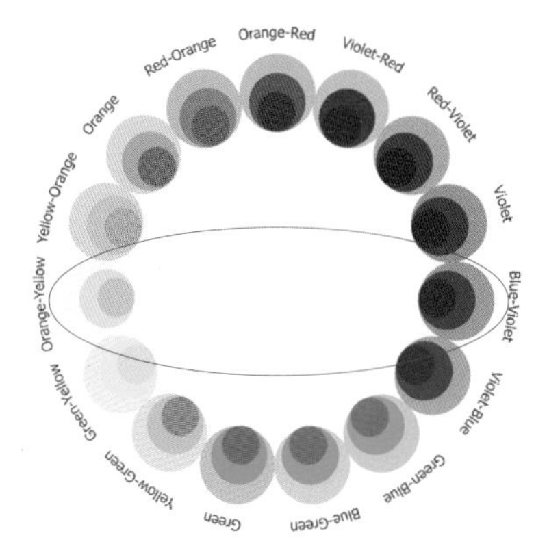

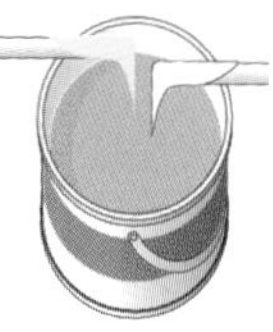

Blue-violet and orange-yellow are mixing partners and will reduce the intensity of each other in mixes.

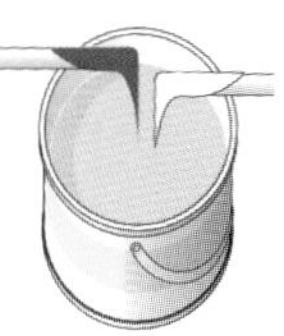

Being a mixing pair, blue-violet and orange-yellow will neutralise each other in mixes. As they are also visual partners they can be used in a way which will enhance each other visually, leading to some very attractive arrangements.

The complementaries

© Red Cover/Mark Bolton

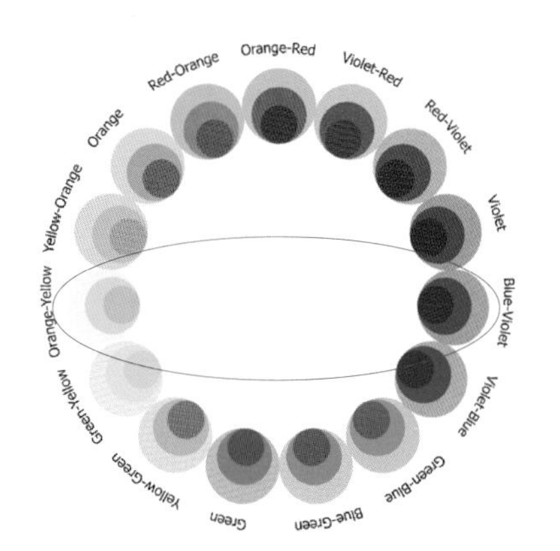

The contrast of temperature is easily set up with this pair.

Various contrasts can add a visual interest to a room. Here a light/dark contrast has been set up by balancing small areas of rich violet-blue against larger but very pale areas of the orange-yellow.

As blue is generally considered to be a 'cool' color and orange-yellow 'warm', a further contrast is added, that of perceived temperature. Such contrasts have an important role to play.

The complementaries

Orange-yellow and blue violet

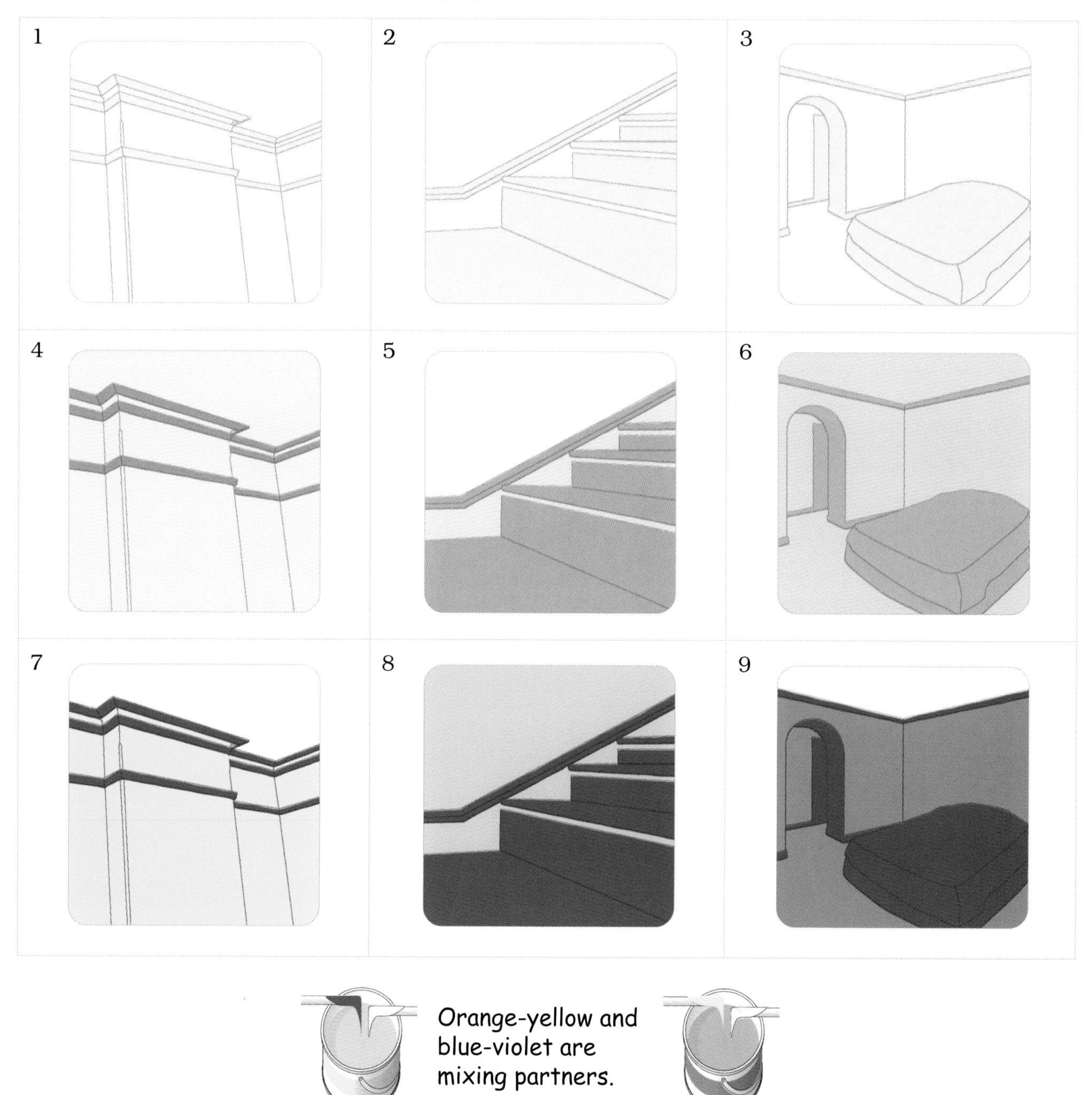

Complementaries act on each other optically, constantly enhancing each other. This fact gives any well matched pair great versatility. By varying intensities and area, a pairing such as these can give soft, quiet harmonies, when they are further reduced with white; bright, strongly contrasting arrangements when at or near full strength and calmer combinations when darkened. A very valuable pair in any setting.

The sequence has been reversed when compared to the previous pages. Here the violet-blue is set against an orange-yellow background. A simple change that can make a great difference in the way that we perceive colors.

The complementaries

© Red Cover/Jake Fitzjones

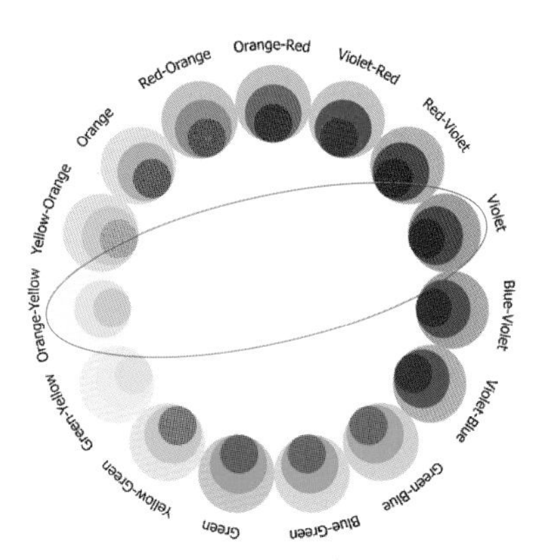

The results can be very pleasing if the two colors are well handled.

Orange-yellow and violet are commonly found together in nature.

Small touches of violet, from bright to grayed, set against a pale orange-yellow background found favour with many earlier artists. This approach can be very effective in the home as well.

As with all color combinations, it will pay dividends if small color arrangements are tried out before committing to mixing and application. A little experimenting can go a long way.

The complementaries

Orange-yellow and violet

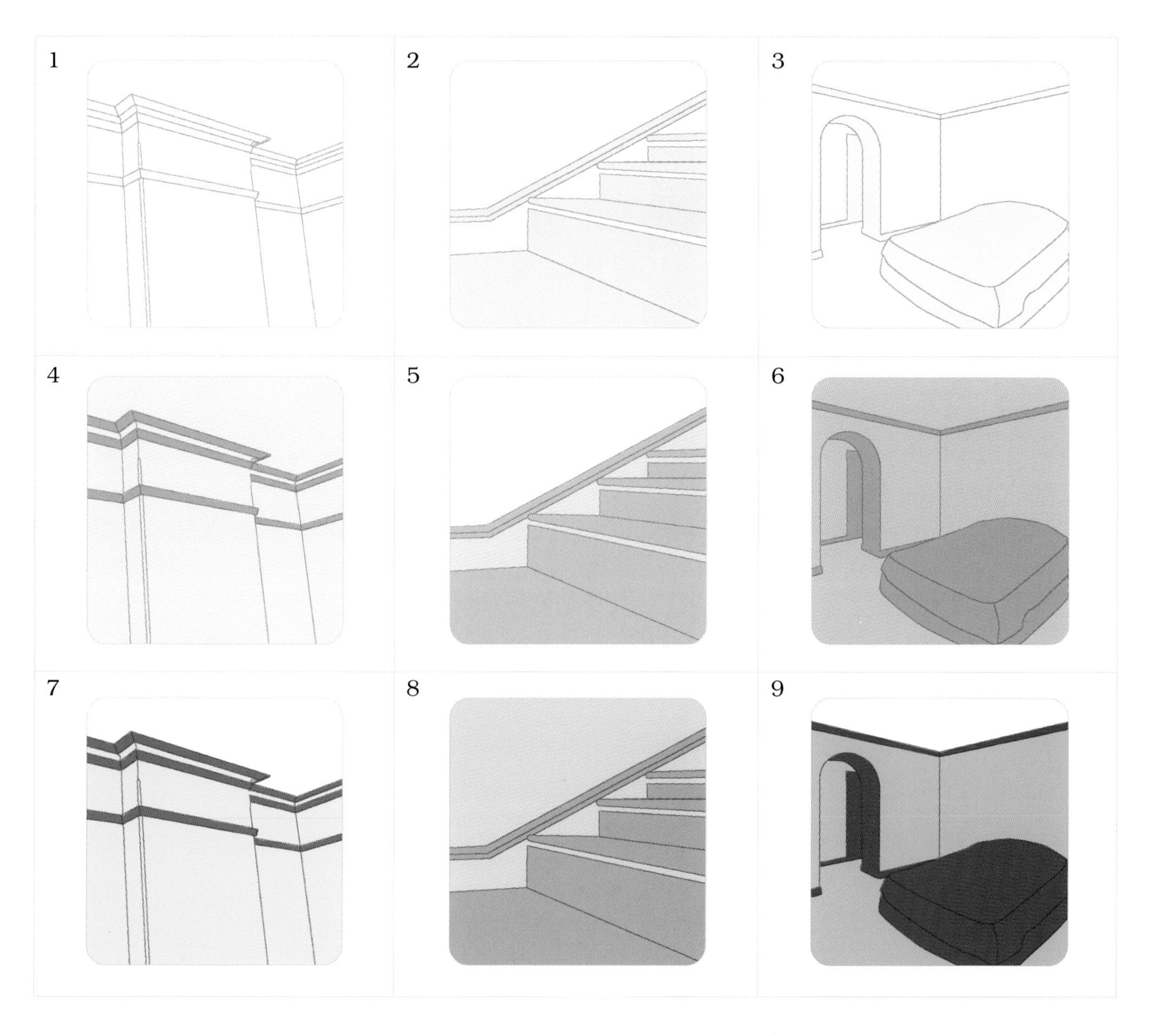

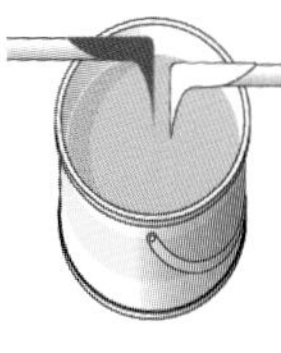

Orange-yellow and violet are a general mixing pair and will absorb each other in mixes.

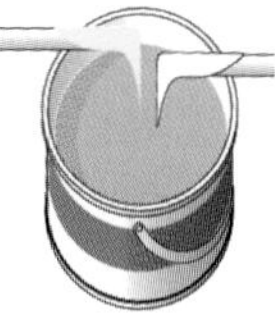

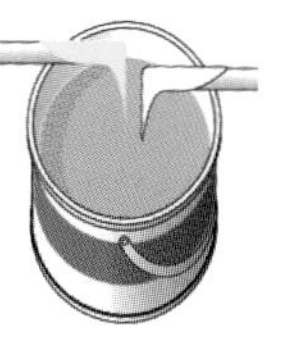

Green-yellow will also neutralise the violet.

As with all of the swatches on this page, the orange-yellow can be desaturated with white, with the mixing partner *violet*, or with white *and* the mixing partner. The violet can be desaturated with the same orange-yellow, with or without white.

With all references to the use of white in this context, please accept that I mean with the addition of white paint *not* with the influence of a white background to thinly applied paint.

Green-yellow will also neutralise the violet with little change to the results but it does mean the introduction of a further color.

The complementaries

© Red Cover/Brian Harrison

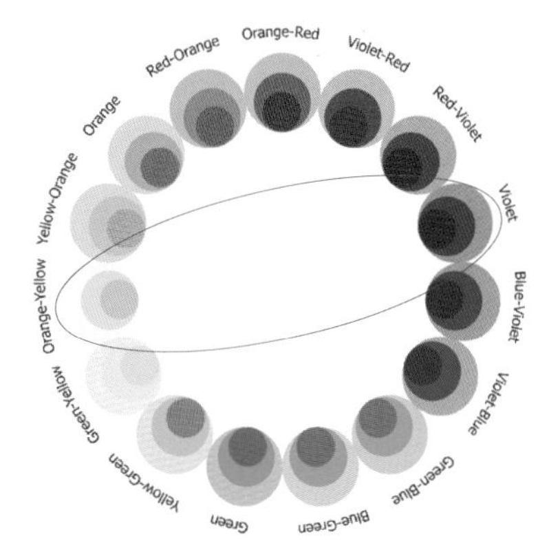

Visual complementaries (which are also mixing partners), can be of particular value when they are played one against the other; light against dark, bright against pale etc. as above.

The Impressionist painters, in particular, were able to produce some very beautiful passages this way. When using such colors do not be afraid to adapt. Perhaps add a touch of blue-violet to the violet as in the furnishing shown here.

The complementaries

Violet and orange-yellow

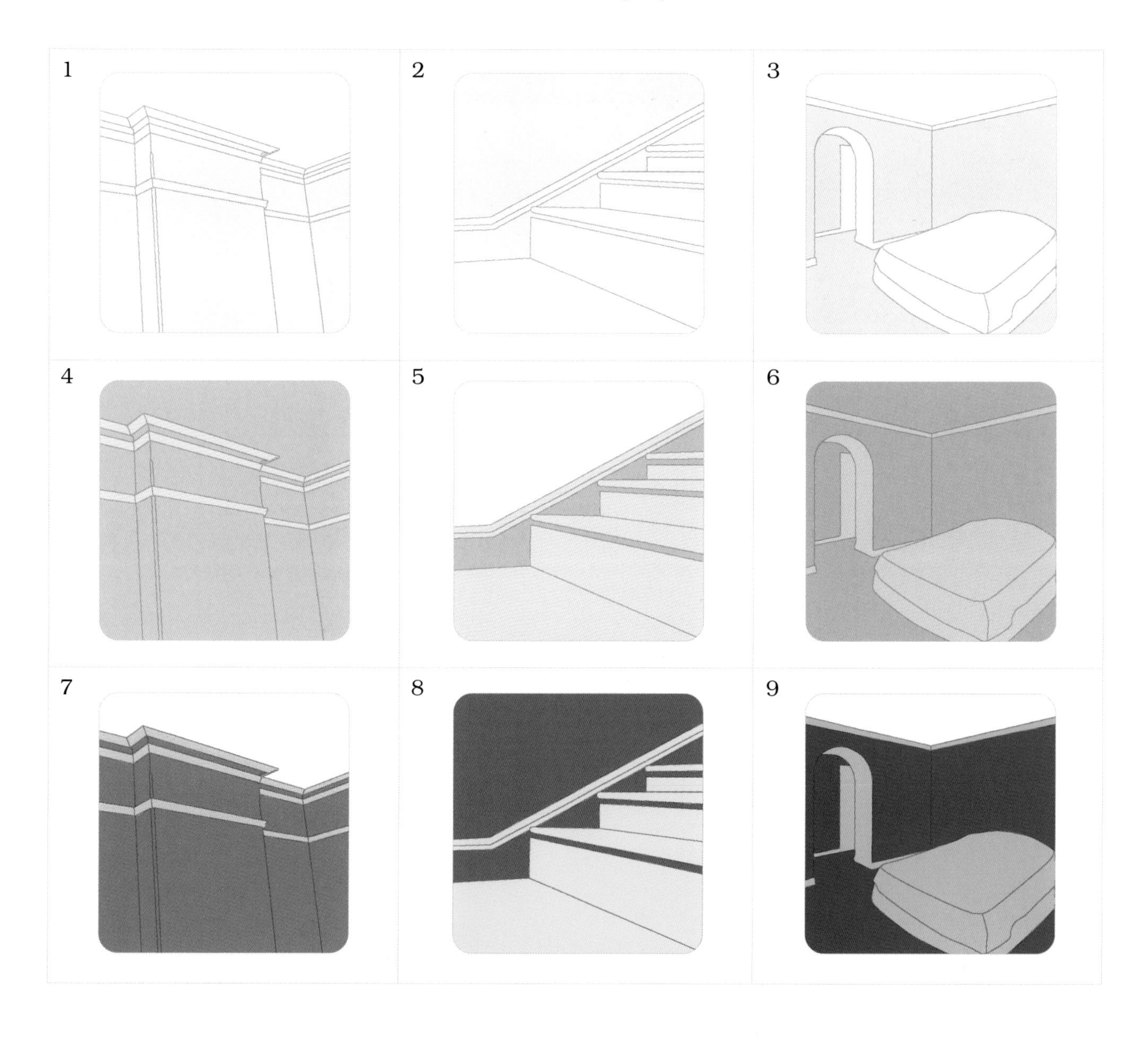

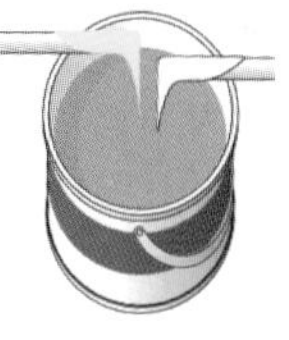

Violet and orange-yellow will neutralise and 'darken' each other in mixes.

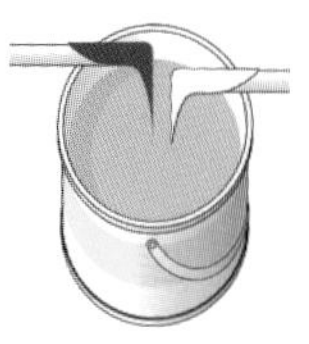

This can be a rather difficult pair to work together as violet is not always well received. However, by varying the strength and proportion of each color, some very interesting and harmonious arrangements are possible. Such alterations can be made by mixing one into the other and using white for further modification. A little experimenting will soon pay off.

The complementaries

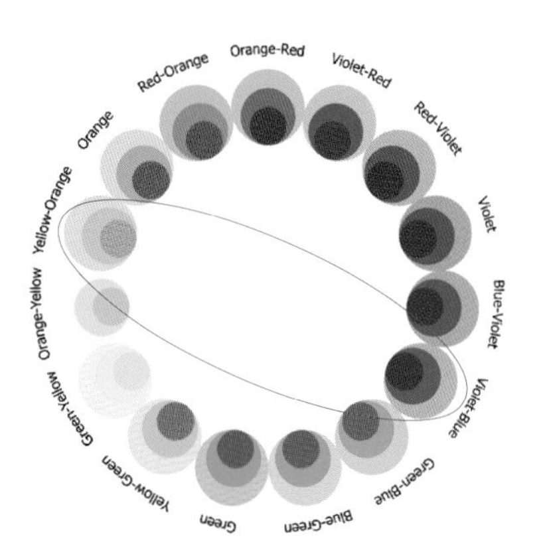

A very practical duo.

Comfortable colors in any setting, from the traditional to the modern.

Large areas of violet-blue, softened with white and with small touches of the yellow-orange can look particularly effective. More so if the latter color is also reduced somewhat.

Versatile and with many applications, this particular complementary pair has been a long time favourite with painters and other users of color world wide.

The complementaries

Violet-blue and yellow-orange

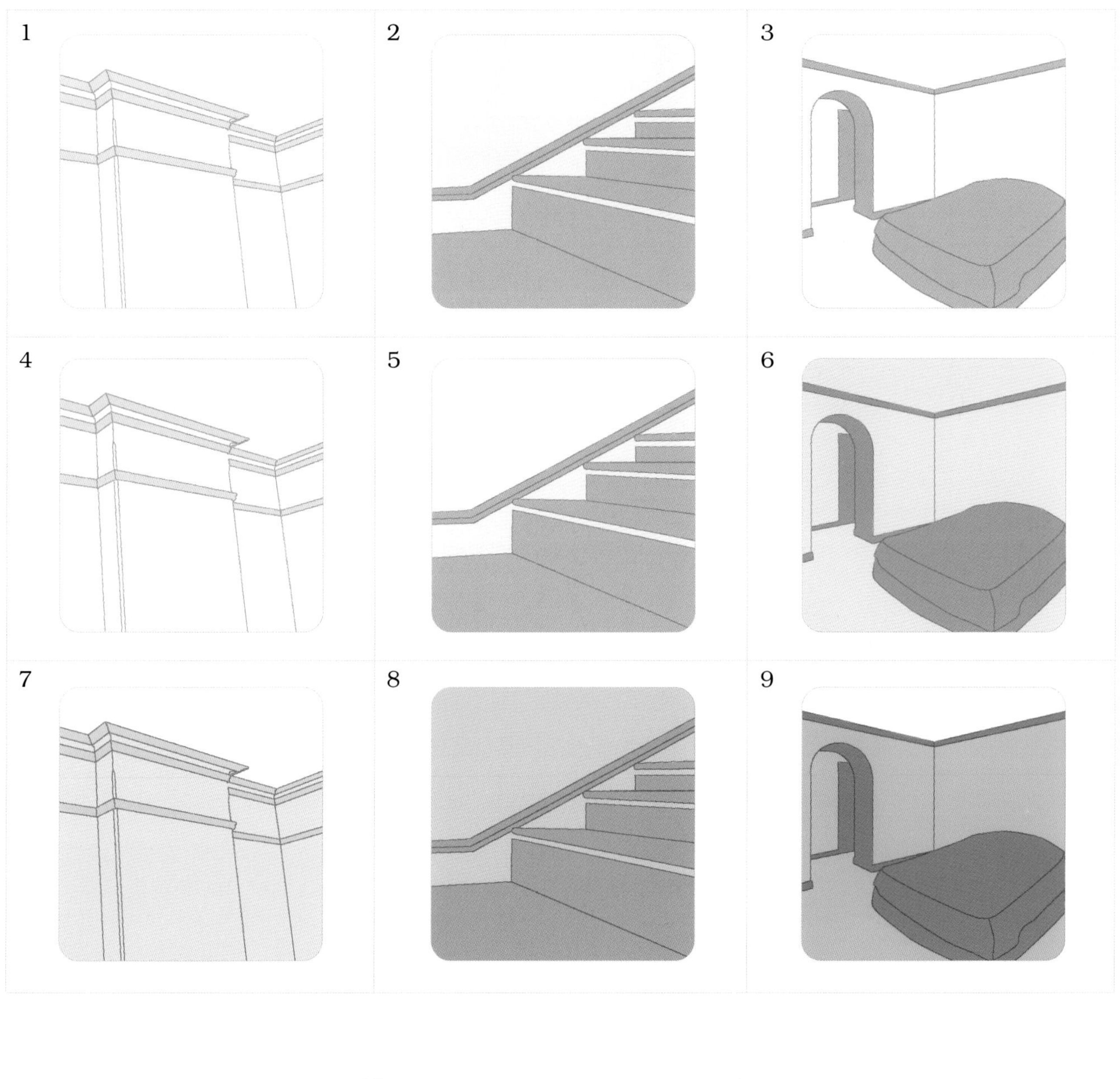

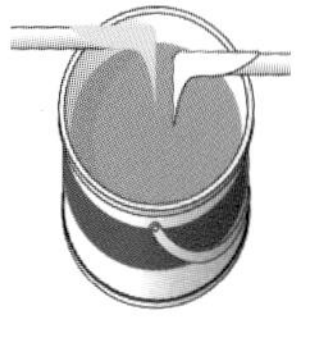

Violet-blue and yellow-orange.

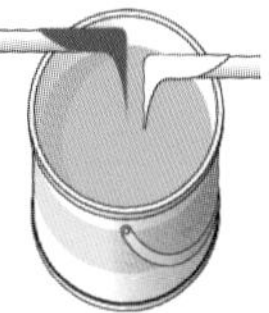

Being mixing partners, these two will reduce each other's intensity in mixes. Being at the same time visual partners (complementaries) they can enhance each other when balanced one against the other. A simple, straightforward and very effective way to work.

The complementaries

© Red Cover/Huntley Hedworth

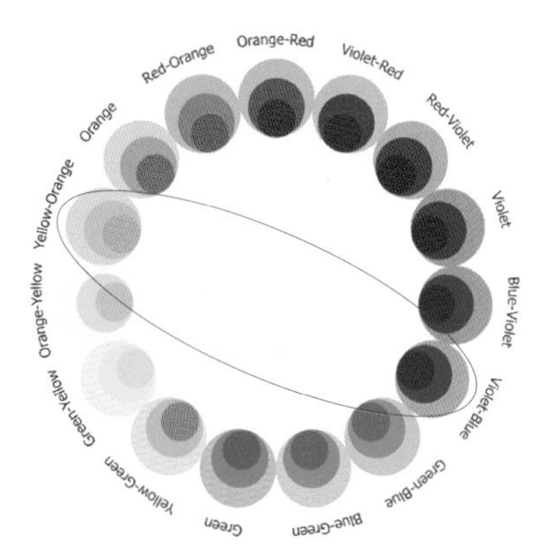

Frequently found in nature, this combination has been used by decorators, artists and craft-workers throughout the ages.

As you look over these pages it will become obvious to you where the pairings work well together. Most combinations can be further altered in area to encourage them to work together. Brighter hues are best applied over small areas, just touches of color.

Yellow-orange and violet-blue

1 2 3

4 5 6

7 8 9

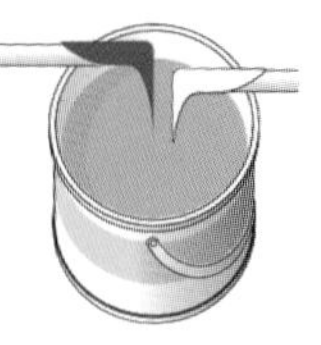

Yellow-orange and violet-blue will absorb each other in mixes, mutually reducing intensity.

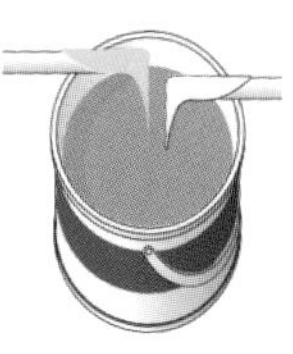

When using this pair to neutralise each other, if the mixes move too far towards green, try adding a little red to reduce the green. (The red will 'absorb' the green as red and green are, of course, also mixing partners).

It might be that the yellow-orange was a little too yellow. With practice you will be able to adjust colors this way. Basically, red will absorb green and vice versa. By adding a touch of red you will be removing the green.

© Red Cover/Jake Fitzjones

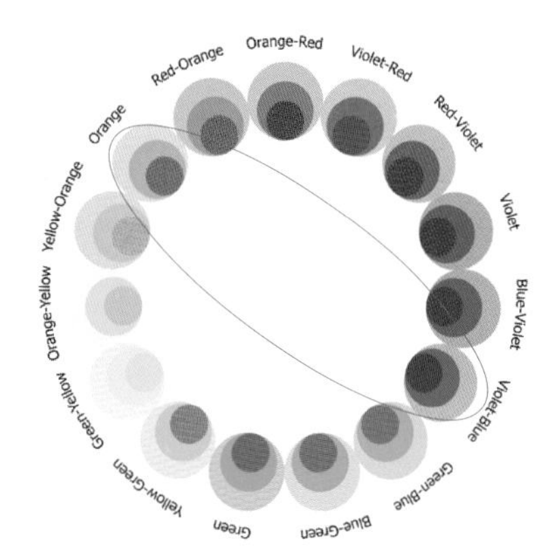

This duo have been very popular with artists, decorators and craft workers through the ages.

The Umbrellas, 1881-6, Pierre-Auguste Renoir
© National Gallery, London

Violet-blue and orange were used again and again by the Impressionists painters. The blue had many applications, clothing, buildings, skies, interiors etc. The orange was the ideal complement, particularly when desaturated for flesh colors, hair and other uses.

This same approach can be used when decorating to bring harmonious arrangements into the home.

Color combinations which have proved to be effective in other applications might well work for you also.

The complementaries

Orange and violet-blue

1

2

3

4

5

6

7

8

9

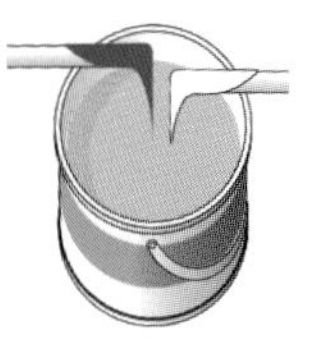

Orange and violet-blue are general mixing partners.

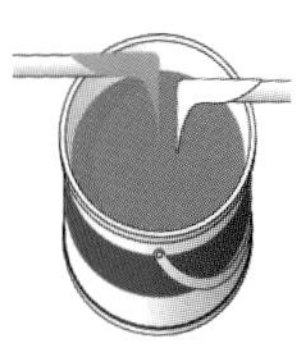

When using this mixing pair for mutual 'darkening', if you find your mixes start to become rather greenish it might be that the orange that you have mixed is a little too yellow.

Add a touch of red to the orange to remove the greenness. Red and green being mixing partners, the extra red will absorb the unwanted green. It will pay to proceed slowly when adding the red.

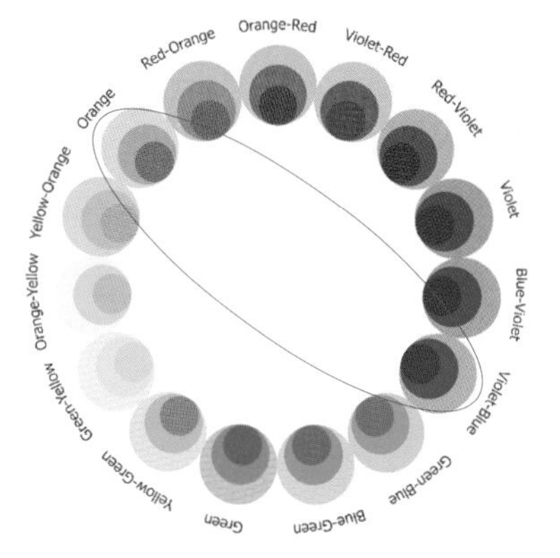

Brown, one of the most 'comfortable' and common of all color groups, can be described as a darkened orange, red or yellow.
In this case; orange darkened by violet-blue.

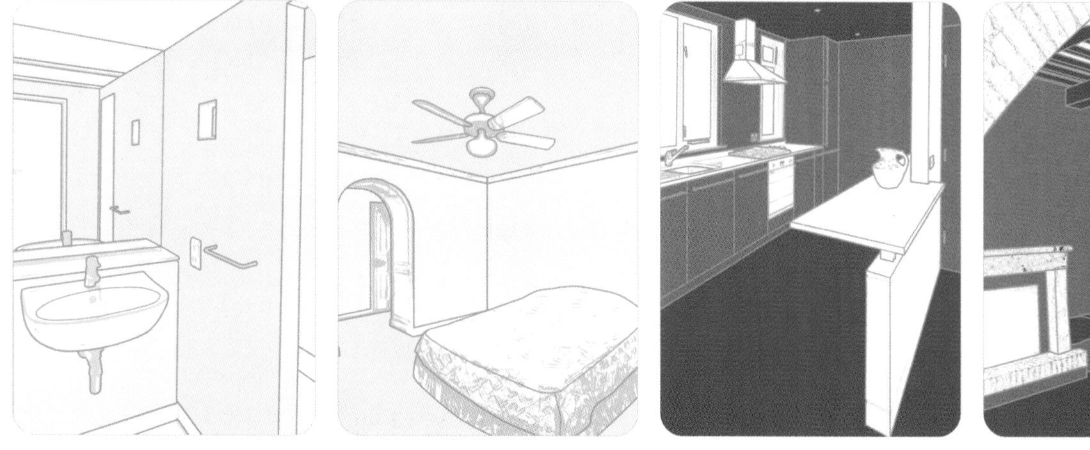

Violet-blue and orange can be harmonised at almost any strength by simply altering the area of color.

Particularly versatile, this pair has applications in almost every area of color use, from fine art to porcelain to your kitchen perhaps?

Violet-blue and orange

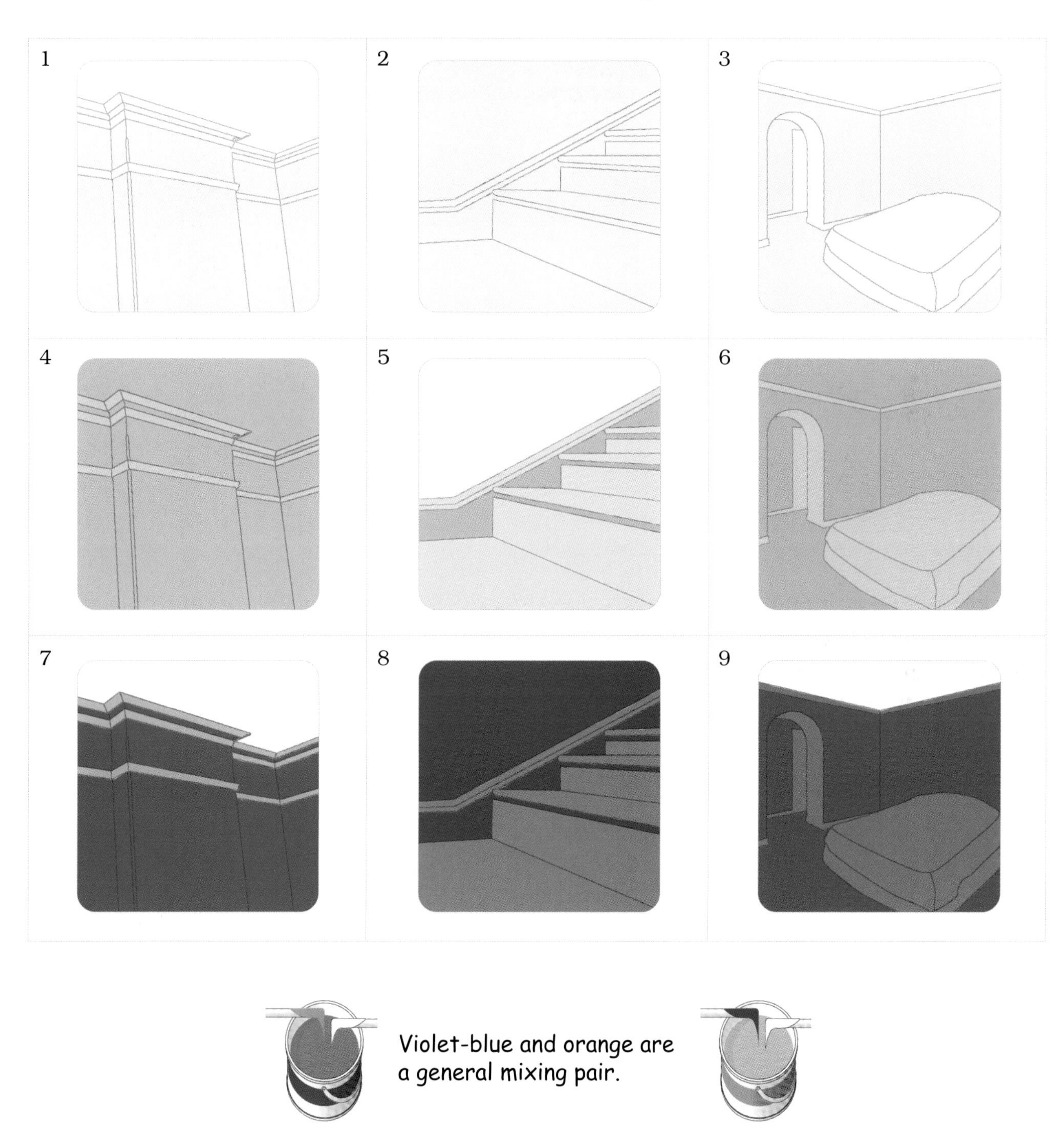

Violet-blue and orange are a general mixing pair.

One of the beauties of working with mixing partners is that one can be used to neutralise the other. This means that only two colors need be in use (one, such as the orange here, might need to be pre-mixed).

Strictly speaking a *yellow*-orange is the mixing partner of violet-blue. But a mid-orange will do the job just as well and will help in color harmony. If one color contains traces of the other they work together very easily.

The complementaries

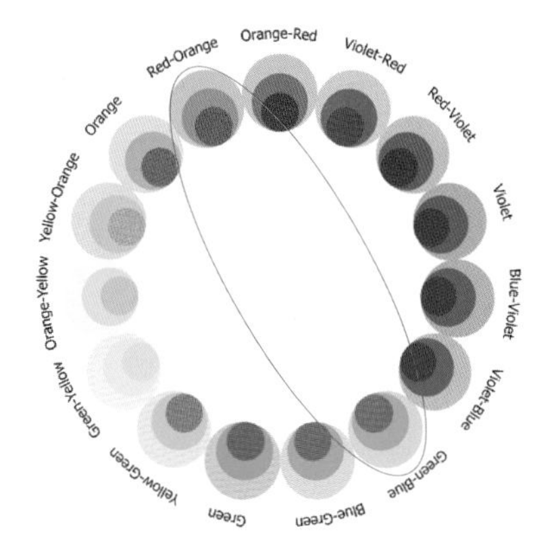

Vibrant contrasts or soft harmonies,
it's up to you with this pair.
They have a lot to offer.

As colors become closer in value, that is, they appear to move towards being equally light or dark, they can be harmonised readily.

Alternatively make one dark and the other light.

This pair are possibly more versatile when the green-blue is used in a pale form in the background with the red-orange appearing a little stronger in smaller highlights, or covering a small area in a room, as in the main illustration.

The complementaries

Green-blue and red-orange

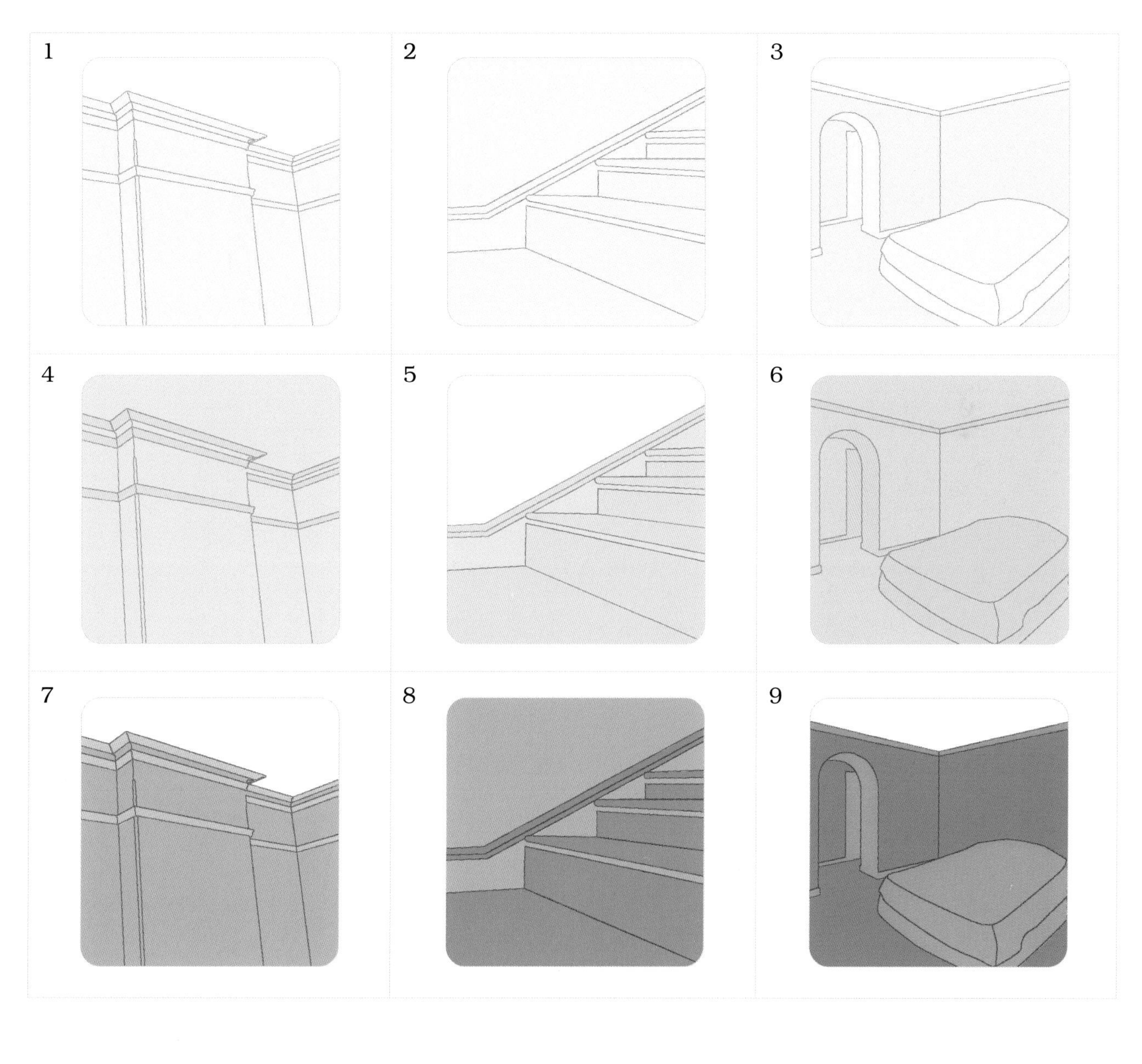

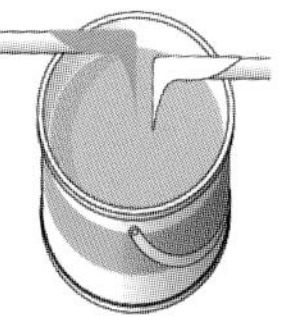

Green-blue and red-orange will 'absorb' each other in mixes.

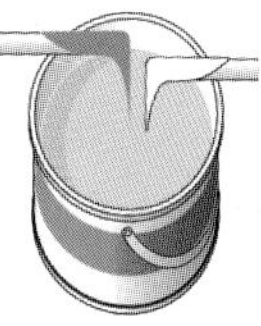

The color mixing tips, above, all show the mixing partner plus white being added.

Individual colors such as the green-blue can, of course, be used unmixed at full strength.

Alternatively they can simply be mixed with white or the mixing partner.

A number of ways can be used to alter the basic hues to give variety.

The complementaries

© Red Cover/Winfried Heinze

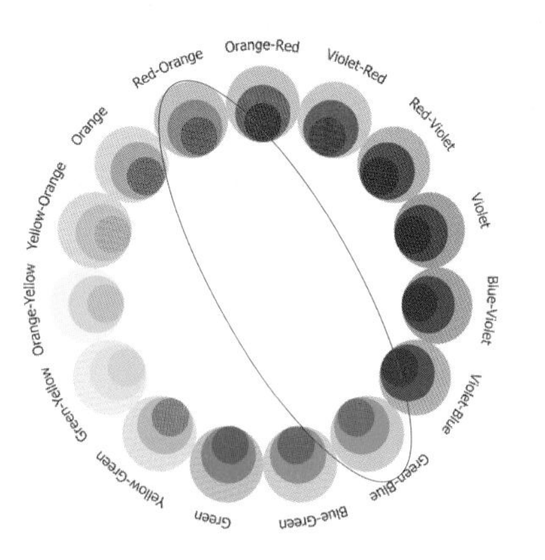

By varying the intensity of one against the other, a wide range of effects are achievable.

Strong, vibrant hues when at or near full saturation, this complementary pair need to be considerably modified if they are to harmonise. There are so many applications for color that a particular pairing might look stunning in a fashion design but unbearable when used to decorate a room. The areas over which colors are applied can often decide color harmony or strong color contrast.

The complementaries

Red-orange and green-blue

1 2 3

4 5 6

7 8 9

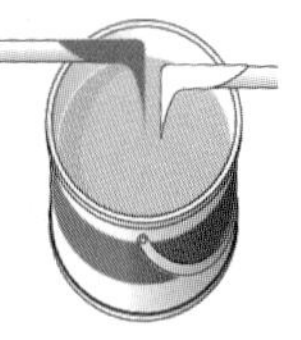

Red-orange and green-blue are mixing partners and will 'absorb' each other very efficiently.

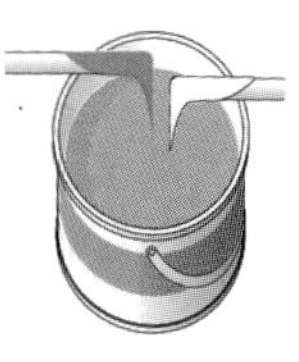

The red-orange can be reduced with white, with the mixing partner *green-blue*, or with white *and* the mixing partner. Lower the intensity of the green-blue with the same orange-red with or without white.

Mixing partners not only modify each other when blended but can enhance each other visually.

For simplicity, color harmony or contrast and visual interest they have it all.

The complementaries

elizabethwhiting.com

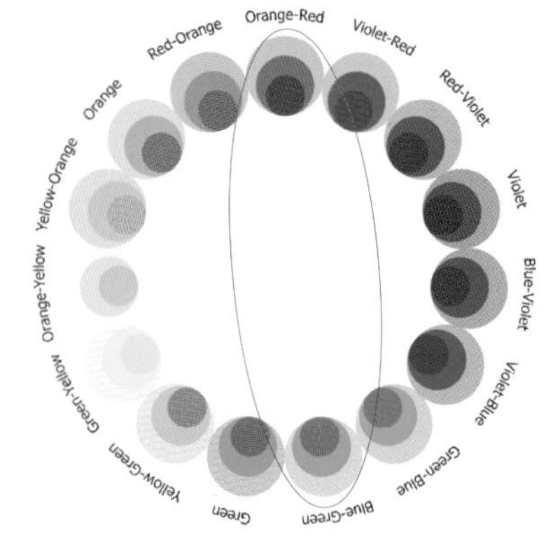

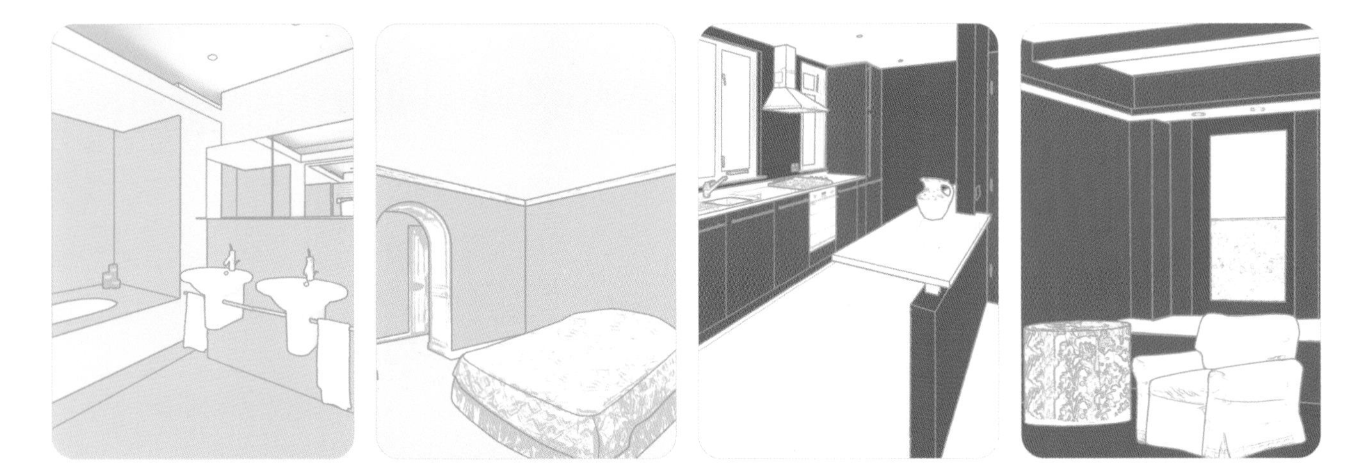

Although they are necessarily set on these pages, try varying the proportions, perhaps spread pale colors over larger areas and reduce the size of brighter colors to small accents, for example. It is a case of deciding on the colors to use and then juggling with proportions and strengths. Careful planning will always pay off.

The complementaries

Blue-green and orange-red

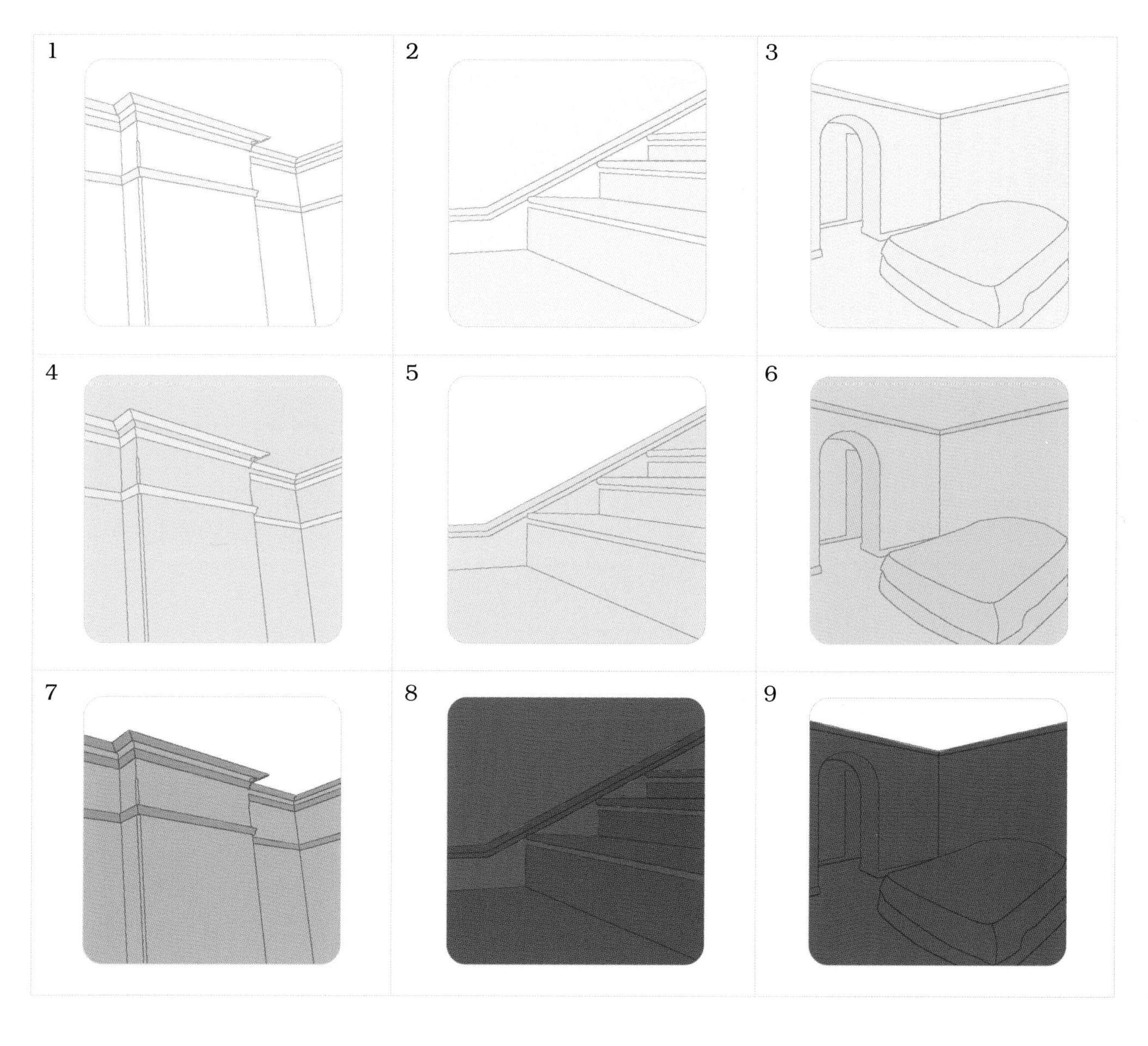

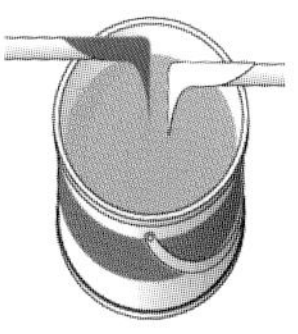

Blue-green and orange-red are close mixing partners.

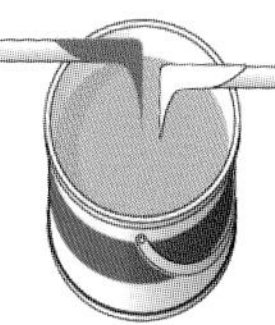

Rather than introduce 'outside' colors, use the blue-green to desaturate the orange-red and vice versa.

Between them they will give a vast range of colors which can be harmonised with ease.

Being mixing partners they will darken each other very efficiently. The 'character' of the desaturated color will be altered slightly but less so than other means of darkening. If white is then added the range becomes enormous.

The complementaries

elizabethwhiting.com

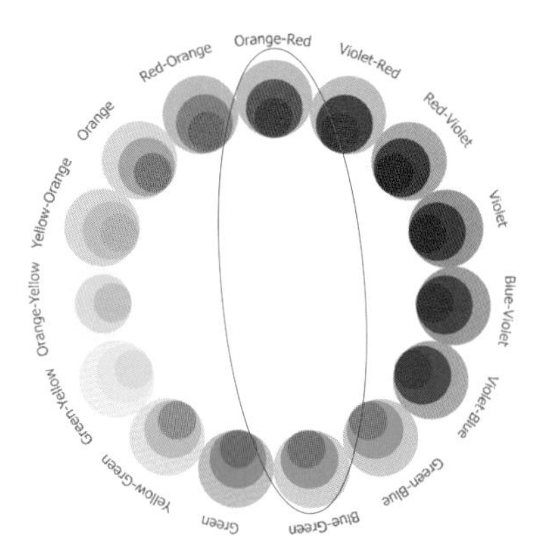

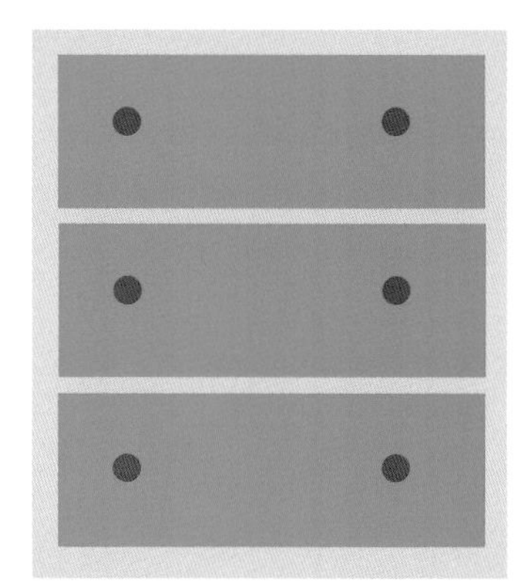

With such vibrant colors, which can contrast very strongly when at or near full strength, it adds to the chances of harmony if they are neutralised one way or the other.

As colors are darkened, for example, they become easier to work with and can be used over larger areas than when brighter.

Unfortunately such darkened hues can become rather oppressive if used on a large scale. One dark and the other relatively light, as above, can be very effective. As with all color use, it is a case of thinking about and juggling with the various colors which are available from a complementary pair (mixing partners).

Orange-red and blue-green

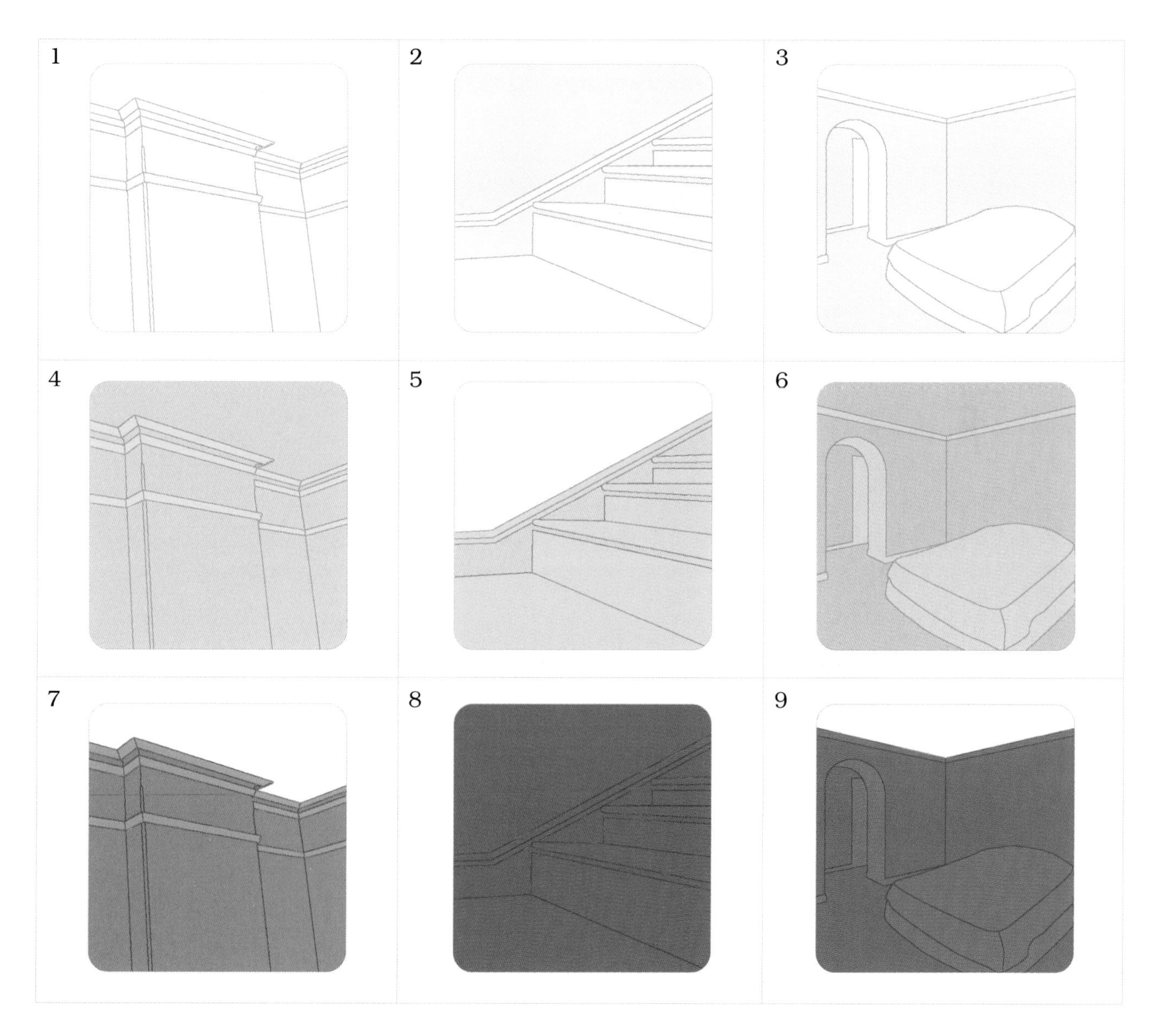

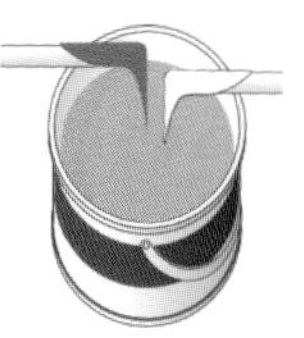

Orange-red and blue-green are a close mixing pair.

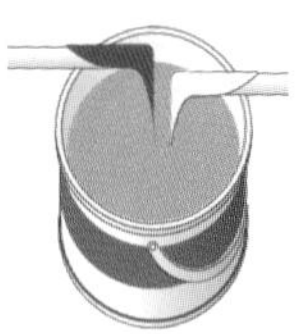

When complementaries (mixing partners) are combined one will start to absorb the other. As the blue-green, for example, is mixed into the orange-red it will start to 'soak it up'. If more blue-green is added it will absorb even more of the orange-red. As the 'orange-redness' disappears through this process it becomes ever darker. Although the red will change somewhat in character, this is the most efficient way to darken it. In turn the orange-red can be used to absorb varying 'amounts' of the blue-green, darkening that hue also.

The complementaries

© Jefferson Smith/arcblue.com

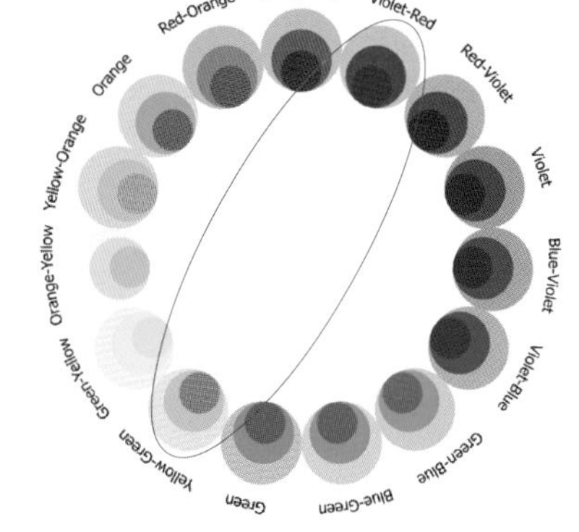

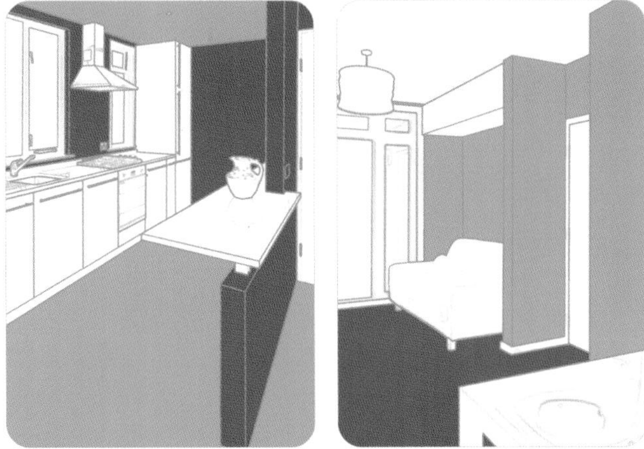

These can be a rather awkward pair to use together. However, any two colors can be enticed into an harmonious arrangement. By varying the intensity of one or both, either with white, with the mixing partner or with the partner plus white, they can give very pleasing and unusual results. At anywhere near full strength they can be rather overpowering.

Violet-red and yellow-green

1	2	3
4	5	6
7	8	9

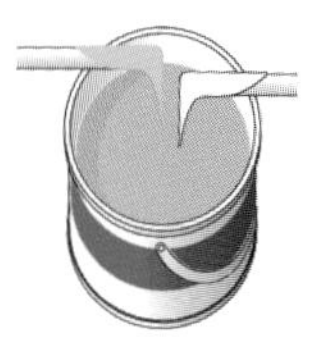

Violet-red and yellow-green are close mixing partners.

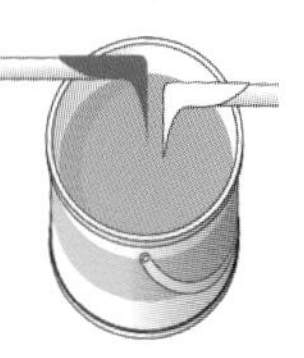

Being close mixing partners these two will act on each other very efficiently. One will neutralise the other and vice versa.

Although the character of the color is altered during such mixing, this is the most efficient way to darken a hue.

The complementaries

© Red Cover/David George

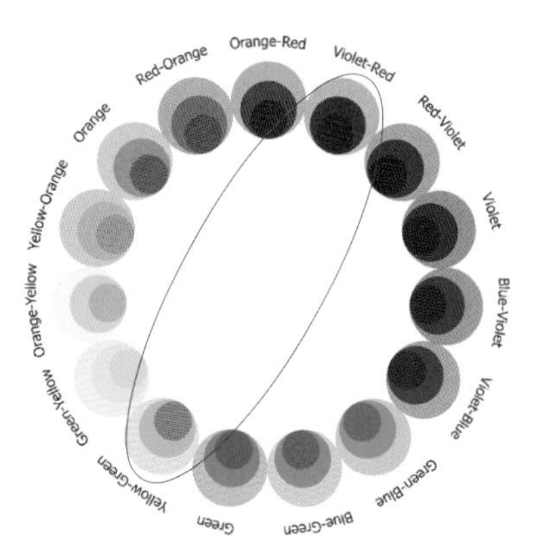

Colors of the furnishing can play a vital role.

Complementary pairings such as these can be very effective when small areas of one color are contrasted with larger areas of the other, particularly if either are at anywhere near full strength. This approach was often taken by the Impressionist painters.

As a small child I helped my rather eccentric Grandmother paint my bedroom a vivid yellow-green, with large bright violet-red spots.

The effect was nothing like an Impressionist painting and I have not been the same since. But it probably used up some old tins of paint.

Yellow-green and violet-red

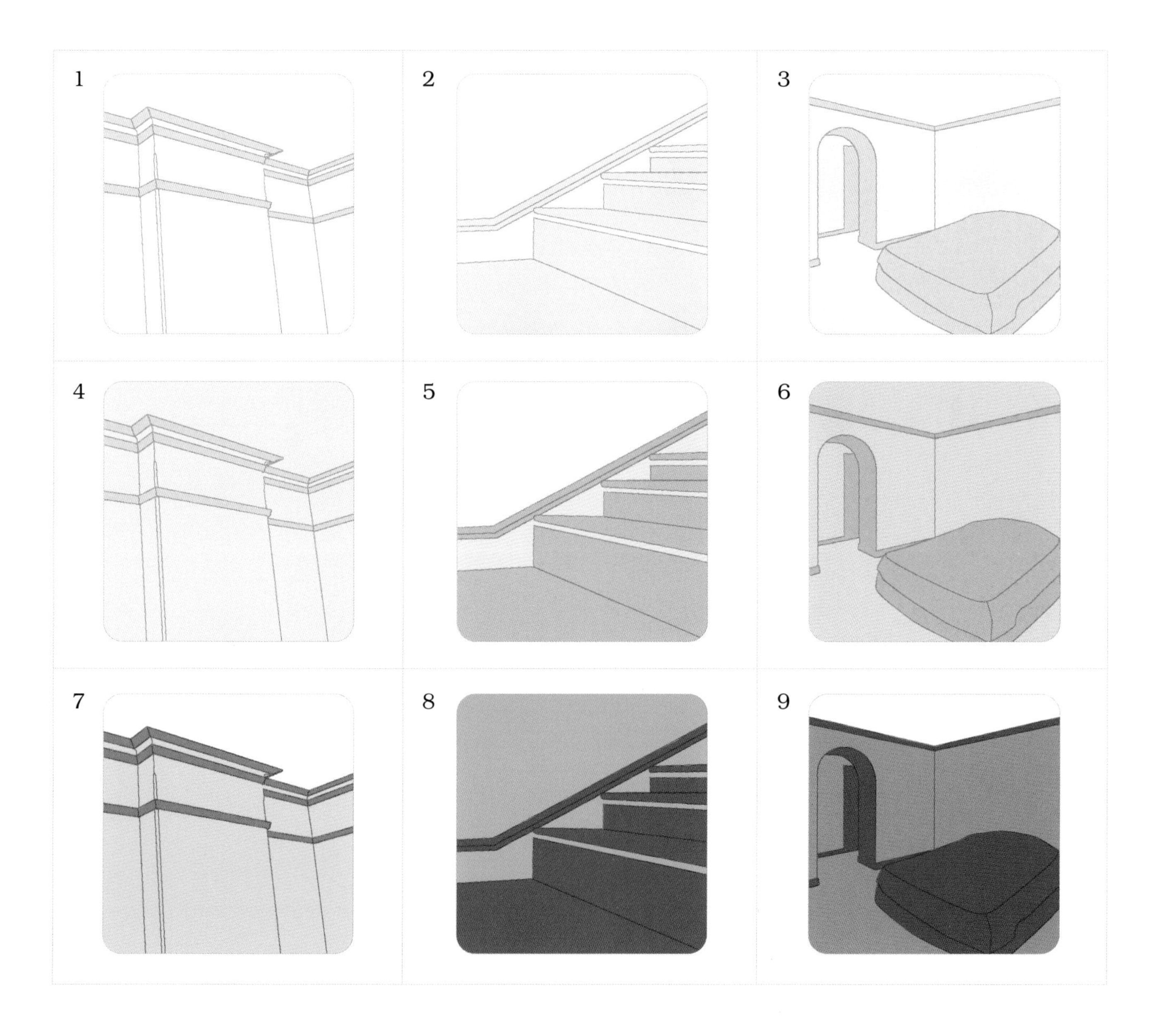

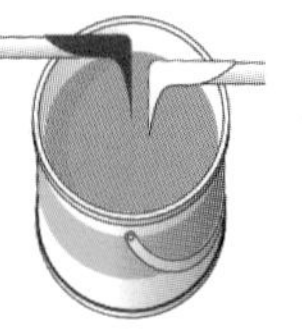

Yellow-green and violet-red will neutralise each other in mixes.

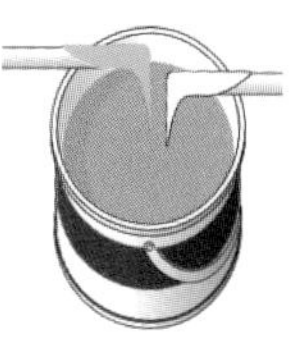

Yellow-green and violet-red will neutralise each other in mixes. They will also produce very useful 'colored grays' when mixed in near equal intensity. 'Colored grays' are reached when the mix does not show either the red or the green to a noticeable extent. When white is added to such mixes the results can be very subtle indeed.

The complementaries

elizabethwhiting.com

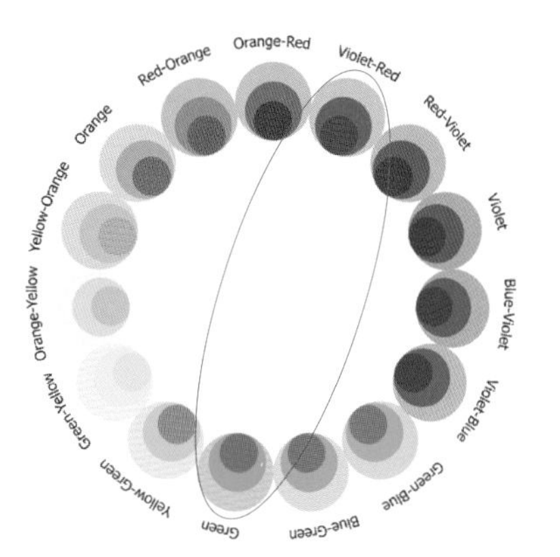

The violet-red can be rather overpowering for many, unless used with caution.

A color scheme can be extended throughout.

The violet-red is probably best kept for use in accents to enhance the green rather than over larger areas. If the violet red is used at full strength against a bright green background, you might have to issue visitors with sun-glasses.

The complementaries

Green and violet-red

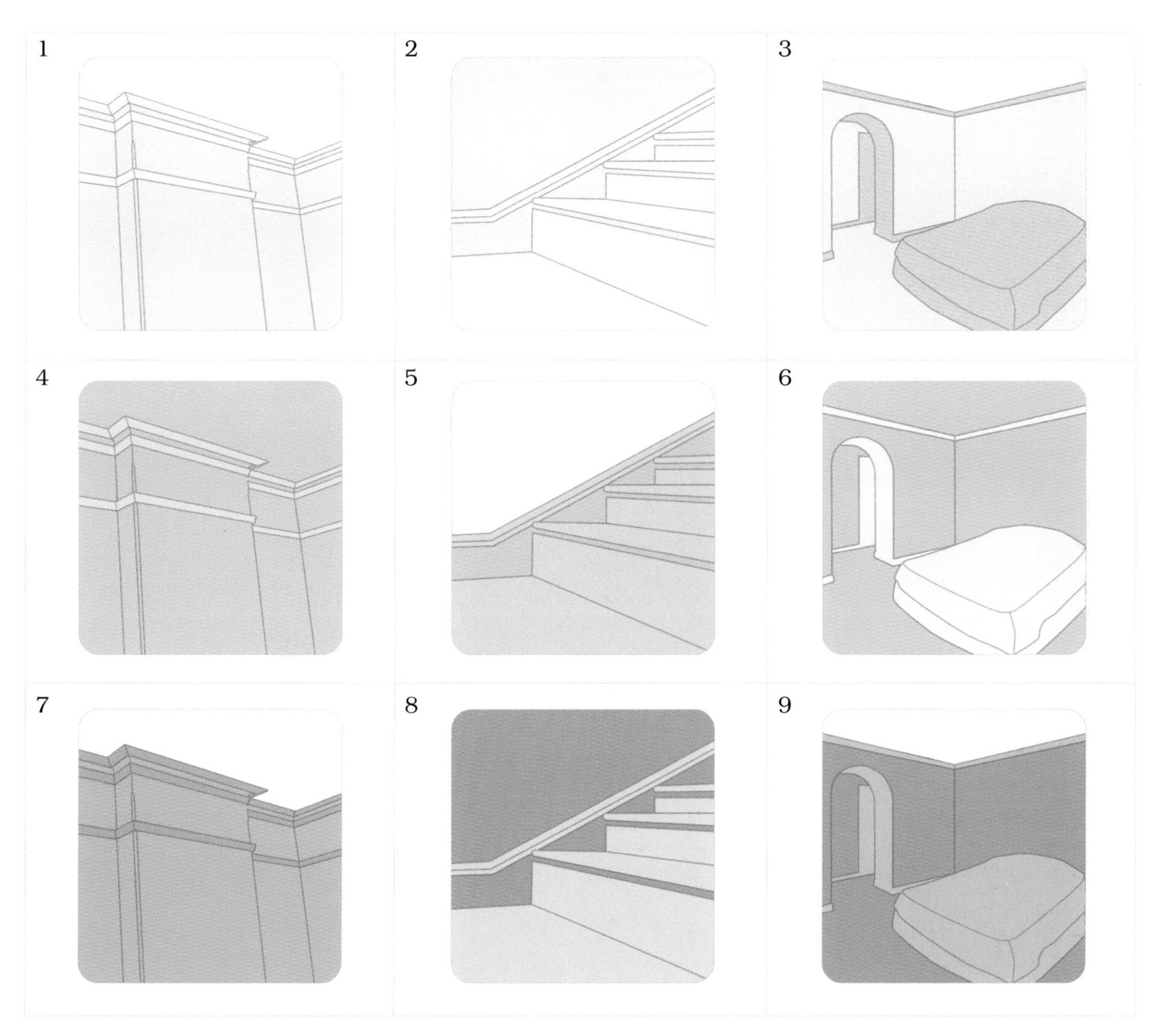

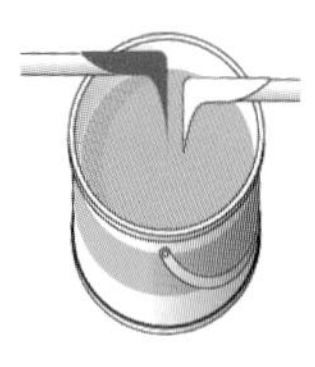

Green and violet-red can be intermixed if you wish to reduce the intensity of either.

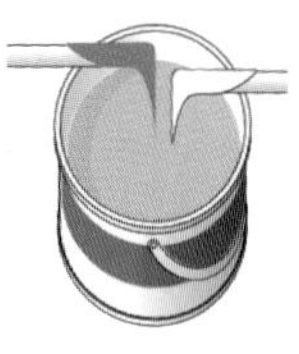

Although either a violet-red or an orange-red will reduce the strength of the green, the ideal will be to use the violet-red, as it is already in use in this arrangement.

Similarly a yellow-green is the close mixing partner of the violet-red but the actual green selected in the arrangement will be the most suitable, it will help to bring the colors together as well as keep the number down as much as possible.

The complementaries

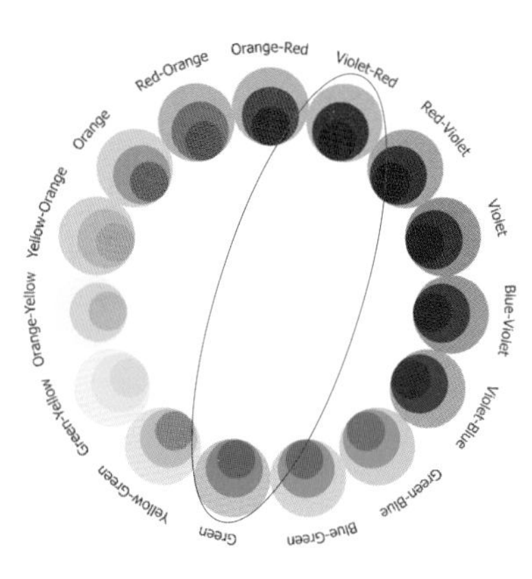

Red and green are complementaries, but which red and which green?

© Jefferson Smith/arcblue.com

Common advice is that red and green are complementaries and can be used together for both contrast and harmony. This is too general as there are many versions of each basic hue.

The green suggested in this combination is best described as a mid green, rather than a green which leans either towards blue (a blue-green), or towards yellow (a yellowish-green).

The complementaries

Violet-red and green

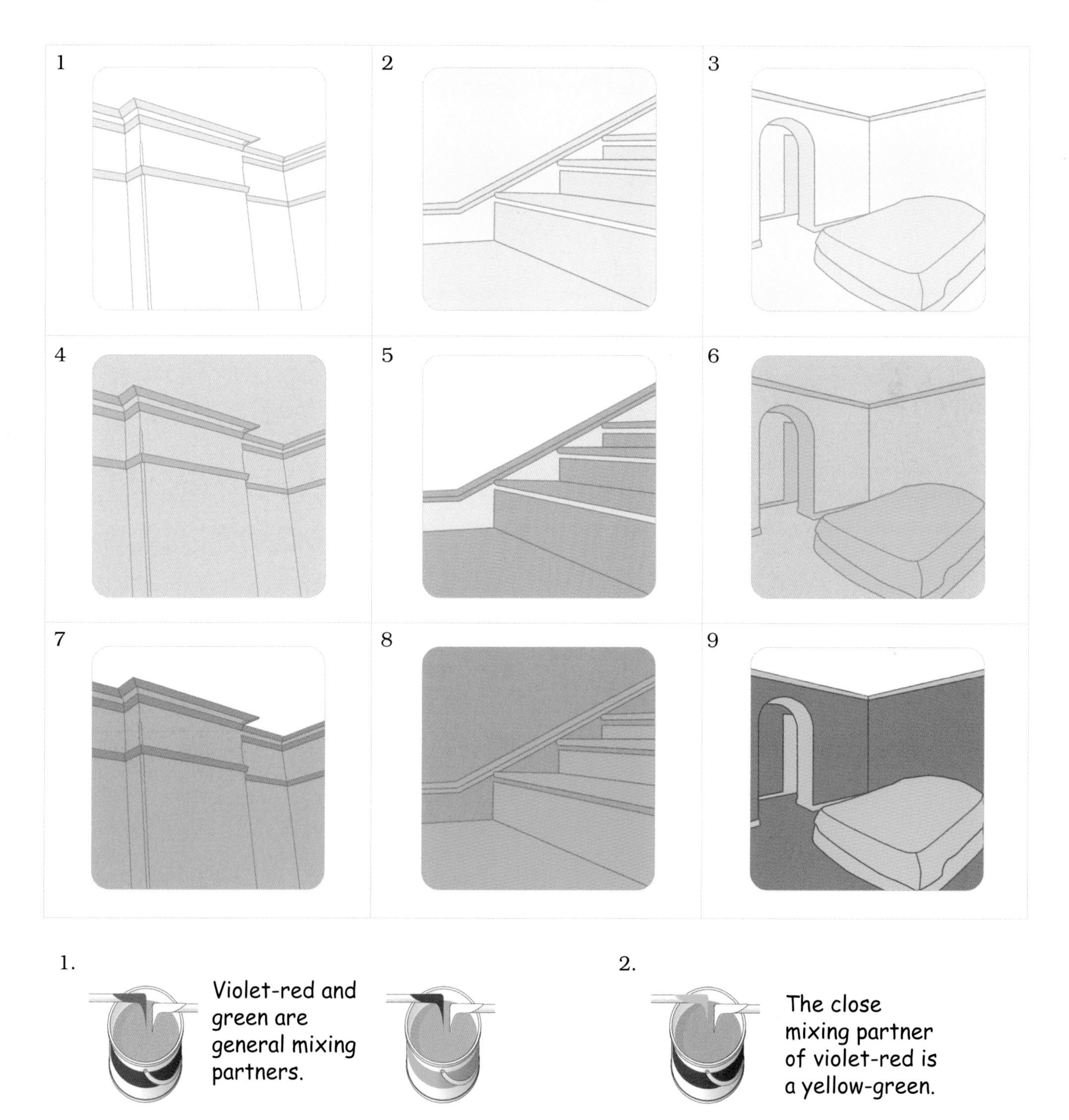

Violet-red and a mid green will neutralise each other very well even though they are not close mixing partners (1).

Any red will act on any green but the results will not always be predictable.

A closer mixing partner to the violet-red would be a yellow-green (2). However, this would mean introducing an additional color for little, if any, benefit. It could also detract from color harmony if over-used.

The complementaries

© Red Cover/Steve Dalton

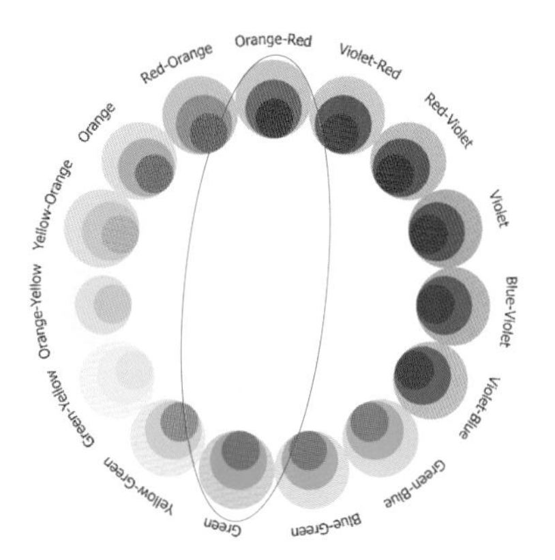

The chosen color scheme can always be extended to other areas such as the patio.

An orange-red tint, pink, can have a calming effect and is sometimes used in prisons for this reason. If using pink to any extent, try the subtle contrast offered by a very pale green.

If used at strength these can be a rather difficult pair to work with as one of their qualities is that they contrast strongly when used in a saturated (full strength), form.

With some modification to strength and area they can be encouraged to harmonise.

The complementaries

Green and orange-red

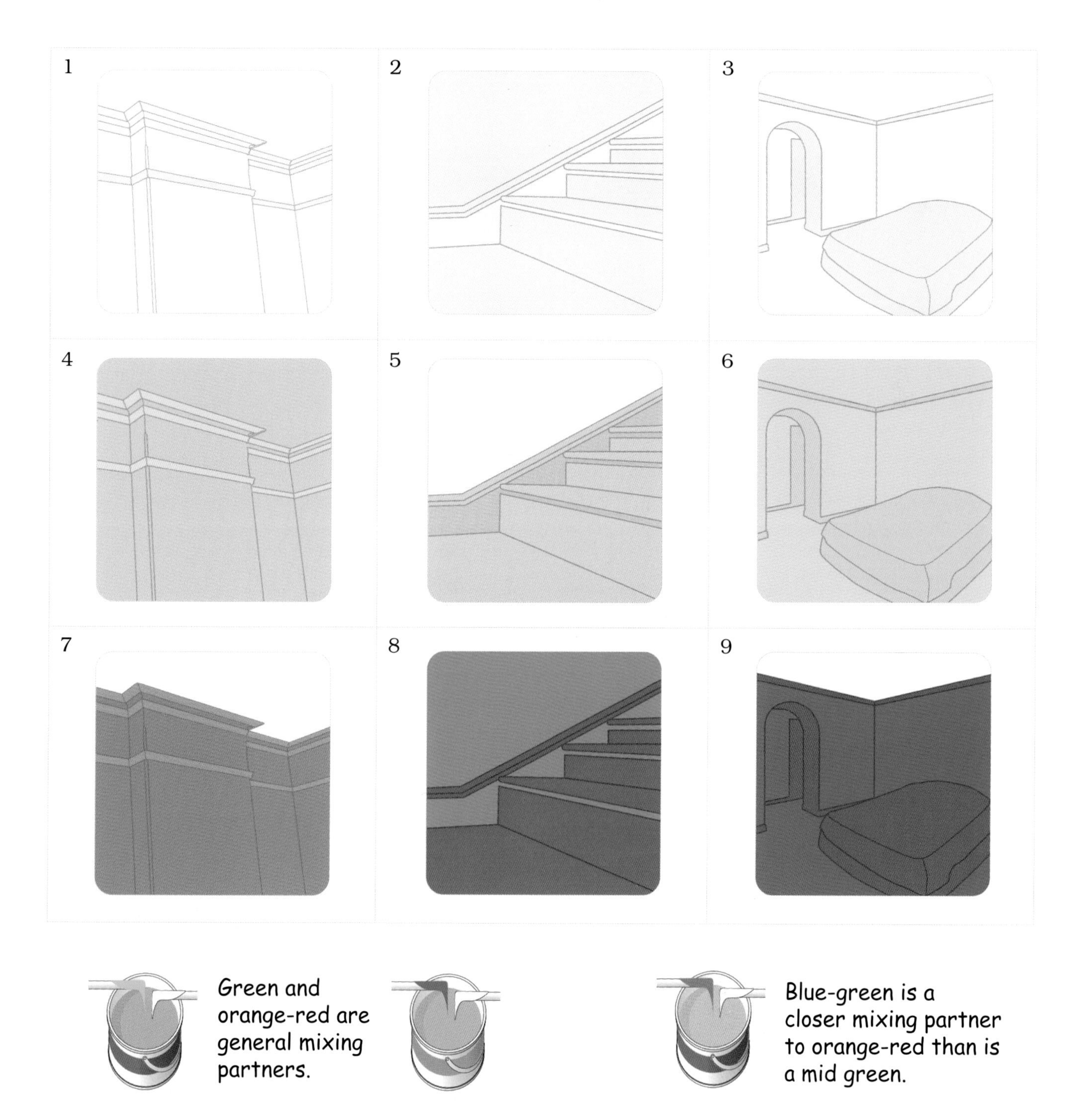

When working with a complementary pair, which are mixing as well as visual partners, use one to neutralise the other. To be exact, (which can be inhibiting), we could say that a *blue*-green should be used to neutralise the orange-red rather than a *mid*-green, as it is the closer partner. In practice we are working with a red-green combination, which is all that really matters. It usually pays to keep the number of colors in use to a bare minimum.

The complementaries

© Red Cover/Jon Bouchier

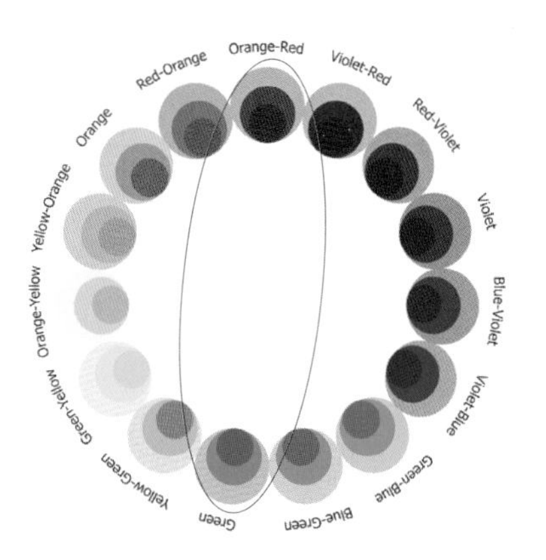

A very wide range of hues are available from this pair, from pale pinks to dark greens.

Small areas of bright, strong color can be offset against larger areas of the complementary reduced with white.

Complementary colors can be encouraged to enhance each other visually.

As they will also 'darken' each other in mixes, giving a wide range of neutralised hues as well as 'colored grays' they are particularly useful in all forms of color work.

The complementaries

Orange-red and green

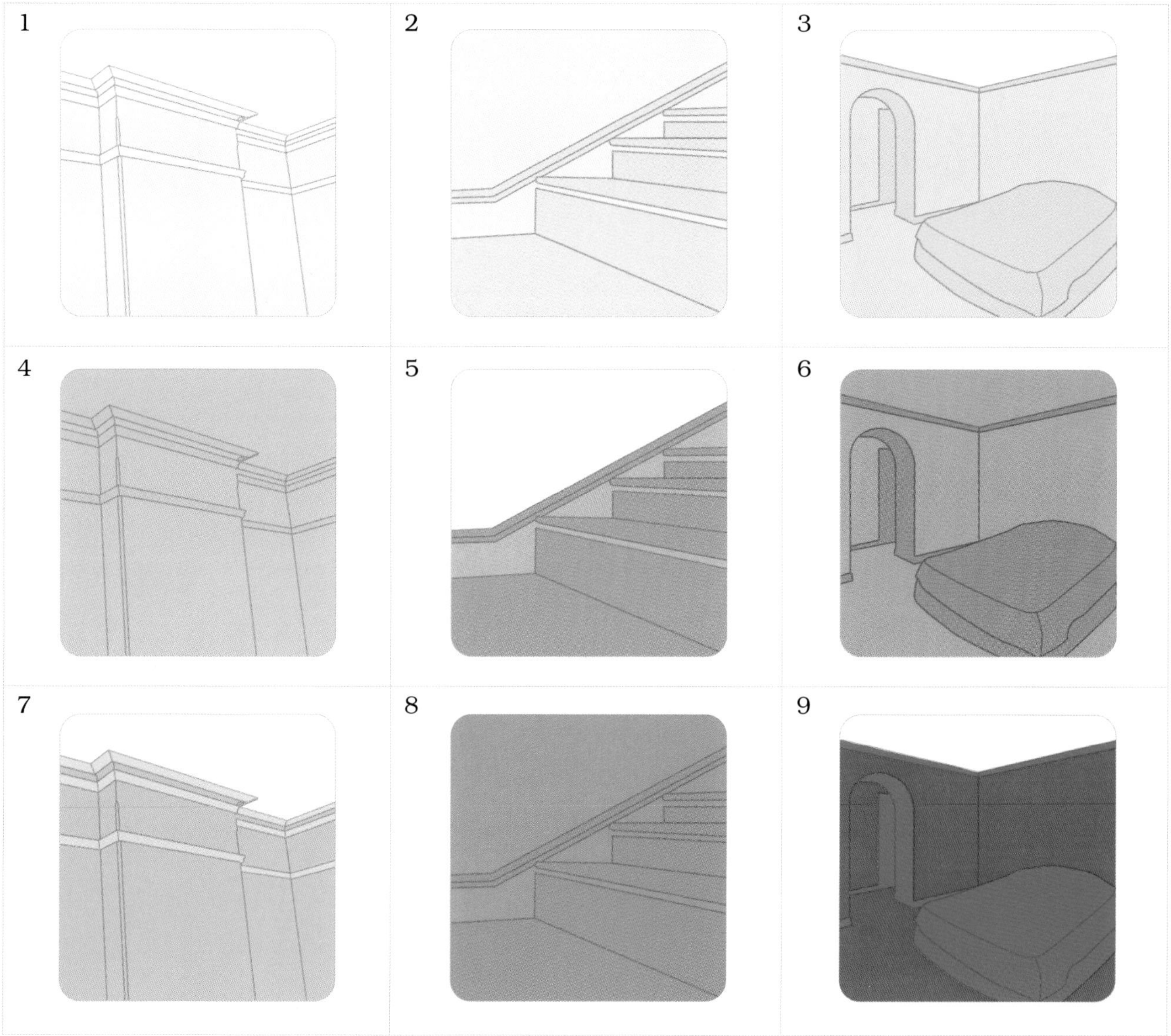

1	2	3
4	5	6
7	8	9

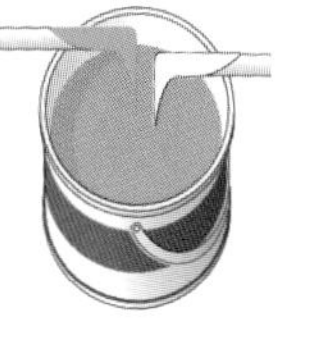

Orange-red and green are a general mixing pair and will neutralise each other very efficiently.

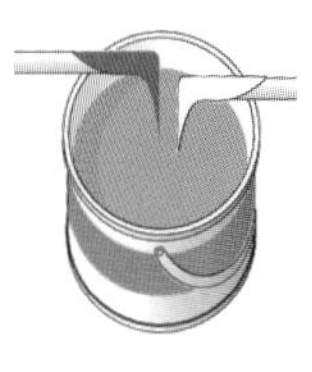

Color swatches such as the above can only offer very general guidance. Before deciding on any color scheme it will pay to pre-mix the colors that appeal to you and paint them out in small areas side by side. Such preparation can prevent later problems.

The complementaries

© Red Cover/Chris Drake

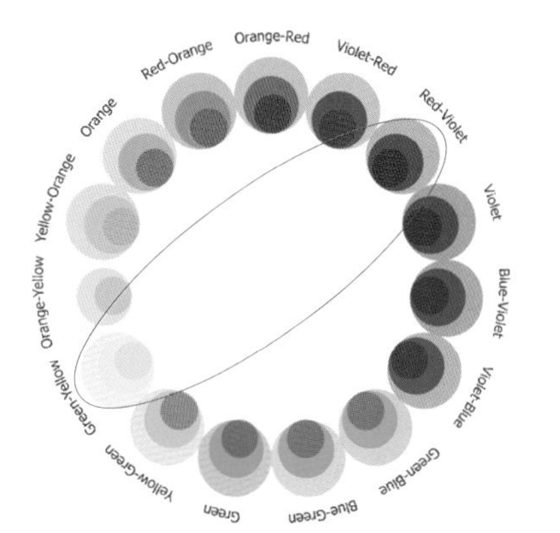

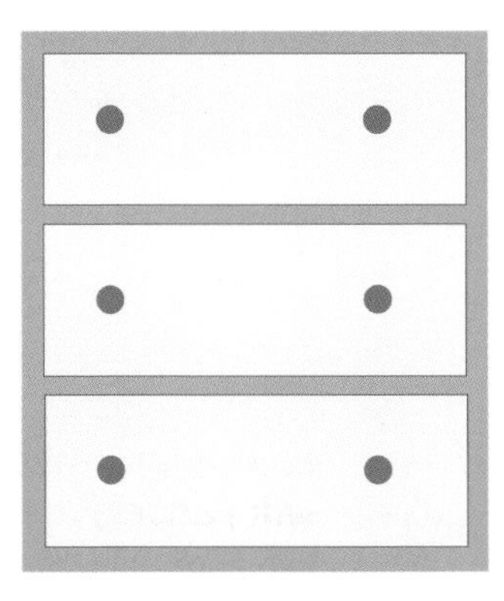

When using any complementary pair do not overlook the 'colored grays' that result when they are combined in near or equal intensity. White can be added to such grays in order to extend the range.

Green-yellow can be very effective when much reduced with white. If it seems too bright with white try adding a little of the red-violet mixing partner to 'take the edge' off the color.

Many find it difficult to work with either hue when they are at or near full strength. As with any pair where one is naturally light and the other dark, when the relationship is reversed (a dark yellow with a pale violet), they can look rather awkward together.

The complementaries

Green-yellow and red-violet

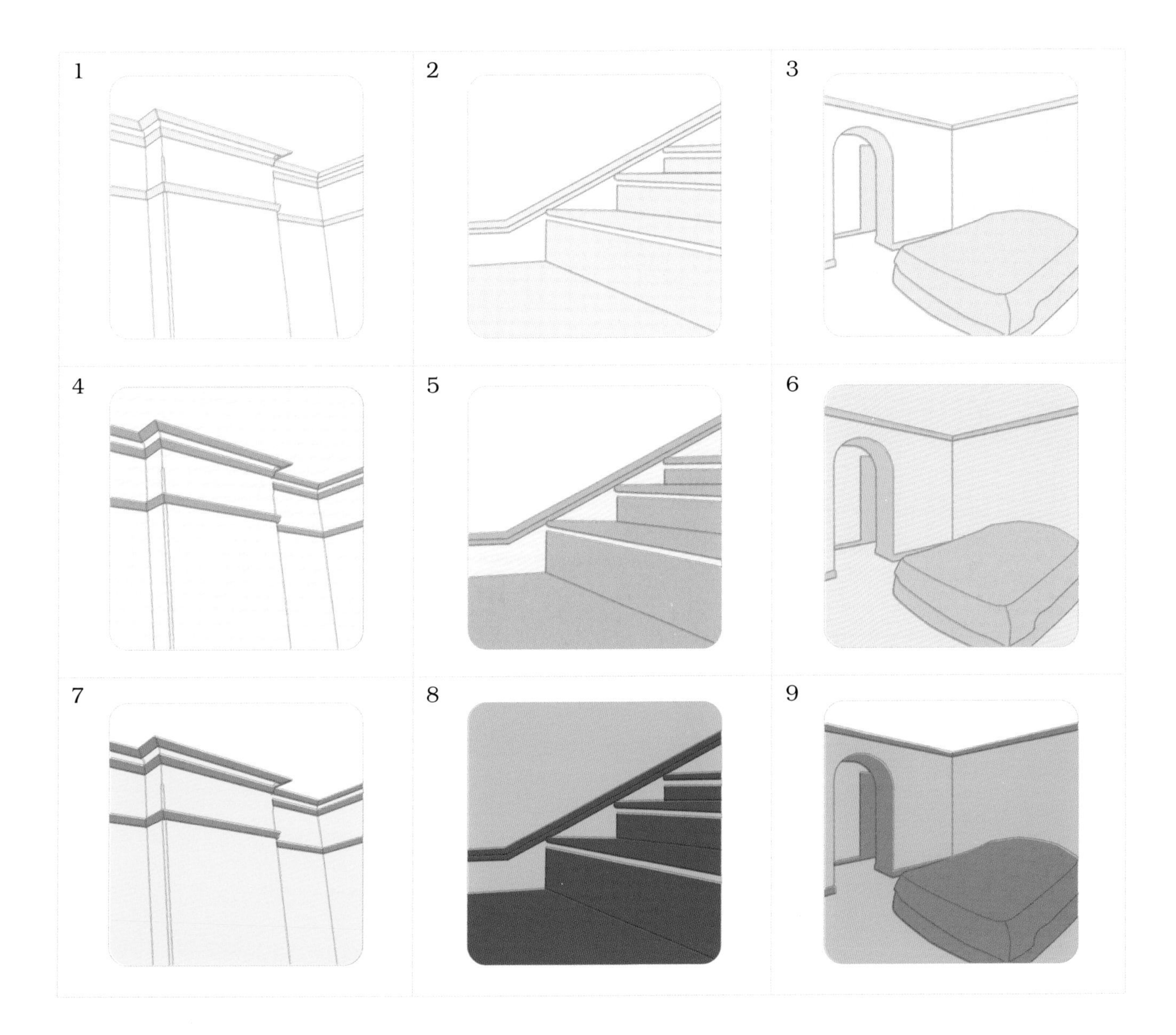

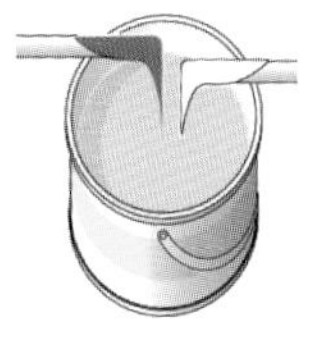

Green-yellow and red-violet are a close mixing pair and will reduce the intensity of each other when combined.

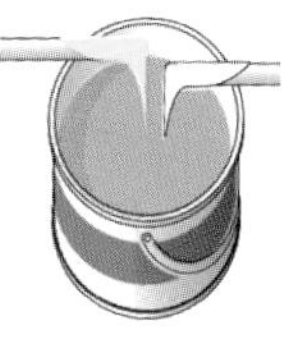

Mixing, as well as visual partners, they will reduce each other in mixes as well as enhance each other visually. It is for these reasons that the complementaries, as they are known, can be so versatile. They can be mixed and matched with absolute ease.

The complementaries

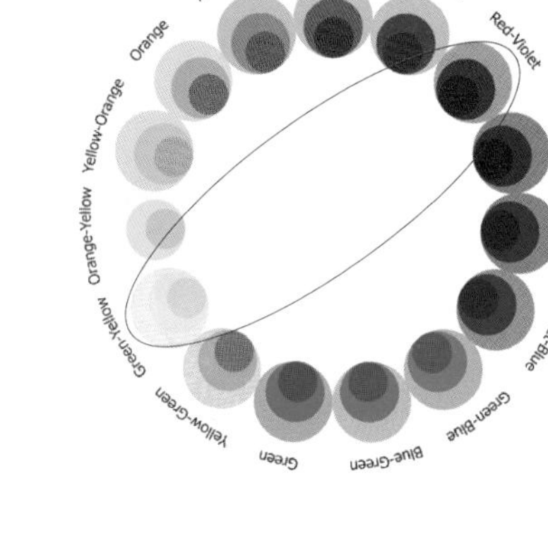

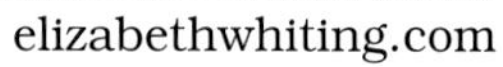
elizabethwhiting.com

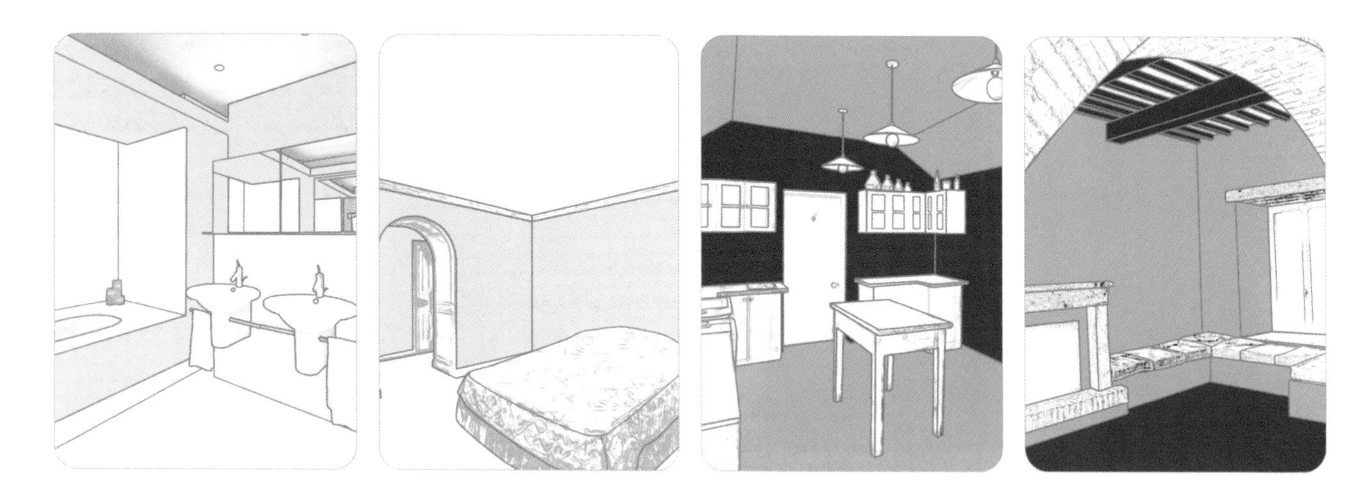

These can be a rather difficult pair to work with at or anywhere near full strength.

When 'taken back' a little by intermixing and with the addition of much white, they can be encouraged to sit together very well. The paler the better for most people.

The complementaries

Red-violet and green-yellow

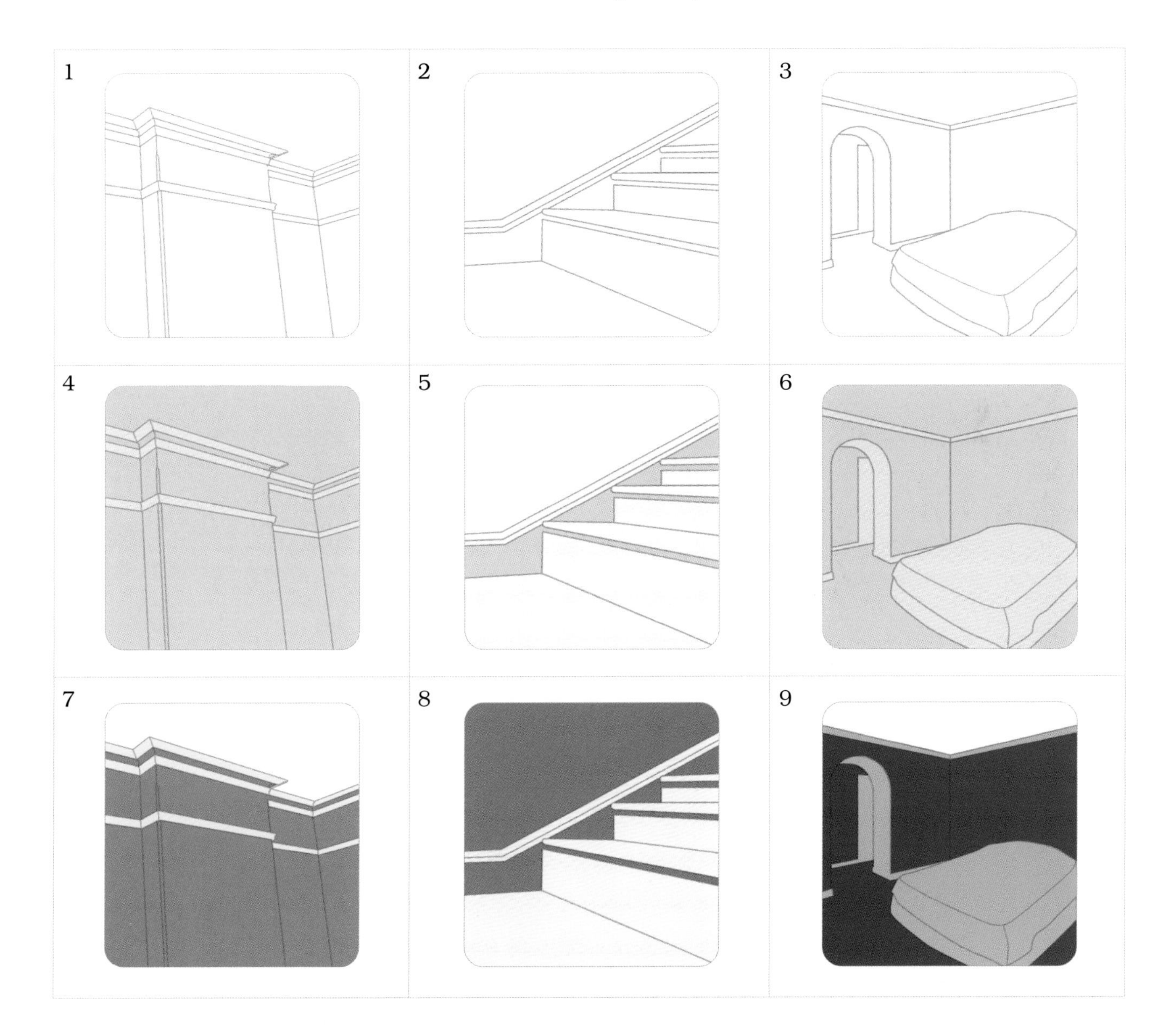

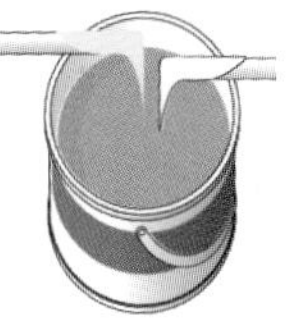

Red-violet and green-yellow, a mixing pair will neutralise each other in mixes.

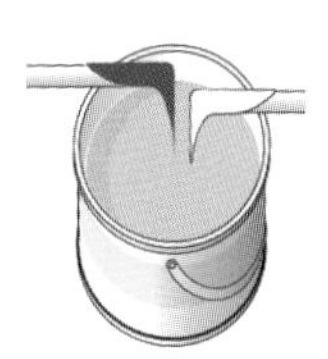

Either color will reduce the intensity of the other. This is the most efficient way to darken a color. Although, strictly speaking the color is not truly darkened, as it will change in character, this is the most efficient means at our disposal.

Add black to the green-yellow, for example, and you do not end up with a darkened green-yellow but a dull, 'heavy' greenish brown.

Our postman ended up with five litres of this color when he tried to darken a yellow with black. Hence the mixing tips on these pages.

The complementaries

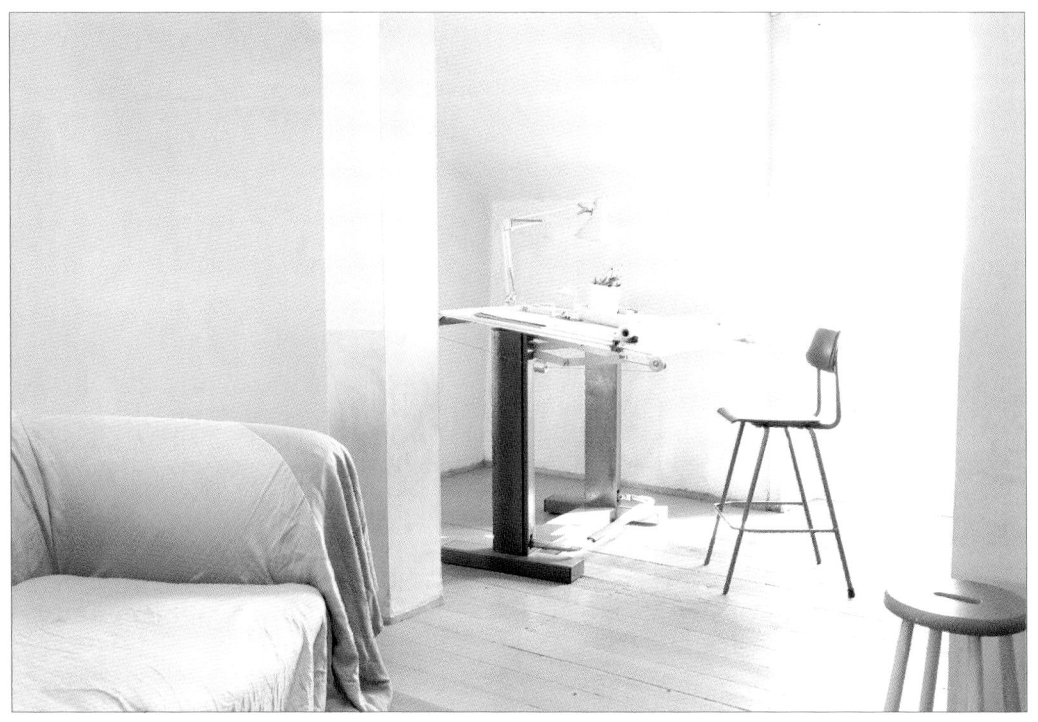

© Red Cover/Verity Welstead

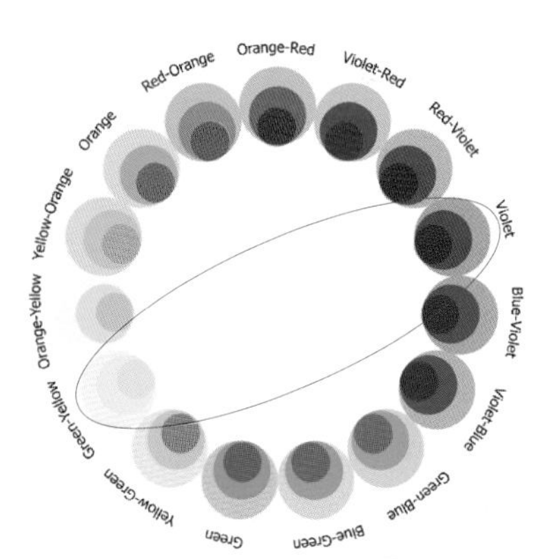

Handled with extra care, this combination can offer very subtle color harmonies.

Furniture painted in the same arrangement as a room can greatly enhance color harmony.

As wide a range as is practical is offered within these pages.

As will be obvious, the series can be expanded in almost unlimited ways, I have hardly made a start.

The combinations offered are no more than suggestions. Cast your eye over them and decide for yourself which color arrangements harmonise, which contrast and which fall somewhere in between.

The complementaries

Green-yellow and violet

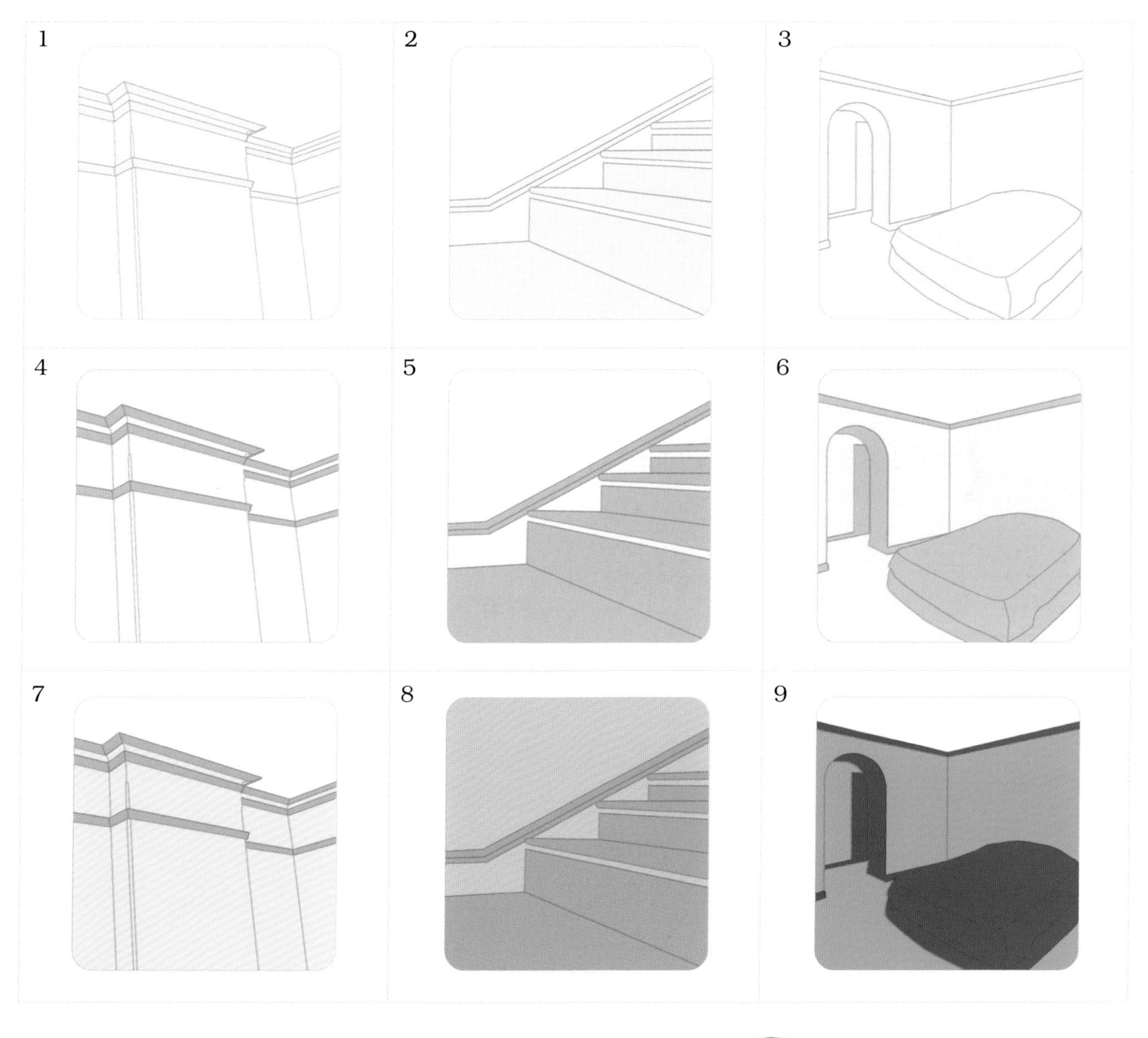

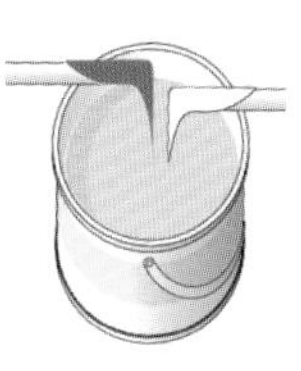

Green-yellow will be reduced in strength with the addition of violet.

Violet can be neutralised with the addition of either green-yellow or orange-yellow.

Found opposite each other on the color mixing wheel, these two hues will readily neutralise each other. Although either type of yellow will reduce the violet, it will aid color harmony and keep the number of colors to a minimum if the green-yellow is used.

The complementaries

elizabethwhiting.com

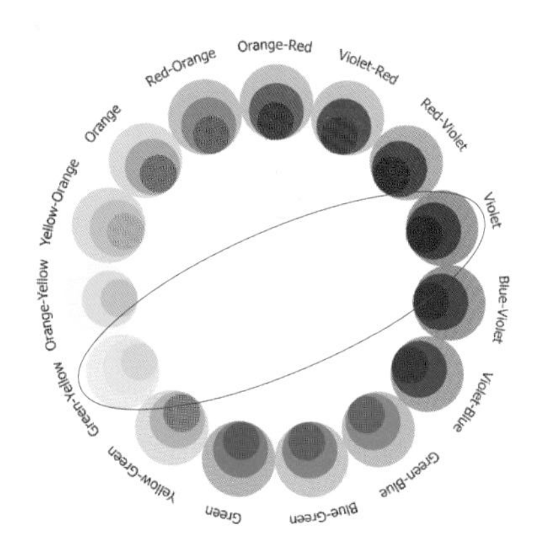

A difficult pair to handle when at or near full strength.

The violet/green-yellow combination can give very soft, subtle harmonies when well handled. However, if used at or close to full strength, without care, they can look very harsh together.

It will usually aid harmony if the color scheme in a room is extended to include fittings and furniture.

Such comments, it must be emphasised, reflect only my views. If you feel differently we will both be right as color combinations are an entirely subjective affair. There is no such thing as 'correct' color use.

The complementaries

Violet and green-yellow

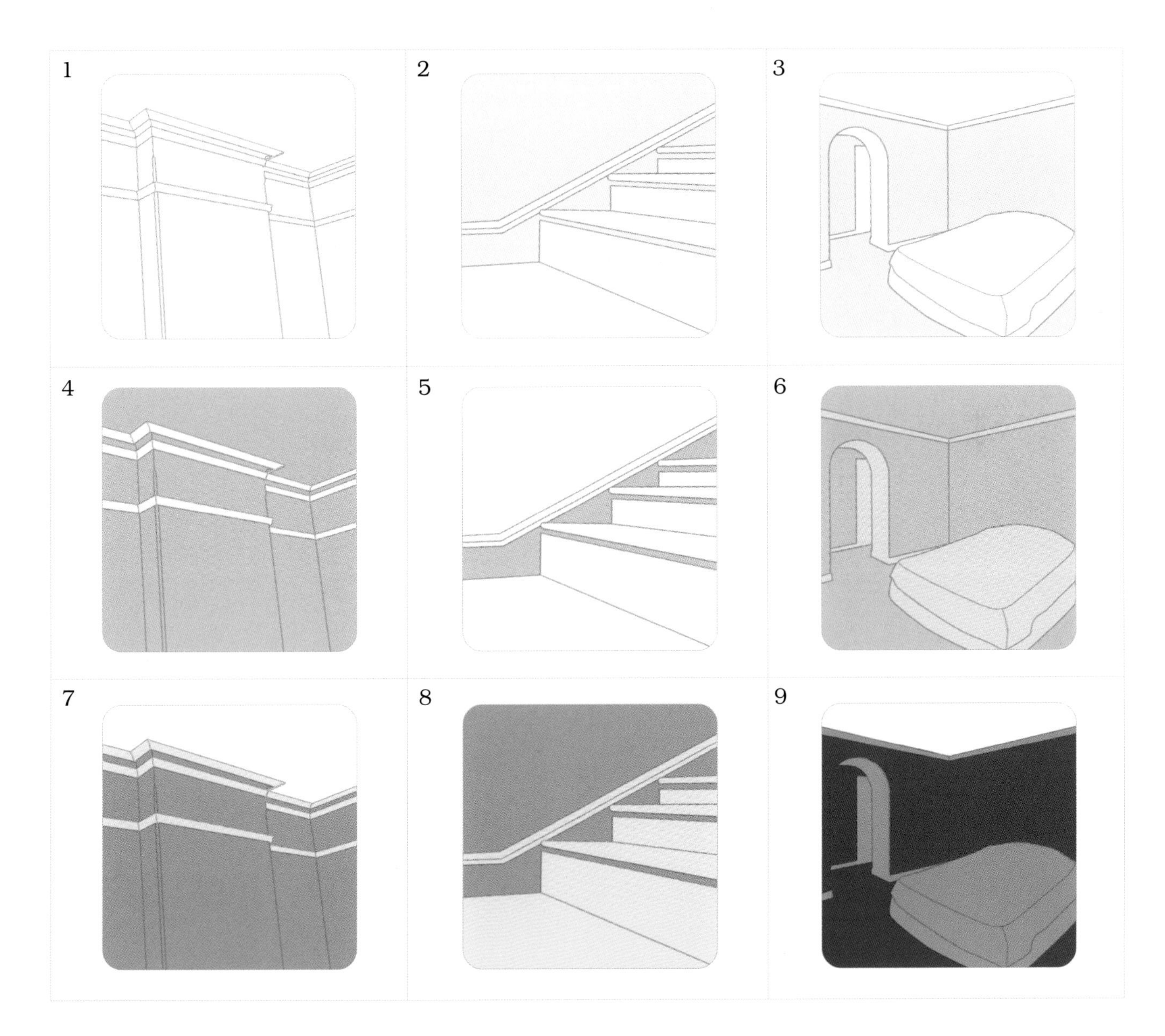

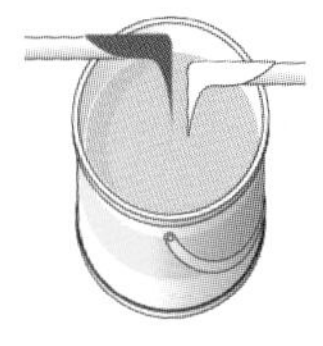

Green-yellow and violet are mixing partners and will reduce each other in mixes.

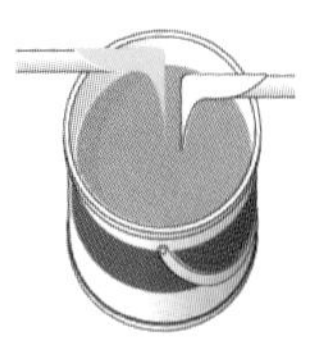

As mixing partners they will desaturate each other with ease and accuracy, keeping each as close to its original character as possible.

As with all color mixing pairs they will give very subtle 'colored grays' when mixed in equal intensities.

Summary

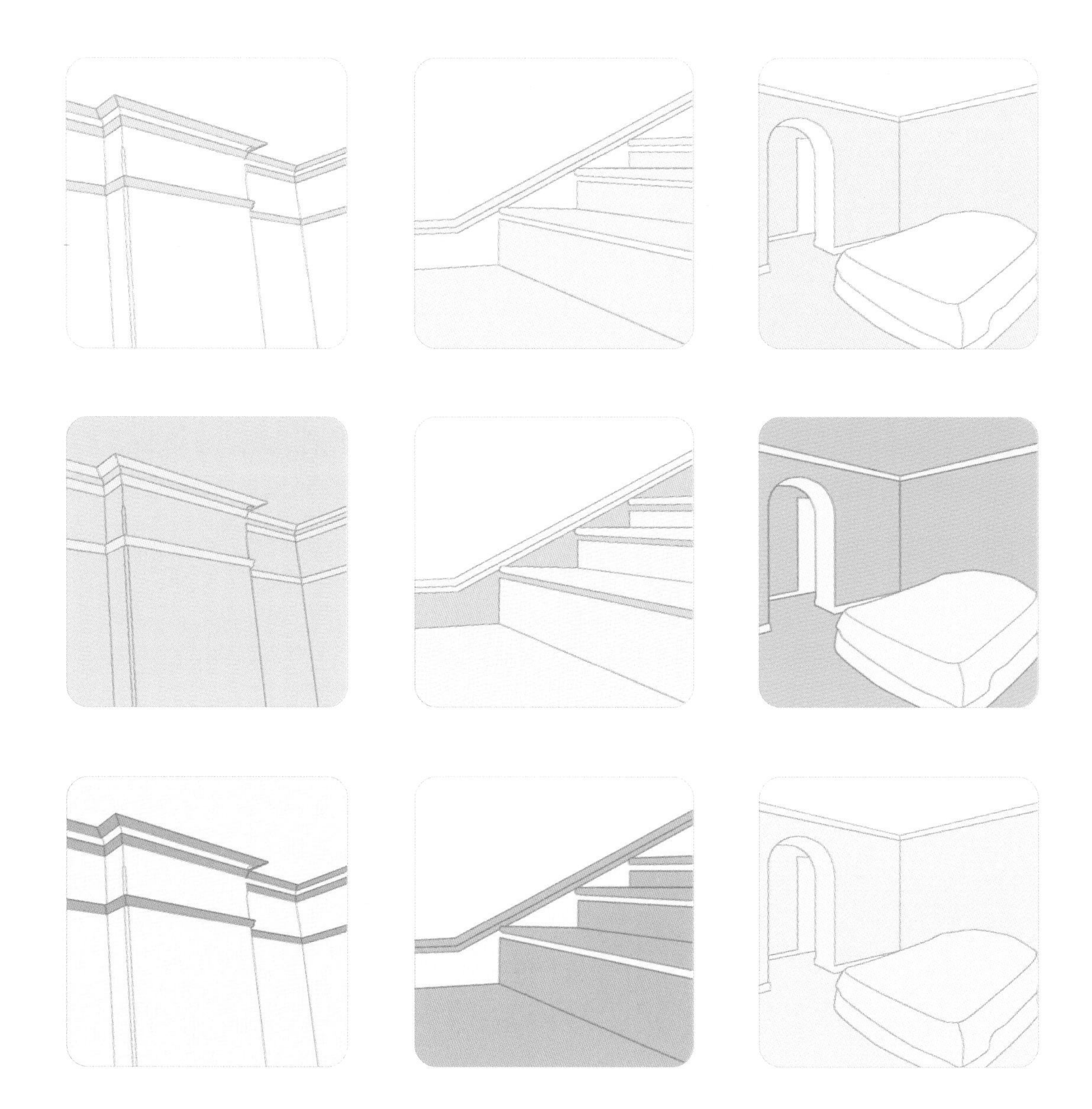

The use of a complementary pair can not only offer strong contrasts but also very subtle harmonies. Based of the effect of the after-image one color can be encouraged to enhance the other.

Although a more adventurous approach than either 'monochrome', 'related colors' or the 'wider family', the complementaries are worth exploring as many of the schemes on offer are quite stunning. It is worth remembering that the work of the Impressionist painters was largely based on the use of complementary pairs. Their color work can be employed in home decorating to great effect.

A complementary and its split opposites

Complementary

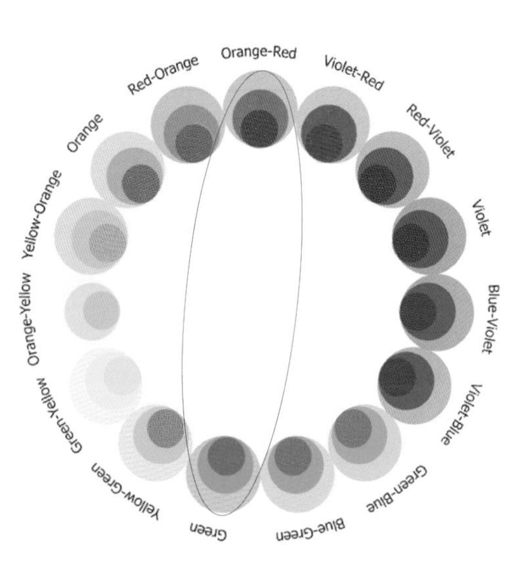

The previous section dealt with complementary pairings. Green could be matched with either an orange-red (as shown here) or a violet-red.

© Red Cover/Steve Dalton

A complementary and its split opposites

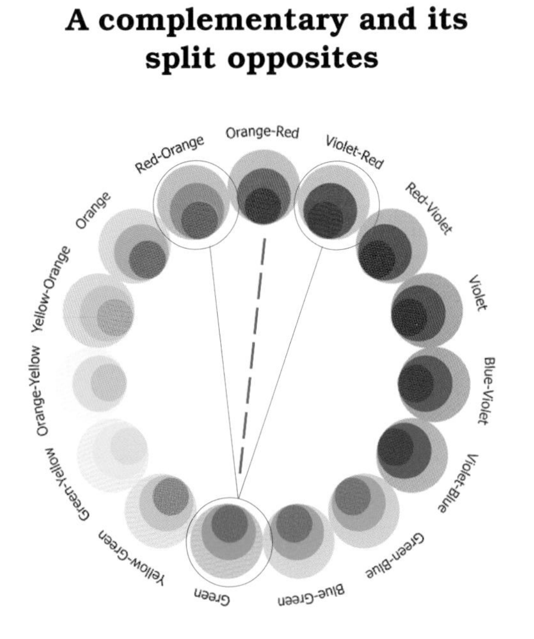

In this approach a complementary pair is selected, but one of the pair is replaced by its neighbours. In this case the arrangement is still based on green and red but red-orange and violet-red are incorporated

© Red Cover/Chris Drake

A basic complementary pair but with three basic colors to play with.

A complementary and its split opposites

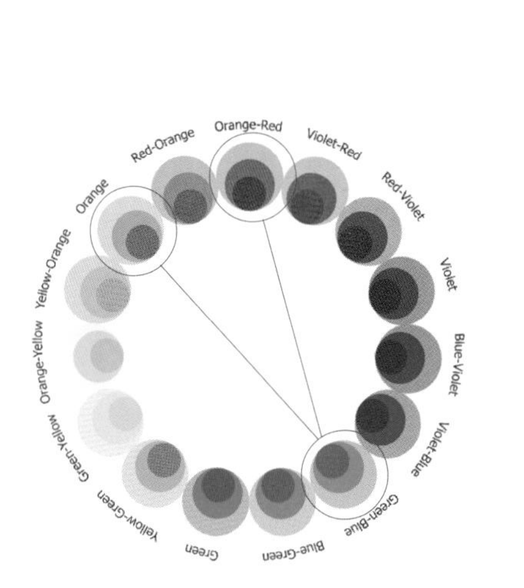

To keep matters simple, try using the green-blue to desaturate the orange and the orange-red, and vice versa. This, rather than use closer mixing partners. The fewer colors the better wherever possible.

© Red Cover/James Mitchell

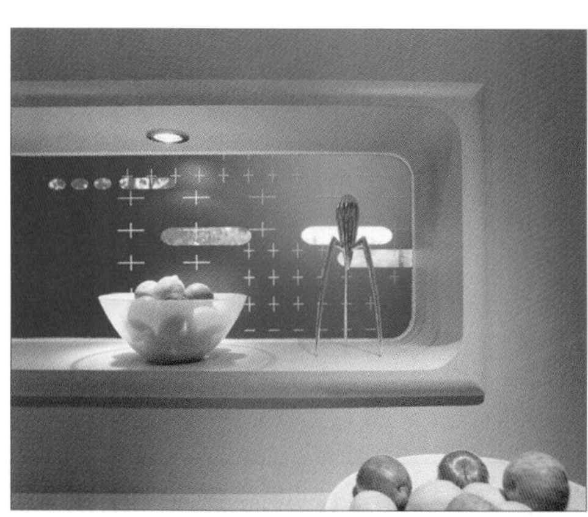

© Red Cover/Adrian Wilson

The green-blue can bring a freshness to the orange and the orange-red; two hues which might otherwise be difficult to work with.

Harmony becomes increasingly difficult when these hues are used at strength. This is particularly so because they are naturally bright with a distinct contrast in 'temperature'. When reduced in intensity one way or the other they can be very versatile.

A complementary and its split opposites

Orange, green-blue and orange-red

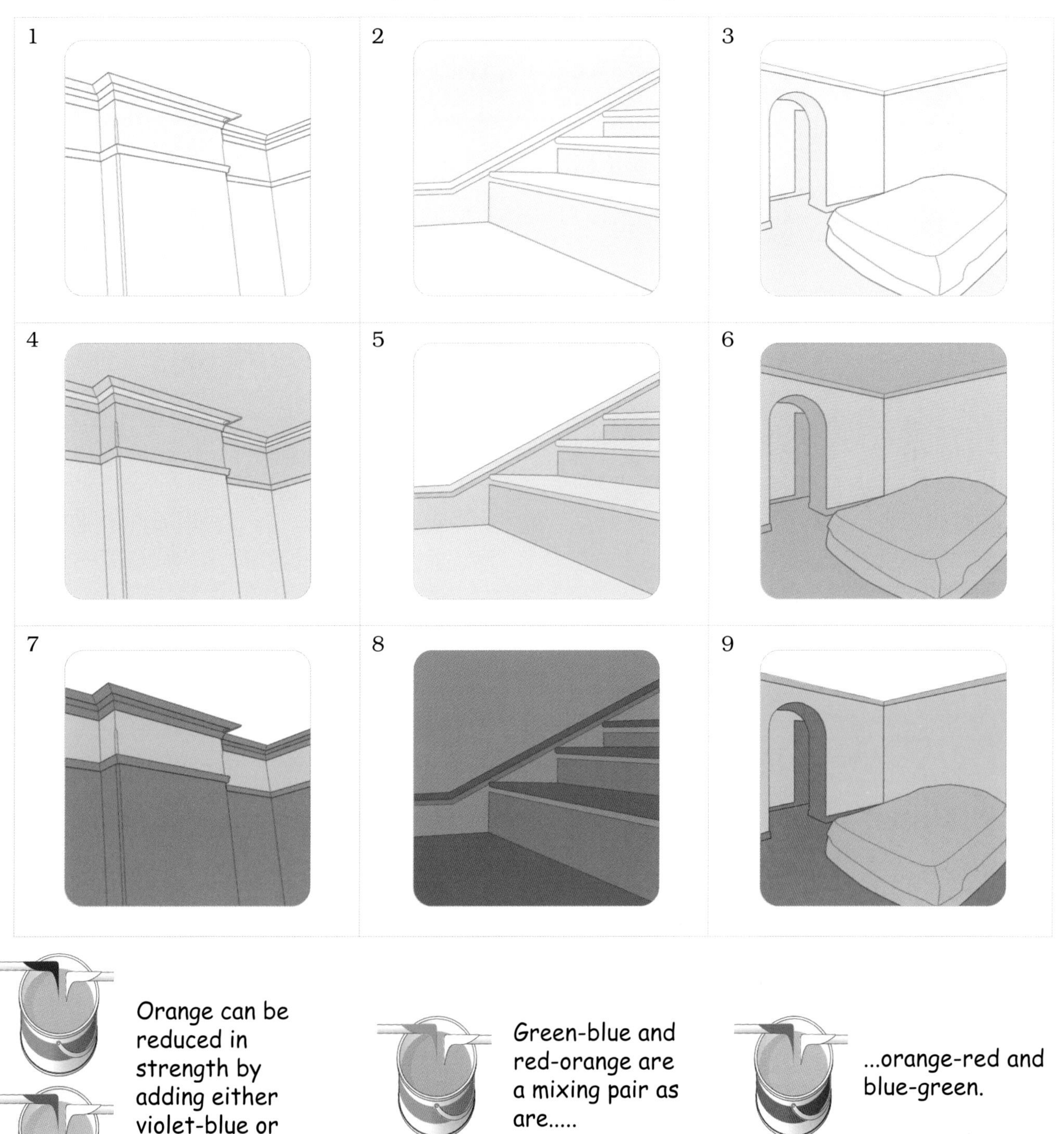

Orange can be reduced in strength by adding either violet-blue or green-blue.

Green-blue and red-orange are a mixing pair as are.....

...orange-red and blue-green.

In normal practice the mixing partner for the orange would be either type of blue, violet-blue or green-blue. However, in order to use colors with a relationship to each other it will be more useful to use the same green-blue that appears in this arrangement. Desaturate the green-blue with the orange or orange-red.

A blue-green is the close mixing partner of the orange-red but the same green-blue as shown here will be more convenient to use.

A complementary and its split opposites

© Red Cover/Chris Drake

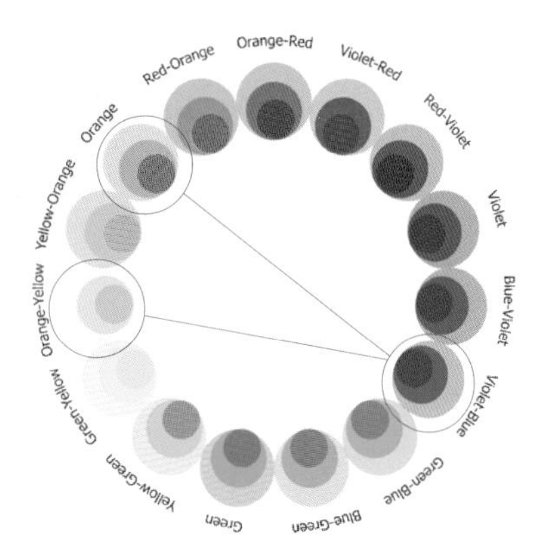

Strong contrasts to delicate color harmonies are available from these three hues.

The colors of nature can offer inspiration to the home decorator.

The orange and the orange-yellow have much in common and can be worked together quite easily. These particular colors can be harmonised quite readily as the violet-blue is matched with a pair which both have the hue 'orange' in common. Such closeness helps towards color harmony.

Being general complementaries (blue and oranges), these three can give rise to strong contrasts as well as subtle harmonies.

A complementary and its split opposites

Orange, violet-blue and orange-yellow

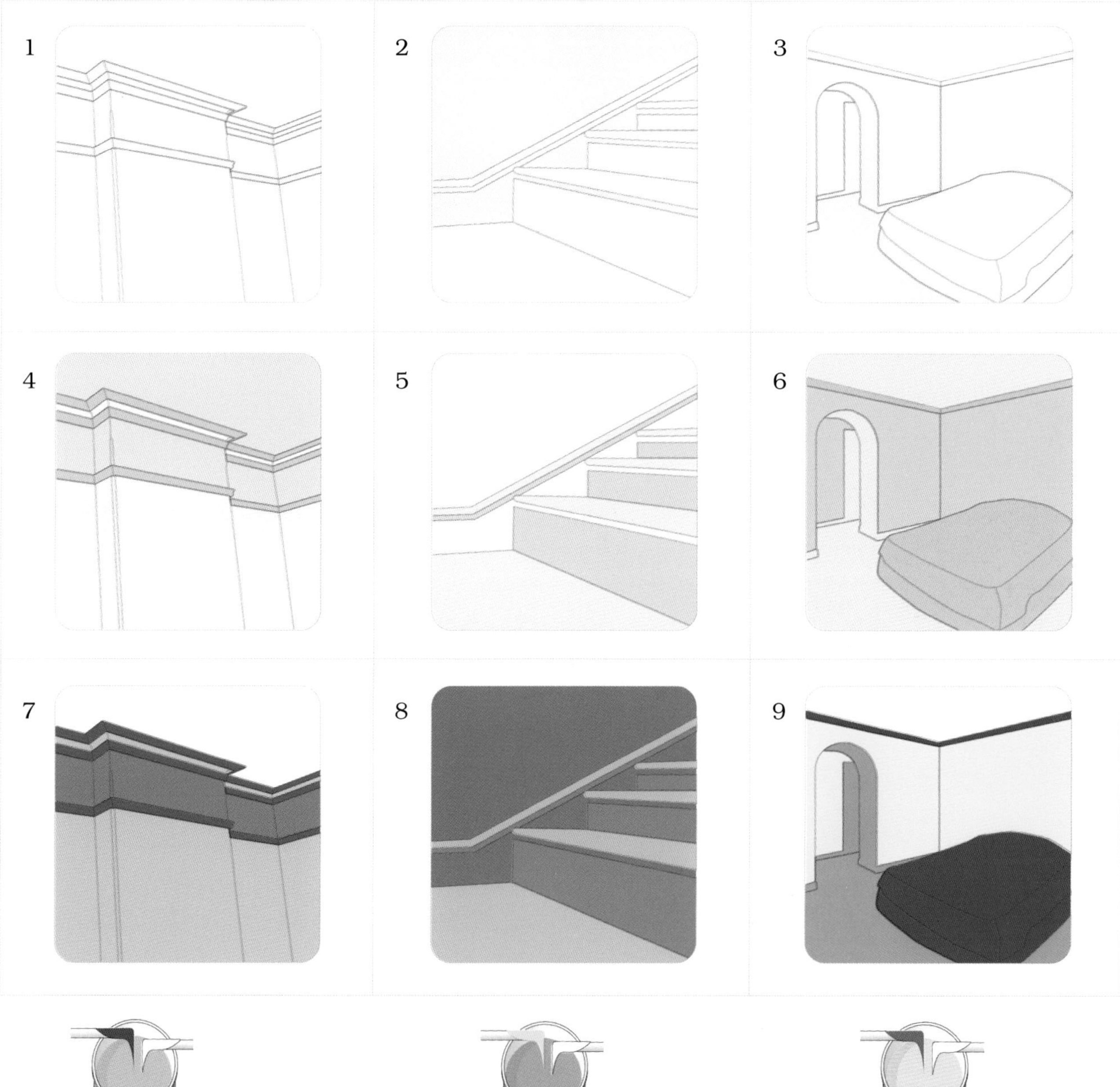

Orange can be reduced with either violet-blue or green-blue but violet-blue (already in use) is a better choice here.

Violet-blue and yellow-orange are close mixing partners but it will be better to use the (in use) orange rather than yellow-orange in this arrangement.

Orange-yellow and blue-violet are also mixing partners but the (in use) violet-blue can be used unless the mix becomes too green.

Ideally use the violet-blue to desaturate the orange, and vice versa. Blue-green could be used with the orange, and the results would not be too dissimilar, but it means bringing in an additional color. It normally pays to use as few colors as possible in home decorating.

A complementary and its split opposites

© Red Cover/Kim Sayer

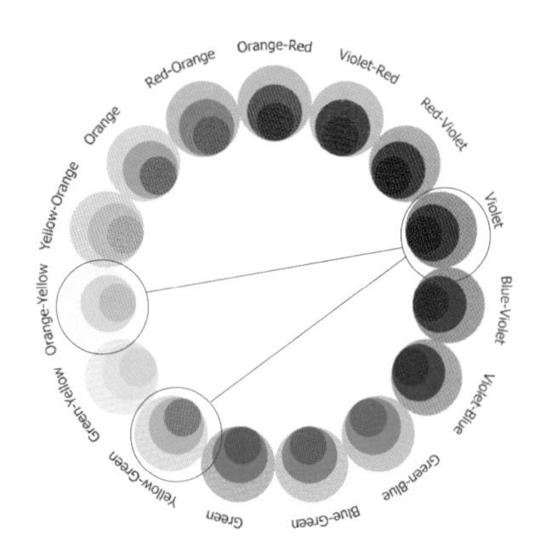

This can be an awkward trio to combine unless they are reduced in intensity.

Orange-yellow and yellow-green can make rather awkward partners unless reduced with white and/or their mixing partners. The violet can be used as a 'go between', allowing a modified contrast to add interest.

These three basic hues can produce some unusual color arrangements. If you are looking for a color scheme which is out of the ordinary, this approach might well give it to you.

A complementary and its split opposites

Orange-yellow, violet and yellow-green

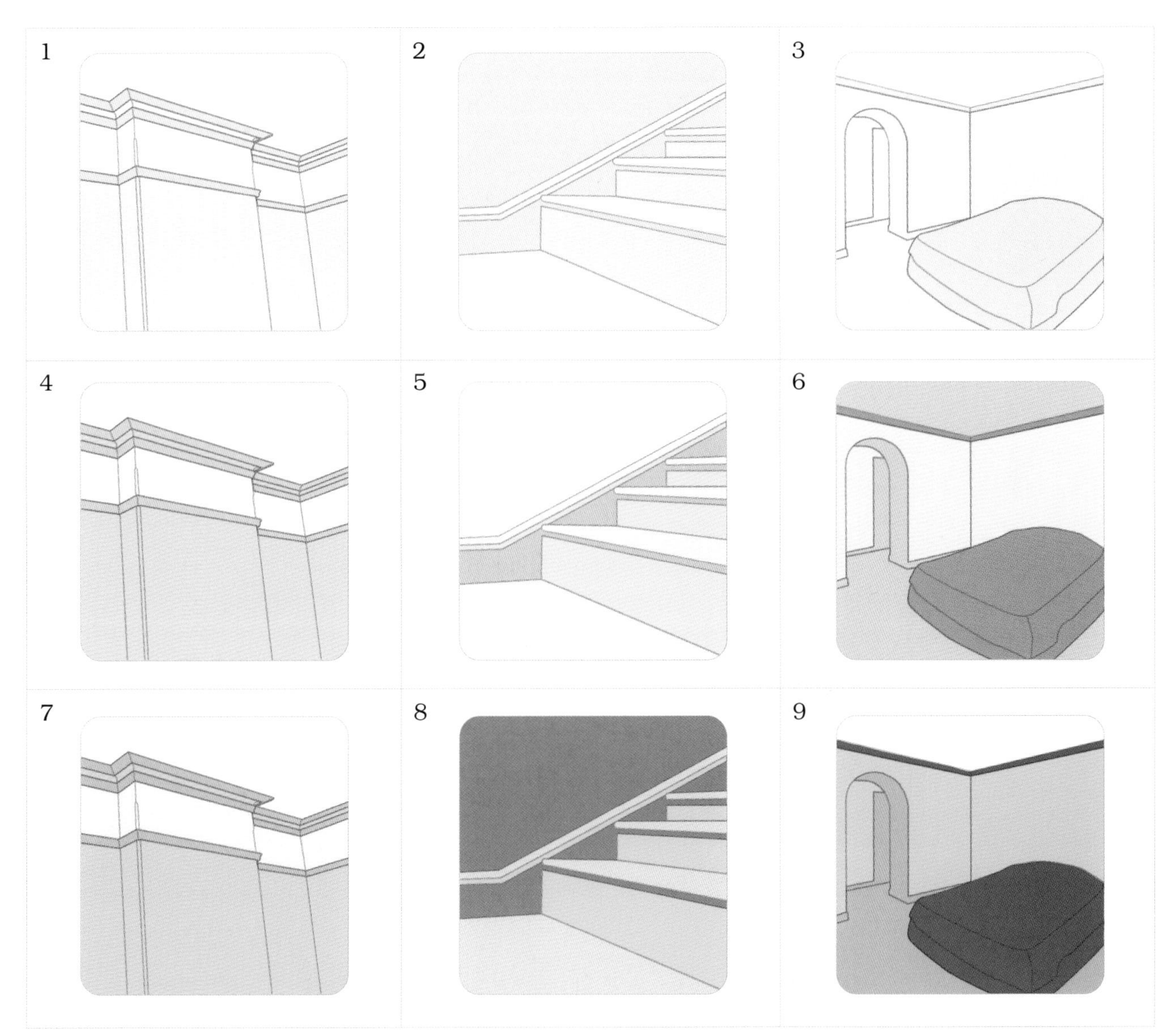

Orange-yellow can be neutralised by blue-violet or with the violet in use here to keep number of colors down.

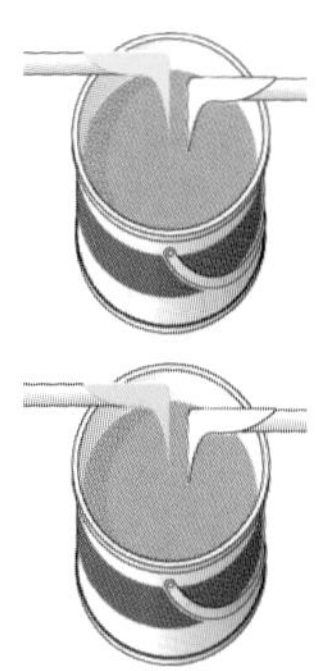

You can either add orange-yellow or green-yellow to reduce the intensity of violet. In this case the (in use) yellow-orange will be better.

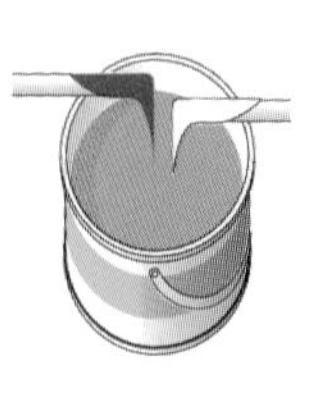

Yellow-green and violet-red are mixing partners but try the violet first to keep numbers down.

The orange-yellow and the violet make a reasonably close mixing pair. Alternatively desaturate the orange-yellow with blue-violet. This will be a closer mixing pair but at the cost of introducing an additional color. Yellow-green will normally require its direct partner violet-red, but try the (in use) violet first to keep the number of colors down.

A complementary and its split opposites

© Red Cover/Brian Harrison

A well balanced color arrangement will include furniture and very often specially chosen floral arrangements.

© Red Cover/Steve Dalton

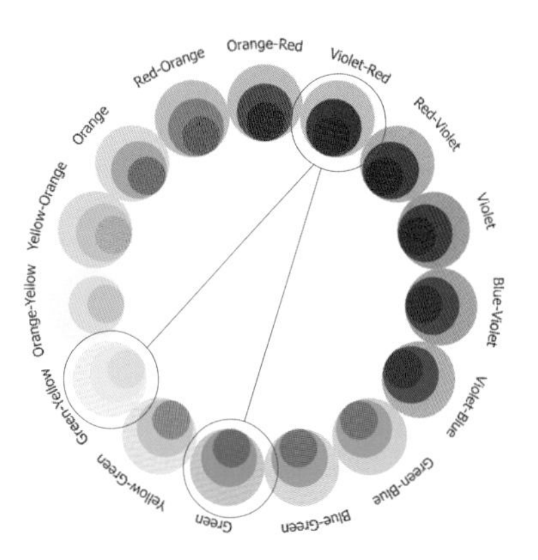

A combination often to be found in nature.

When colors are selected on the 'split opposite' basis from the color wheel, some unusual combinations can come together. These three are no exception and can give varied and interesting color schemes.

To achieve harmony it might be better to work on the violet-red first. When reduced with white and/or its mixing partner, it can be used easily with its neighbours even when they are comparatively strong.

A complementary and its split opposites

Green-yellow, violet-red and green

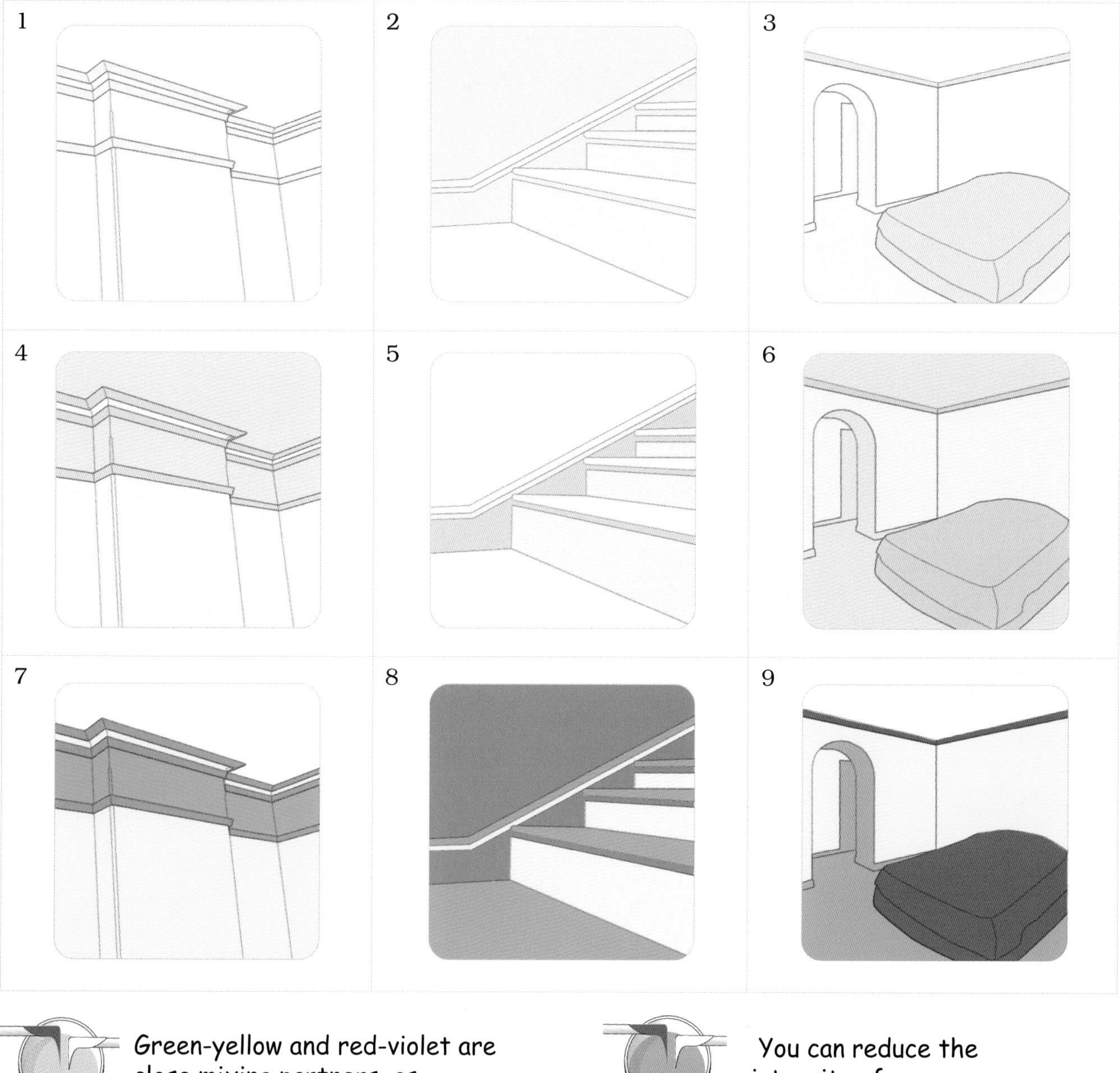

Green-yellow and red-violet are close mixing partners, as are violet-red and yellow-green. But try using the violet-red and mid-green together to keep numbers down, as they are already in use.

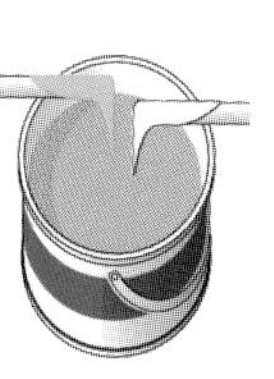

You can reduce the intensity of green with either an orange-red or a violet-red. The violet-red should be used here as it is one of the main hues.

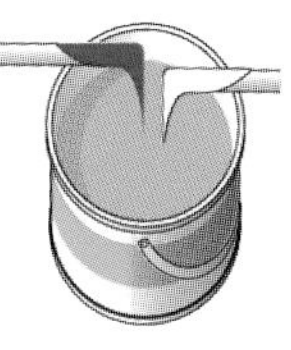

A red-violet will desaturate the green-yellow, yellow-green will lower the intensity of the violet-red and either red will reduce the green. Alternatively use the central violet-red to neutralise both the green-yellow and the green. The end result will be similar to using close mixing pairs and the number of colors required will be kept to a minimum.

A complementary and its split opposites

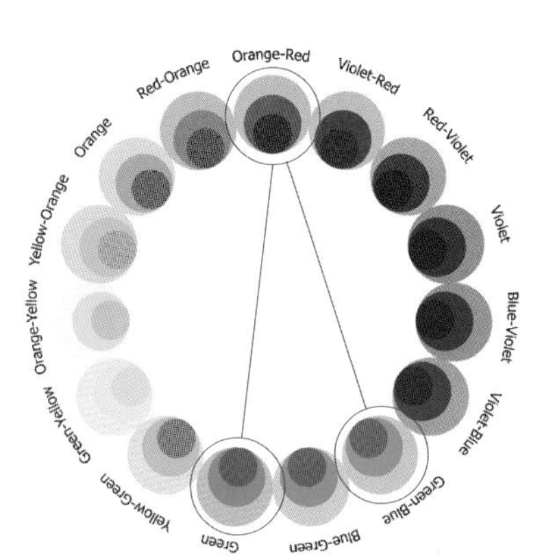

elizabethwhiting.com

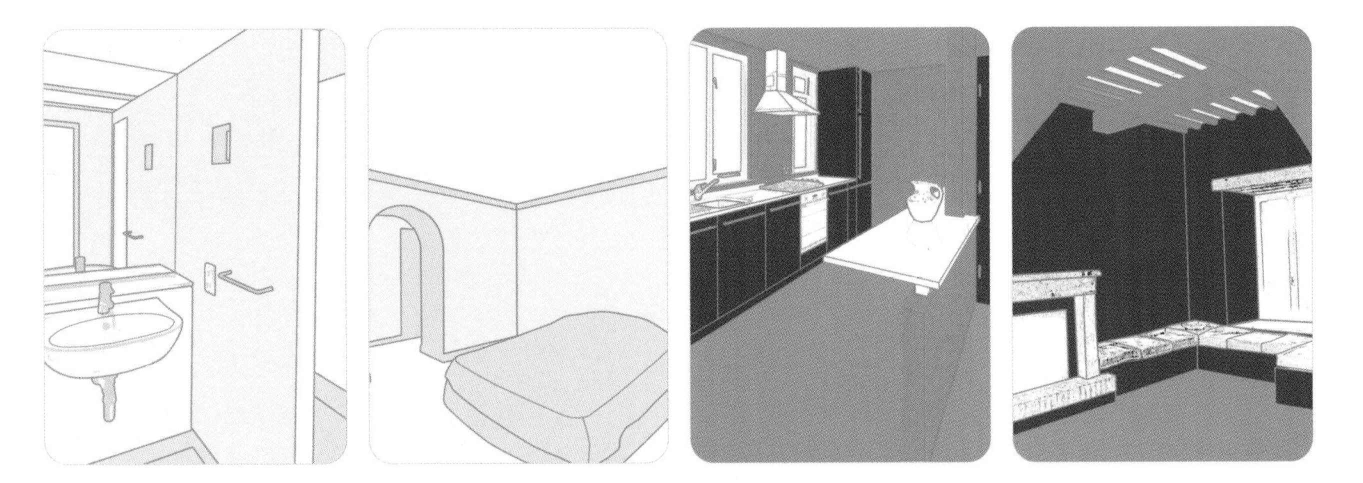

As combinations based on complementaries are taken from the opposite sides of the color wheel, there will always be a contrast of 'temperature'. This contrast will be extreme when these combinations are used at full strength.

Not only will the orange-red have a strong temperature contrast with its partners but complementaries also contrast visually in their own right. For these reasons it usually pays to lighten or darken these hues, or use in small 'touches' when at or near full strength.

A complementary and its split opposites

Green, orange-red and green-blue

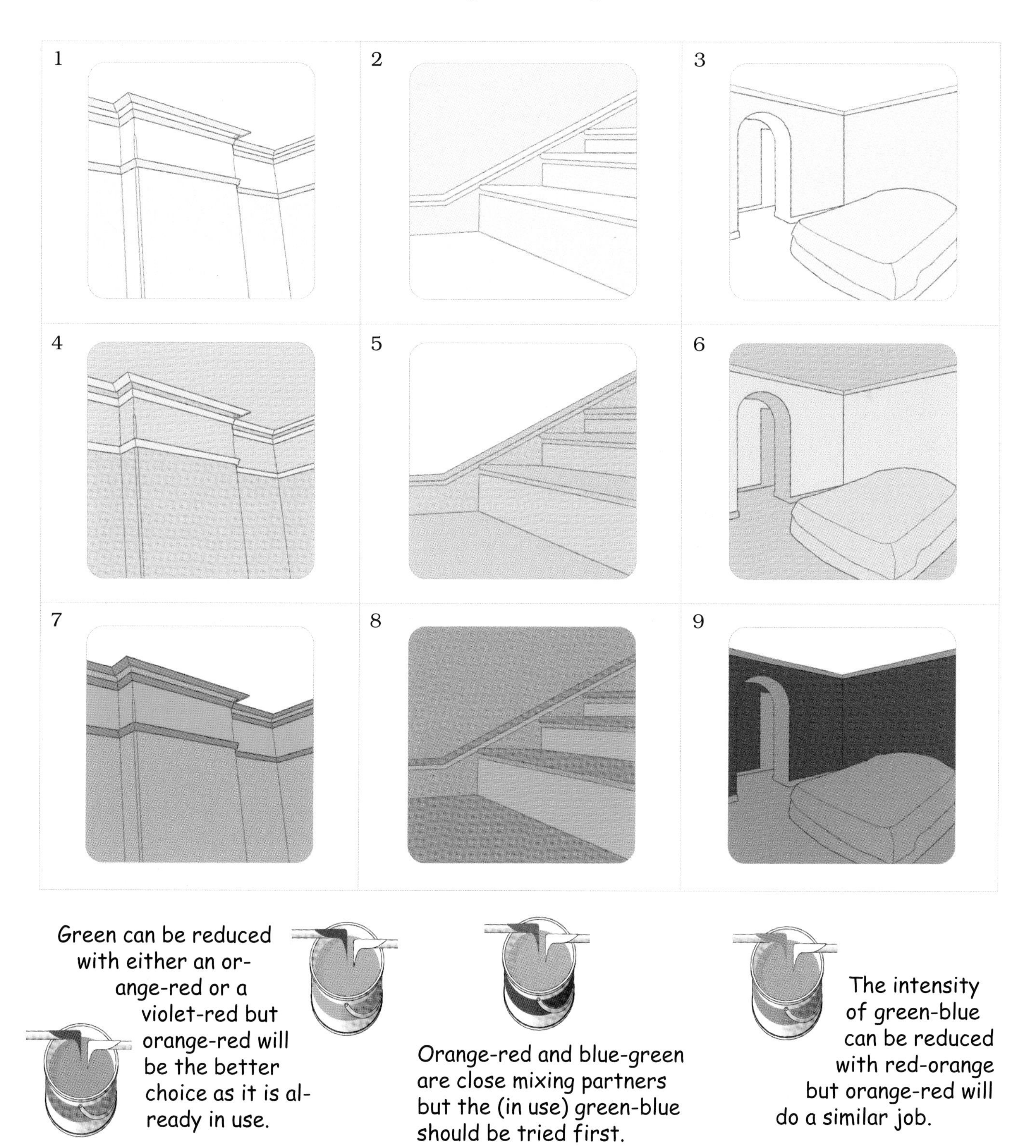

Green can be reduced with either an orange-red or a violet-red but orange-red will be the better choice as it is already in use.

Orange-red and blue-green are close mixing partners but the (in use) green-blue should be tried first.

The intensity of green-blue can be reduced with red-orange but orange-red will do a similar job.

Either type of red can be used to desaturate the green. A blue-green will reduce orange-red and a red-orange will lower the saturation of green-blue. To keep the number of colors to a minimum, use the same central orange-red to reduce the green and the green-blue.

A complementary and its split opposites

elizabethwhiting.com

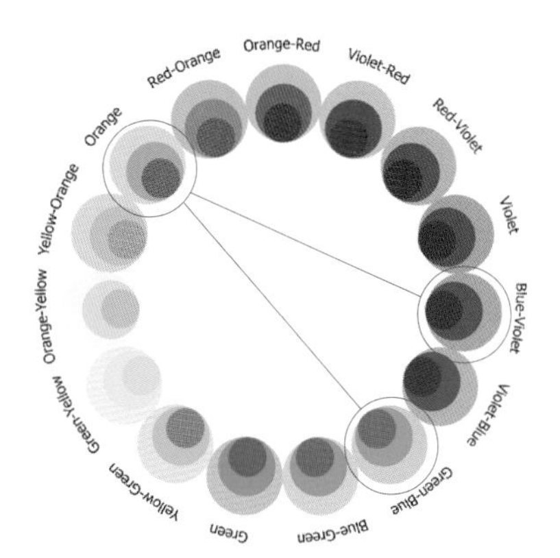

There are only slight differences between blue-violet (a type of violet) and violet blue (a type of blue). Do not be over concerned with these slight differences when selecting or mixing colors as the two hues are so close to each other.

Used with some modification, blue-violet and green-blue make a versatile couple. If the orange, their basic complementary, is also either lightened or darkened, you have a wide range of possible combinations to work with.

With regard to orange, it seems to be one of the most widely disliked hues when applied at or near full strength. As with certain pinks, many either love it or loathe it. With this in mind it often pays to take orange towards a tint by adding white. Alternatively it can work well as a shade (darker version). Particularly dark shades are often described as browns, a color group enjoying wide acceptance.

A complementary and its split opposites

Blue-violet, orange and green-blue

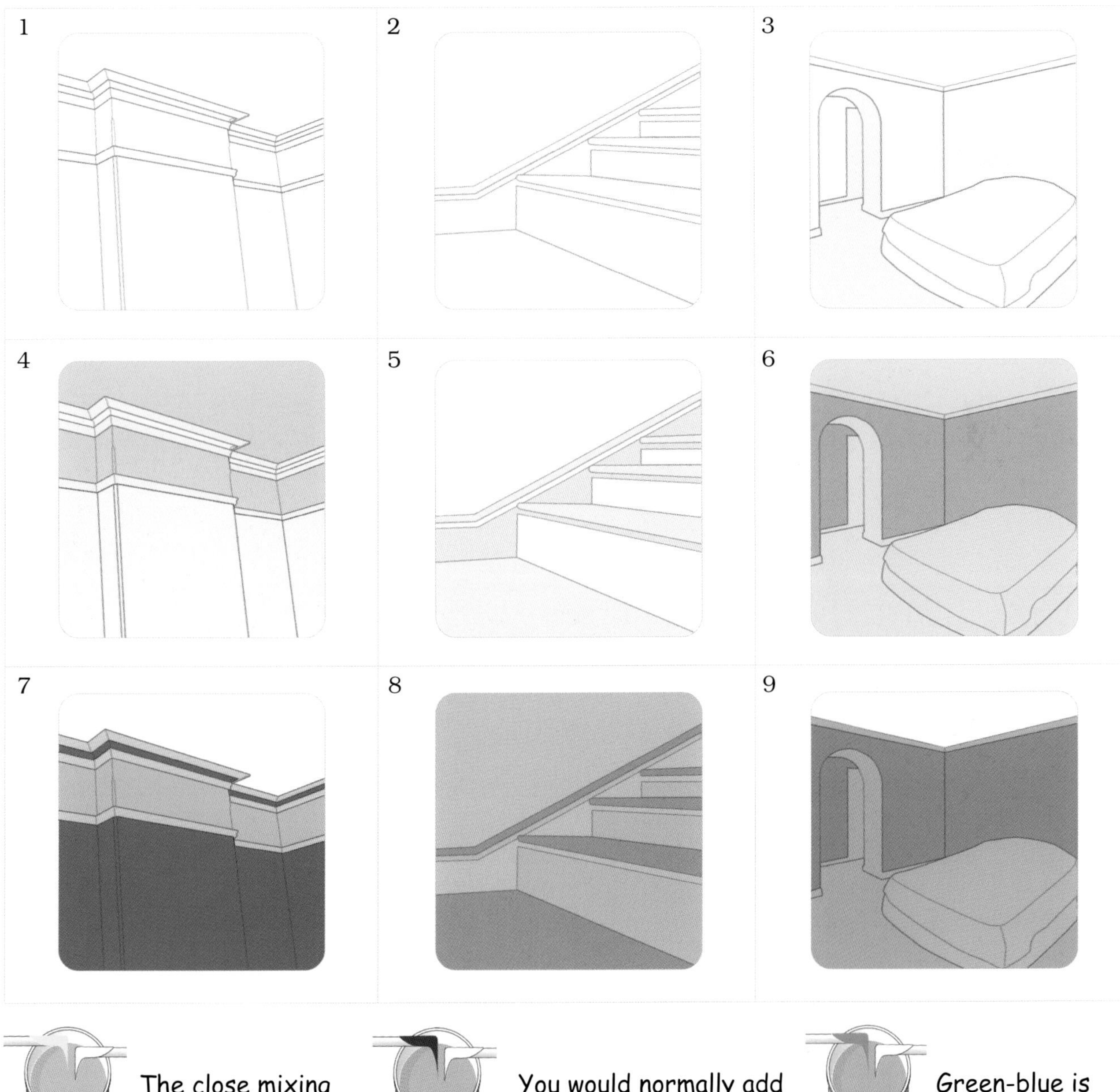

The close mixing partner of blue-violet is orange-yellow but try the (in use) orange first to keep color numbers down.

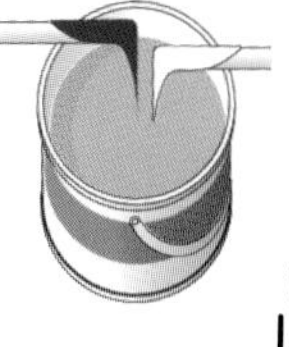

You would normally add either violet-blue or green-blue in order to lower the intensity of orange but use the blue-violet as results will be similar to violet-blue.

Green-blue is normally reduced with red-orange but try the orange (already in use) first.

Close mixing partners do not always have to be used as there are other ways to modify a color. You could try adding the central orange to both the blue-violet and the green-blue. This would keep the number of colors involved to a minimum and the final mixes should work well together. As I cannot know the actual paints that you will be using I can only suggest a trial mix first. The fewer the colors in use, the better for color harmony.

A complementary and its split opposites

© Red Cover/Huntley Hedworth

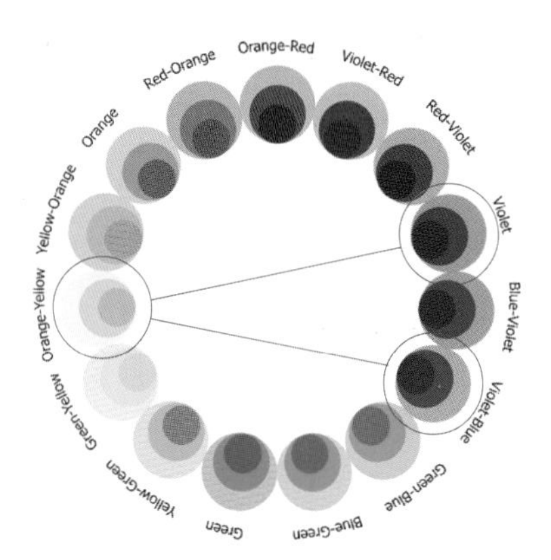

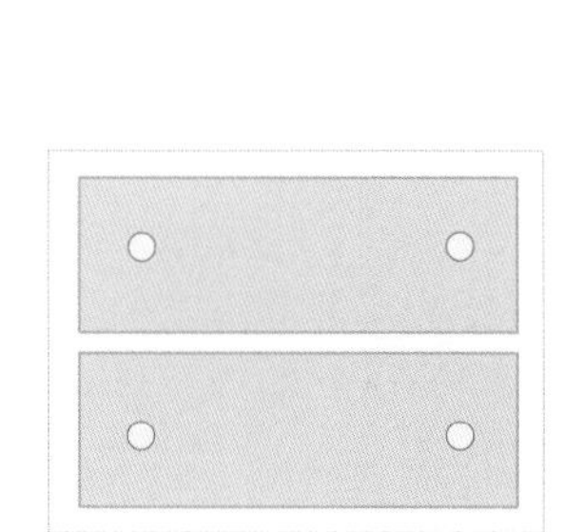

Painted furniture can greatly assist in the overall color scheme.

The violet and the violet-blue make a well balanced pair as they have much in common, both reflecting violet in varying degrees.

Color combinations based on the split opposite approach point the way not only to color harmony but also to arrangements which can contrast strongly. For an extensive range, vary the relative strength of the colors and juggle with the areas that they cover. A little experimenting will soon show the way.

A complementary and its split opposites

Violet, orange-yellow and violet-blue

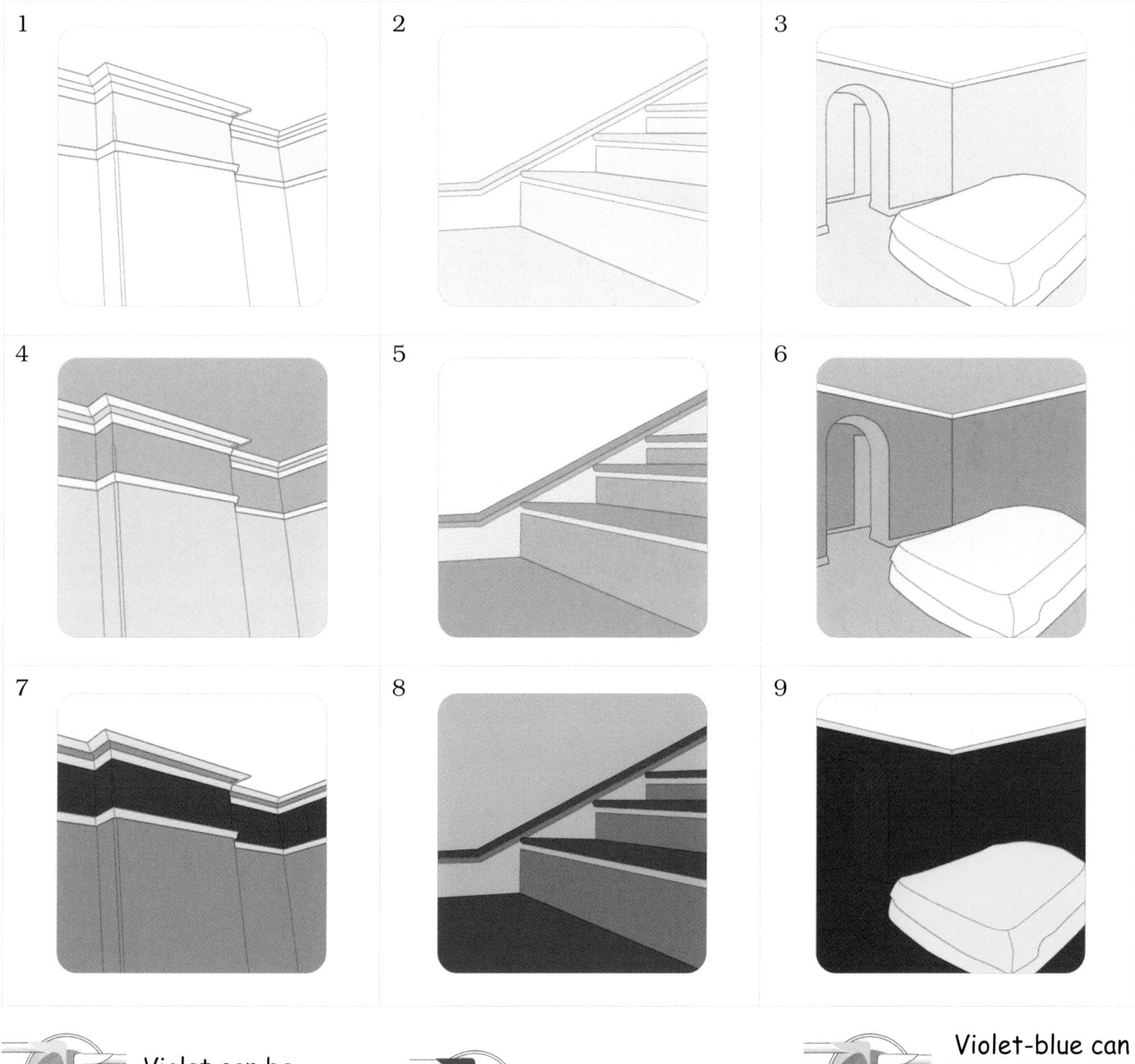

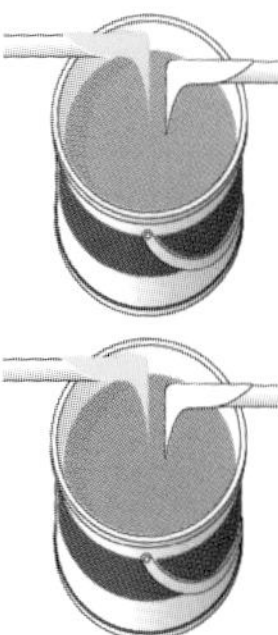

Violet can be desaturated with either green-yellow or orange-yellow the latter is the better choice here as it is already in use.

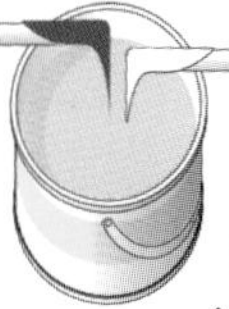

Blue-violet is the close mixing partner of orange-yellow but try the (in use) violet-blue first. Add a touch of red if the mixes become too green.

Violet-blue can be reduced with its close mixing partner yellow-orange (a type of orange). But try the orange-yellow (a type of yellow) first. Add red to remove any greenness.

For the sake of simplicity you might wish to use the central orange-yellow to neutralise both the violet and the violet-blue.

Although the mixing partner of the violet-blue is a yellow-orange (a type of orange), it will be worth trying the orange-yellow if only small changes are being made.

Tiny amounts are needed to alter a color.

A complementary and its split opposites

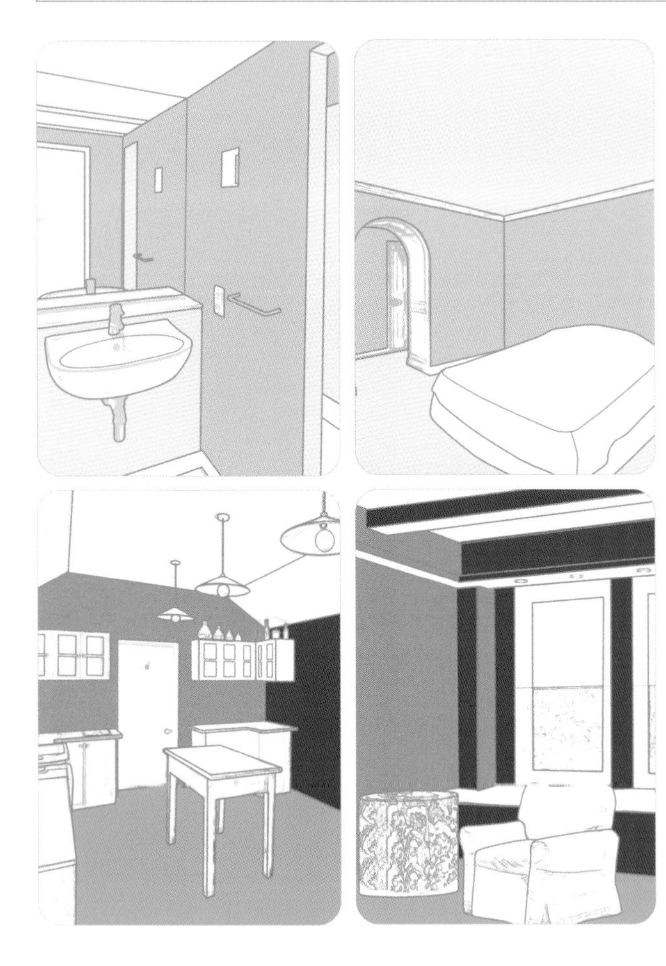

© Red Cover/Chris Drake

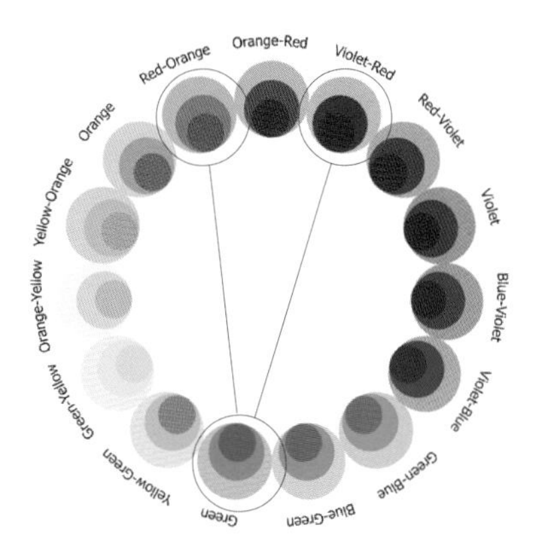

A particularly useful arrangement with very many applications.

We can learn a great deal from the way that colors mix in nature.

Red and green are a versatile pair which can give results ranging from soft harmonies to very strong contrasts.

This is a combination which occurs very frequently in nature. The red and green coloring matter in plants often blend to give the browns and dull red-violets of the stems, leaves and buds. We can certainly learn from this. If, in a room where red and green are in close proximity you wished to use various 'browns' and dull red violets, it will pay to mix them from the same red and green.

A complementary and its split opposites

Red-orange, green and violet-red

1 2 3

4 5 6

7 8 9

Red-orange is normally best reduced with its close partner green-blue. But try the green that you have selected first. If it does the job it will keep the total number of colors down.

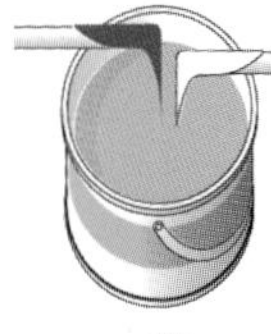

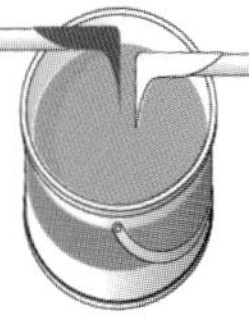

Green can be lowered in intensity with either a violet-red or an orange-red, but the (in use) violet-red should be your first choice here.

You would normally add a little yellow-green to the violet-red to reduce it. But try your selected green first.

As green and red are mixing partners, either the red-orange or the violet-red will lower the intensity of whichever green you are using. However, the results will vary depending on the selected green. It will help to mix small amounts before committing yourself.

A complementary and its split opposites

elizabethwhiting.com

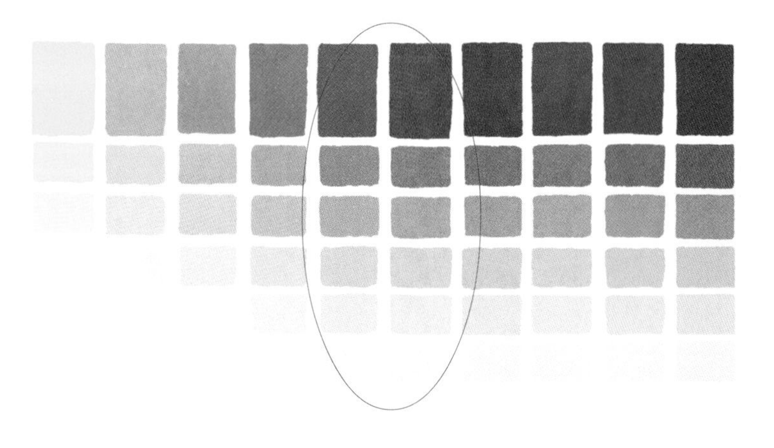

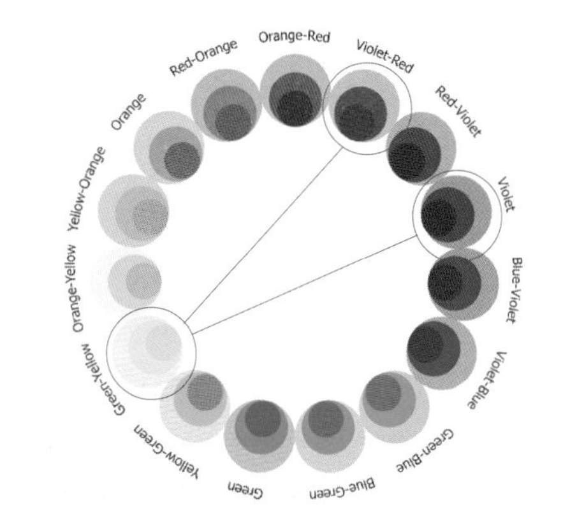

'Colored grays', circled above, result when close or exact mixing partners are blended in or near equal intensity. In practice this means mixing them until the colored grays appear.
They are a very important part of the potential color range, particularly when lightened through the addition of white.
The above mixing swatch shows a combination of green-yellow and violet.

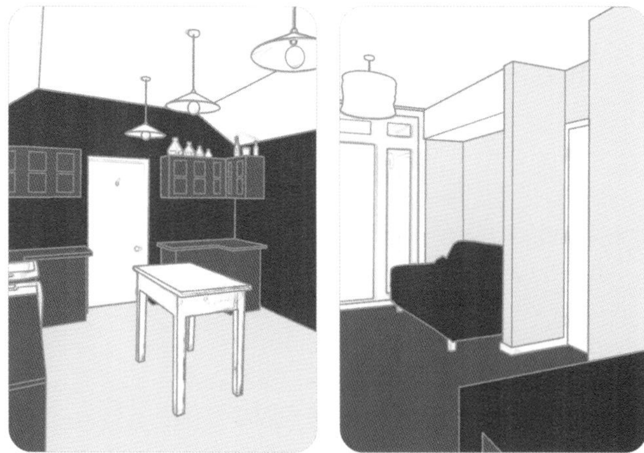

The 'colored grays' also have a part to play. Colored grays occur around the middle of the range and are the result of a mixing pair absorbing much of each others color.

If these colored grays are further reduced with white the results can be very subtle. This is a vital area of color use which is much neglected.

A complementary and its split opposites

Violet-red, green-yellow and violet

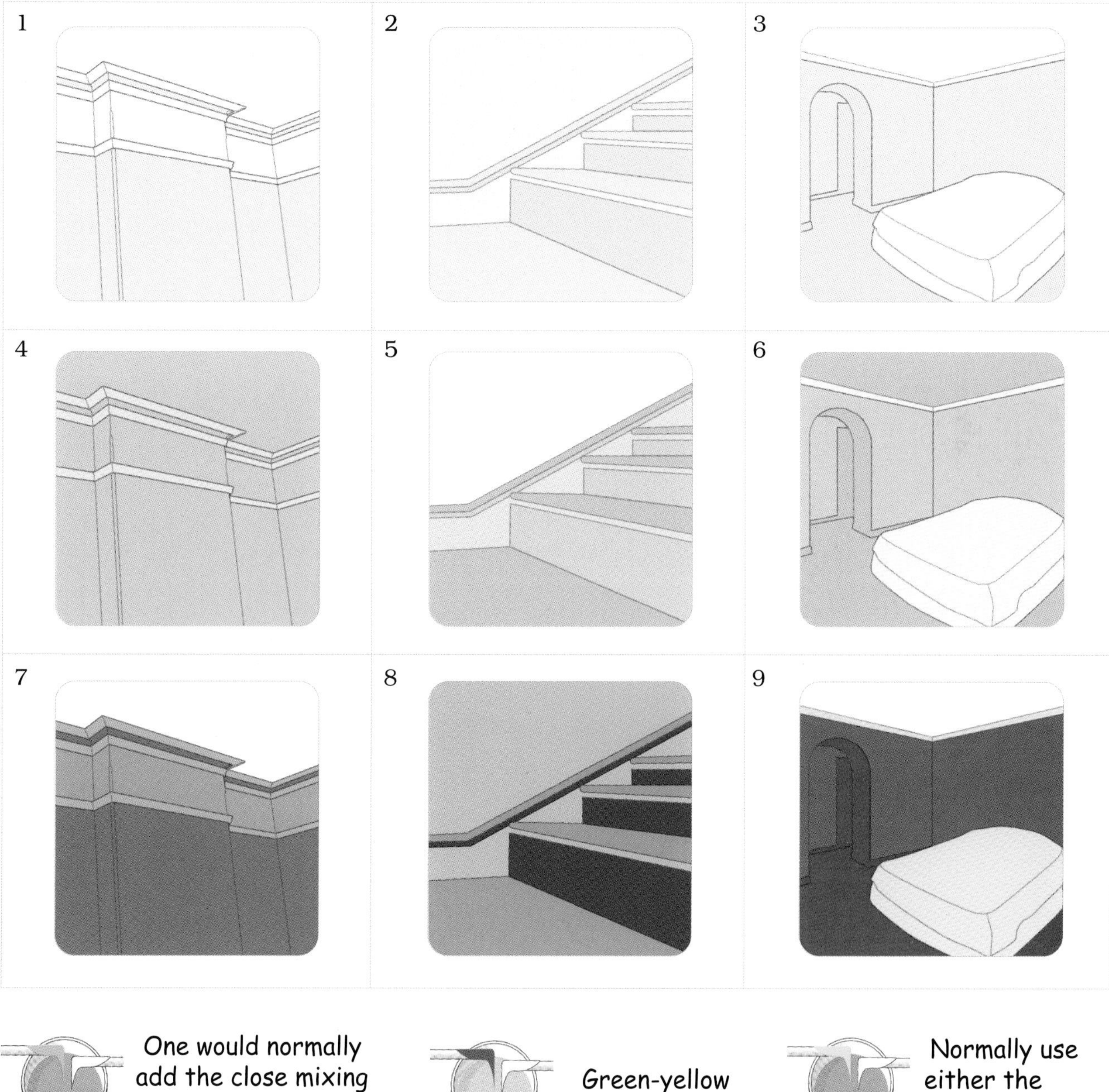

One would normally add the close mixing partner yellow-green to lower the intensity of the violet-red. However, you should try the green-yellow first as it is already in use.

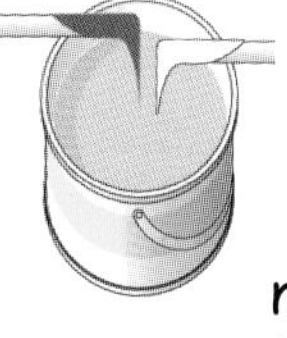

Green-yellow and red-violet are close partners but the violet-red should be tried first.

Normally use either the orange-yellow or the green-yellow to lower the strength of violet. But the latter should be used here.

Although the close mixing partners are shown above, you could use the central green-yellow to neutralise both the violet-red and the violet. This would keep the number of colors to a minimum. As only relatively small amounts of one color are required to alter the other, the end result should be much the same whether you used the yellow-green or the green-yellow.

A complementary and its split opposites

Summary

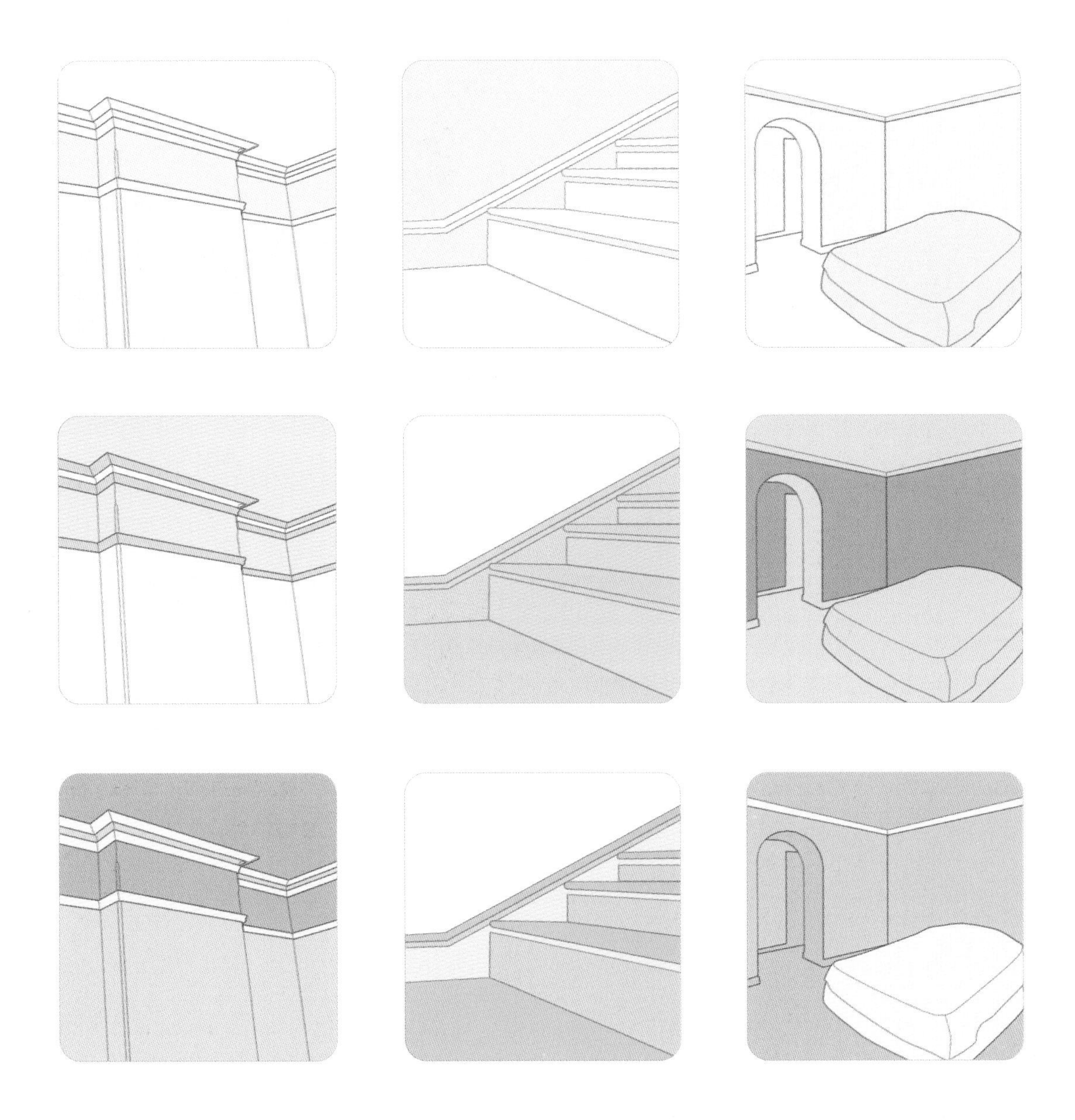

The use of a complementary pair with the addition of the neighbour of one of the hues can give a wide range of harmonising color schemes.

Such arrangements can look very subtle and sophisticated where the colors are balanced one against the next with a certain amount of care.

Related hues & the general complementary

Introduction

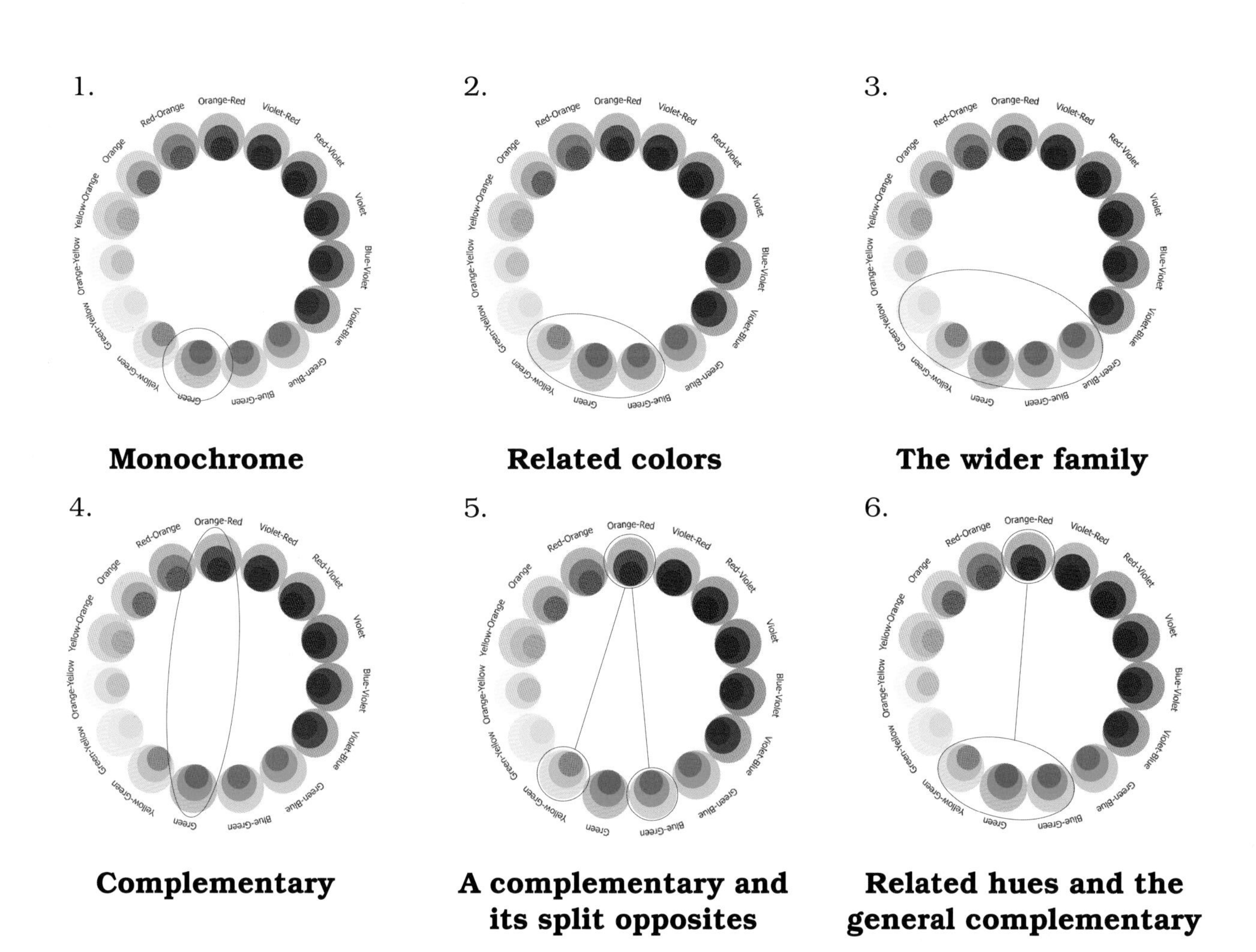

Monochrome **Related colors** **The wider family**

Complementary **A complementary and its split opposites** **Related hues and the general complementary**

The color arrangements that we have examined so far have grown steadily in their complexity:

1. Monochrome, a single color is very straightforward but can tend towards blandness.
2. Related colors, neighbours on the color wheel, offer greater interest and can be harmonised with ease.
3. When the related color arrangement is extended to the 'wider family' group, greater potential is on offer but care has to be taken when balancing one color against the next.
4. Complementary pairings bring in the effect of the after-image. They offer strong contrasts as well as the possibility of subtle harmonies.
5. When a complementary color is set against the neighbours of its partner the complexity grows but at the gain of potentially greater visual interest.
6. In the area that we will now be examining, 'related hues and the general complementary' we will be working with a related group (2) plus the general complementary of that group.

The potential for advanced color work increases.

Related hues & the general complementary

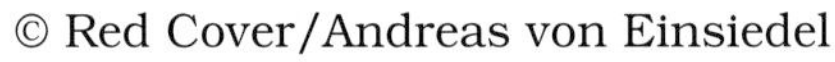

© Red Cover/Andreas von Einsiedel

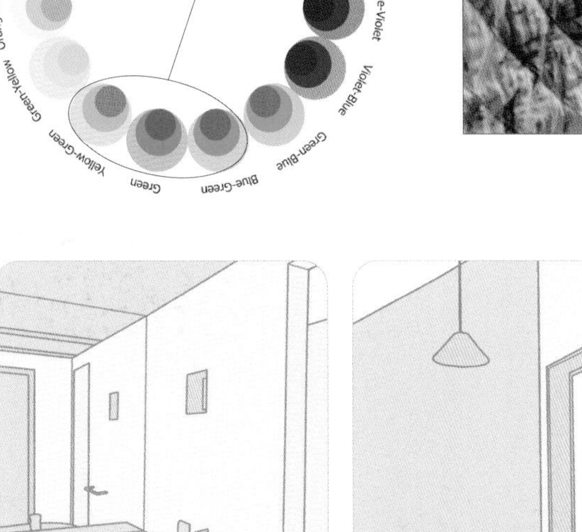

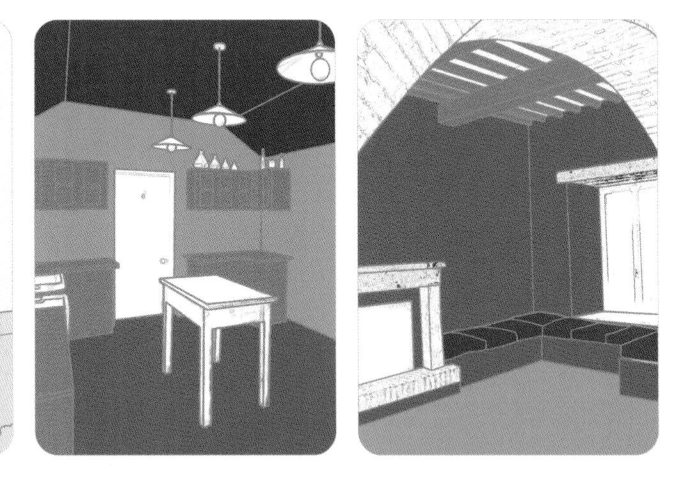

The violet-red tends to be easier to work with when applied as a pale tint. As it becomes more saturated it can upset the balance unless the other colors involved are also fairly strong.

When all are darkened this combination of hues can take on a rather sombre appearance. However, if one or two of the colors are made a little brighter, this effect can be lifted somewhat.

Related hues & the general complementary

Blue-green, violet-red, green and yellow-green

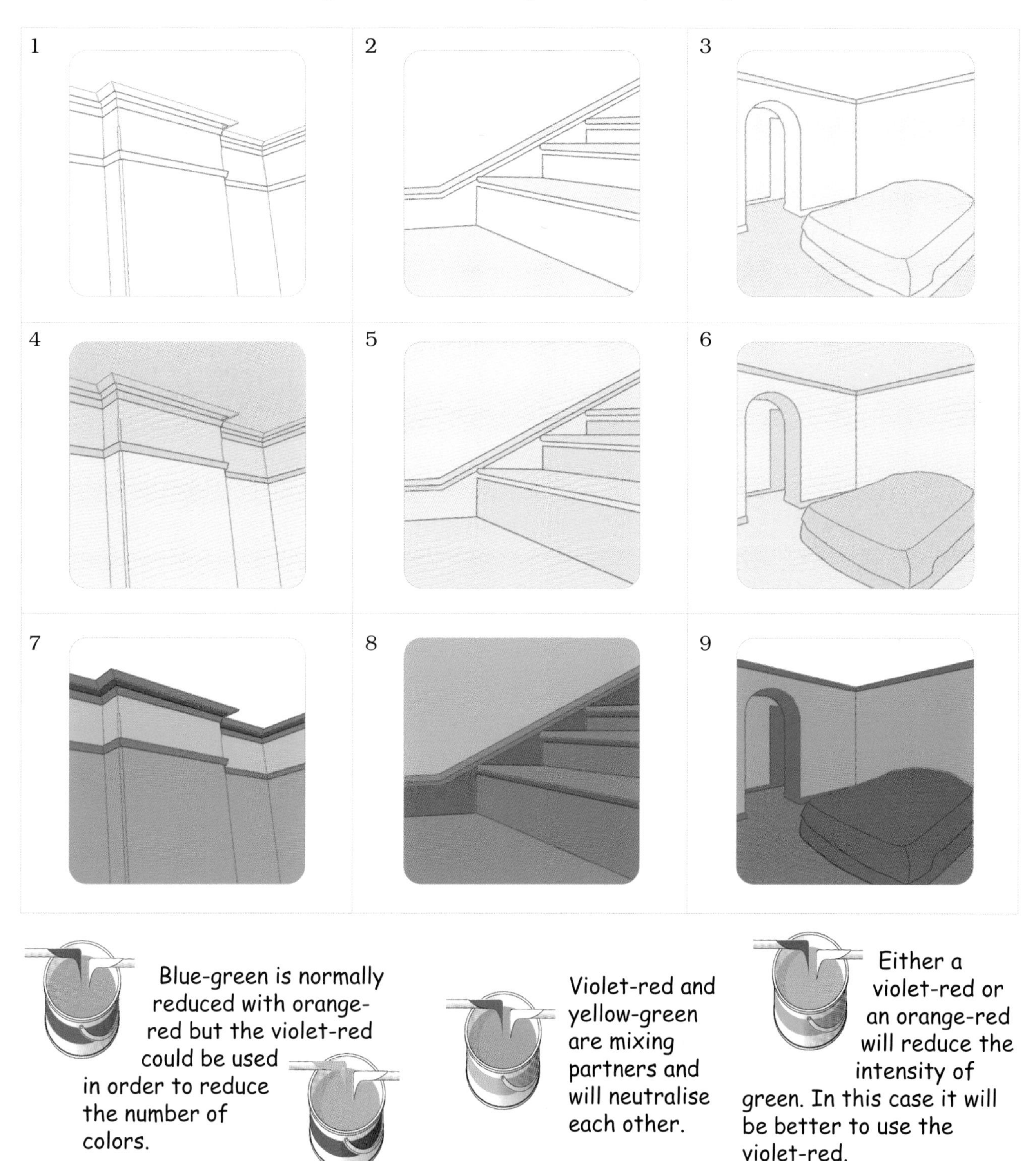

Blue-green is normally reduced with orange-red but the violet-red could be used in order to reduce the number of colors.

Violet-red and yellow-green are mixing partners and will neutralise each other.

Either a violet-red or an orange-red will reduce the intensity of green. In this case it will be better to use the violet-red.

The blue-green can be desaturated with white, with its general mixing partner violet-red, or with white and the mixing partner. Either type of red can be used with the green and yellow-green can be desaturated with violet-red. In order to keep the number of colors down as much as possible, the violet-red can be used with all three opposites.

Related hues & the general complementary

© Red Cover/Huntley Hedworth

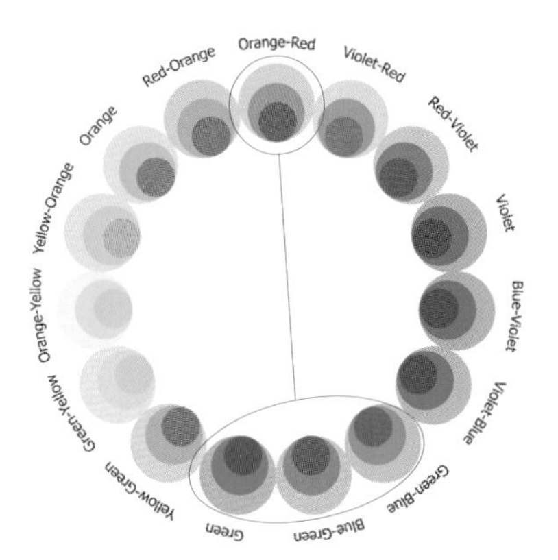

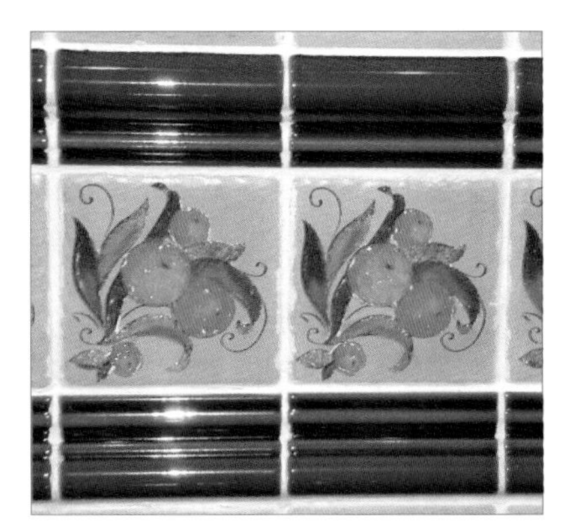

The three 'cool' hues can be balanced very well against the 'warm' orange-red.

Although it takes a little practice and care to harmonise (rather than contrast) these three, the end result can be very pleasing.

Obviously, only a tiny fraction of the possible combinations available from these three hues can be shown in these pages.

It will be worth a little experimentation if you find this general arrangement to be of interest.

Related hues & the general complementary

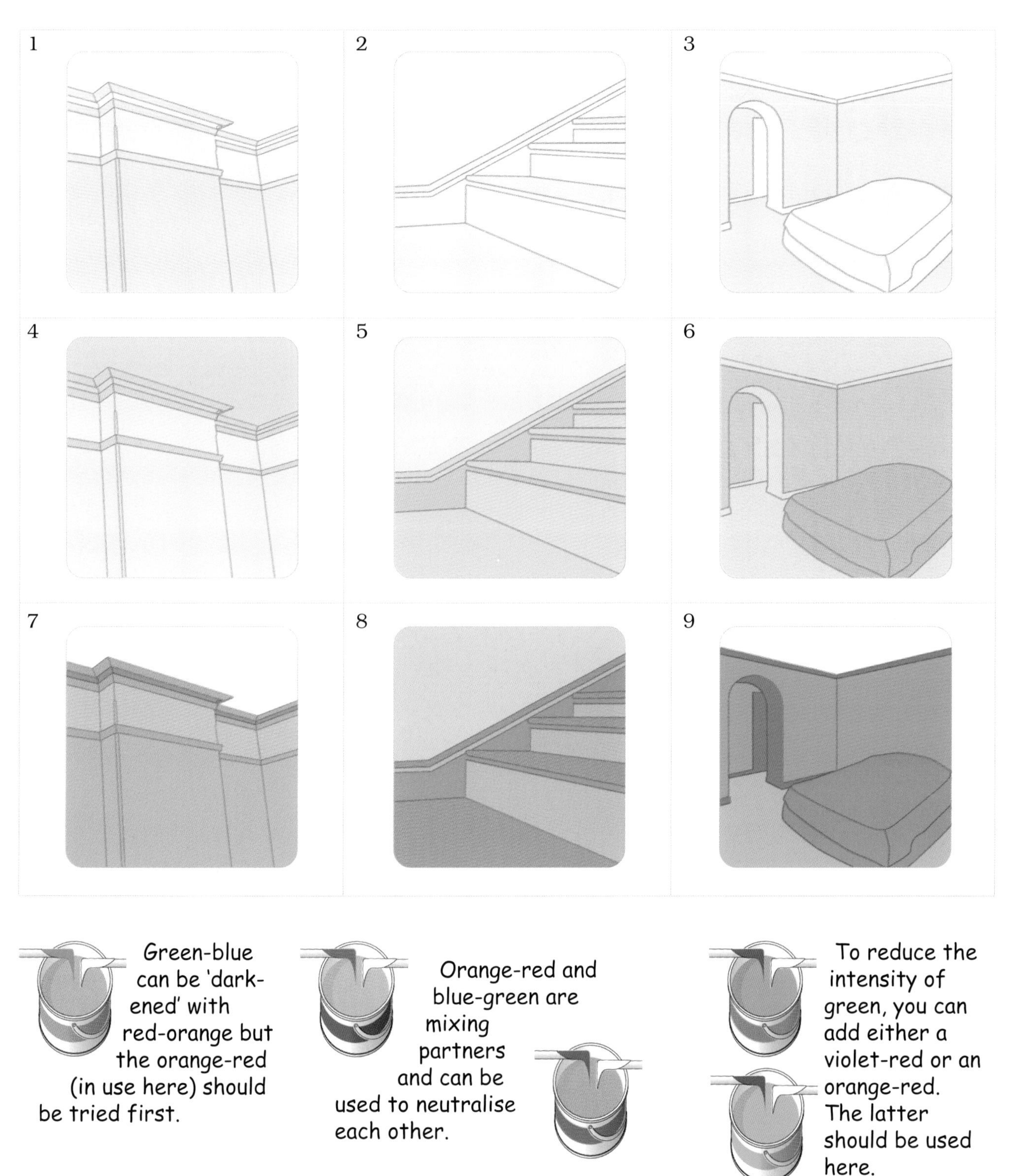

Green-blue can be 'darkened' with red-orange but the orange-red (in use here) should be tried first.

Orange-red and blue-green are mixing partners and can be used to neutralise each other.

To reduce the intensity of green, you can add either a violet-red or an orange-red. The latter should be used here.

As there is not a great deal of difference between a red-orange (a type of orange) and an orange-red (a type of red) you can use the same orange-red to reduce intensity in the green-blue, the blue-green and the green. This will reduce the number of colors involved.

Related hues & the general complementary

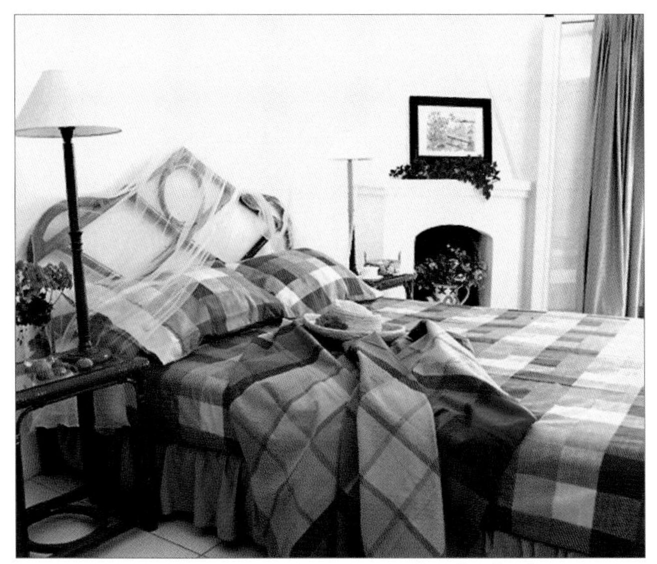
elizabethwhiting.com

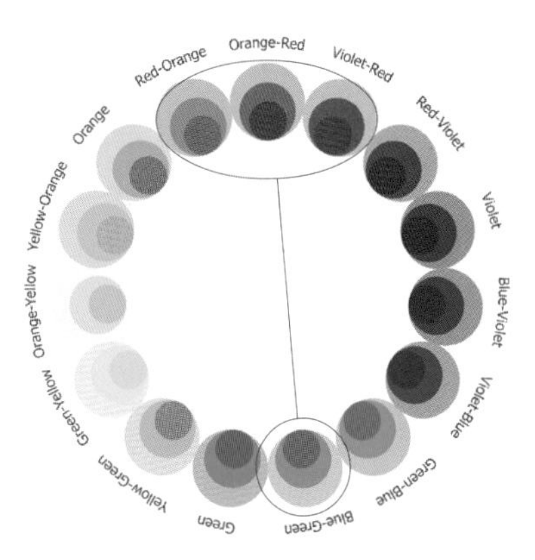

In the space available I can only show a few of the possible combinations. The color wheel will guide you to very many more.

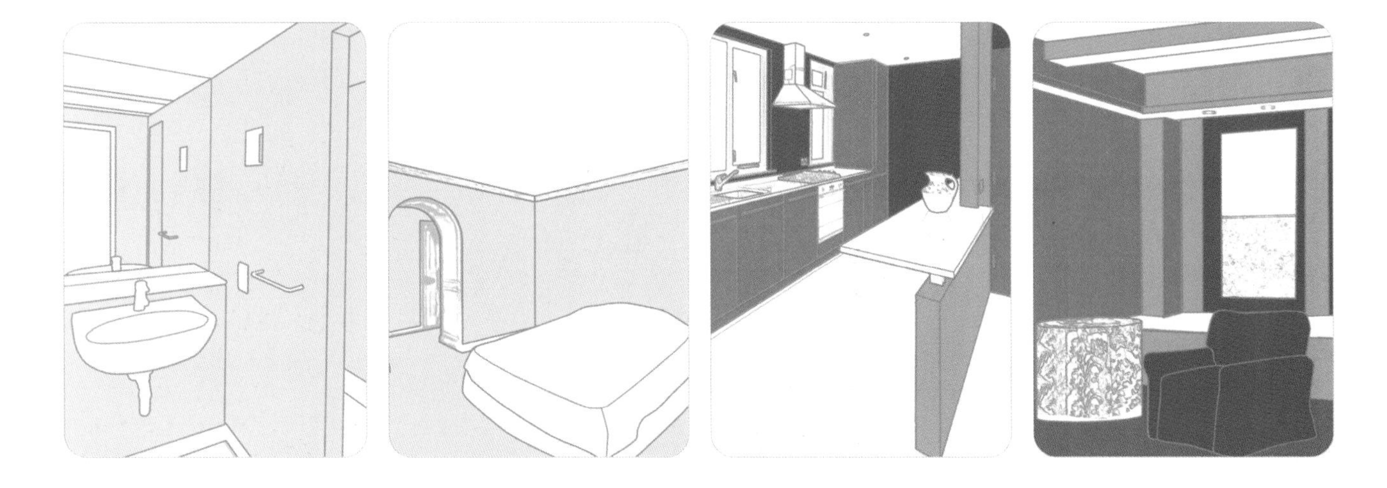

The two reds, orange-red and violet-red can be rather difficult to work with. Much in the same way that the two types of yellow can give problems. To help overcome this tendency it pays to vary the intensity of one to another. One light and the other dark for example.

Related hues & the general complementary

Red-orange, blue-green, orange-red and violet-red

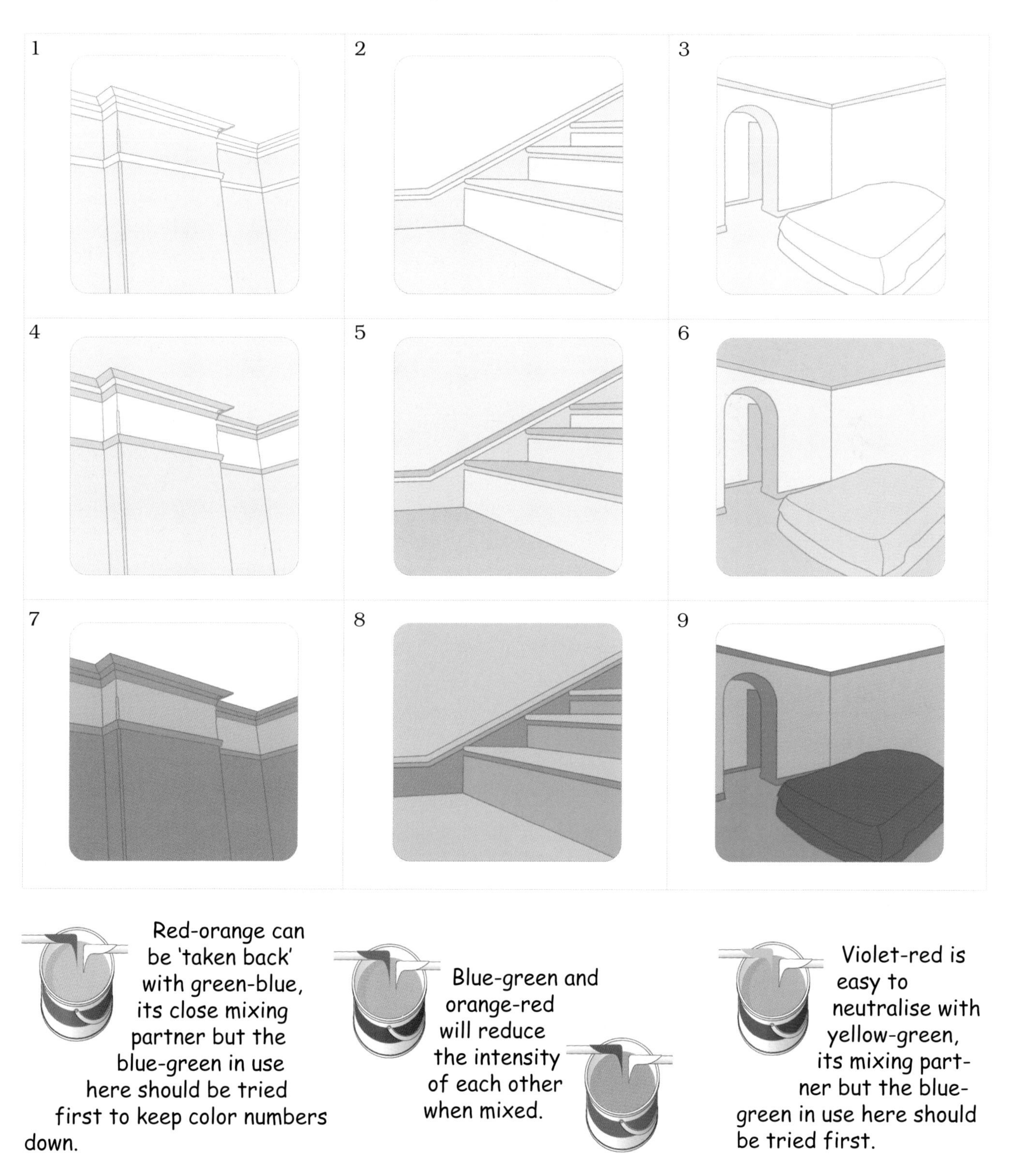

The basic hues can be used in various ways: either at full strength without mixing; made into any of a range of tints with white; reduced in intensity with the gradual addition of the mixing partner; or blended with white *and* the mixing partner.

Related hues & the general complementary

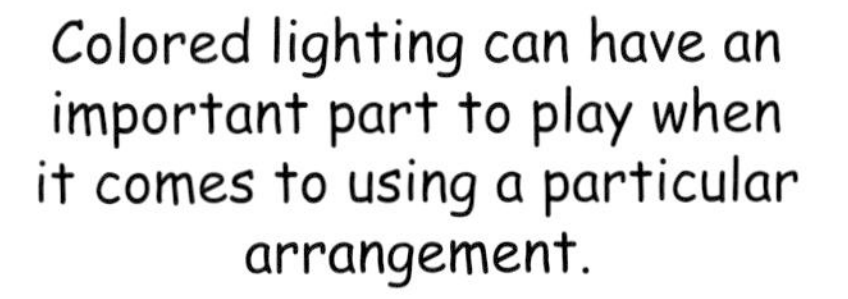

Colored lighting can have an important part to play when it comes to using a particular arrangement.

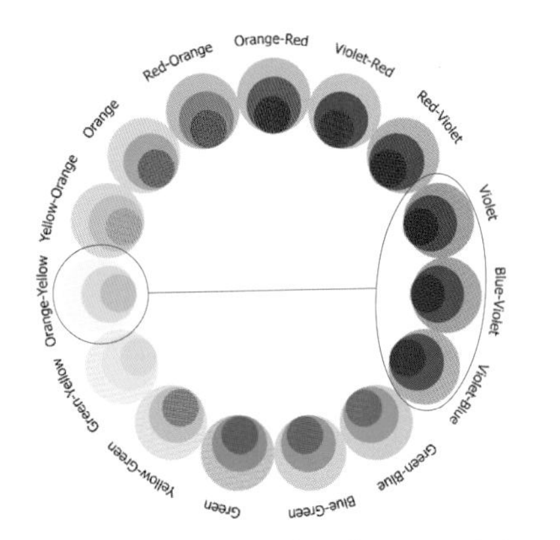

Some very attractive harmonising arrangements are available from this combination.

Orange-yellow can be rather difficult to work with when at or near full saturation as it can appear a little brash.

However, when modified and well balanced with the other hues the results can be very attractive (to my eyes, that is, you might well have other ideas, in which case we will both be right). Although seldom handled well, in my opinion, this combination can give outstanding harmonies when balanced with care.

Related hues & the general complementary

Violet, orange-yellow, blue-violet and violet-blue

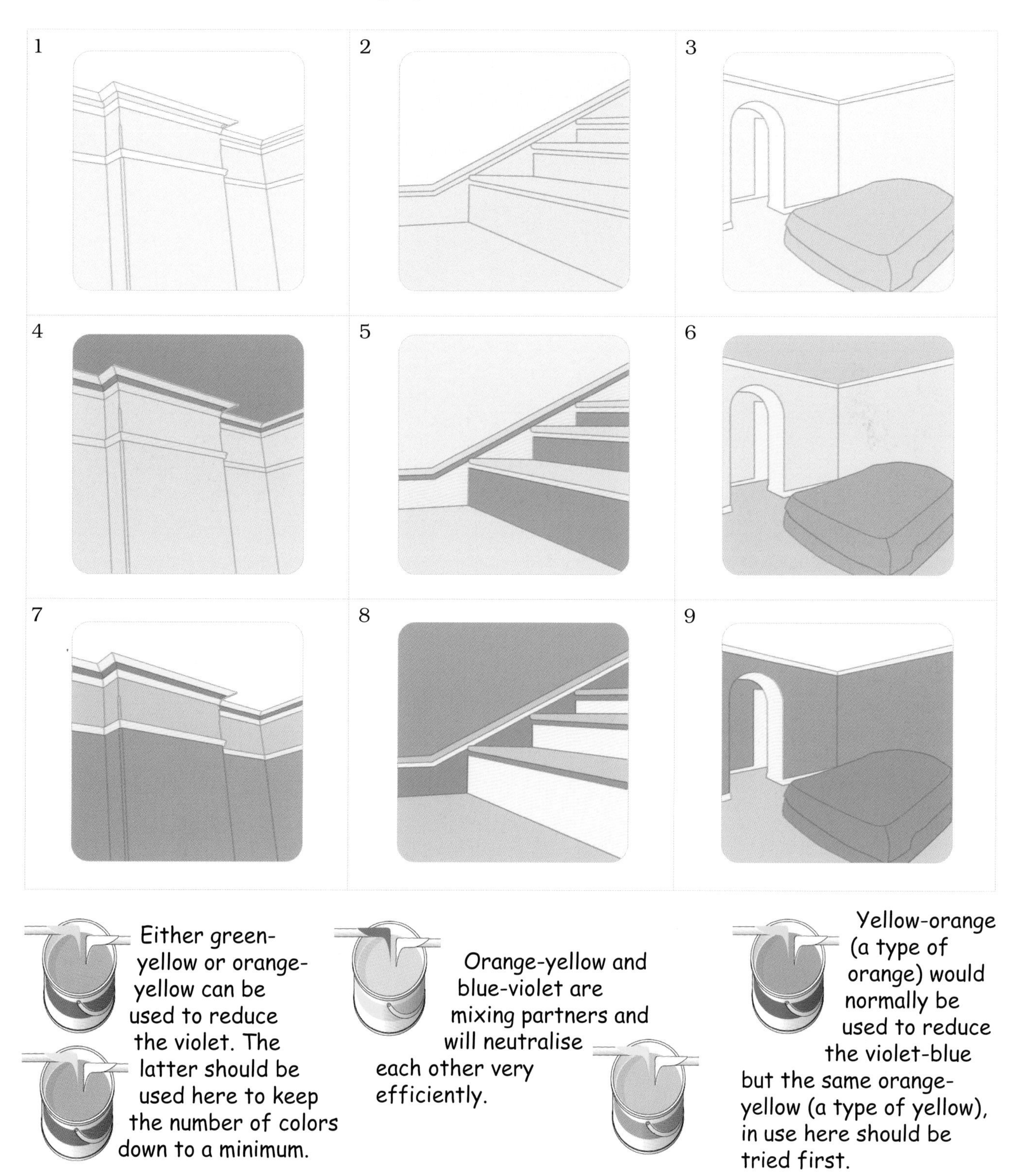

Either green-yellow or orange-yellow can be used to reduce the violet. The latter should be used here to keep the number of colors down to a minimum.

Orange-yellow and blue-violet are mixing partners and will neutralise each other very efficiently.

Yellow-orange (a type of orange) would normally be used to reduce the violet-blue but the same orange-yellow (a type of yellow), in use here should be tried first.

You might need to read the color descriptions several times. A violet-blue is a type of blue and a blue-violet is a type of violet.

Although the differences are subtle they are quite separate colors and should normally be treated as such.

Related hues & the general complementary

elizabethwhiting.com

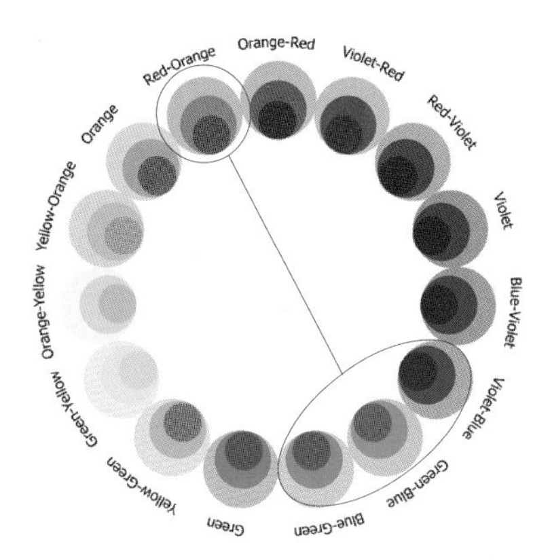

The two types of blue, violet-blue and green-blue, set up an interesting but subdued contrast which is often found in early Chinese and Persian work. When well balanced they can be very effective.

The complementary red-orange, when used with skill, can add a contrast varying from the subtle to the extreme. The blue-green is somewhat of an outsider and should be treated with a little care. When reduced in intensity it can have an important role to play in this versatile arrangement.

Related hues & the general complementary

Violet-blue, red-orange, green-blue and blue-green

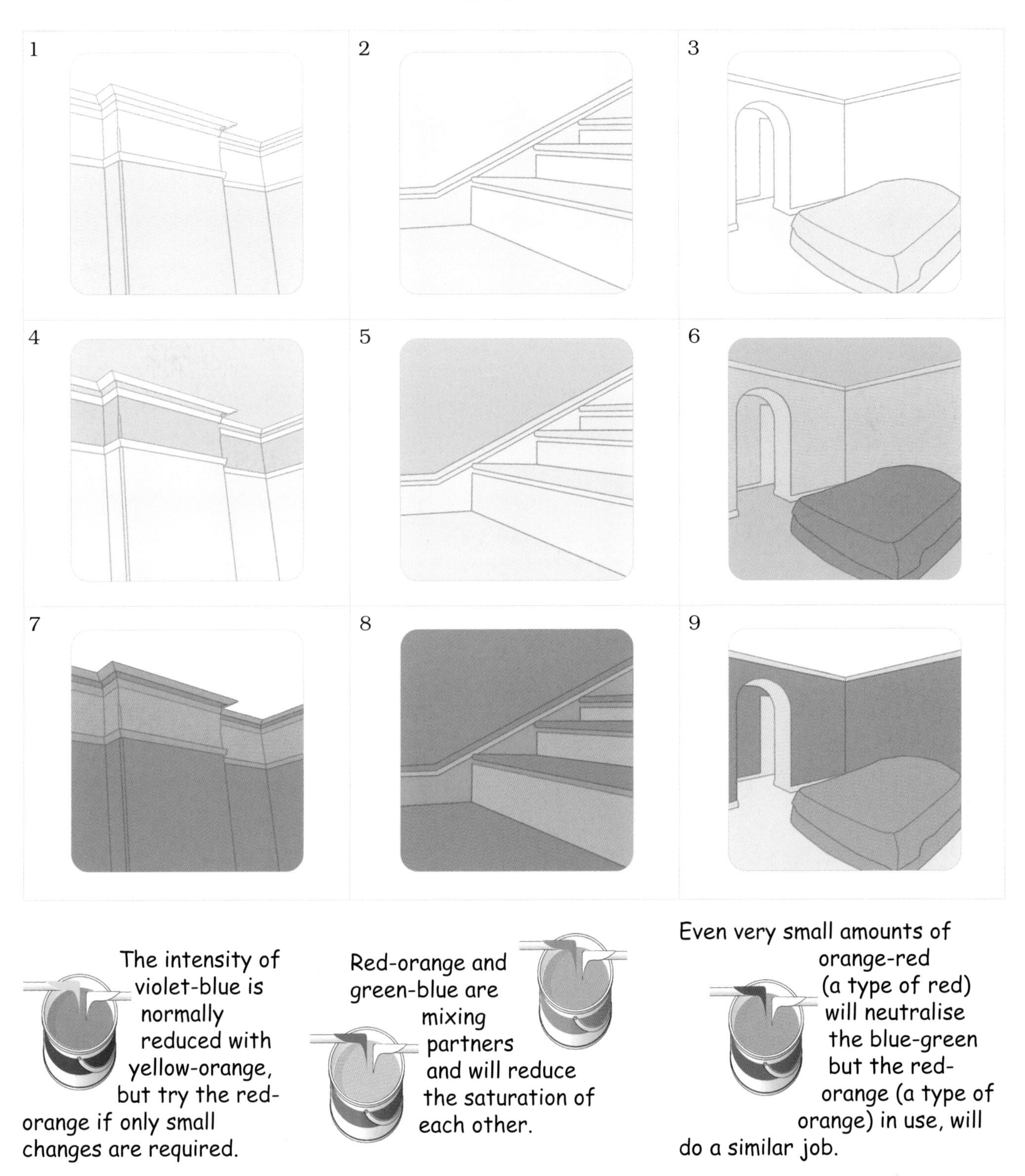

The intensity of violet-blue is normally reduced with yellow-orange, but try the red-orange if only small changes are required.

Red-orange and green-blue are mixing partners and will reduce the saturation of each other.

Even very small amounts of orange-red (a type of red) will neutralise the blue-green but the red-orange (a type of orange) in use, will do a similar job.

Use a close or general mixing partner if you wish to reduce the intensity of a hue.

Although the character of the color will change and, strictly speaking you do not end up with an exact darker version of the hue, this is the most efficient way to deepen a color. Adding black will simply destroy its very nature and take it in another direction.

Related hues & the general complementary

© Jefferson Smith/arcblue.com

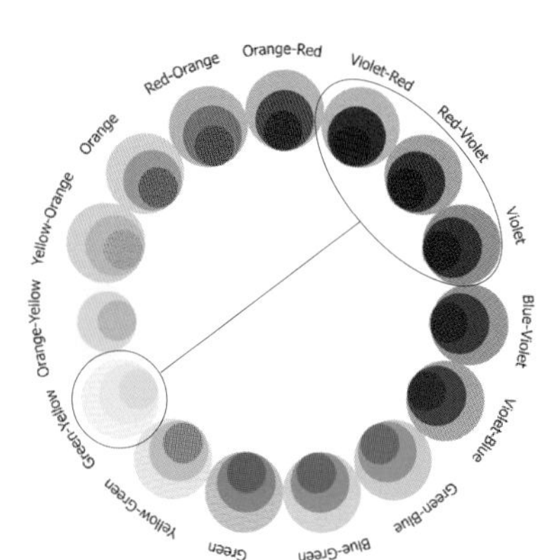

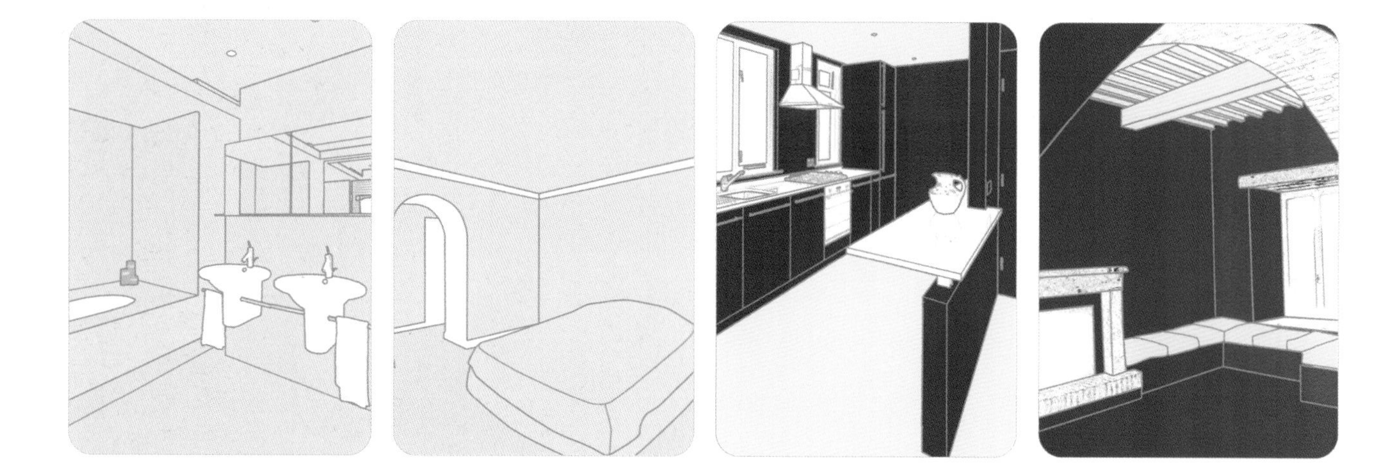

To many, these four hues tend to harmonise only when they are all reduced with white, or with white and the mixing partner.

The green-yellow, in particular, can add unwanted contrast at strength and needs to be used with some care. If you are actually seeking such contrasts use the green-yellow at full saturation. There is no such thing as an incorrect use of color. If you like a certain arrangement and the next person does not, you are both right, in much the same way as you might not both like apples.

Related hues & the general complementary

Violet-red, green-yellow, red-violet and violet

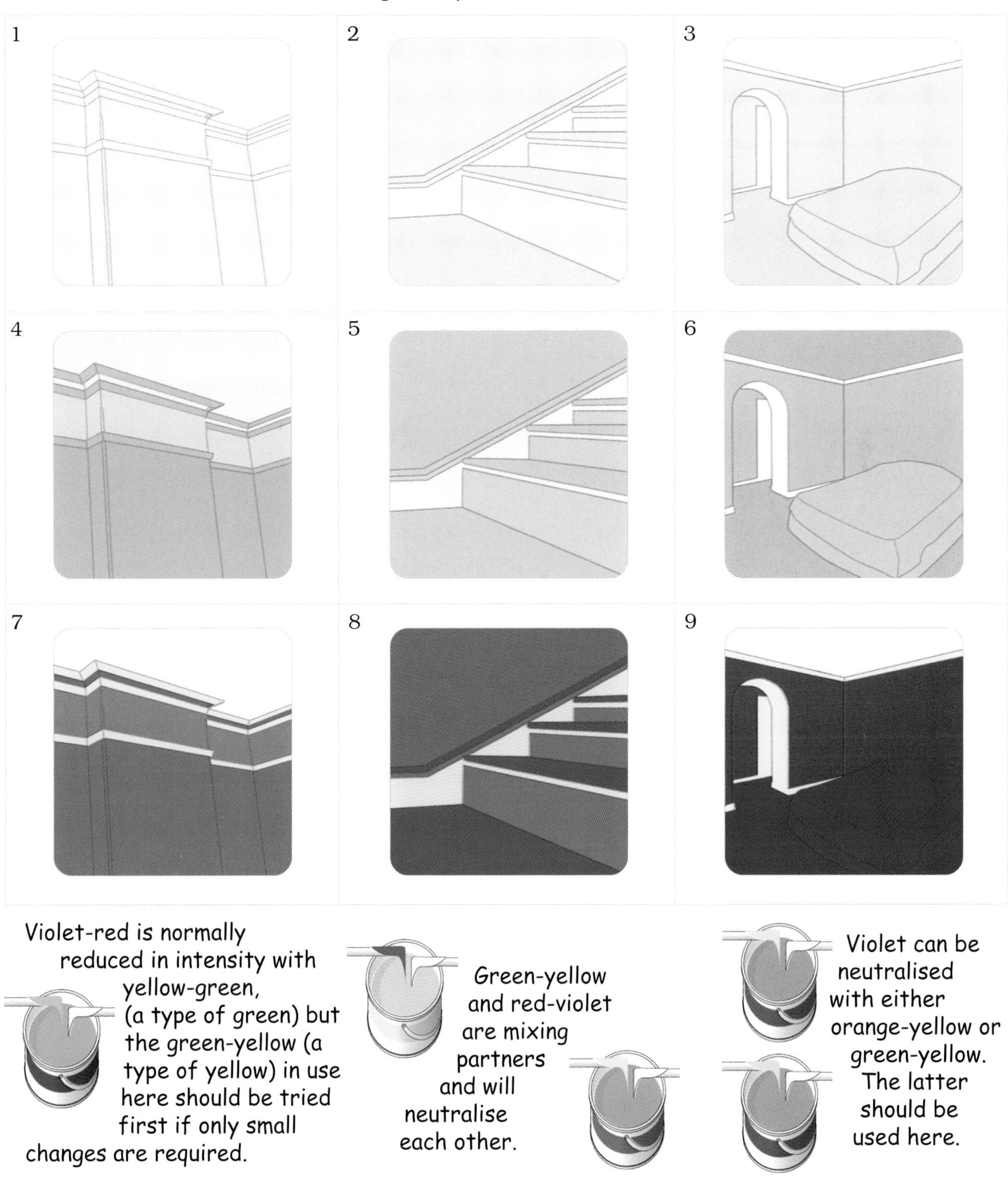

If you are looking for a soft 'colored gray' add more of the close mixing partner, as identified above, until a mid 'colored gray' results. If white is then added you will have a very subtle pale 'colored gray'.

The results will vary: Violet-red and yellow-green will give 'colorful' grays, violet mixed with either type of yellow will give soft neutral grays which are more like our idea of a gray mixed from black and white.

Related hues & the general complementary

© Red Cover/Mark Bolton

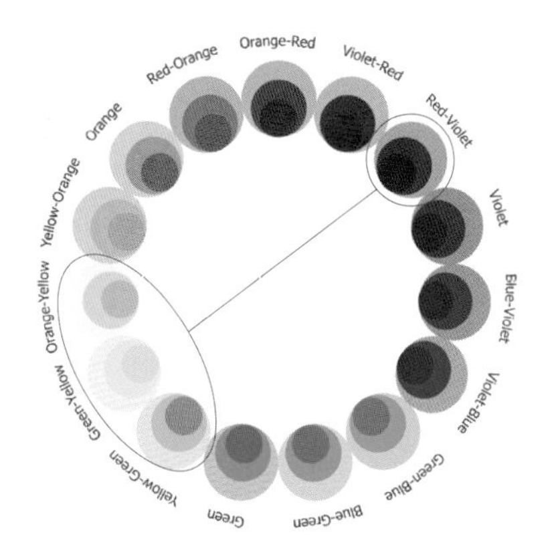

A yellow which leans towards green (a green-yellow) and one which is biased towards orange (an orange-yellow) are usually best separated by other hues.

© Red Cover/Andreas von Einsiedel

The use of the two types of yellow in the one room, green-yellow and orange-yellow, can introduce slight discord as they do not always sit well together.

If might pay to lighten or darken one or both to reduce intensity. Alternatively use them over relatively small areas or keep them separated by other colors.

Related hues & the general complementary

Yellow-green, red-violet, green-yellow and orange-yellow

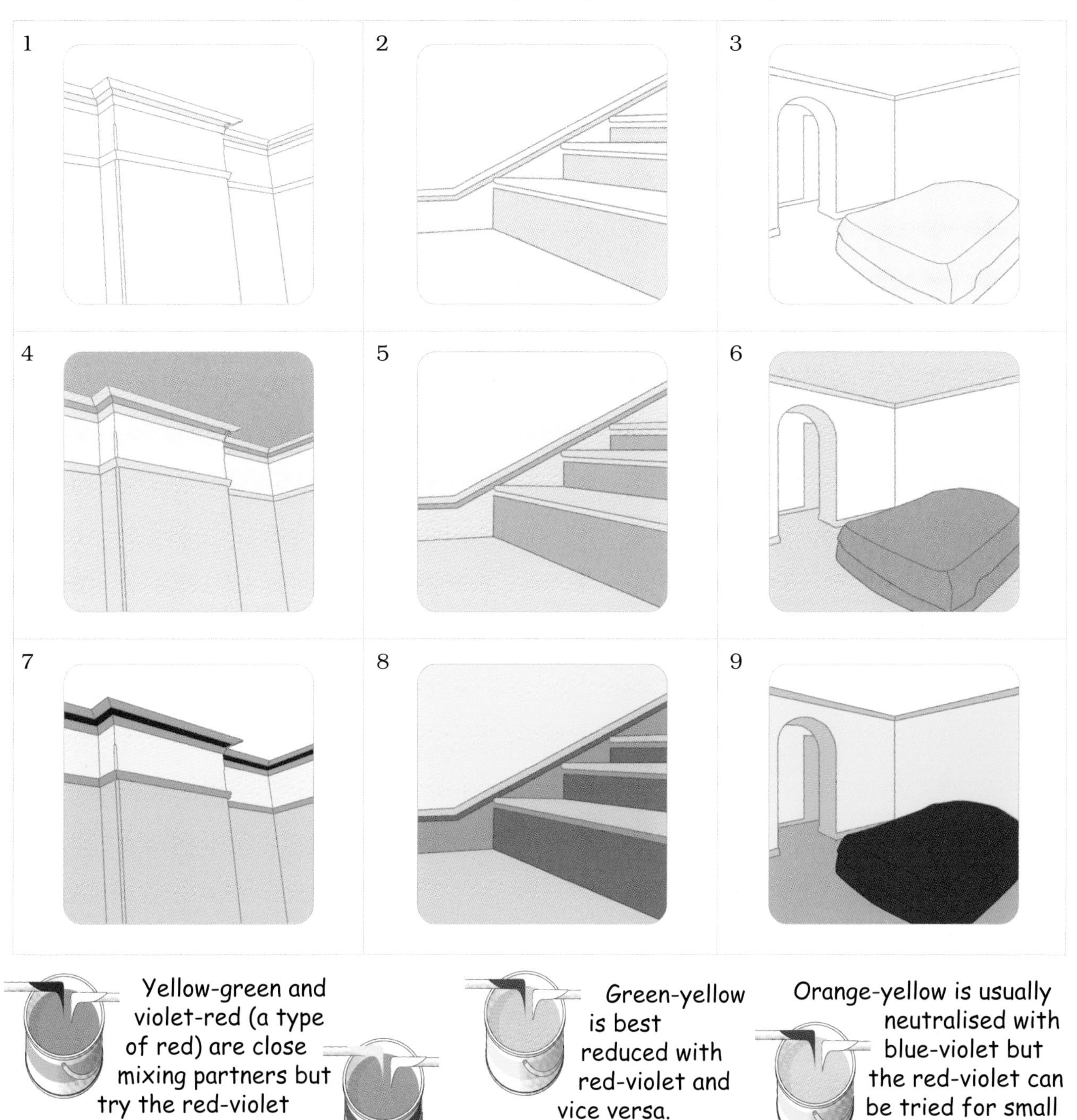

Yellow-green and violet-red (a type of red) are close mixing partners but try the red-violet (a type of violet) in use here.

Green-yellow is best reduced with red-violet and vice versa.

Orange-yellow is usually neutralised with blue-violet but the red-violet can be tried for small changes.

Once you have decided upon a color scheme, it pays to prepare small amounts of the chosen colors and apply them side by side before mixing larger quantities. Please bear in mind that due to the severe limitations of color printing and the varying colored paints and tinters on the market, these pages can be no more than a general guide. Do not expect the final result to look exactly as above as there are so many variables to take into account; the actual colors that are available to you, the surface onto which you are painting, the available light, whether you choose gloss, semi gloss or matt paint etc.

Related hues & the general complementary

© Red Cover/Brian Harrison

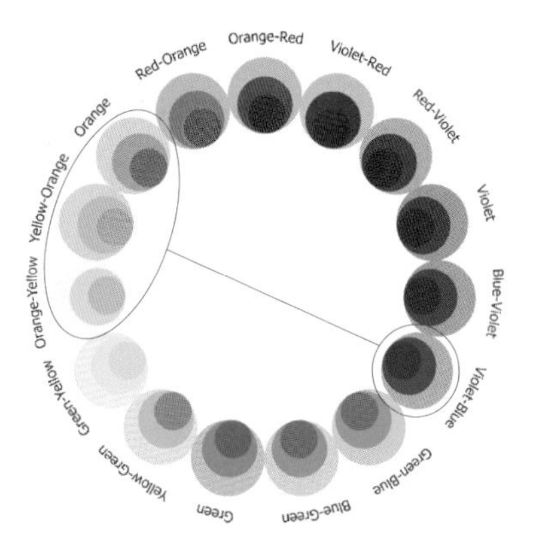

The combinations shown on these pages are only suggestions. Drop a color and use just three or 'borrow' a hue from another swatch.

With the almost unlimited range of possible combinations neither this, or any guide (that I can imagine), could ever be definitive.

It is a case of deciding on a color scheme which appeals, then mixing small amounts of each color and trying them side by side.

Make sure that you are entirely happy with your selection before mixing large amounts of paint. It can be cheaper to decorate that way.

Related hues & the general complementary

Orange-yellow, violet-blue, yellow-orange and orange

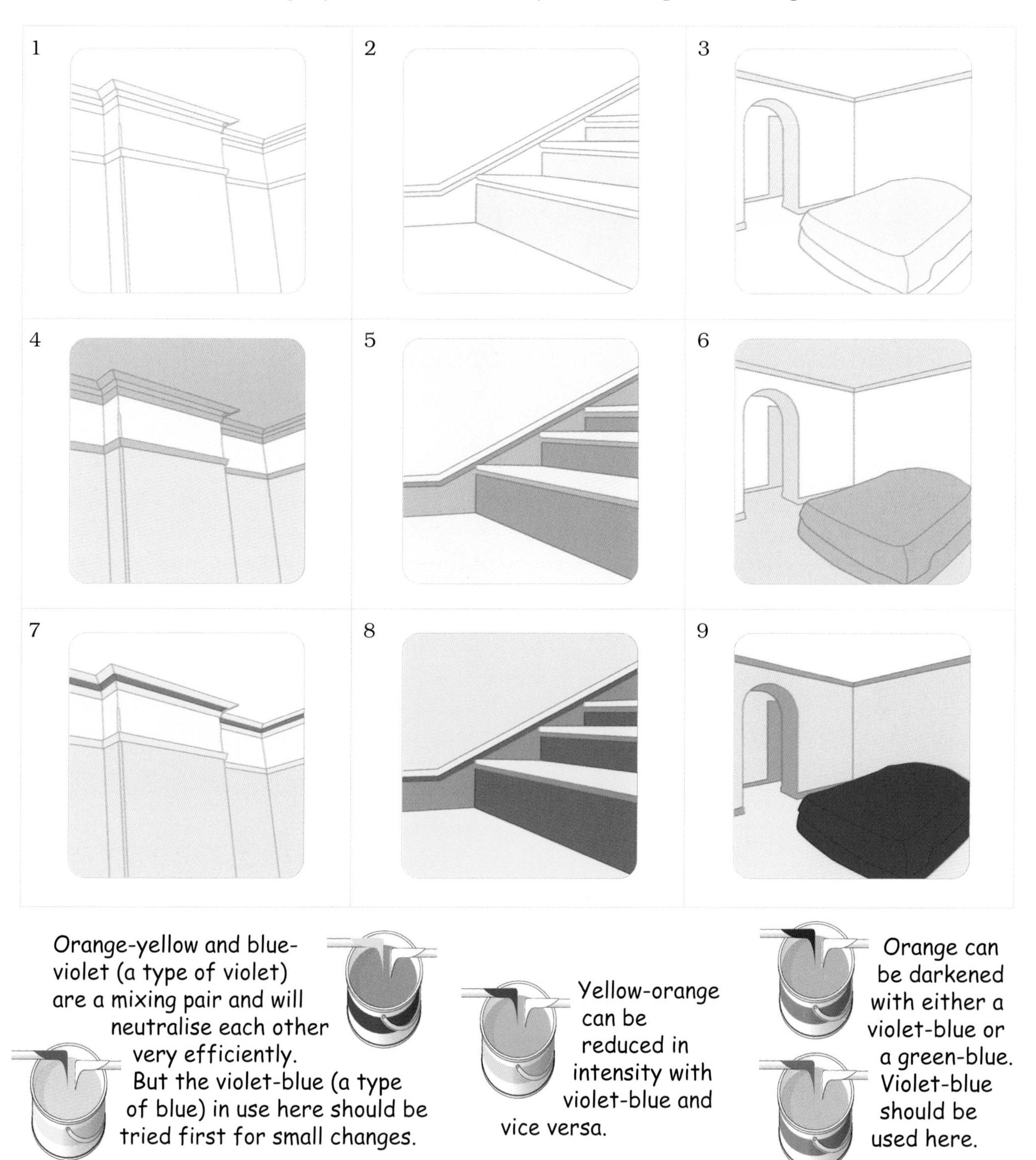

A variety of approaches have been taken to alter the intensity of the colors in these swatches.

The mixing partner and white might have been added to neutralise and then lighten individual hues (as above). Alternatively they have been used unmixed, in a bright, intense form or simply lightened with white.

Related hues & the general complementary

© Peter Durant/arcblue.com

Orange-Red
Violet-Red
Red-Violet
Violet
Blue-Violet
Violet-Blue
Green-Blue
Blue-Green
Green
Yellow-Green
Green-Yellow
Orange-Yellow
Yellow-Orange
Orange
Red-Orange

As with all color combinations it can never be the case that a particular two, three or four colors automatically harmonise. It depends entirely on how they are used, at what strength and over what area. Ultimately of course, color harmony depends on the viewer.

Related hues & the general complementary

Orange, green-blue, red-orange and orange-red

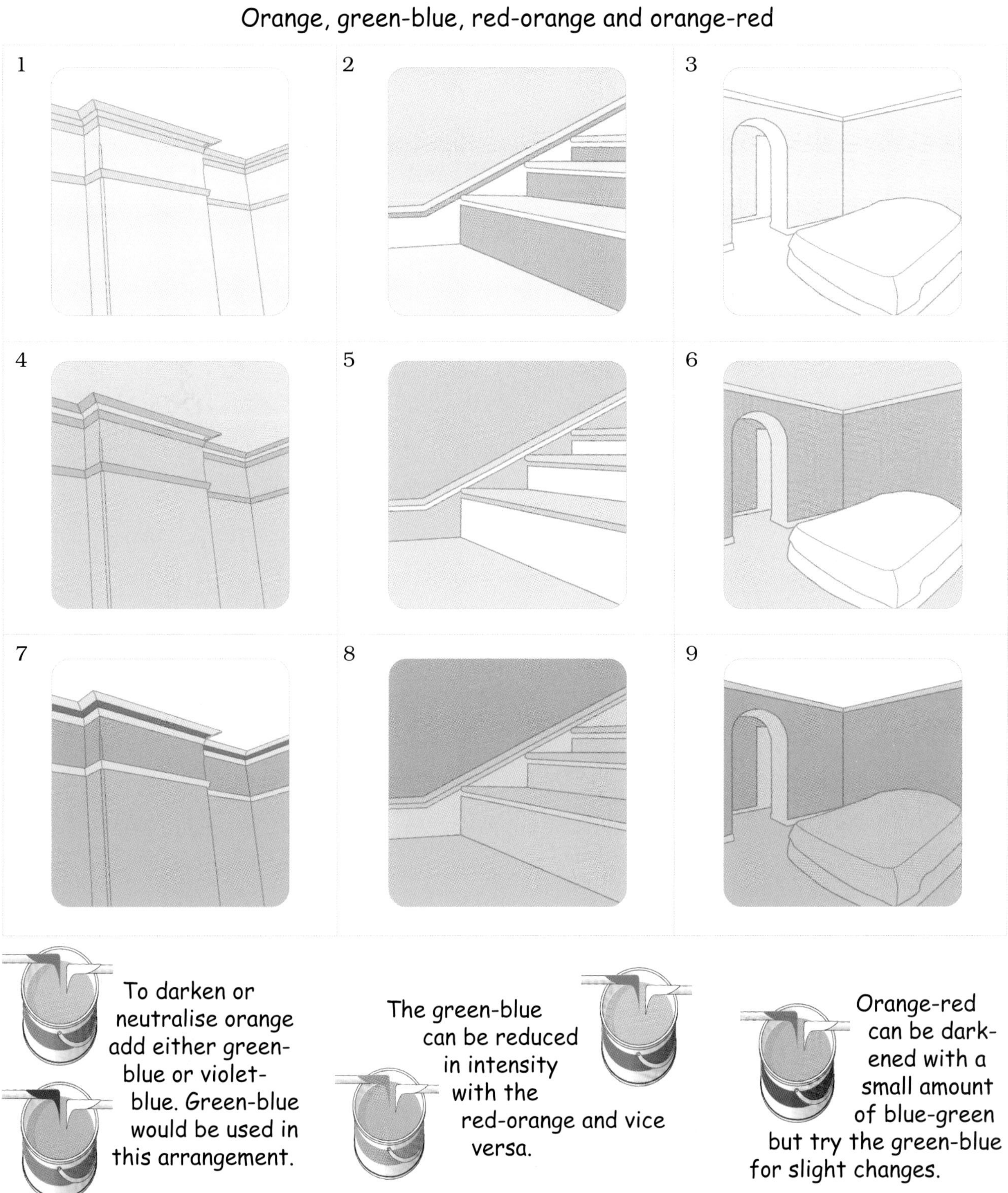

To darken or neutralise orange add either green-blue or violet-blue. Green-blue would be used in this arrangement.

The green-blue can be reduced in intensity with the red-orange and vice versa.

Orange-red can be darkened with a small amount of blue-green but try the green-blue for slight changes.

Although the color mixing information above shows the use of the mixing partner (together with white), you may choose to use the colors in an entirely different way.

The orange, for example can be employed unmixed in a very bright form. Or alternatively mixed with white only. The mixing partner only comes into its own when you need to darken, or more accurately, neutralise a particular color.

White may or may not then be added to the neutralised color.

Summary

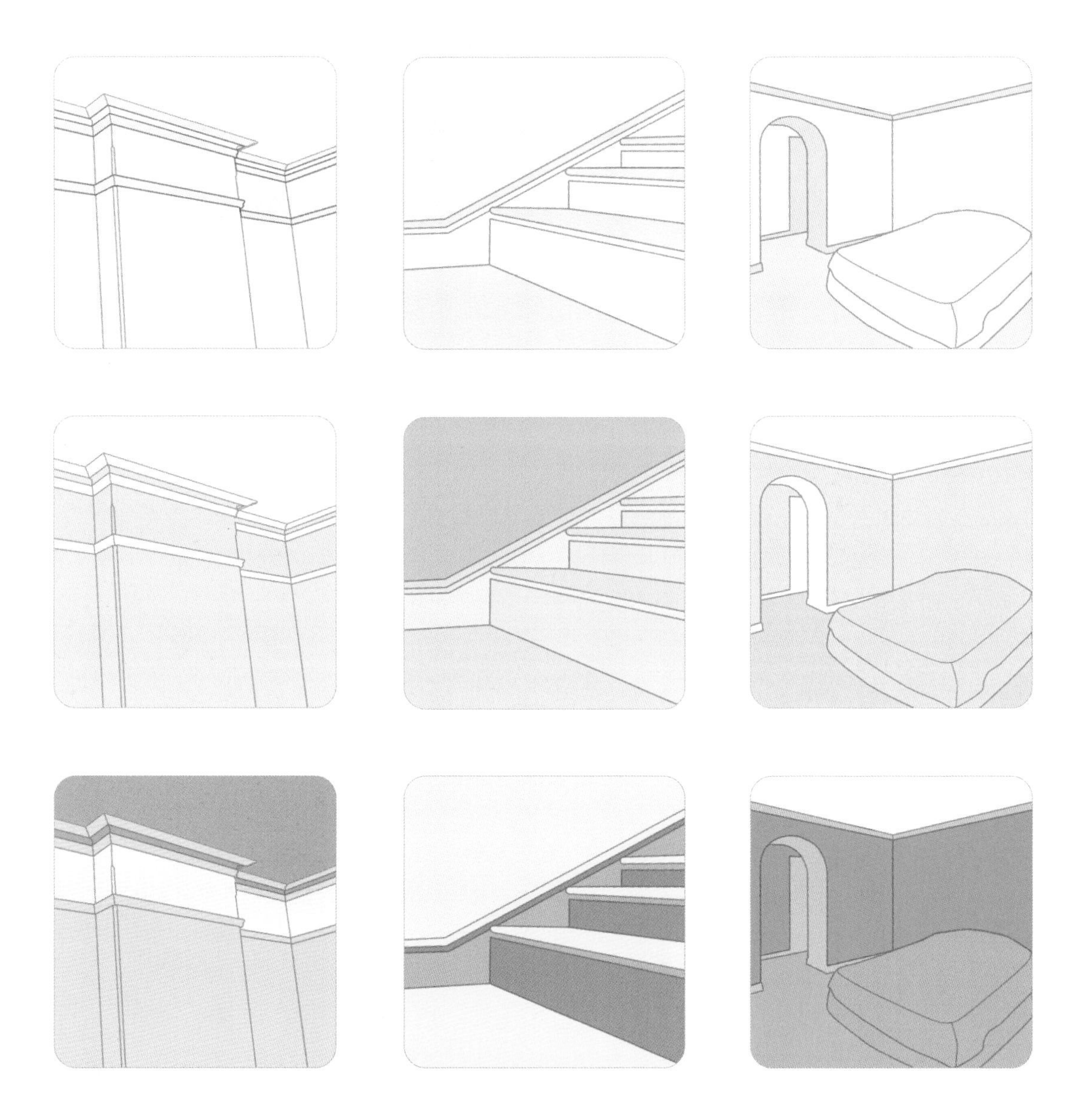

This approach can offer a wide range of interesting and potentially harmonious color schemes. The variety is almost endless.

However, as with all arrangements the colors need to be balanced carefully one against the other.

Two complementary pairs

Introduction

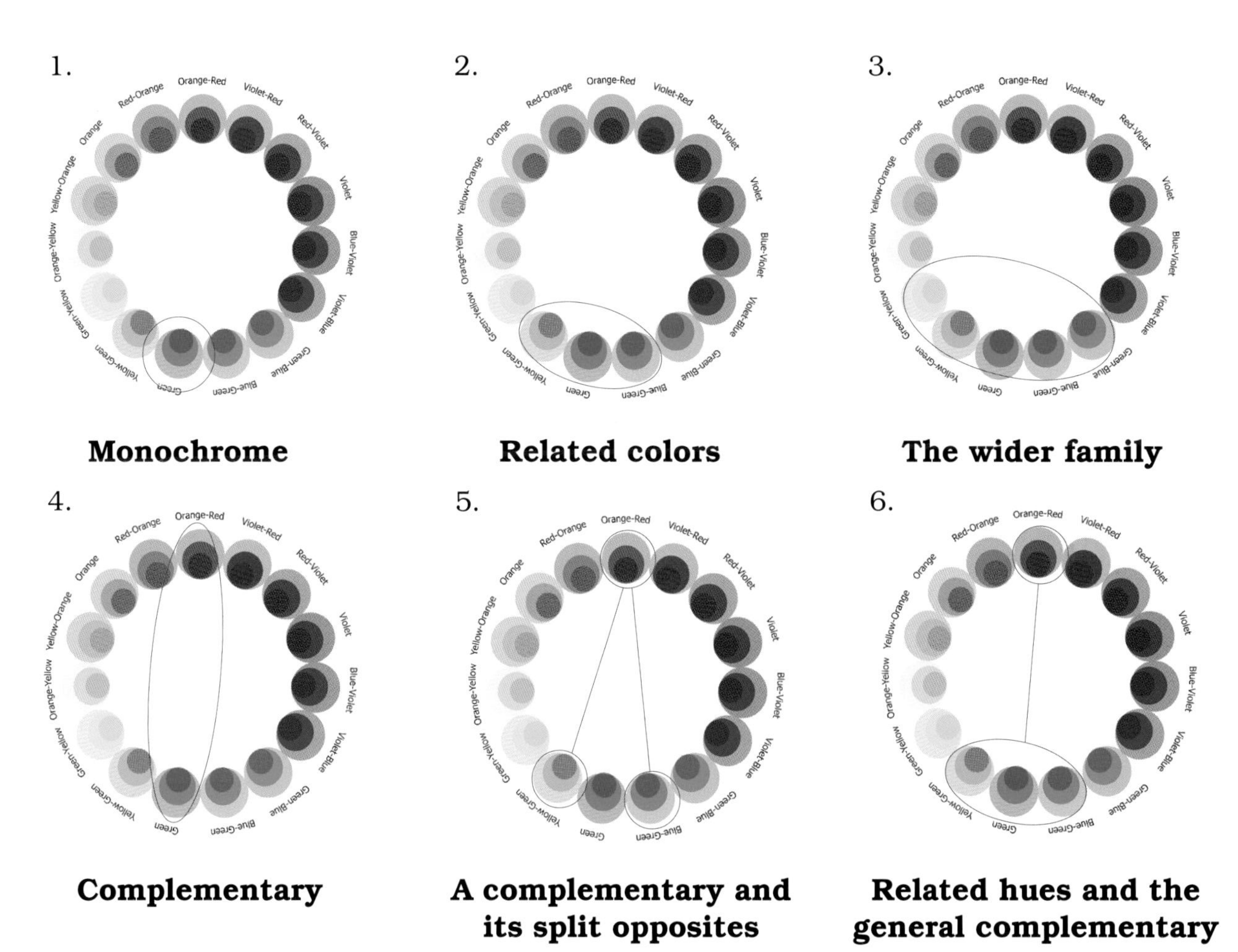

Monochrome | **Related colors** | **The wider family**

Complementary | **A complementary and its split opposites** | **Related hues and the general complementary**

As we have progressed through the different color arrangements they have become slightly more involved each time.

The additional colors which become available can allow for more variety and possible visual interest. However, the opportunities for awkward color arrangements are also increased.

The final suggestion is for an approach which offers the potential for color schemes based on much of the work of the Impressionist painters. Two sets of complementaries in use at the same time.

The potential is there for the most amazing and beautiful of color schemes but the possibility for things to go wrong also exists. Just take a little care if using the following suggestions.

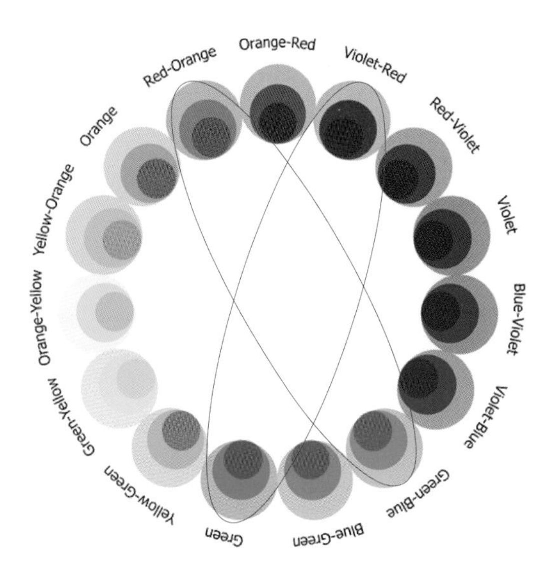

Two complementary pairs

Two complementary pairs

© Red Cover/Jon Bouchier

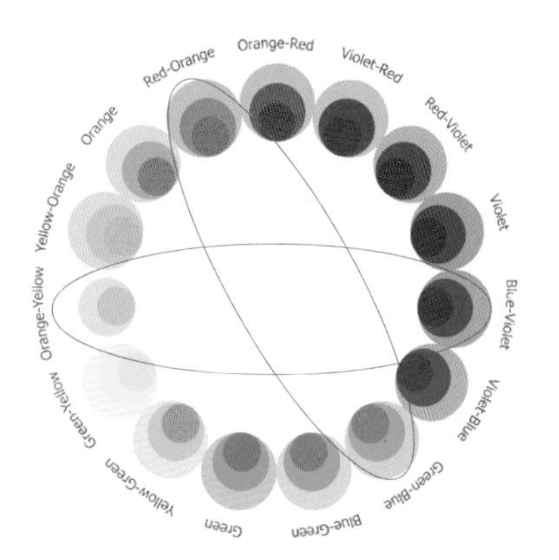

As darkened orange-yellows and red-oranges can be classified as 'browns', this combination is incredibly flexible, with many applications.

Few find fault with the colors of nature and they can certainly be an inspiration when it comes to deciding on a color scheme.

Subtle and unusual harmonies are available from these hues if the potentially strong contrast of complementary as well as the contrast of 'temperature' is modified.

If you wish to introduce contrast this arrangement at anywhere near full strength is a very effective way to draw attention. Very powerful contrasts are possible.

Two complementary pairs

Blue-violet, orange-yellow, green-blue and red-orange

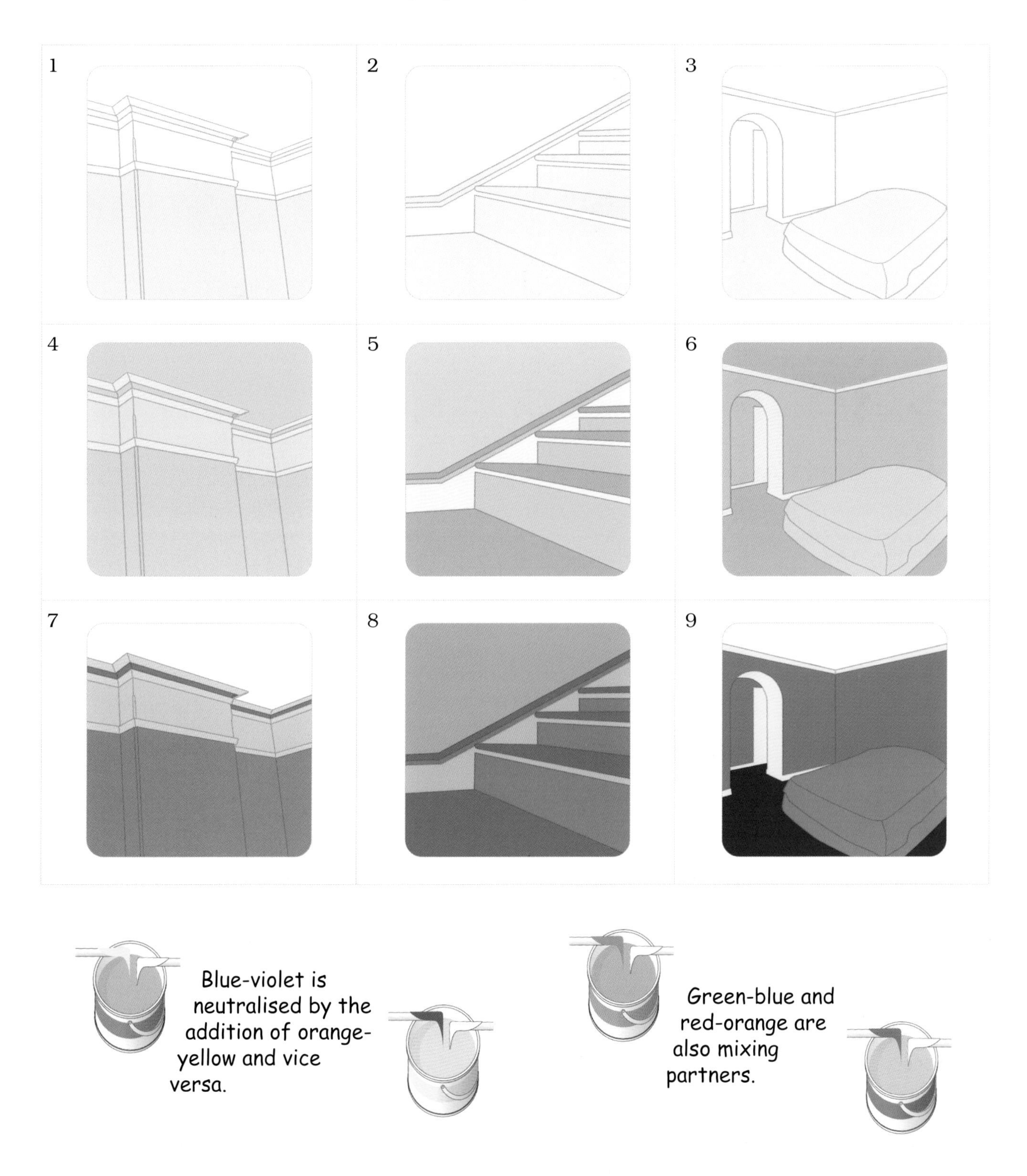

Use the color pairs to desaturate each other. This they will do very efficiently. Be careful when dulling the orange-yellow with the blue-violet as the yellow quickly turns to green.

Two complementary pairs

© Red Cover/Brian Harrison

The violet-red can add a touch of subtle sophistication when used with caution. Lighten, darken or use over small areas.

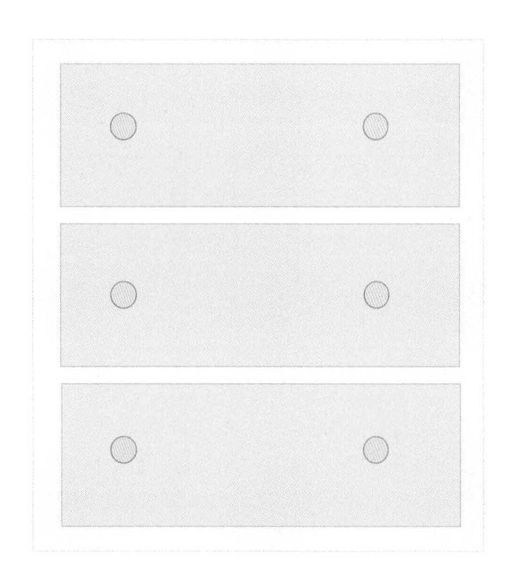

To give an idea of the versatility of this way of working, a small amount of red-orange added to a green-blue will dull it slightly.

This mix, lightened with white might be used on, say, the frame of a chest of drawers.

In my experience, these combinations are a lot easier to employ when all four are further reduced with white. You might find otherwise.

A little more red-orange and the green-blue will darken for perhaps the drawers themselves. A quick and easy way to produce a range of green-blues which can be harmonised with ease.

For a touch of contrast the drawer handles might be painted with the red-orange. If this is too bright you can of course darken it with a little green-blue or it can be made lighter.

Another piece of furniture could be painted with the other complementary pair or, alternatively, all four colors could be used together.

Two complementary pairs

Green-blue, red-orange, green and violet-red

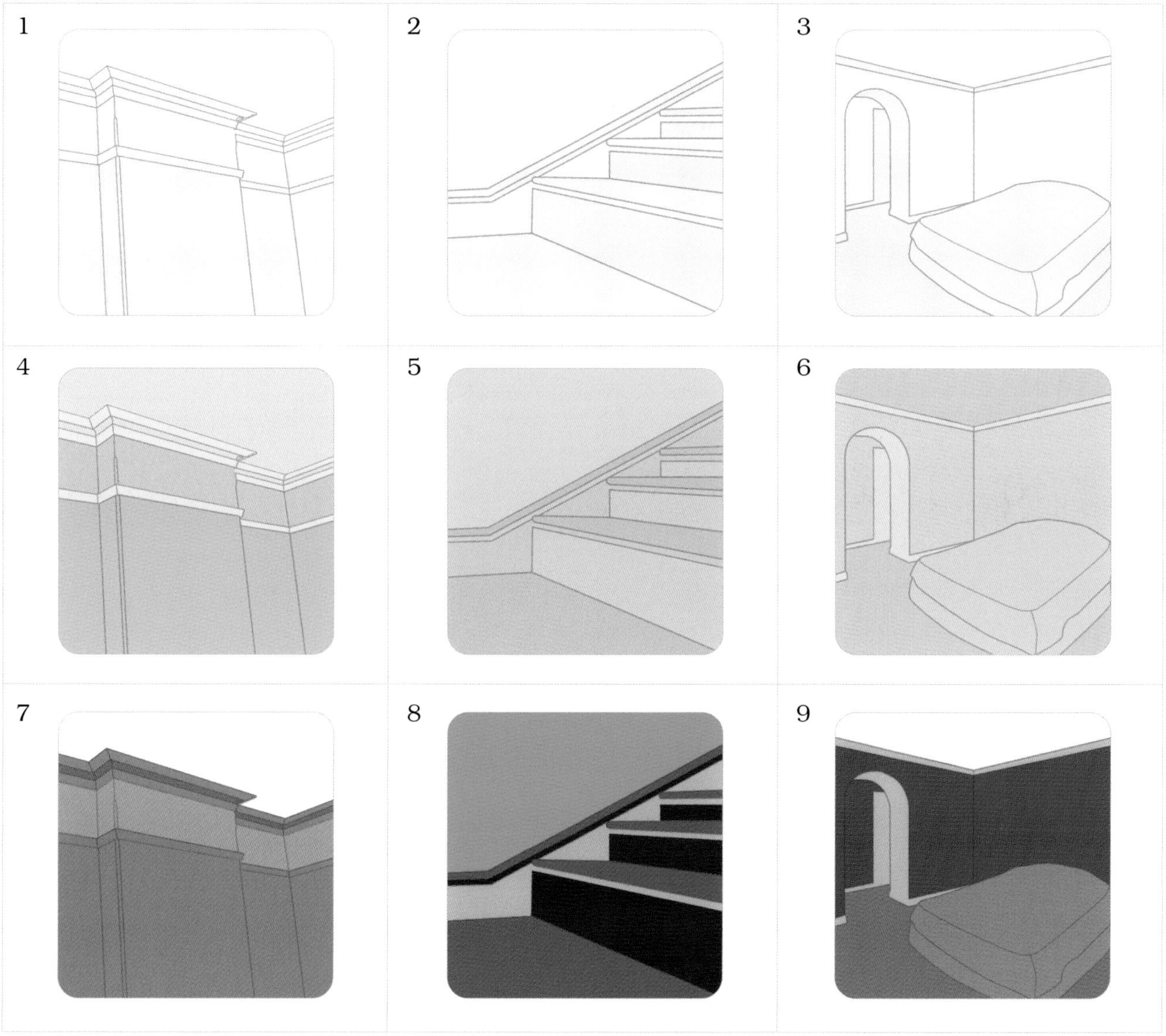

1 2 3

4 5 6

7 8 9

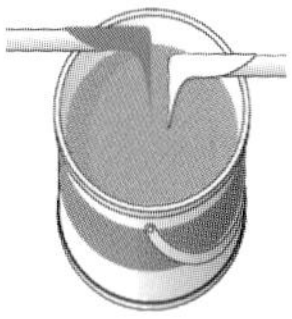

Green-blue and red-orange are a mixing pair. Once selected, they can be used to darken each other.

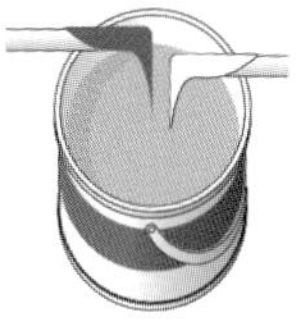

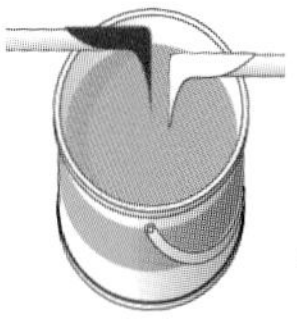

Green and violet-red are also partners. This approach to color mixing is quick, accurate and versatile.

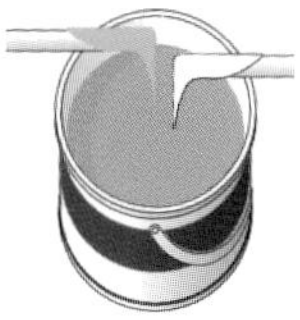

The green-blue and the red-orange will reduce the intensity of each other as will the green and violet-red. White will reduce this even further.

As soon as you start to work with the mixing partners you will see how easy and versatile this approach becomes. It also makes achieving color harmony very easy.

Two complementary pairs

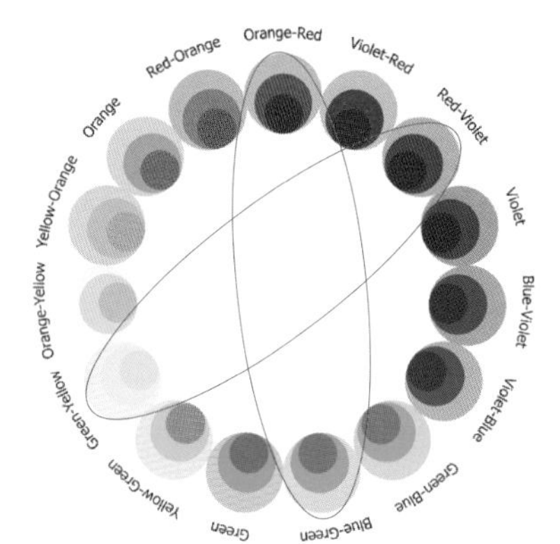

elizabethwhiting.com

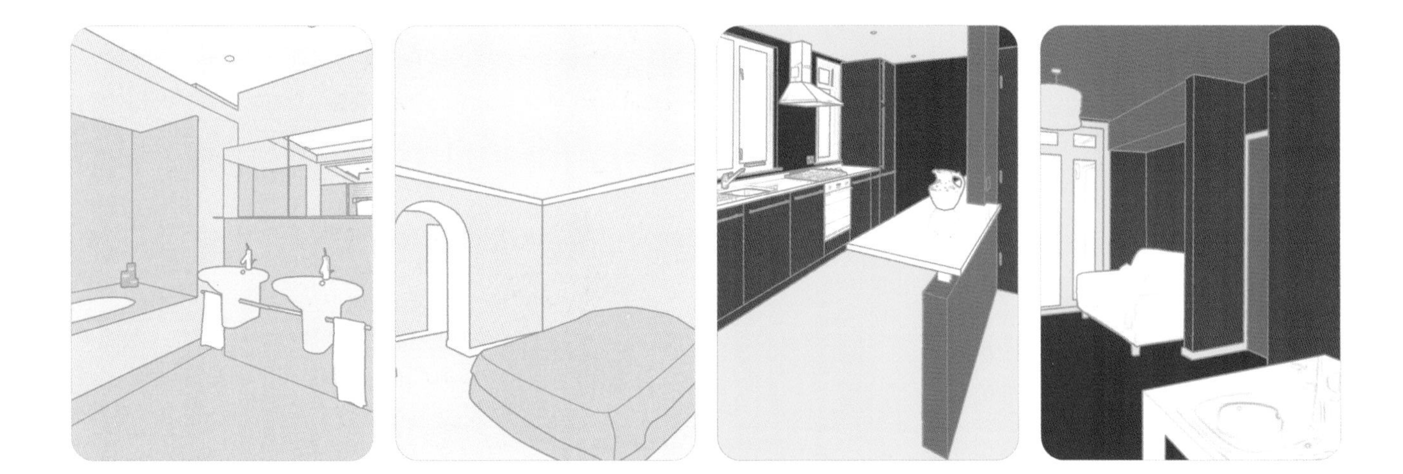

At or close to full strength (fully saturated), this foursome can take on a 'carnival' atmosphere.

When considerably reduced in intensity, especially when made much lighter, they can be harmonised with relative ease.

Two complementary pairs

Orange-red, blue-green, red-violet and green-yellow

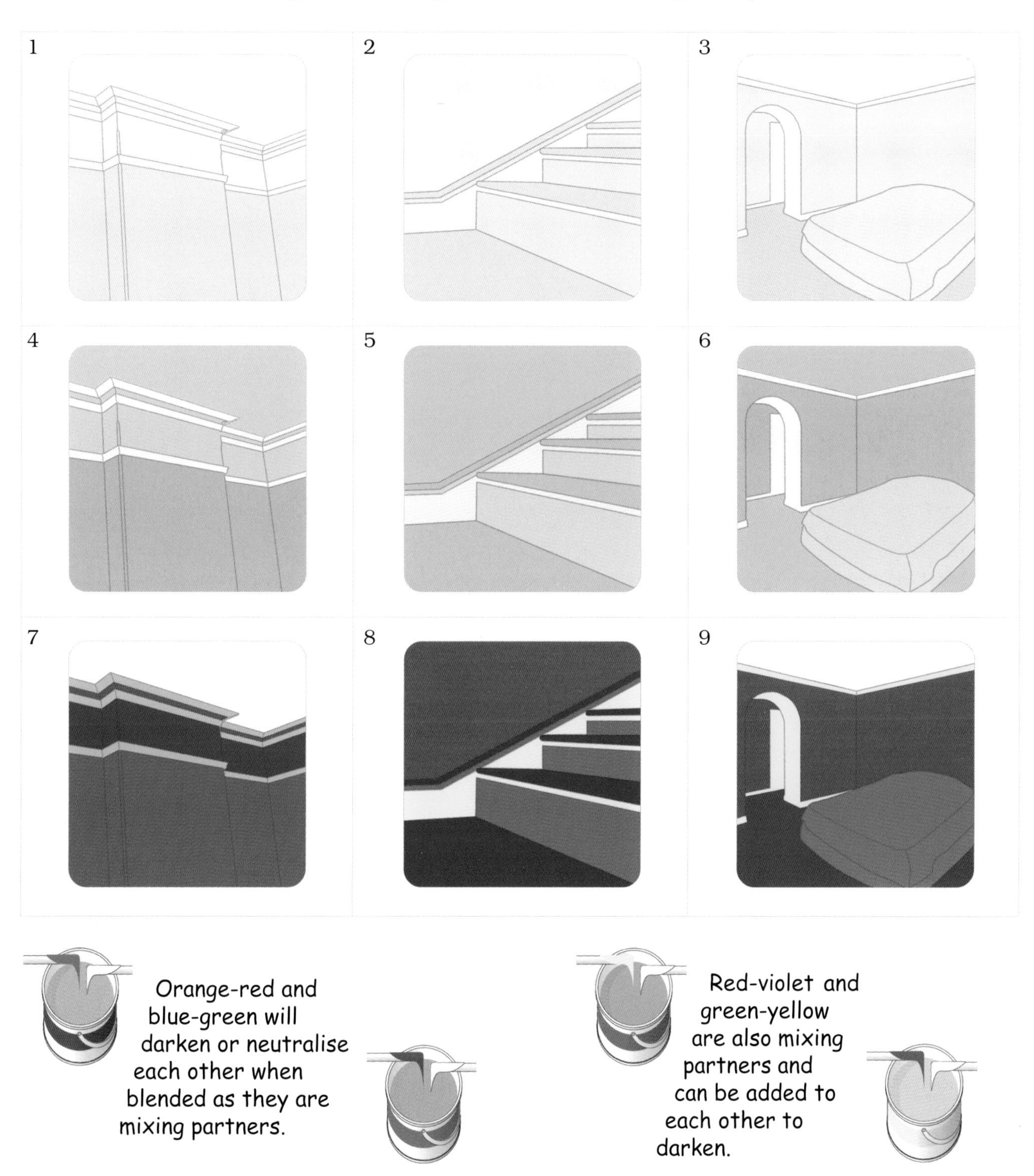

To reduce intensity add white and/or the mixing partner. Whenever you come across reference to the addition of white on these pages, take it to mean white paint.

The other means of creating a lighter version of a hue is to apply it thinly over a white background. This approach is often used by the artist but is not practical in decorating.

Two complementary pairs

© Red Cover/Chris Drake

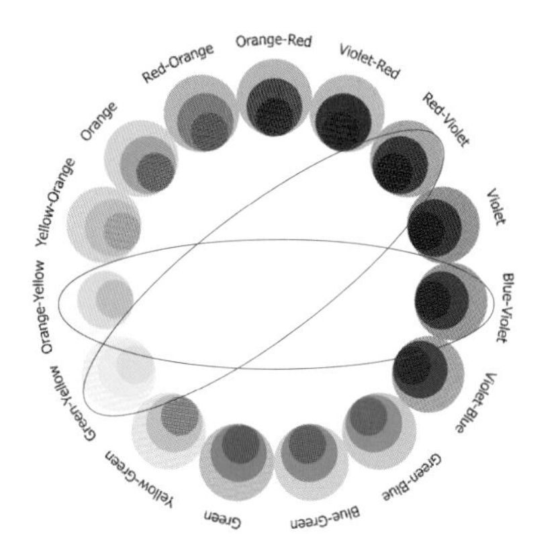

A very versatile arrangement offering an almost endless range of contrasts and harmonies.

This is basically a violet/yellow combination, with variety added by the use of two versions of each color. A simple approach which can give very pleasing results.

If the color arrangement selected for a room is repeated in the furnishings some very subtle harmonies can be achieved.

Strong contrasts are set up when these hues are used at anywhere near full strength.

They usually require subduing with the mixing partner and/or white.

Two complementary pairs

Red-violet, green-yellow, blue-violet and orange-yellow

1

2

3

4

5

6

7

8

9

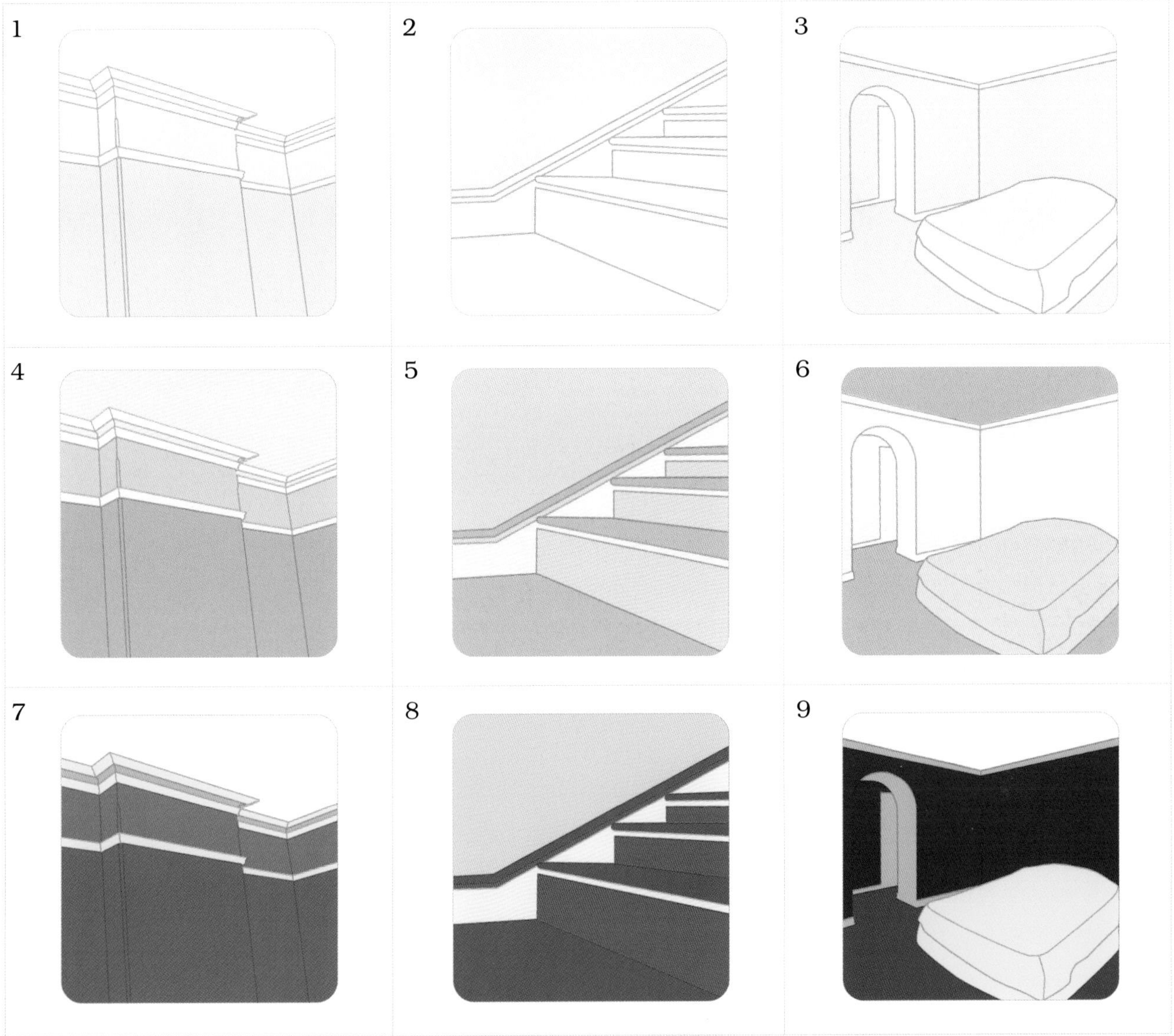

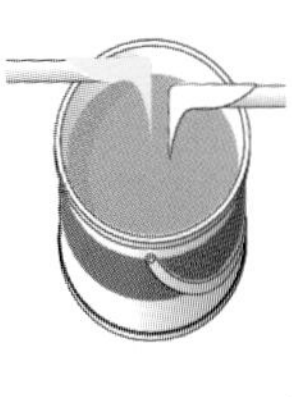

Red-violet and green-yellow are mixing partners and will darken or neutralise each other very successfully.

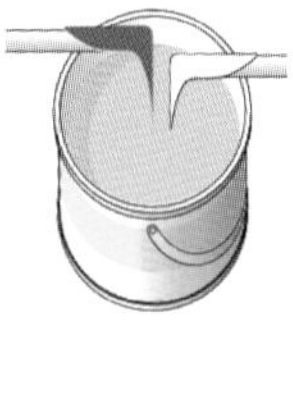

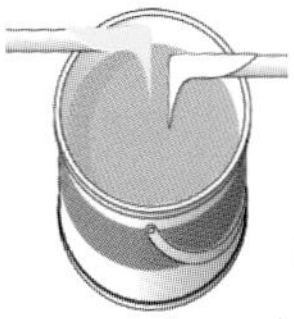

Blue-violet and orange-yellow are also mixing partners. Be careful when adding the blue-violet to orange-yellow as the mix can very soon turn green. A touch of red will remove this greenness.

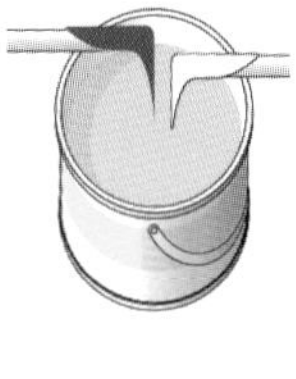

The above mixing partners are also optical pairs. Therefore they will not only darken or dull each other in mixes very effectively but will enhance each other visually when applied with care. At full strength such enhancement can lead to overpowering contrasts.

Two complementary pairs

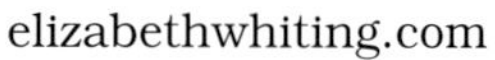
elizabethwhiting.com

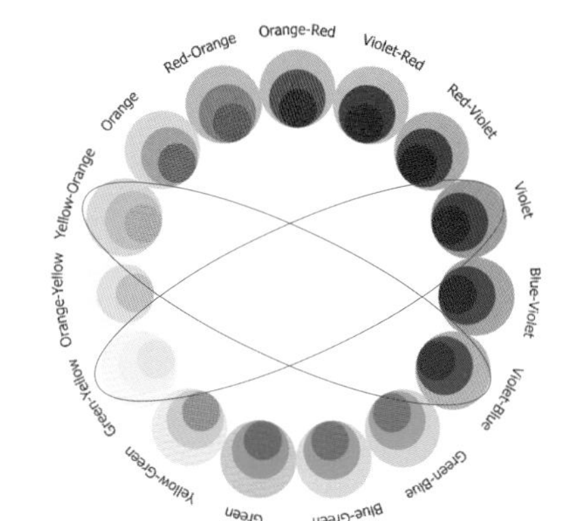

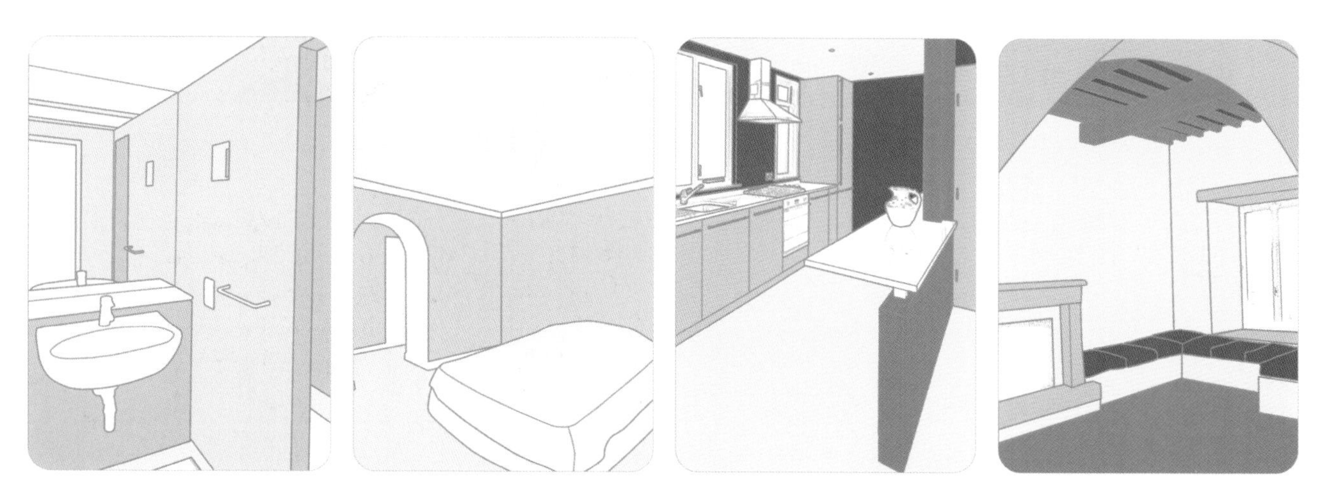

If any of these four hues are used at or near full strength they can quickly dominate and cause discord. This is particularly the case with green-yellow which usually needs to be used in a very light form. When reduced in intensity by one means or the other this foursome can give rise to some very attractive color arrangements.

Two complementary pairs

Violet, green-yellow, violet-blue and yellow-orange

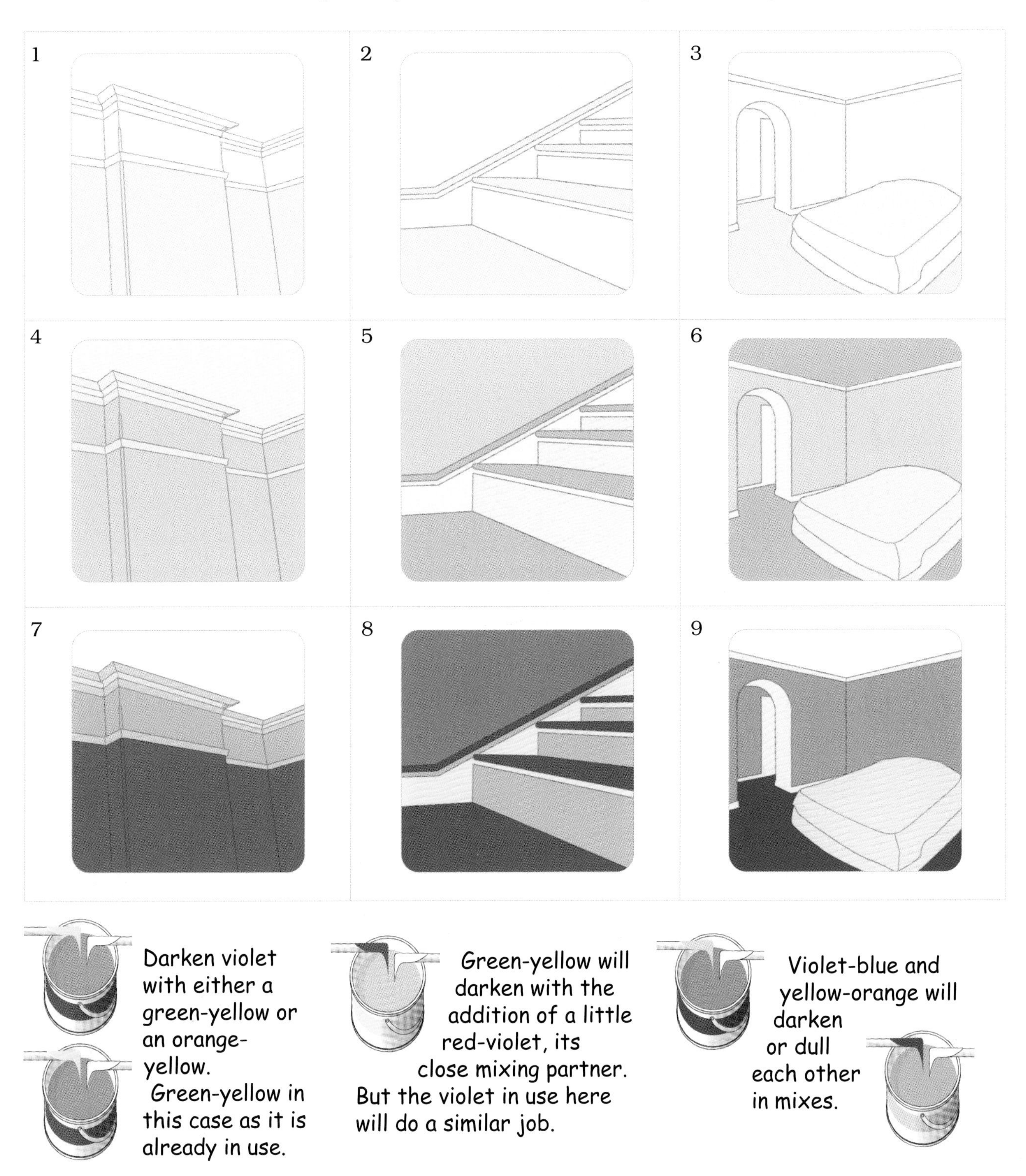

As with all mixing partners, they will darken or neutralise each other. As more of one is added to the other the mix will move towards gray.

For example, either yellow will darken the violet, but if enough is added the mix will become a type of gray. These grays are known as 'colored grays' and are very useful.

Two complementary pairs

© Red Cover/Mark Bolton

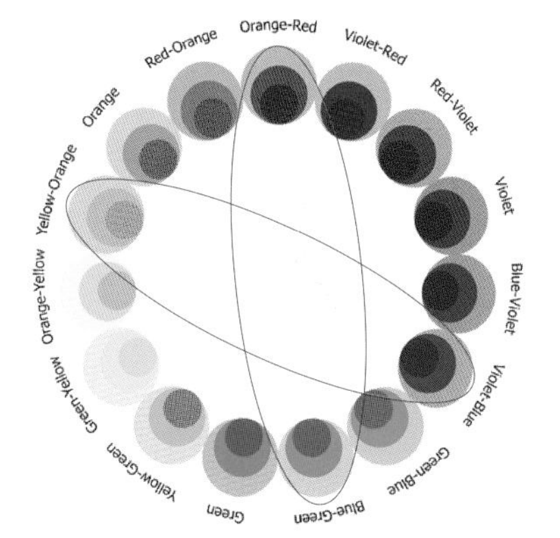

Strong contrasts when used at strength but very balanced harmonies are also available.

At or anywhere near full strength these hues will set up strong contrasts at the possible expense of color harmony. Used with plenty of white added, or the mixing partner and white, they can provide some very unusual and versatile combinations.

This particular combination is worth exploring in any form of color work, whether on the walls, ceilings and floor or accessories such as cushions and cupboards etc.

Very pale walls and strongly colored highlights can look particularly good together.

Two complementary pairs

Violet-blue, yellow-orange, blue-green and orange-red

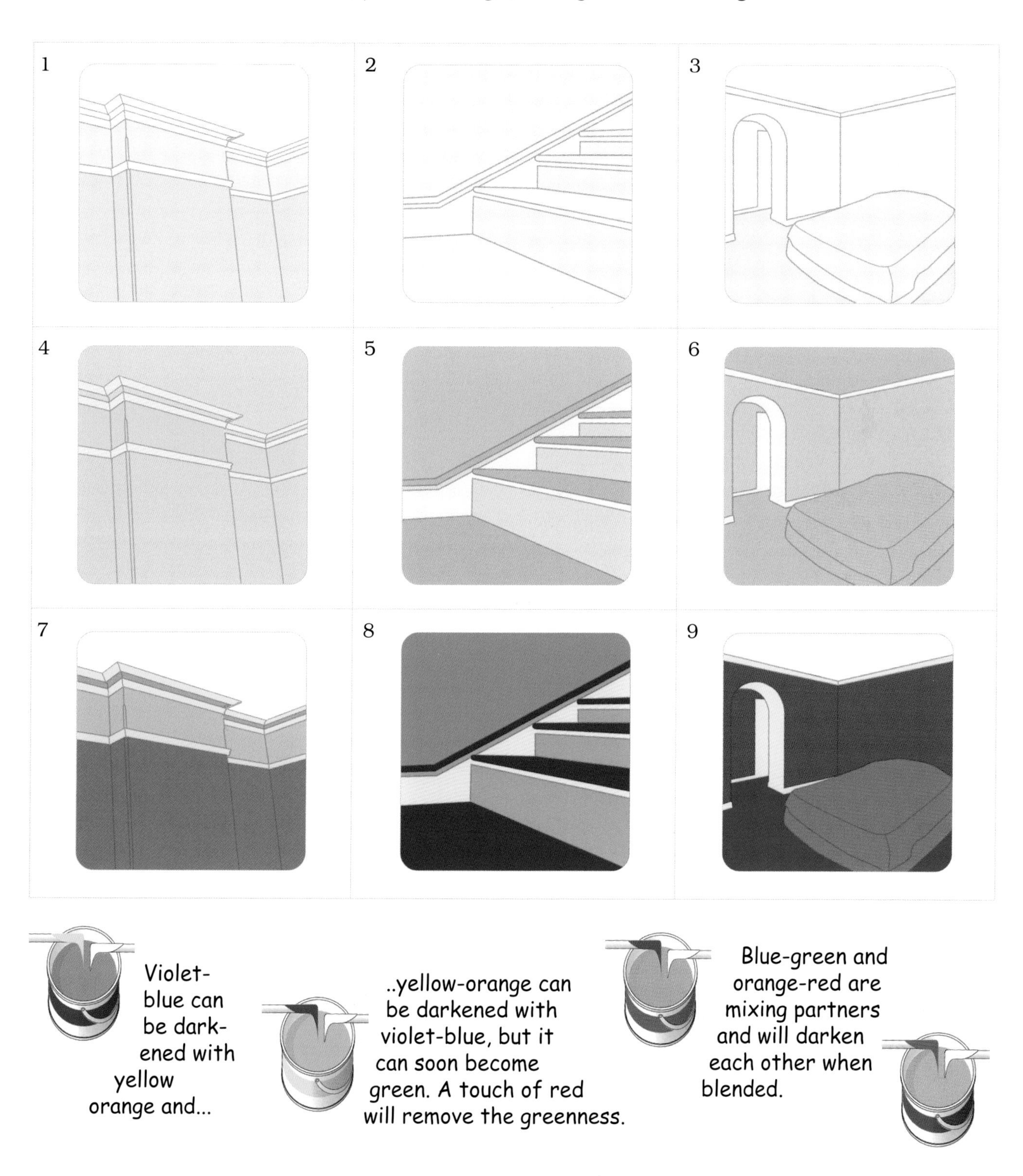

Yellows and yellow-orange are the most difficult colors to darken as they tend to become green rather quickly.

This is because our eyes are very sensitive to green and we can detect even the slightest trace of it.

The complementary pairs

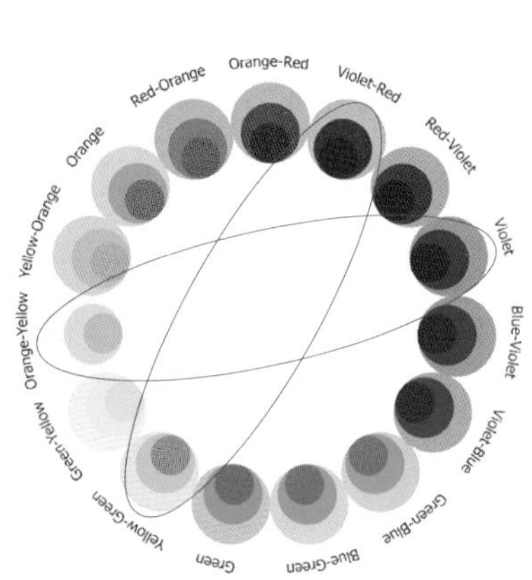

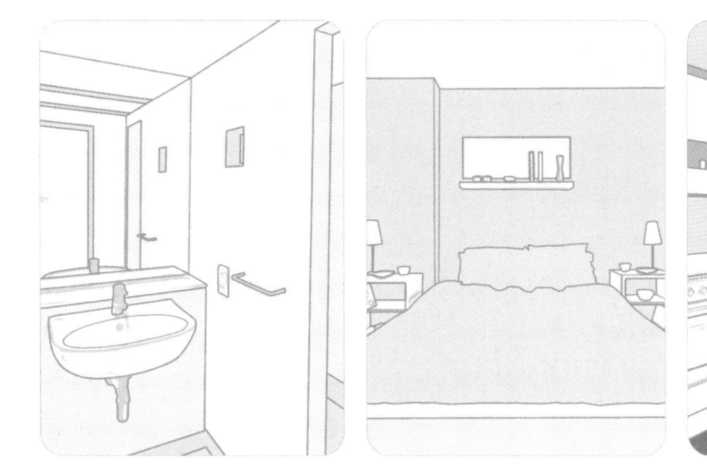

These pairings can give unusual harmonies but the orange-yellow tends to dominate unless checked.

It might be better to add a lot of white to it or first to darken it slightly with violet before adding to white.

As with all complementary pairs they can be encouraged to enhance each other and contribute towards color harmony. This will be helped if the pairing are placed alongside each other, the violet-red with the yellow-green and the violet with the orange-yellow.

The complementary pairs

Violet-red, yellow-green, violet and orange-yellow

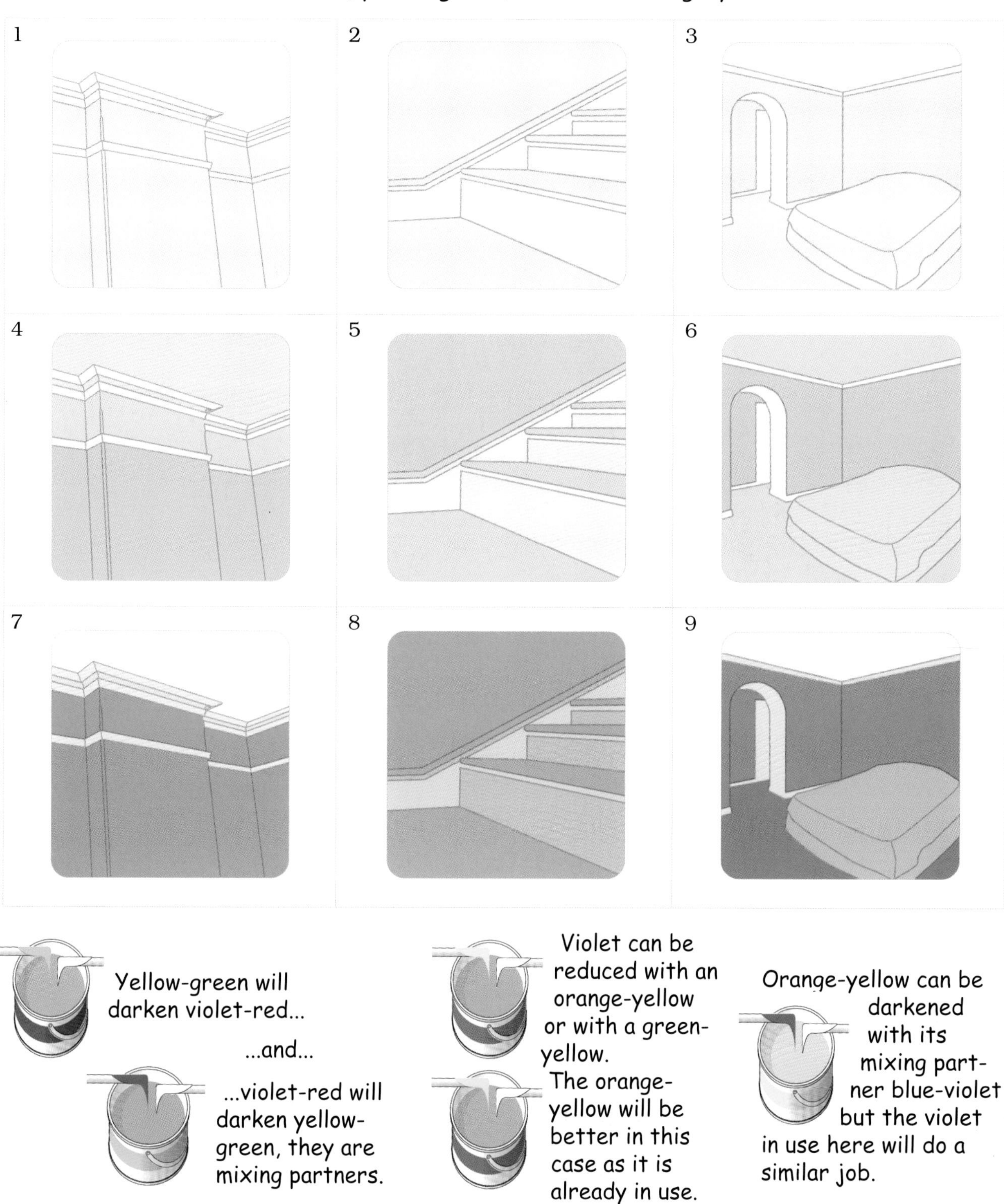

Use either type of yellow to darken the violet. There will be slight differences depending on the yellow that you use, but these will be virtually unnoticeable. The mixes shown above are the ideal starting points if you wish to darken the basic hues. However, you might prefer to use them unmixed at full strength, or made lighter by the addition of white.

White, gray, black & tints in the background

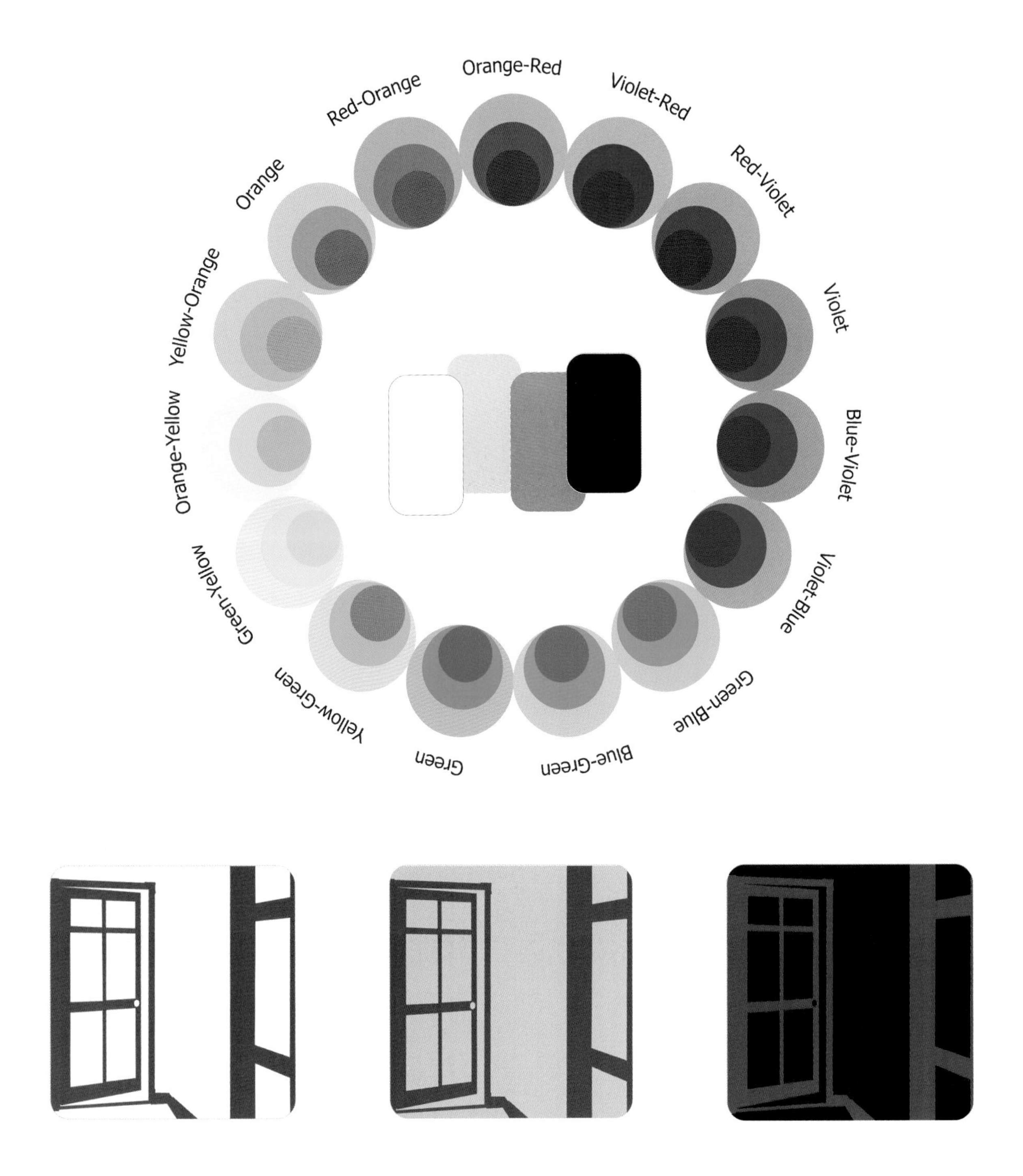

The addition of white, gray or black to an arrangement will add a further dimension and can help to create additional harmonies.

Indeed, colors which might otherwise be difficult to harmonise can often be made workable this way.

As you will see, your knowledge of the effects of the after-image will be a great help in forecasting the results of incorporating white, gray or black into your work.

If you skipped that section it will pay to take another look. It is all quite simple really.

White, gray, black & tints in the background

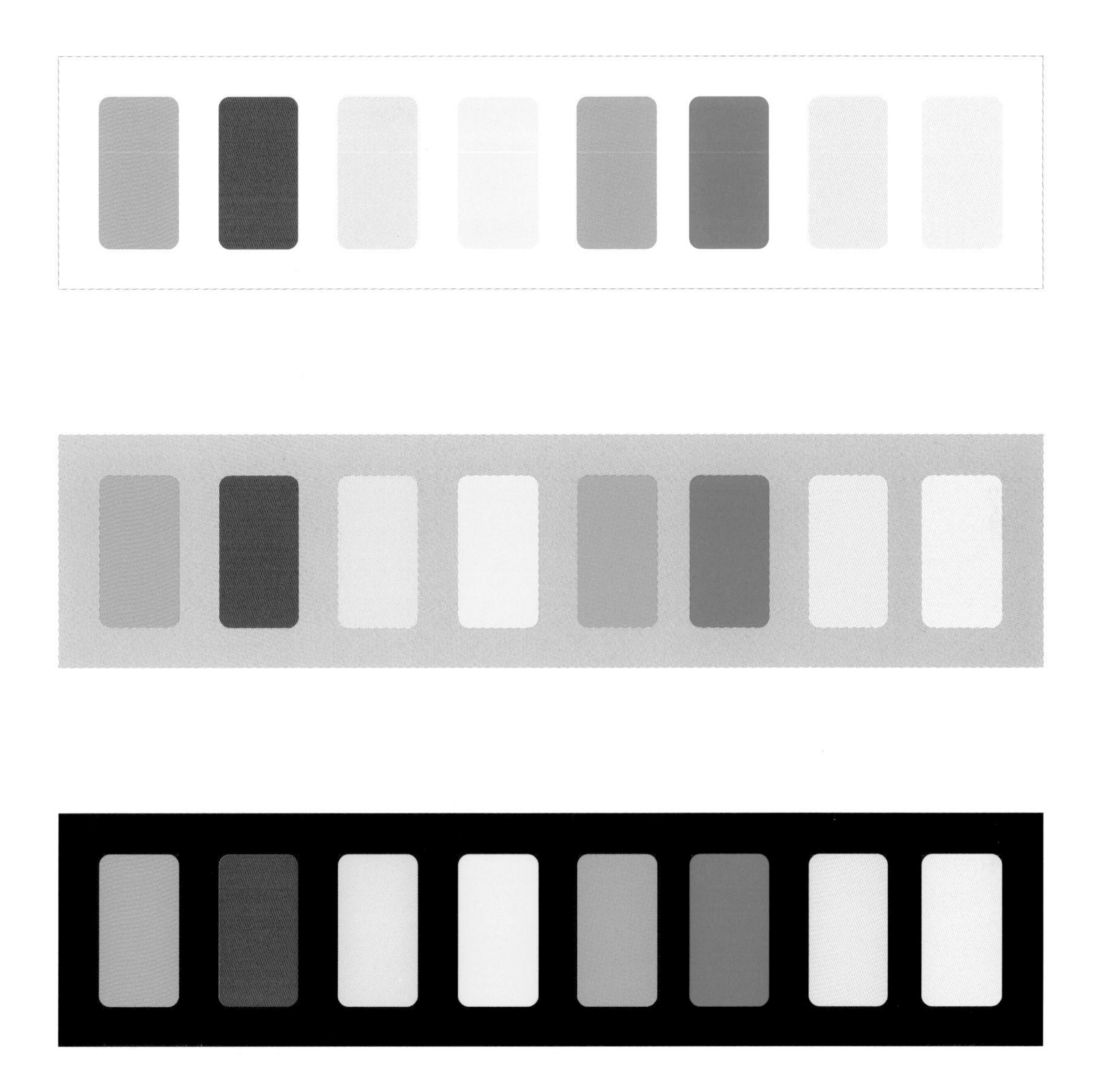

Surrounding a hue with white tends to darken it and reduce its brilliancy. This is particularly noticeable with the light, otherwise bright hues such as yellow.

Gray has a calming, neutralising effect, particularly when combined with the brighter hues. The use of gray will reduce contrast, often aiding harmony.

Black, (or possibly a mixed dark), surrounding a hue causes it to appear richer, almost glowing. This is particularly so with red. The two colors have often been used together to give added vibrancy to each other.

The bright red/black combination should be used sparingly in a room unless you are determined to draw attention, which could come from miles around.

White

Although white used over an area, rather than in line form, will darken and reduce the brilliancy of other colors, it can certainly add a great deal of freshness.

The type of white employed will bring its own range of influences. Some are very 'cold' and bright whilst others might be a little 'warmer', slightly creamy. The density of the white will also have its influence when it comes to color mixing. It pays to settle on a good quality white, which covers well, and use it throughout.

This will also be a definite help when it comes to color mixing.

Gray

The same hues have been repeated in the centre of the above swatches. Notice how the colors intensify (due to after-image), as the gray background becomes darker.

Gray has a soft, calming effect on all colors, whether used as a surround or as a separator. The effect will vary depending on the intensity of the gray.

Very pale grays will bring a dark after-image to the scene (light and dark being complementaries). Whilst a dark gray will throw a light after-image over other colors. (See page 97).

Much, of course, will depend on the area of gray involved.

The after-image from small 'touches' of gray will hardly influence neighbouring colors. (After images remain the same size as the originating color).

Surrounding a color with a much larger area of gray will have a greater effect.

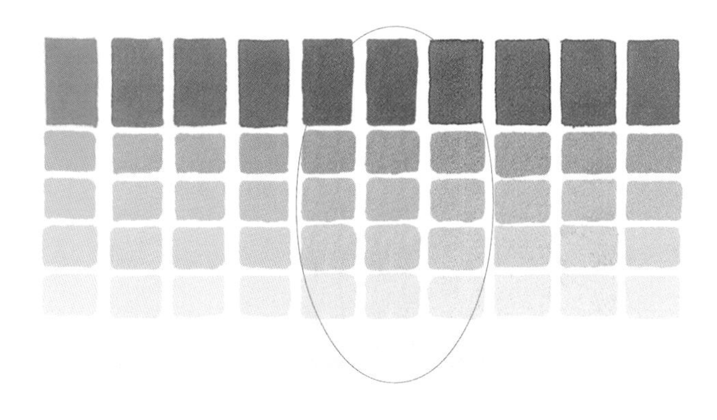

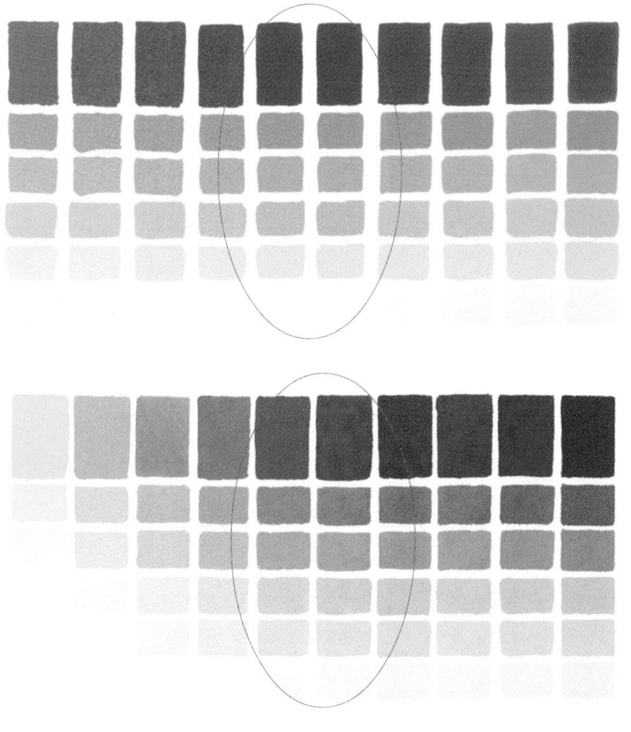

'Colored grays' will emerge around the centre of the range whenever a complementary pair (also mixing partners) are combined.

This is because each will have absorbed most of the other's color. When further reduced with white they can give some very subtle tints.

A vast range of colored grays can be mixed from the complementary pairings (also mixing partners), red/green, yellow/violet and blue/orange etc. This factor opens up enormous possibilities when working with the complementaries and at the same time seeking color harmony. If you are working with blue and orange, for example, the ideal gray to use will come from a mix of those same two colors.

With the addition or otherwise of white, such colored grays will give a very wide range of values.

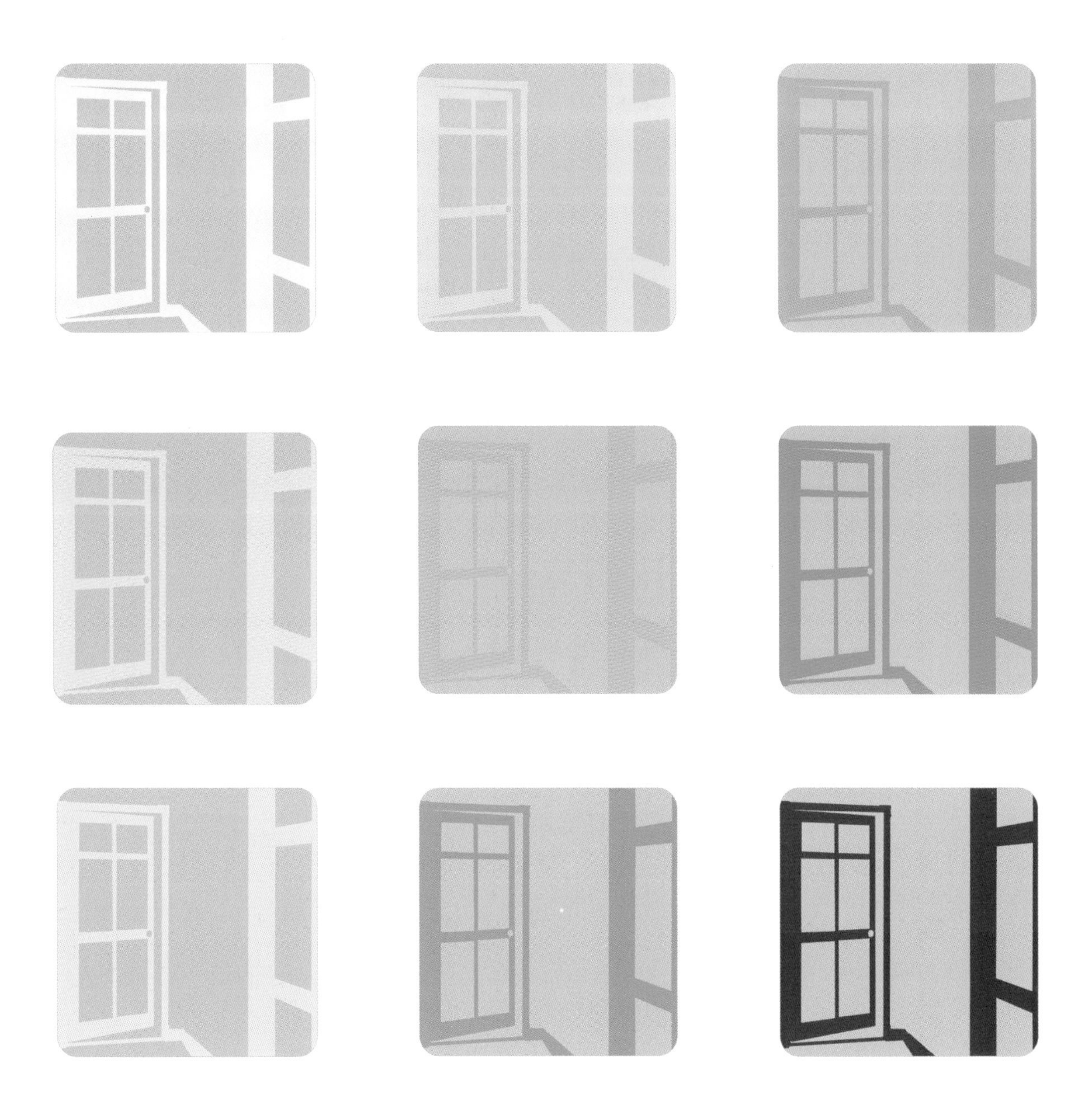

The neutralising effect of gray is particularly noticeable on the brighter, stronger colors.

By reducing contrast, otherwise discordant hues can be brought into line and persuaded to harmonise. Used with skill, 'colored grays' (from the complementaries), can have a vital role to play.

They can certainly enhance a room dramatically. The relationship between colored grays and the two colors from which they emerge is vital where color harmony is sought.

For this reason they are best mixed where possible.

Black

Contrast can be heightened by the use of black. Whereas white and gray tend to blend into a room with ease, black becomes a very definite additional color in its own right and must be treated accordingly,

A black surround (and to a lesser extent) a black edge or outline) will tend to enrich red, make yellow appear 'cooler' and blue almost luminous.

Black will make these and all other hues seem particularly brilliant.

The area of black involved will have a direct influence on the result. The more that a hue is surrounded in area the greater the effect of after-image thrown by the black. Black outlines will have less of an effect.

The Irish playwright Brendan Behan once offered to decorate a friends house whilst he took a week long break. Brendan, with several of his drinking cronies, painted the entire house black, walls, ceilings and probably floors. This might be overdoing it somewhat.

Tints

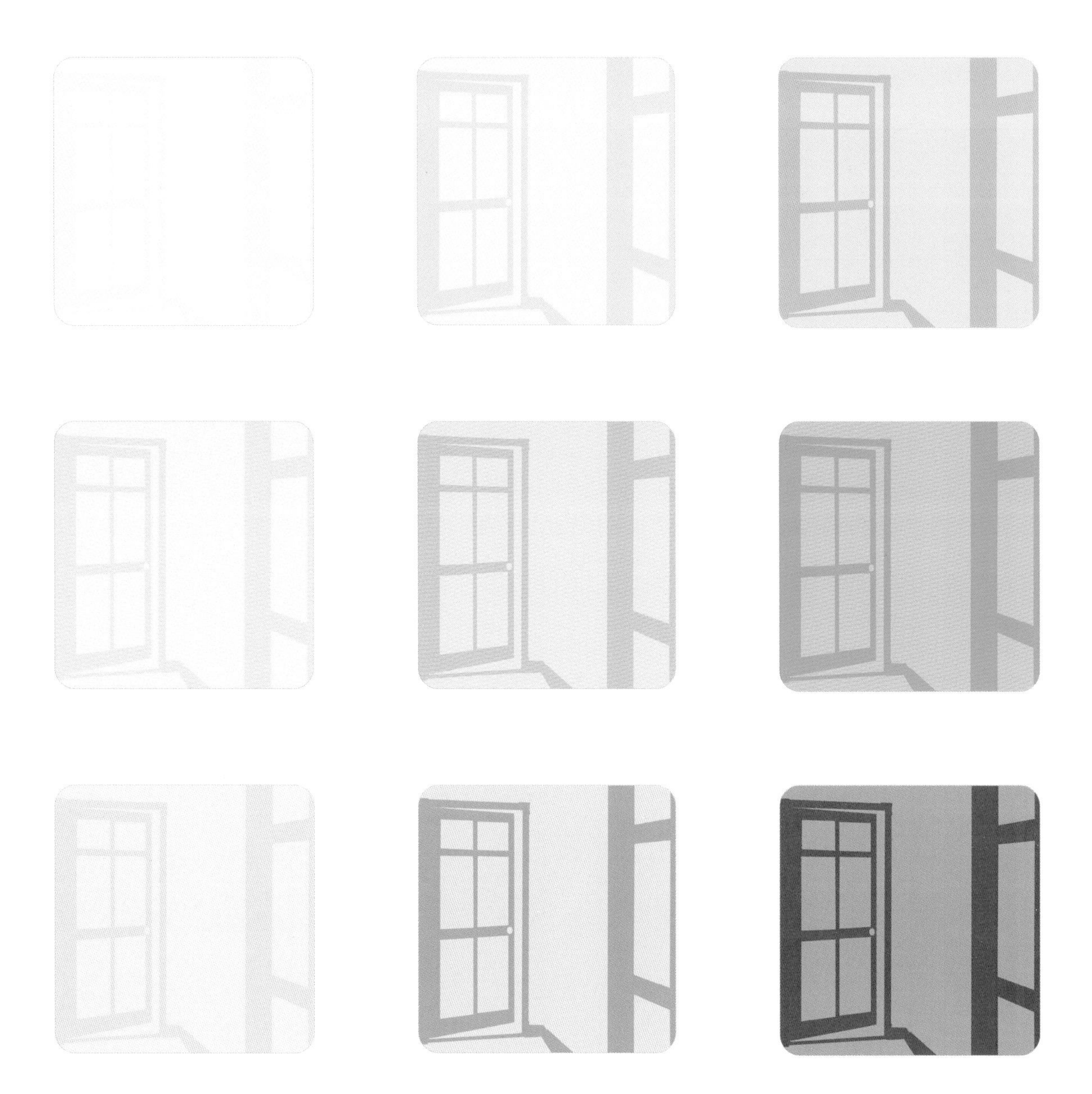

As an alternative to the use of black, white or gray, the tint (a lightened version), of one of the colors can be used in the background.

When used in this fashion, the tint acts almost as a 'go between', reducing color contrast and very often aiding color harmony. It is also another example of the fact that when colors in an arrangement have something in common, they are on the way to color harmony for many people.

White, gray, black & tints in the background

A comparison of the varying backgrounds that we have been discussing will be of value. The foreground colors are the same in each column. The difference can be quite dramatic.

The contrast of temperature

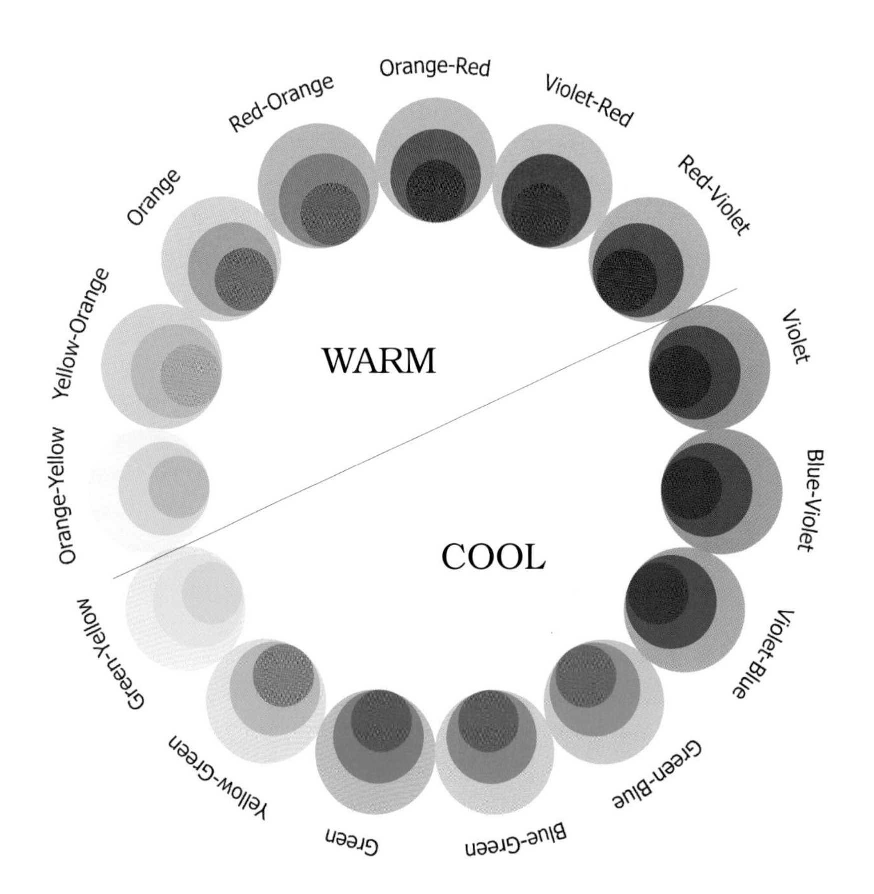

As a general guide the color wheel can be divided into two parts, warm and cool.

Colors are frequently described as being of a certain temperature, whether hot, warm, cool or cold.

Colors associated with fire and heat; reds, oranges and yellows, are often described as being warm or hot while the blues and greens of ice and water are thought of as being cool.

As a general guide the conventional color wheel is divided into two parts, warm and cool.

This can only be a rough guide as the final 'temperature' of a color is largely decided by the way in which it contrasts with others.

A fairly straightforward contrast to use, it can either be drawn on as the principal contrast or become an element of the color arrangement almost by default.

Whenever a complementary pair is used, for example, a certain contrast of temperature is inevitable.

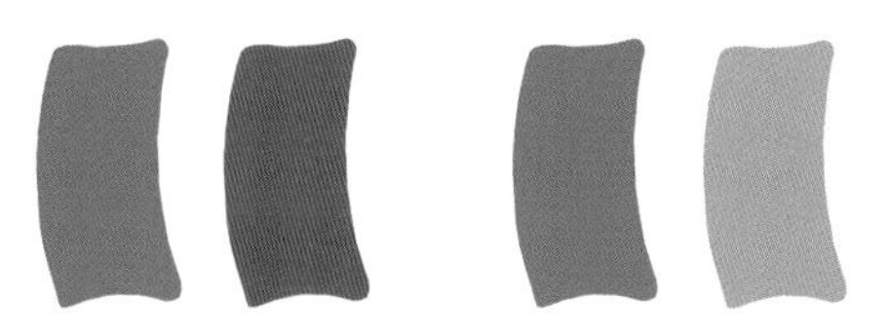

A mid blue can appear decidedly 'chilly' when set against an orange-red but takes on a relatively 'warm' appearance when it is compared to a greenish blue, particularly if the latter has a little white added.

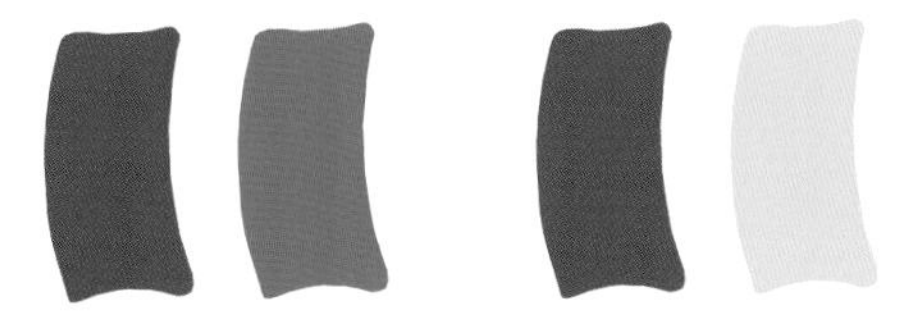

Ultramarine, a blue leaning towards violet, seems slightly 'warm' against green but 'cool' when contrasted with orange-yellow. So it can be both warm and cool.

The contrast of temperature

The red-violet can be shifted from 'warm' to 'cool' through the choice of background color.

I have placed the above in a random fashion so that you can decide for yourself how the central color is being moved.

Likewise, a greenish-yellow can be moved from 'warm' to rather 'cool' when contrasted with certain background colors.

It is rather limiting to describe colors as being either warm or cool as so much depends on comparison.

1.

2.

1. The addition of white will 'cool' a color.

2. Darkening will also tend to make it appear 'cooler'. The orange 'darkened' with blue, its mixing partner, takes on a far 'cooler' appearance as it become progressively darker.

Although we can divide the color wheel into two as a general guide to 'warm' and 'cool' colors, such guidance can only ever be of limited use as so much depends on the contrast of one color to another.

Temperature and depth

Visual interest can be added to a room through the manipulation of the contrast of temperature. An arrangement which is entirely 'warm' or entirely 'cool' can be rather bland. By contrasting 'cool' and 'warm' a room can be brought to life and have much greater impact.

The contrast of temperature can be of considerable help in giving the illusion of depth.

Blue, which is considered to be a 'cool' color, is synonymous with distance and will appear to recede partly due to our association of it with distant scenery, hills and mountains etc.

In addition to this factor, our eyes actually change focus slightly when we look at blue.

'Cool' colors such as blue recede visually and 'warm' colors appear to advance.

By using 'warmer' hues in the foreground (by the entrance to a room perhaps) and 'cooler' colors in the distance, a feeling of great depth can be created.

The effect of the edge

The way that the paint is applied at the edges of an area influences our perception of color and therefore has a bearing on whether colors harmonise or perhaps contrast.

In the above illustrations the paint was applied thinly and brushed out well at the edges. This technique can give a glowing, almost atmospheric effect, particularly when complementaries are involved.

When a complementary pair such as orange-red and blue-green (2nd from left) are juxtaposed in this fashion, they react at the 'join' in much the same way as light behaves on velvet. An intense visual reaction is set up as the after-image from one color is transferred to the other. The effect takes place over a much longer joint outline than it would had the outlines been straight. In much the same way that a zig zag line becomes a lot longer when stretched out. Like velvet, such edges can appear very rich in color.

Although this approach has few applications in conventional decorating, it is certainly worth knowing about as it can have an influence when fabrics are involved.

In stark contrast to the approach illustrated at the top of the page, here the colors are flatly applied and touch at sharply formed edges.

This format highlights the interaction between colors, each affecting the perception of its neighbour. This is particularly noticeable where a dark color butts against a lighter color, causing the edge of the lighter color to appear even paler.

The effect of the edge

Yet another approach has been taken in the above illustration. The same flat, evenly applied colors are separated by thin white lines.

Each color is independent of and barely affected by its neighbour.

Although the areas of color do not influence each other directly through after-image, the use of white can enhance contrast between colors. The way that one color can affect another at its edge has a definite part to play in both color harmony and color contrast.

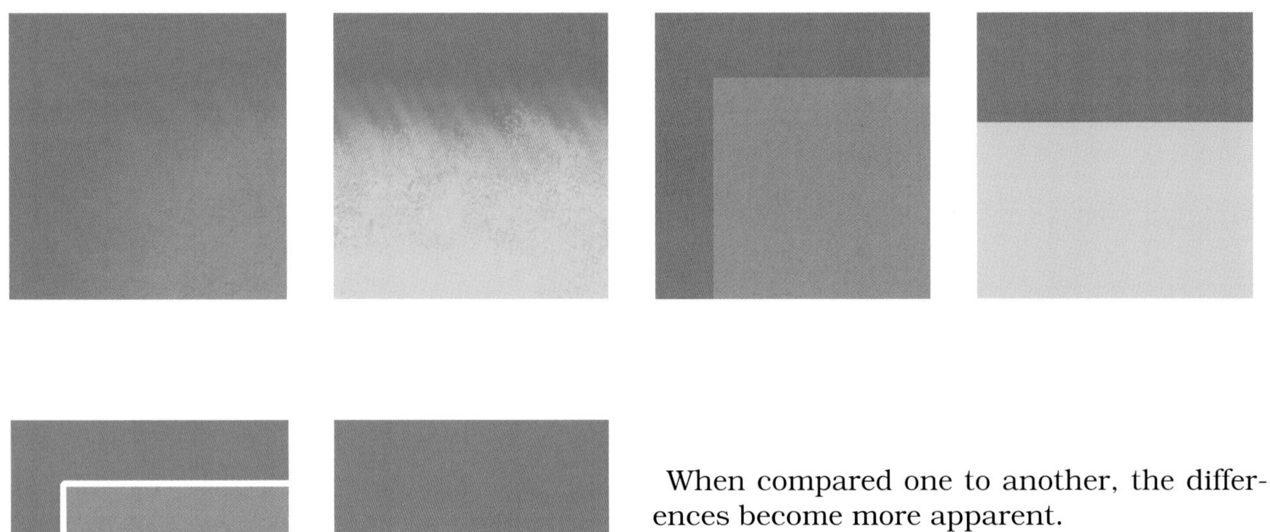

When compared one to another, the differences become more apparent.

The varying effects might not be of concern to you if you always work with one approach or the other. However, there might be an occasion when you wish to extract that little bit more from color.

The effect of the line

Contrast can be heightened by separating hues with white.

Gray will reduce contrast, often aiding harmony.

Separating hues with black can cause them to appear richer, almost glowing.

Using a tint of one of the main hues can often be an to aid color harmony. Here the blue has been made lighter to form a tint of itself.

Separating colors by a line can lead to varying effects:

White tends to darken and reduce the brilliancy of colors when used as a background (page 211).

However, *contrast* can be heightened by separating hues with white in the form of lines or narrow surrounding bands.

Whereas white heightens contrast when used to separate colors, gray will reduce contrast, often aiding color harmony.

Black, (or a mixed dark), surrounding a hue causes it to appear richer, almost glowing.

When black is used to separate colors they have less opportunity to influence each other, depending, of course, on the width of the separation.

This effect can be seen on leaded church windows as well as on paintings with areas outlined in black ink or paint.

Using a tint of one of the main hues can often aid color harmony.

White

When white is used to separate colors, visual interest is added in the form of contrast. This contrast increases as the colors being surrounded become either darker or richer.

Many color arrangements which might otherwise be rather bland can be brought to life and freshness added, when thin strips of white separate other colors.

Freshness and 'sparkle' are probably the two main benefits to be gained by the use of white and many an otherwise dull room can be brought to life by the careful use of white.

Gray

Gray has a soft, calming effect on all colors, whether used as a surround or as a separator.
The neutralising effect of gray is particularly effective on the brighter, stronger colors. By *reducing* contrast, otherwise discordant hues can be brought into harmony.

Applied in an almost endless variety of ways, mixed, 'colored grays' are vital to a full color repertoire. I say mixed 'colored grays' because the conventional idea of gray, a black and white mix can look rather dull and lifeless unless part of pure black and white work.

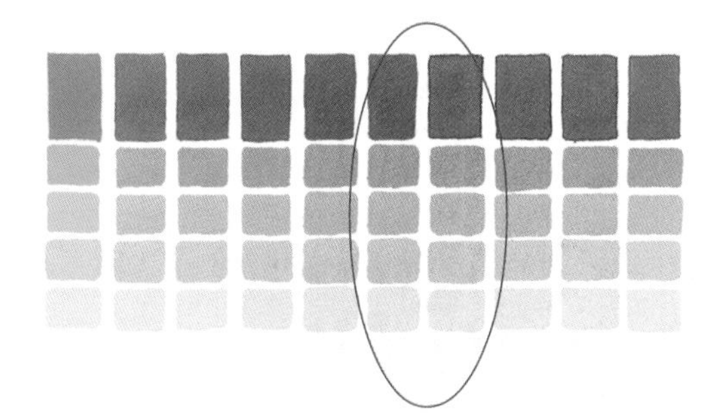

To aid harmony it pays to mix your grays from hues already in use. If a complementary pair such as blue and orange are involved they will produce 'colored grays' which will be a definite aid to harmony.

Black

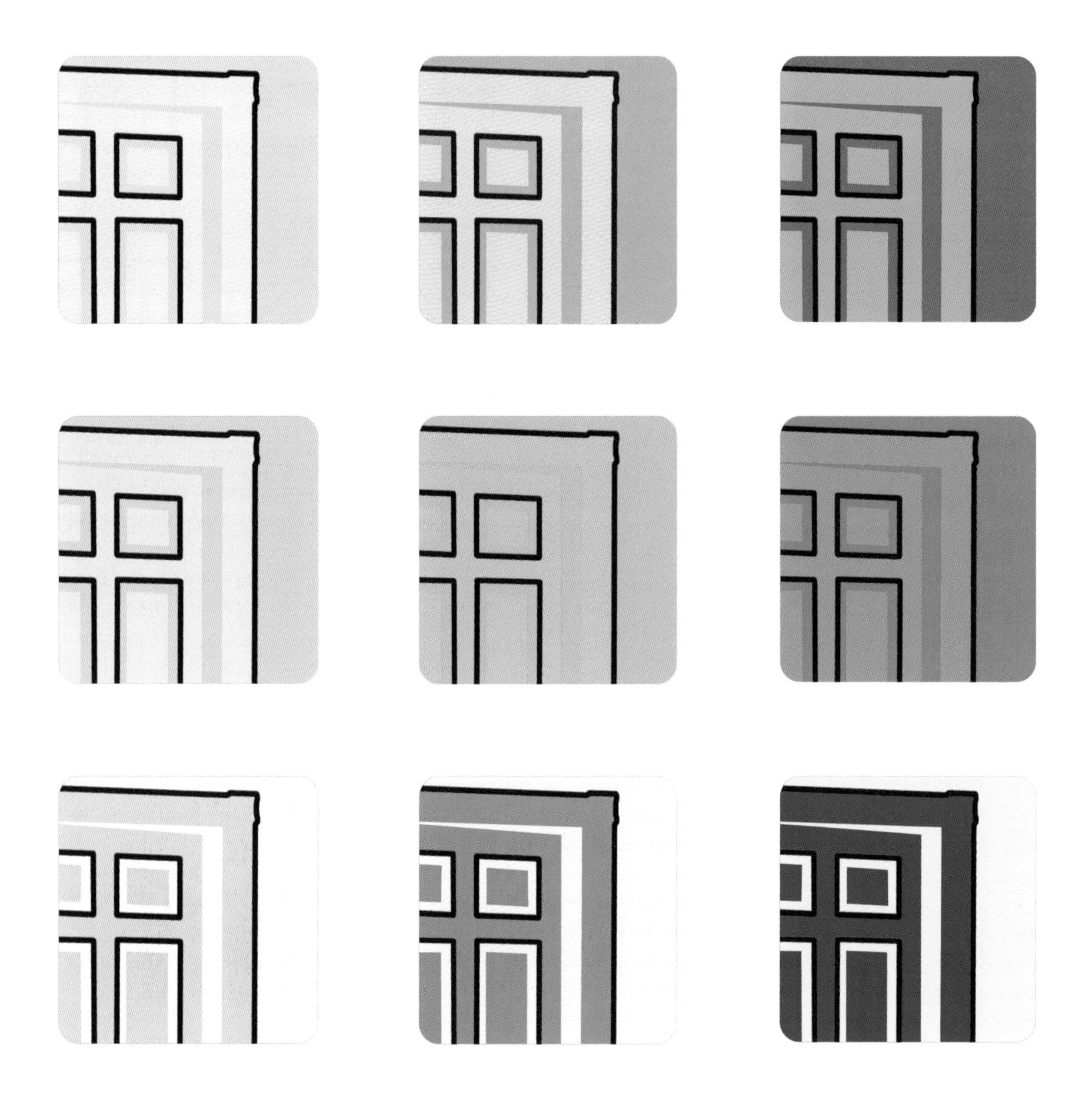

Black, or a very dark mixed 'colored gray', used either as a background or surrounding line will tend to visually enrich red, make yellow appear 'cool' and cause blue to appear almost luminous.

When used as an outline it tends to separate other colors. By being somewhat isolated they have less opportunity to directly influence each other. This isolation seems to accentuate their particular characteristics.

The lead strips in a stained glass window, for example, seem to have this effect on the individual colors of the glass work.

The interior decorator can also employ this approach by the use of black or very dark outlines.

Tint

As an alternative to the use of white, gray or black, the tint (lightened version), of one of the colors can be used to separate the others.

When used in this fashion, the tints act almost as go-betweens, reducing color contrast and aiding color harmony.

In one sense this situation can be considered similar to many found in nature, with a single color cropping up here and there, at different strengths, in different parts of the scene.

Although the tints from several, or even all of the colors used in a room can be employed, the use of just one, (maybe the most prominent color), is often sufficient.

Seldom seen, the use of a tint to outline other colors is a simple approach with many applications. It is certainly worth exploring on a rainy day if you are seeking subtle and harmonious color arrangements. A few experiments will quickly help you to decide.

The complementary

The use of the complementary (to the background), for the outline can bring a great deal of 'zing' to a room. It is a technique which is difficult to ignore. The effect of after-image from the background (please see page 84), on the line will enhance it quite dramatically.

This approach can be used in part of a room, or overall.

I cannot say that I have often seen this technique used fully, but it has great potential. If the lines are kept reasonably thin it gives the potential, from a short distance, of bringing an unusual 'light' to an area.

Much in the same way that the small dabs of complementary color applied by the Impressionist painter did to their work.

A personal matter

© Red Cover/Ken Hayden

It is quite impossible to fully identify the meaning of the term 'color harmony'.

Just as we have individual tastes in, say, fruit, so we have our own individual ideas of what colors look good (or otherwise) together.

You might be very pleased with the color scheme that you have chosen to use for a particular room. But if your friend or neighbour goes rather quiet when you ask their opinion, do remember that color is an entirely subjective matter. There is no such thing as the 'correct' use of color.

The person who chose the above color scheme would have had responses varying from 'fantastic' to 'I like the color of the towel'.

Be bold and always do your own thing.

The colors of nature

One thing seems fairly certain; the peoples of the world find that the colors which surround them work together with ease.

From the muted yellows of the desert to the lush greens of the rain forest, everything in the landscape seems to balance.

Around the world and over the centuries, few people have found fault with the color schemes which occur naturally.

Complementary pairings are very common in nature; red and greens together, yellows and violet and blues and oranges.

Most of nature's color schemes are deceptively simple, being based on very few base colors. However, these same colors are presented in a wide range of intensities.

I have based my approach to color harmony and contrast on these arrangements. This particularly applies to the selection of a limited range of colors. Through intermixing one color influencing the next.

Hence the color mixing tips, with the emphasis being placed on the use of mixing partners.

The colors of nature

The color schemes of nature are usually quite simple. In the example above, violet-red plus green, together with their mixes and influence from the light provide the full picture. Violet-red appears in the flower, the stems and around each immature berry.

The presence of chlorophyll (green), modifies this redness, giving the range from the 'un-mixed' hue of the flower to the dulled violet-red of the stems and onto the 'brown' around the fruit. In nature, only two pigments provided the range of hues. These two, plus variations in brought about by the light provide the entire range.

This simplicity can be adopted when it comes to the selection of the paints to employ in decorating. The range provided by just two colors, particularly if they are mixing partners, can be more than sufficient for many a room.

In the above color mixing swatch, a mid-green (leaning neither towards blue or yellow) has been mixed with a violet-red. Colors from this range appear in the plant. The 'browns' around the fruit for example appear around the centre in the top row of mixes.

If the mixing pair, the green and violet-red, are used with a little care, any of the mixes in the above range can be used together in the one room. This pair appears on page 138.

1. 2. 3.

In the main, the vast range of colors found in the plant world result from the intermingling of three color groups; violet, yellow and green.
The violets vary from blue to red-violet (1), the greens from blue to yellow-green (2) and the yellows between green-yellow and orange-yellow (3).

4. 5. 6.

Of these three color groups only two are usually found together.
A very wide range of wild flowering (as opposed to cultivated*) plants rely on internal chemicals which provide either yellow and green coloring (4) or violet (blue to red-violet) and green (5).
Where violet and green are the main colors, a touch of yellow often appears within the violet (6).

** Cultivated plants frequently exhibit color combinations not seen in wild flowering species. We are more concerned with the latter.*

The colors of nature - the plant world

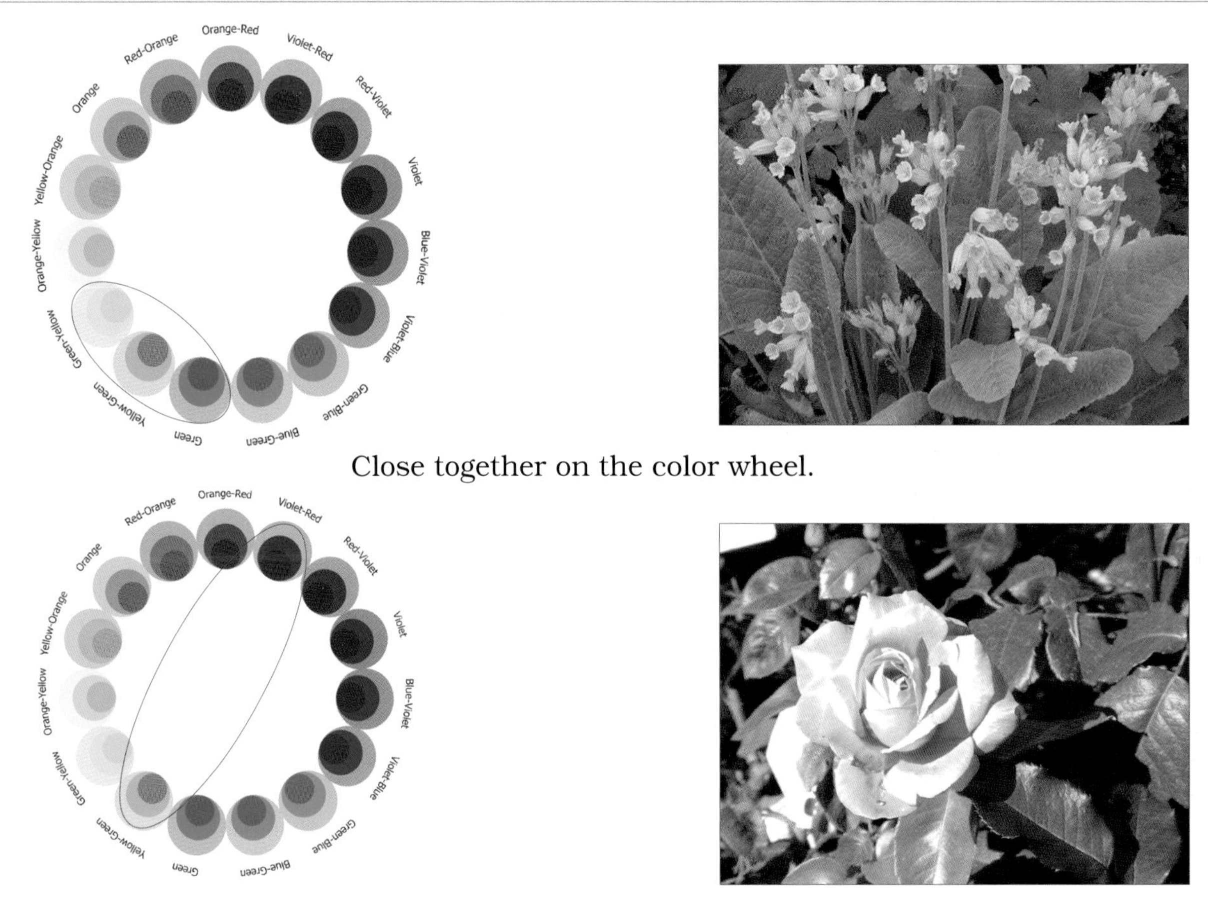

Close together on the color wheel.

Complementary, opposite each other on the color wheel.

Many of the color schemes within plants are either found close together on the color wheel or are complementary and opposite on the wheel. It is perhaps due to such simple arrangements that most plants exhibit harmonious color schemes.

The close groupings such as green, yellow green and yellow tend to sit together very well as they are closely related.

The complementary pairings, such as red and green, usually work well as the two principal colors are extended and made more compatible by their intermixing in the stems, veins, buds or leaves.

This is something that we can definitely learn from.

Not all arrangements are simple: Orchids, for example, often exhibit a very wide range of colors in the one plant. A flower might move from violet in the centre to blue-violet, then onto green-blue and yellow.

As I have mentioned, nature can provide the inspiration for many a color scheme.

A few quick notes taken when interesting color arrangements present themselves can be the basis for a future redecoration. A scene such as that shown above might prompt you to take note of the colors. Perhaps decide to use some lighter and others darker etc.

A small section of sky might be enough to get your creative juices flowing. Mental or written notes, or indeed a photograph might lead to some very unusual and attractive arrangements. Or maybe they will just be unusual.

In this case the seagulls would be an optional extra, unless you are fond of unruly pets. Perhaps a stuffed budgerigar would do much the same job.

The colors of nature - the wider world

Various color arrangements are, of course, all around us and are constantly on the move.

If you have a developed interest in color it can certainly be an enjoyable exercise to actually take in what is, after all, an amazing free show.

The creative person will find inspiration everywhere. The scene depicted in the top left picture, for example, might lead you to consider a pale orange-red in the kitchen with green utensils. Moving around the cart you might decide to add a touch of green-blue to the cupboard doors.

The lower scene might see a very pale yellow added for the work-tops.

Even if you never use any of the combinations, at least you will have observed them. And some fantastic arrangements might suggest themselves that you will use. Inspiration is all around for those who can respond to it.

This interest could result in you constantly changing the color arrangements in your home and spending a fortune on materials.

If this becomes the case, and you wish to complain, please write to anybody but me.

Color Cleaver™

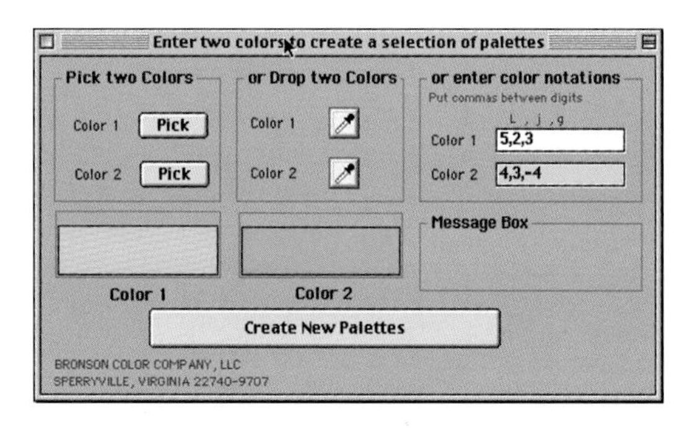

At the time of writing, the *School of Color* is finalising the development of two computer programs to assist in the selection of color combinations.

The first of these will be known as *Color Cleaver.*

Some time after WWII, leading scientists from the Optical Society of America began intensive research into color relationships. Their work, based on color vision, spanned more than thirty years.

The research led to a model in which hues blend smoothly from color to color and every difference in lightness and purity is represented.

The result is a visually uniform, three-dimensional color world known as the Uniform Color Scales, or OSA-UCS. The model was not based on any individual's ideas of color relationship but on color vision.

It is the most advanced program of its kind in the world.

Color Cleaver™

The color sequences are not an individuals color selection and they do not depend on any color theory. They represent instead the color sequences found everywhere in nature. It is for this reason that the *School of Color* has become involved in the project.

The original research was carried out before the days of the desktop computer. Joy Turner Luke, a leading expert on color vision, took over the project and developed a working computer program.

Joy later joined the School of Color team and we are jointly developing the program to the point where it will become a working tool for all who are looking for quick and highly effective color arrangements.

Color Cleaver™, as the program is known, introduces a fresh approach to the creation of harmonious groups of colors. It provides a way to explore and expand color possibilities, but does not limit either your choices or your imagination.

This program will be of interest to those with a need to be able to select effective color arrangements quickly.

The interior designer, advanced artist, teachers, the graphic artist, designers and web designer would be typical users.

For the keen home decorator we are also developing a program based on the color swatches to be found in this book.

If you wish to follow these, as well as other developments please see details on page 240.

Other titles

Described as the first breakthrough in the field of color mixing in 200 years. Enlarged and updated 2002. Full color, 200 pages. The standard text of artists and art teachers world wide.

The most comprehensive guide to artist's watercolor paints ever published. All leading manufacturers assessed. Their pigments identified and lightfastness examined. 408 pages in full color.

Whether selecting watercolors, oils, acrylics, gouache or alkyds this book will guide you to paints are superb and warn against those which fade or darken. User information on all paint media. 120 pgs. Full color.

This book examines the age old search for harmonious color combinations and offers the artist the most comprehensive guidance and advice that has ever been given in this vital area. 424 pages. Full color.

The 'Color Mixing Swatch book' offers 2,400 mixed hues from just 12 colors. An instant color mixing guide. 56 pages in full color.

An easy to follow, step by step guide towards the quick and accurate mixing of greens. 64 pages in full color with spiral 'lay flat' binding.

The 'Color Notes' series. Step by step guides towards mixing and using colors for a variety of subjects. 64 pages in full color, with spiral 'lay flat' binding. Each book is like a mini-course in the subject. A must for the realist painter.

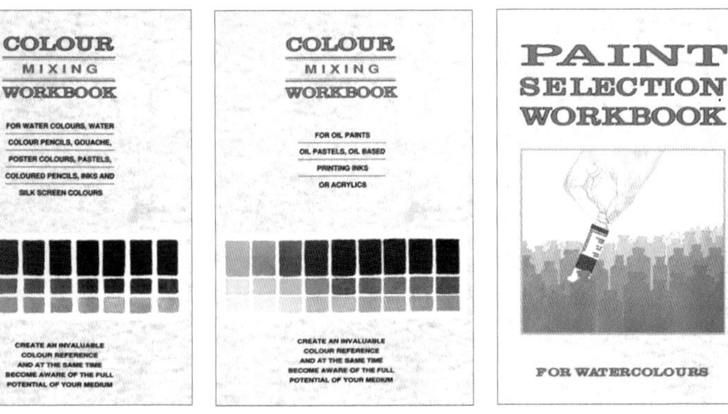

Practical 'paint-in' color mixing workbooks. Each builds into a complete color reference.

Get to know your watercolor paints.

Getting the most from your Color Coded Mixing Palette. We also publish courses on color mixing and color harmony.

Future developments

The intention is to produce a range of products to assist in the selection and mixing of paints for the home decorator.

Specially selected tinters to allow for easy color mixing, a color mixing video and a book on mixing colors for the home are in progress at the time of writing.

If you wish to be kept informed of these development please see contact details on page 240.

Contact details

A range of products has been designed and books and courses published to help bring about a fuller understanding of color and technique. These products are principally for the artist but might also be of interest to other users of color.

We offer artist's paints, color mixing palettes, books, courses, videos and workbooks.

For further information please contact either of the offices listed below:

The Michael Wilcox School of Color UK
Gibbet Lane
Whitchurch
Bristol
BS14 OBX
United Kingdom
Tel: 01275 835500
Fax: 01275 892659
e-mail: wilcoxsoc@aol.com

The Michael Wilcox School of Color USA
25 Mauchly #328
Irvine
CA 92618 USA
Tel: 949 450 0266
Fax: 949 450 0268
Free Phone: 1888 7 WILCOX
e-mail: wilcoxschool@earthlink.net

www.schoolofcolor.com